The
Representation
of
Knowledge
and
Belief

Arizona Colloquium in Cognition

GENERAL EDITORS

Myles Brand
Peter Culicover
Keith Lehrer

The Representation of Knowledge and Belief

Myles Brand and Robert M. Harnish, Editors

THE UNIVERSITY OF ARIZONA PRESS
Tucson

About the Editors

MYLES BRAND, President for Academic Affairs and
Provost, and Professor of Philosophy at the Ohio State
University, is author of numerous articles in philosophy,
editor of several books, and is author of *Intending and
Acting,* Bradford/MIT Press.

ROBERT M. HARNISH, Professor of Philosophy and Linguistics, and Associate Director of the Program in Cognitive Science, has published articles in various areas of
cognitive science, and co-authored (with K. Bach) *Linguistic Communication and Speech Acts,* MIT Press, and
(with A. Akmajian and R. Demers) *Linguistics: An Introduction to Language and Communication,* MIT Press.

THE UNIVERSITY OF ARIZONA PRESS

Copyright © 1986
The Arizona Board of Regents
All Rights Reserved

This book was set in 10/12 Linotron Galliard.
Manufactured in the U.S.A.

Library of Congress Cataloging-in-Publication Data

The Representation of knowledge and belief.

(Arizona colloquium in cognition)
Bibliography: p.
Includes index.
1. Knowledge, Theory of—Congresses. 2. Cognition—
Congresses. 3. Belief and doubt—Congresses.
I. Brand, Myles.   II. Harnish, Robert M.
III. Series.
BD161.R465   1986   121   86-24961

ISBN 0-8165-0971-9

British Library Cataloguing in Publication data are available.

Contents

Arizona Colloquium in Cognition

With this volume we initiate the series "Arizona Colloquium in Cognition." The series is associated with the program in Cognitive Science at the University of Arizona and reflects a portion of its ongoing activities.

The multidisciplinary approach of this series aims at a unified theory of the mind/brain. Current efforts under the rubric of "cognitive science" suggest that this theory, when it is fully articulated, will prove to be a computational one. Disciplines contributing toward an understanding of computations in the mind/brain are linguistics, neuroscience, philosophy, and psychology, and offerings in this series will be concentrated primarily in these areas.

Arizona Colloquium in Cognition will include timely contributions to cognitive science without regard to school or methodology. The purpose of the series is to provide a forum for the interplay of important new ideas and to stimulate debate on significant and theoretically controversial issues. In order to address the widest possible audience, books in this series will not be focused primarily on technical results that are pertinent only to particular subdisciplines. Rather, they will seek to bring to bear the insights of a range of disciplines and methodologies on important questions of general concern.

This first volume in the series, *The Representation of Knowledge and Belief*, is a collection of papers garnered from two recent conferences, one of which was held at the University of Arizona. It is planned that the proceedings of future conferences at the University of Arizona and elsewhere, as well as individually authored manuscripts, will be represented in this series.

MYLES BRAND
PETER CULICOVER
KEITH LEHRER

Introduction

An issue crucial to the foundations of cognitive science—indeed, one that lies at the very heart of this research program—is the nature of mental representation. Of particular concern is high-level representation, representation of knowledge and belief. The issue of Mental Representation, both in its general form and in its focus on knowledge and belief, was the occasion of two recent conferences: one at the University of Arizona during February 1984, and another at the Massachusetts Institute of Technology during May 1984. Both conferences brought together philosophers, linguists, and psychologists, as well as persons from other disciplines. This volume includes most of the papers presented at the University of Arizona conference, some of those presented at the MIT conference, and several others that bear importantly on this issue. The papers by Robert Cummins, Fred Dretske, Alvin Goldman, William Lycan, and Lance Rips were presented at the University of Arizona; and those by Noam Chomsky and Daniel Dennett were originally presented at the MIT meetings.

Although these papers speak for themselves, we should take a moment to highlight some of their main claims. In "Changing Perspectives on Knowledge and Use of Language," *Noam Chomsky* considers the questions of the nature of knowledge of language, its origins, and its use, from the perspective of his recent Governing and Binding (GB) framework. Knowledge of language is a certain state of the mind/brain described, in part, by core grammar consisting of principles of Universal Grammar with values of parameters fixed, and a periphery of marked exceptions. This state (an internal or "I-Language," as contrasted with an external or "E-Language") is attained by an experientially undetermined process of parameter setting and periphery formation. This state also provides for "rule following" in speech production and comprehension. Chomsky defends this view against a conception drawn from Kripke's recent revival of Wittgensteinian arguments.

In a typically engaging paper, "The Logical Geography of Computational Approaches," *Daniel Dennett* sketches the competing attempts by cognitive scientists to understand the mental. Suppose that MIT is the East Pole and that all dispersion from it is directed toward the West Pole. East Polers (such as Jerry Fodor) hold what Dennett labels "High Church Computationalism (HCC)," the view that thinking is information processing and information processing is computation (i.e., symbol manipulation). In contrast to HCC is Zen Holism, worshipped, for example, at Berkeley by John Searle. This view to date has been largely negative; Zen holists hold that HCC could not possibly be true because it cannot explain the intentionality (the "aboutness") of thought.

Dennett observes that there is a newly developing constructive West Pole view. New Connectionism, as he labels it, takes seriously the neural architecture of the brain; it is a bottom-up research strategy, when compared with HCC. Typical New Connectionist claims are that memory and other cognitive processes are distributed, parallel, and without central control. The problem for New Connectionists is reaching the semantic level. But it may be, as Dennett suggests, that semantic properties result from rule-described processes, not processes that are rule following, and that inexplicit information (to anticipate Cummins' description of the situation) plays a key explanatory role.

The idea that information processors processing *"standard" information* can naturally be viewed as *"associative" nets* has encouraged some psychologists and computer scientists to propose such networks as possible models of cognitive capacities (both person and subpersonal). According to *Jerry Fodor,* these two notions have interlocking inadequacies. Networks transmit information without encoding it, but it is the encoding that is relevant to exercising cognitive capacities and explaining behavior. Though we need the notion of "information encoded" for our psychology, the standard notion of information yields only the "information transmitted." We can have the objective notion of information, one that puts the information "in the world," but it will not do the work of the pretheoretic notion of "the information available" to an information processor. Alternatively, we can have a notion of "the information available," but it will not be receiver neutral or *naturalistic* because it will depend on what the receiver knows and is able to infer. The notion of information that it is required for cognitive science is *nonnaturalistic*, unreduced, and intentional. Is there a use for the standard notion of information? Psychosemantics: perhaps what fixes the interpretation of formulas in the internal code is the covariance (standard notion of information) of their tokening in the head with tokenings of situations in the world.

In "Aspects of Cognitive Representation," *Fred Dretske* argues that a cognitive system is a representational control mechanism that indicates how matters stand with respect to specific properties of external objects. To take a simple case, a fuel gauge indicates through a read-out how full a tank is. A cognitive system accomplishes this function by means of information provided by lawful connections between it and the external objects.

Dretske sketches a defense of the claim that this model of cognitive systems can explain attribution of semantic content. Representational states are states that indicate something and mark what is represented, how it is represented, and which elements in the representation play a causal role in determining behavior. What is represented is the reference or denotation of the control state and how it is represented is the content of the state. For the fuel gauge, a certain reading indicates something about the tank, that it is, say, half-full. The model has a natural extension to humans: in particular, Dretske claims that the model has resources sufficient to explain propositional attitudes (such as believing and knowing) and nonpropositional ones (such as seeing). Indeed, the entirety of folk-psychological accounts of perceiving, believing, and knowing are to be reinterpreted in the framework of cognitive systems as information-driven control mechanisms.

Robert Cummins in "Inexplicit Information" argues that the behavior of cognitive systems, their outputs, can be explained by the execution of rules, by, as it were, "inexplicit information." For instance, an instruction is the rule "embodied" in the device that executes it; it is information the system has in virtue of the program's being executed on a physical device. Another example is the flow of control in a cognitive system. Explanation by inexplicit information contrasts with that provided by knowledge structures. Knowledge structures are represented in memory, whereas rule execution is not. Both knowledge structures and inexplicit information are capable of explaining systems intentionally characterized, that is, specified in terms of propositional states; but, unlike explanation by knowledge structures, explanation by inexplicit information does not make reference to contentful representations.

In his contribution "Functionalism and Belief," *Stephen Schiffer* takes up the tenability of functionalism. Functionalism with respect to belief (and, *mutatis mutandis,* every other kind of propositional attitude) holds that some psychological theory determines a correlation of belief states and functional states in such a way that each belief state is identical to the functional state with which it is correlated. But what psychological theory does this? Schiffer argues that, for a variety of reasons, it is neither folk psychology nor some scientific psychological theory. Functionalism thus refuted, he then considers the possibility of extended functionalist theories: but they fare no better than their purer predecessors.

In "Thoughts About Things," *William Lycan* attempts to provide order to the seeming chaos in the philosophic literature about *de re* attitudes. As a point of departure Lycan adopts a representational theory of belief, in which belief states are assimilated to linguistic items. Just as sentences and phrases can be about things in the world, so too can the contents of belief. There are several grades of aboutness, where the main division is between those belief contents containing referring terms that make "contact" with objects and those that do not. To make contact, reference must somehow result from a causal process. Of those grades that make contact, there are some that contain terms referring directly to an object (rather than making reference via description) and there are others that contain terms making direct reference while relying on some intimate epistemic connection, such as perception. A belief is *de re*, on Lycan's view, when the truth-conditions of the sentential content of the belief is about objects in the world at least to the degree that there is causal contact between the contained referring terms and the external objects.

Lycan argues that *de re* beliefs (as well as other attitudes) understood in this way have a real role to play in psychology. Methodological solipsism, the view that psychology should only concern itself with what happens in a subject's head, as it were, is rejected. For such a view leads to a psychology that is too restrictive to explain learning and informing others, goal achievement, and indexing (counting) internal states.

In "Thought and Object," *Kent Bach* develops a theory of *de re* belief roughly corresponding to Lycan's fourth grade of aboutness. This theory, restricted to *de re* beliefs about concrete individuals other than oneself, is motivated by the consideration that without such beliefs our conception of the world could only be qualitative and not be about particular objects at all. However, *de re* beliefs do not literally contain their objects or even singular terms that semantically denote their objects. Rather, a *de re* belief contains a representation which functions as a mental indexical and whose object is determined not satisfactionally but relationally. Its object is the one to which the representation (token) bears a certain causal relation, where the relation depends on whether the *de re* representation is a percept, a memory, or a mental name.

De re beliefs can be based on perception, memory, or communication. For each Bach schematizes both its "narrow" content and its context-relative truth-condition ("wide" content). Noting that memory-based ones are derived ultimately from others' perceptual beliefs, Bach formulates a recursive definition of what it is for a *de re* belief to be of a certain object. He uses his relational conception of *de re* belief to account for Kripke's intuitions about the rigidity of proper names. Finally, arguing against what Evans calls "Russell's Principle," according to which thinking of an object requires knowing which object it is, Bach defends the view that *de re* relations are causal but not epistemic.

Lynn Nadel, Jeffrey Willner, and *Elizabeth Kurz* argue in their chapter that when cognitive scientists attended to biology they typically "assumed that the hardware of the brain was general enough to support almost any proposal that we found useful to postulate" (Rumelhart and Norman 1981, p. 2). Recent research leaves little doubt that many of the assumptions upon which this abiological view is based are wrong, but the implications of these new findings for the relation between mental and biological states remain unclear. The authors review some of these findings here and attempt to relate them to issues of mental representation. They begin with a brief exposition of the traditional views which sanctioned a lack of concern with biology and the ways in which these views have been proven inadequate. They then analyze neural representations in sensory/perceptual systems, in particular those which show the striking feature of maintaining in an apparently isomorphic way some of the spatial or temporal aspects of experience. The possible functions of those internal "maps" are analyzed in some detail, especially as they shed light on the ways in which neural activity might "represent" knowledge. In the third section they discuss mental imagery and evaluate some of the implicit neurobiological claims made by the participants in the debate over the internal mechanisms responsible for the "analog" properties of imagery. They turn from there to a discussion of several contemporary approaches to representation—Connectionism and Computationalism—and how they square with contemporary neuroscience. Finally, they discuss briefly some of their tentative answers to the questions of mental representation.

A number of cognitive scientists have recently proposed that many aspects of human understanding and problem solving can be explained if we suppose people to possess "mental models" of knowledge domains. On one view, these mental models are representations that differ formally from propositions, networks, and images, and that directly reflect the objects and relations they are about. Proponents of this approach claim that mental models can also provide a classical semantics for beliefs and can explain certain types of inductive and deductive reasoning. However, *Lance Rips* in "Mental Muddles" examines the arguments and evidence for mental models and finds that they provide few advantages beyond those of standard cognitive theories. Despite their advocates' assertions, mental models provide no account of referential semantics; and in most situations, reasoning is better explained by deductive schemas and inductive rules-of-thumb operating on internally represented logical forms.

In "Constraints on Representation," *Alvin Goldman* investigates the parameters of human representation, with an eye toward their epistemologically relevant properties. He explores representational preferences for patterns which realize Gestalt-type principles, and preferences for hierarchically linkable representations in both visual and auditory materials (especially music). Representational preferences suggest the presence of a fairly restricted repertoire of mental operations or transformations, perhaps with a preference ranking among the elements of the repertoire. These transformations may underlie the perception or judgment of analogical relations. Goldman surveys some possible epistemic assets and liabilities of the hypothesized representational constraints. He argues that the set of "natural," or "highly marked," operations are tacitly employed in making evaluative appraisals of people's ideas and beliefs, including evaluations of the "originality" and their "justifiedness."

In "The Aesthetic Basis for Cognitive Structures," *Tom Bever* argues that aesthetic experience, at least in the case of folk art, is to be understood in terms of current cognitive explanations of problem solving. Sometimes in perception a subject automatically forms conflicting representations on the basis of different perceptual schemata. Such conflicts are resolved by accessing another representation that incorporates the original ones. Similarly, in aesthetic experience there is a conflict of representations that is resolved when another is accessed. In a piece of music, an expectation of the next notes can be unfilled; the conflict between what was expected and what was heard is then resolved by another, higher-level representation of the musical phrase. This process produces a sense of satisfaction, often characterized as a feeling of "Aha!" Bever illustrates his analysis by examining in detail several examples of folk art, among them the "shave and a haircut, two bits" rhythm and the Goldilocks fairy tale.

If Bever is right about aesthetic experience, there are significant consequences for the modularity thesis, discussed for example by Chomsky and Fodor. Aesthetic judgments follow the same principles independently of modality and hence appear to be a "nonmodular" cognitive process. Moreover, if aesthetic activity of conflict resolution is intrinsically satisfying and if, as Bever argues, it ubiquitously applies to all levels of language representation, then aesthetic principles constrain the form of learnable languages, independently of representational level.

Acknowledgments

The University of Arizona conference, from which the majority of these papers came, was titled "Problems in the Representation of Knowledge and Belief." It was supported by the Arizona Humanities Council, the Faculty of Social and Behavioral Sciences at the University of Arizona, and private donations. The conference was administered by the Cognitive Science Program at the University of Arizona, with the local arrangements very ably organized by Ann Farmer. The conference at MIT was sponsored by the Sloan Foundation. Local arrangements were well organized for that conference by James Higgenbotham.

The Editors would like to thank all those who helped in the preparation of the volume, especially members of the Cognitive Science Program at the University of Arizona. Special thanks are due to James Taylor who cheerfully assisted in the preparation of this volume in innumerable ways, and to Francis Sheehan for help in preparing the index.

M. BRAND
R. HARNISH

Contributors

Kent Bach is Professor of Philosophy at San Francisco State University. He received his Ph.D. from the University of California at Berkeley. He has published numerous articles, as well as (with R. M. Harnish) *Linguistic Communication and Speech Acts,* MIT Press, 1979.

Thomas Bever is a Professor in the Departments of Psychology and Linguistics at the University of Rochester. He received a Ph.D. from MIT. Along with numerous articles, his publications include, with Fodor and M. Garrett, *The Psychology of Language,* McGraw-Hill, 1974.

Noam Chomsky is a Professor in the Department of Linguistics and Philosophy at MIT. He received his Ph.D. in Linguistics from the University of Pennsylvania. Professor Chomsky is the author of books and articles on linguistics, philosophy, intellectual history, and contemporary issues. Among his works are the following: *Syntactic Structures,* Mouton, 1957; *Aspects of the Theory of Syntax,* MIT Press, 1965; *Logical Structure of Linguistic Theory,* Plenum, 1975; *Rules and Representations,* Columbia University Press, 1980; *Lectures on Government and Binding,* Foris, 1981; *Some Concepts and Consequences of the Theory of Government and Binding,* MIT Press, 1982.

Robert Cummins is Professor of Philosophy at the University of Colorado at Boulder. He received his Ph.D. degree from the University of Michigan.

He has published many articles, and also the book *The Nature of Psychological Explanation,* MIT Press, 1983.

Daniel Dennett is Professor of Philosophy at Tufts University. He received a D. Phil. degree from Oxford University. He is the author of several books and articles including the following: *Content and Consciousness,* Routledge and Kegan Paul, 1969; *Brainstorms,* MIT Press, 1978; *Elbow Room: The Varieties of Free Will Worth Wanting,* MIT Press, 1984. He also writes a biennial column for the *Journal of Artificial Intelligence* on recent work in philosophy.

Fred Dretske is Professor of Philosophy at the University of Wisconsin at Madison. He received his Ph.D. in Philosophy from the University of Minnesota. His books include *Seeing and Knowing,* Univ. of Chicago Press, 1969; *Knowledge and the Flow of Information,* MIT Press, 1981.

Jerry Fodor is Professor of Philosophy and Psychology at MIT. He received his Ph.D. from Princeton University. He is the author of several books and articles including the following: *Psychological Explanation,* Random House, 1968; *The Language of Thought,* Thomas Y. Crowell, 1975; *RePresentations,* MIT Press, 1981; and *The Modularity of Mind,* MIT Press, 1983.

Alvin Goldman is Professor of Philosophy at the University of Arizona. He received his Ph.D. in Philosophy from Princeton University. Among his publications is *A Theory of Human Action,* Prentice-Hall, 1970. He is currently working on a book titled *Epistemology and Cognition.*

Elizabeth Kurz is in the Department of Psychology at the University of California, Los Angeles. She received her Ph.D. from Cornell University and held a post-doctoral position at the University of California at Irvine. She has published a series of papers with Lynn Nadel and Jeffrey Willner on the hippocampus and related topics.

William G. Lycan is Professor of Philosophy at the University of North Carolina at Chapel Hill. He received a Ph.D. in Philosophy from the University of Chicago. He has published numerous papers and the recent book *Logical Form in Natural Language,* MIT Press, 1984.

Lynn Nadel is Professor of Psychology and Research Professor of Cognitive Science at the University of Arizona, Tucson. He received his Ph.D. in Biopsychology from McGill University. Among his publications is the following book (with J. O'Keefe): *The Hippocampus as a Cognitive Map,* Clarendon Press, 1978.

Lance Rips is Associate Professor in the Department of Behavioral Sciences at the University of Chicago. He received his Ph.D. from Stanford University. He is a consulting editor for *Cognitive Psychology* and *Cognition,* and he has published extensively in the area of cognitive psychology.

Stephen Schiffer received a D. Phil. from Oxford University, and is Professor of Philosophy at the University of Arizona. He is the author of *Meaning,* Oxford Univ. Press, 1972, and of the forthcoming *Remnants of Meaning,* MIT Press.

Jeffrey Willner is a Visiting Assistant Research Social Scientist at the University of Arizona, Tucson. He received his Ph.D. from Dalhousie University and held a post-doctoral position at the University of California at Irvine. He has published a series of papers with Lynn Nadel and Elizabeth Kurz on the hippocampus and related topics.

Changing Perspectives on Knowledge and Use of Language

Knowledge of Language as a Focus of Inquiry

The study of generative grammer, as it has developed since its origins—or, perhaps, reincarnation—about 30 years ago, represented a significant shift of focus in the approach to problems of language. Put in the simplest terms, the shift was from behavior or products of behavior to states of the mind/brain that enter into behavior. If one chooses to focus attention on this topic, the central concern becomes knowledge of language: its nature, origins, and use. The three basic questions that arise, then, are these:

(1)　(i)　What constitutes knowledge of language?
　　　(ii)　How is knowledge of language acquired?
　　　(iii)　How is knowledge of language used?

In the mid-1950s, certain proposals were advanced as to the form that answers to these questions might take, and a research program was inaugurated to investigate the adequacy of these proposals and to sharpen and apply them. This program was one of the strands that led to the development of the cognitive sciences in the contemporary sense, sharing with other approaches the belief that certain aspects of the mind/brain can be usefully construed on the model of computational systems of rules that form and modify representations and that are put to use in interpretation and action.

This general research program has been developed along a number of different paths. I will be concerned here with only one of these—with the problems it faced and the steps that were taken in an effort to deal with them.[1] During the past four to five years, these efforts have converged in a somewhat unexpected way, yielding a rather different conception of the nature of language and its mental representation, one that offers interesting answers to a range of empirical questions and opens a variety of new ones to inquiry while suggesting a rethinking of the character of others.

I want to consider, then, two major conceptual shifts, one that inaugurated the contemporary study of generative grammar, and a second, more theory-internal, that is now in process and that offers some new perspectives on traditional problems.

Traditional and structuralist grammar did not deal with the questions (1), the former, because of its implicit reliance on the unanalyzed intelligence of the reader, the latter because of its narrowness of scope. The concerns of traditional and generative grammar are, in a certain sense, complementary: a good traditional or pedagogical grammar provides a full list of exceptions (irregular verbs, etc.), paradigms and examples of regular constructions, and general and often quite informative observations about the form and meaning of expressions. But it does not examine the question of how the reader of the grammar uses such information in attaining the capacity to form and interpret new expressions, essentially questions (1), above. With not too much exaggeration, one could describe such a grammar as analogous to the data presented to a child learning a language. Generative grammar, in contrast, was concerned primarily with the intelligence of the reader, the principles and procedures brought to bear to attain full knowledge of a language. Structuralist theories, both in the European and American traditions, did concern themselves with analytic procedures for deriving aspects of grammar from data, as in the work of Troubetzkoy, Harris, Bloch, and others, but primarily in the areas of phonology and morphology. The procedures suggested were seriously inadequate and in any event could not possibly be understood (and were not intended) to provide an answer to the question (1ii), even in the narrower domains where most work was concentrated. Nor was there an effort to determine what was involved in offering a comprehensive account of the knowledge of the speaker/hearer.

As soon as these questions were squarely faced, a wide range of new phenomena were discovered, including quite simple ones that had passed unnoticed, and severe problems arose that had previously been ignored or seriously misunderstood. A standard belief 30 years ago among psychologists and linguists was that language acquisition is a case of "overlearning"; that is, the habit system that was taken to underlie language use was assumed to be vastly overdetermined by available evidence. Production or interpretation of new forms was taken to be a simple matter of "analogy" (Bloomfield, Hockett) or "analogic synthesis" (Quine), posing few problems.[2] Attention to the questions (1) quickly reveals that exactly the opposite is the case: language poses in a sharp and clear form what has sometimes been called "Plato's problem," the problem of "poverty of stimulus," of accounting for the richness, complexity, and specificity of shared knowledge given the limitations of the data available. This difference of perception concerning where the problem lies—overlearning or underdetermination—reflects very clearly the effect of the shift of focus that inaugurated the study of generative grammar.

A great many examples have been given over the years to illustrate what clearly is the fundamental problem: the problem of poverty of stimulus. A familiar example is the structure dependence of rules, the fact that without instruction or direct evidence, children unerringly use computationally complex structure-dependent rules rather than computationally simple rules that involve only the predicate "leftmost" in a linear sequence of words.[3] To take some other examples, to which we will return, consider the sentences (2)–(7):

(2) I wonder who [the men expected to see them]
(3) [the men expected to see them]
(4) John ate an apple
(5) John ate
(6) John is too stubborn to talk to Bill
(7) John is too stubborn to talk to

Both (2) and (3) include the clause given in brackets, but only in (2) may the pronoun be referentially dependent on the antecedent *the men*. Numerous facts of this sort, falling under what is now generally called "binding theory," are known without relevant experience to differentiate the cases. They pose a serious problem that was not recognized in earlier work: how does every child know, unerringly, to interpret the clause differently in the two cases? Why does no pedagogic grammar have to draw the reader's attention to such facts (which were, in fact, noticed only recently in the course of the study of explicit rule systems in generative grammar)?

Turning to examples (4)–(7), sentence (5) means that John ate something or other, a fact that one might explain on the basis of a simple inductive procedure: *ate* takes an object, as in (4), and, if the object is missing, it is "understood" as arbitrary. Applying the same inductive procedure to (6) and (7), it should be that (7) means that John is so stubborn that he (John) will not talk to some arbitrary person, on the analogy of (6). But the meaning is in fact quite different: namely, that John is so stubborn that some arbitrary person will not talk to him (John). Again, this is known without training or relevant evidence.[4]

Children do not make errors about such matters as these, and, if they did, the errors would be largely uncorrectable. It is doubtful that even the most compendious traditional or teaching grammar notes such simple facts as those illustrated in (2)–(7), and such observations lie far beyond the domain of structural grammars. A wide variety of examples of this sort immediately come to attention when one faces the questions formulated in (1).

Knowledge of language is often characterized as a practical ability to speak and understand, so that questions (1i) and (1iii) are closely related, perhaps identified. Ordinary usage makes a much sharper distinction between the two questions and is right to do so. Two people may share exactly the same knowledge of language but differ markedly in their ability to put this knowledge to use. Ability to use language may improve without any change in knowledge. It may also be impaired, selectively or in general, with no loss of knowledge, a fact that would become clear if injury leading to impairment recedes and lost ability is recovered. Many such considerations support the common-sense assumptions that knowledge cannot be properly described as a practical ability. Furthermore, even if this view could somehow be maintained, it leaves open all of the serious questions. Thus, what is the nature of the "practical ability" manifested in our interpretation of (2)–(7), how is it properly described, and how is it acquired?

Note also that it is often not immediately obvious what our knowledge of language entails in particular cases, a fact illustrated even with short and simple sentences such as (8)–(10):

> (8) his wife loves her husband
> (9) John is too clever to expect us to catch Bill
> (10) John is too clever to expect us to catch

In the case of (8), it takes some thought to determine whether *his* can be referentially dependent on *her husband* if *her* is dependent on *his wife*.[5] Examples (9) and (10) are in fact analogous to (6) and (7), respectively, but again, it takes some thought to discover that (10) means that John is so clever that an arbitrary person cannot expect us to catch him (John), though it is clear at once that it does not mean that John is so clever that he (John) cannot catch some arbitrary person, on the analogy of (9) [and (4), (5)]. Our abilities seem limited somehow in such cases (and there are far more complex ones), but it would make little sense to speak of our knowledge of language as "limited" in any comparable way.

In the present case, it seems that we should think of knowledge of language as a certain state of the mind/brain, a relatively stable element in transitory mental states, and furthermore as a state of some distinguishable faculty of the mind—the language faculty—with its specific properties, structure, and organization, one "module" of the mind.[6]

Turning to the questions of (1), let's begin by distinguishing the intuitive, pretheoretic common-sense notion of language from various technical concepts that have been proposed with the intent of developing an eventual science of language. Let us call the latter "scientific approaches" to language, with an eye toward a possible future more than a present reality, some might argue. The scientific approaches, I believe without exception, depart from the common-sense notion in several ways; these departures also affect the concepts of knowledge or understanding of language, use of language, rule of language, rule-guided linguistic behavior, and others.

In the first place, the common-sense notion of language has a crucial sociopolitical dimension, as when we speak of German, Dutch, Chinese, English, etc., as "languages." It is doubtful that any coherent account can be given of "language" in this sense; surely, none has been offered or even seriously attempted. Rather, all scientific approaches have simply abandoned these elements of what is called "language" in common usage.

The common-sense notion also has a more subtle normative-teleological element, also disregarded in scientific approaches. I do not refer here to prescriptive grammar, but to something else. Consider the way we describe a child or a foreigner learning English. We have no way of referring directly to what that person knows: it is not English, nor is it some other language that resembles English. We do not, for example, say that the person has a perfect knowledge of some language L, like English but still different from it. What we say is that the child or foreigner has a "partial knowledge of English," or is "on his/her way" toward acquiring knowledge of English, and if the person reaches the goal, he/she will then know English. Whether or not a coherent account can be given of this aspect of the common-sense terminology, it does not seem to be one that has any role to play in an eventual science of language.

I will follow standard practice in disregarding these aspects of the common-sense notions of language, rule following, etc., though the departure should be noted and one may ask whether it is entirely innocent.

Modern linguistics commonly avoided these questions by considering an idealized "speech community" that is internally consistent in its linguistic practice.[7] For Leonard Bloomfield, for example, a language is "the totality of utterances that can be made in a speech community," regarded as homogeneous (Bloomfield 1928). The legitimacy of this idealization has sometimes been questioned but on dubious grounds.[8] Suppose that there is some property of the human mind/brain P that would enable a child in a homogeneous speech community of the Bloomfieldian sort to acquire the language of that community. Suppose further that P is actually put to use in acquiring language under the more complex conditions of real life, with conflicting evidence, etc. It is difficult to see how either of these assumptions can reasonably be questioned (could one believe, for example, that conflicting data are a prerequisite for language acquisition, or that P exists but is never used, some kind of "vestigial organ"?). In fact, it seems clear that any reasonable study of the nature, acquisition, and use of language in real-life circumstances accepts these assumptions and proceeds on the basis of some tentative notion of the property P. In short, the idealization is hardly controversial.

Scientific approaches to language, in the sense of the term used earlier, proposed various technical notions of language to replace the common-sense notion. The term "grammar" was also used in a variety of ways. In conventional usage, a grammar is a description or theory of a language, an object constructed by a linguist. Let us keep to this usage. Then associated with the various technical notions of language there are corresponding notions of grammar.

One technical notion of language is Bloomfield's, which became conventional. A language, in this sense, is a certain set of sentences, construed in subsequent work as an infinite set. Others (e.g., Lewis 1975) took a language to be an infinite set of sentence–meaning pairs, where "meanings" are taken to be certain set-theoretic objects. Let us refer to such technical concepts as instances of "externalized language" (E-language), in the sense that language, so construed, is something "external" to the mind/brain. Under the same rubric we may include the notion of language as a collection (or system) of behaviors, speech acts, etc. From this point of view, a grammar may be regarded as a function that enumerates the elements of the E-language. And universal grammar (UG) will be the set of conditions satisfied by those E-languages that count as human languages. The possibility of UG was often denied, at least implicitly, as, for example, when Martin Joos put forth what he called the "Boasian" view that "languages could differ from one another without limit and in unpredictable ways," echoing Sapir's notion that "language is a human activity that varies without assignable limits" (Joos 1957; Sapir 1921). Although such proposals could hardly have been meant literally, they did reflect a relativistic impulse that denigrated the study of UG.

From this point of view, the choice of grammar is a fairly arbitrary matter, not raising questions of truth and falsity, as long as the grammar does identify the E-language in question. Quine, for example, argued that it is senseless to take one grammar rather than another to be "correct" if they are extensionally equivalent, characterizing the same E-language (for him, a set of expressions). And Lewis doubts that there is any way "to make objective sense of the assertion that a grammar G is used by a population P whereas another grammar G', which generates the same language as G, is not" (where language is E-language—a set of sentence–"meaning" pairs—and a language is "used" by a population if there are certain regularities in action and belief in this population, sustained by an interest in communication).

The notion E-language is, of course, familiar from the study of formal systems, as is the conclusion just cited: given the "language of arithmetic," there is no objective sense to the idea that one set of rules that generates the well-formed formulas is correct and another wrong.

A rather different approach was taken, for example, by Otto Jespersen, who held that there is some "notion of structure" in the mind of the speaker "which is definite enough to guide him in framing sentences of his own," in particular, "free expressions" that may be new to the speaker and to others (Jespersen 1924). Let us refer to this "notion of structure" as an "internalized language" (I-language). The I-language, then, is something in the mind of the person who knows the language, acquired by the learner, and used by the speaker–hearer. If language is taken to be I-language, the grammar would then be a theory of the I-language, which is the object under investigation. And if indeed such a "notion of structure" exists, as Jespersen argued, then questions of truth and falsity arise for grammar as they do for any scientific theory.

Knowing the language L is a property of a person P and one task of the brain sciences is to determine what it is about P's brain by virtue of which this property holds of P. Returning to our earlier discussion, we suggested that for P to know the language L is for P's mind/brain to be in a certain state; more narrowly, for the language faculty (one module of this system) to be in a certain state S_L. One task of the brain sciences, then, is to discover the mechanisms that are the physical realization of the state S_L.

Suppose we analyze the notion "P knows language L" in relational terms, that is, as involving a relation R (knowing, having, or whatever) holding between P and an abstract entity L.[9] Suppose that we proceed further to regard talk of mind as talk about the brain undertaken at a certain level of abstraction at which we believe, rightly or wrongly, that significant properties and explanatory principles can be discovered. Then statements about R and L belong to the theory of mind, and one task of the brain sciences will be to explain what it is about P's brain (in particular, its language faculty) that corresponds to P's knowing L, i.e., by virtue of which R(P, L) holds and the statement that R(P, L) is true.

It is natural to take L to be I-language, Jespersen's "notion of structure," regarding this as an entity abstracted from a state of the language faculty, this being one component of the mind. Then, for P to know L is for P to have a certain I-language. The statements of grammar are statements of the theory of mind about the I-language; hence, they are indirectly statements about structures of the brain presented at a certain level of abstraction from mechanisms. These structures are specific things in the world, with their specific properties. The statements of a grammar and the statement that R(P, L) are similar to statements of a physical theory that characterizes certain entities and their properties in abstraction from whatever may turn out to be the mechanisms that account for these properties: say, a nineteenth-century theory about valence or properties expressed in the periodic table. Statements about I-language or the statement that R(P, L) are true or false, much in the way that statements about the chemical structure of benzene or the valence of oxygen or about chlorine and fluorine being in the same column of the periodic table are true or false. The I-language L may be the one used by a speaker but not the I-language L', even if the two generate the same class of expressions in whatever precise sense we give to this derivative notion; L' may not even be a possible human I-language, one attainable by the language faculty. UG now is construed as the theory of human I-languages, a set of conditions deriving from the human biological endowment that identifies the I-languages that are humanly accessible under normal conditions. These are the I-languages L such that R(P, L) may be true (for normal P, under normal conditions).[10]

There is, of course, no guarantee that this way of approaching the problems of (1) is the correct one. It may turn out to be thoroughly misguided, even if it achieves substantial successes—just as a theory of valence might have turned out to be completely off the track, despite its substantial successes in nineteenth-century chemistry. It is always reasonable to consider alternative approaches, if they can be devised, and this will remain true no matter what successes are achieved. The situation does not seem different in principle from what we find in other areas of empirical inquiry. I will suggest directly that in certain fundamental respects early ideas about I-language were misguided and should be replaced by a rather different conception, though one formulated in the same general framework.

If we assume the approach to be generally sound, many factors may bear on the question of what is the I-language apart from the expressions or sound–meaning pairs characterized: perceptual experiments, studies of acquisition and deficit, neurophysiological or biochemical evidence, etc. Furthermore, evidence from other languages has a crucial bearing on the choice of grammar for a given language (that is, bearing on what is in fact the I-language) if we accept the plausible assumption that the capacity to acquire language, the subject matter of UG, is common across the species.[11] This capacity, which we may consider to be incorporated in the initial state S_0 of the language faculty, maps linguistic data into an attained I-language. Since evidence from Japanese can evidently bear on the correctness of a theory of S_0, it can have indirect, but very powerful, bearing on the choice of the grammar that attempts to characterize the I-language attained by a speaker of English. For this reason alone it is quite wrong to suppose that there are no grounds to choose among "extensionally equivalent grammars"; for example, one may require a theory of S_0 that is demonstrably inadequate for some other language. Questions of choice of grammar and UG are, then, typical questions of science.

Generative grammar shifted the focus of attention from E-language to I-language. The point of view was essentially this. The language faculty is a distinct system of the mind/brain, with an initial state S_0 common to the species (to a very close first approximation, apart from pathology, etc.) and apparently unique to it in essential respects. Given appropriate data, this faculty passes from the state S_0 to some relatively steady state S_s, the latter constituting an I-language. UG is the theory of S_0; particular grammars are theories of the various attainable states S_s. Each I-language assigns a status to every expression, indeed every physical event. Some are sentences with a definite meaning (literal, figurative, or whatever); others are intelligible with, perhaps, a definite meaning, but are ill formed in one or another way ("the child seems sleeping," "what do you wonder who saw?"); others are well formed but unintelligible; others are identified as possible sentences of some language, but not mine; others are mere noise. Different I-languages will assign status differently in each of these and other categories. The notion of E-language has no place in this picture. There is no issue of correctness with regard to E-languages, however characterized, since E-languages are artifacts, not real things in the world or even related in any clear way to real things in the world as I-languages are. We can define "E-language" in one or another way; or not at all, since it appears to play no role in the theory of language.

The qualms expressed by Quine, Lewis, Dummett, and many others are unwarranted. It is true, as often observed, that for every E-language, however we choose to define this notion, there are many grammars (i.e., many grammars, each of which is a theory of a particular I-language which, under the convention selected, determines an E-language). But this is a matter of no consequence. In the case of arithmetic, we assume the class of well-formed formulas in some notation to be "given," and we select the "grammar" as we wish. But the E-language is not "given." What is "given" to the child is some finite array of data, on the basis of which the child's mind (incorporating S_0) constructs an I-language which, in turn, we may think of as generating some E-language in one or another manner (or we may not); what is given to the linguist is finite arrays of data from various speech communities, on the basis of which the linguist will attempt to discover the nature of S_0 (i.e., to discover UG) and the particular I-languages attained (i.e., to discover the particular grammars). The account presented by Lewis and others has the story backwards: E-languages are not given but are derivative, more remote from data and from mechanisms than I-languages and the grammars that are theories of I-languages. The choice of E-language therefore raises a host of new and additional problems beyond grammar and I-language, and it is not at all clear that it is worthwhile addressing or attempting to solve them, since the concept appears to have no significance. The belief that E-language is a fairly clear notion, whereas I-language or grammar raises serious (perhaps unsolvable) philosophical problems, is quite mistaken. Just the opposite is true. There are numerous problems concerning the notions I-language and grammar, but not the ones raised in these discussions.

The shift of focus instituted by generative grammar, reviving and modifying much older traditions, is a shift toward realism: I-languages are abstracted directly from particular states of the mind/brain, under the relational interpretation of states of knowledge; and theories of I-languages are on a par with scientific theories in other domains, whereas theories of E-languages, if sensible at all, have some different and more obscure status. Linguistics, so conceived, becomes part of psychology, ultimately biology. It will be incorporated within the natural sciences insofar as mechanisms are discovered which have the properties revealed in these more abstract studies; indeed, one would expect that these studies will be a necessary step toward serious investigation of mechanisms.[12]

The shift of focus was also, arguably, a shift toward the common-sense notion of language. This matter is less important than the move toward realism and is also much less clear, since, as noted, all of these approaches deviate from the common-sense concept in certain respects. But it seems that when we speak of a person as knowing a language, we do not mean that he/she knows an infinite set of sentences or sound–meaning pairs taken in extension; rather, the person knows what it is that makes sound and meaning "hang together," a particular characterization of a function, perhaps. The person has "a notion of structure," and I-language, characterized by the linguist's grammar. The rules of the language are not rules of some infinite set but are rules that form or constitute the language, like Articles of the Constitution or rules of chess (not an infinite set of moves but a game, a particular rule system). Of the various technical notions that have been developed in the study of language, the concept of I-language seems closer to the common-sense notion than others, though again, the matter is not of great importance and is also hardly very clear. Note that traditional analogies between languages and games or codes also point toward I-language rather than E-language; a code is not an infinite set of signal–message pairs but instead some particular system of encoding which characterizes this set.[13]

As noted earlier, the conceptual shift just discussed was one of the steps that led toward the contemporary cognitive sciences. The character of this quite fundamental shift was in part obscured by some unfortunate terminological decisions and in part by accidents of publishing history.[14] Within generative grammar the term "language" was used for E-language, following familiar usage in linguistics and logic. The term "grammar" was then used with systematic ambiguity, in the sense of I-language and of theory of I-language; the same was true of the term UG, introduced later with the same systematic ambiguity, referring to S_0 and the theory of S_0. Thus we find the paradoxical situation that in work devoted to language, the term "language" barely appears. In my *Aspects of the Theory of Syntax*, for example, there is no entry for "language" in the index but many entries under "grammar," generally referring to I-language. I suspect that the debate in past years over the alleged problems that are raised by the concepts grammar and knowledge of grammar may in part be traced to these unfortunate terminological choices, which reinforced inappropriate analogies to the formal sciences.

Keeping now to a more appropriate terminology, generative grammar was concerned with the language faculty in its initial state S_0 and steady state S_s, with UG and particular grammars. Its primary concern is knowledge of I-language, in the initial and steady state. Consider then the proposed answers to the three central questions (1) that arise. The answer to (i) was taken to be that knowledge of language is knowledge of a certain rule system; the answer to (ii), that this knowledge arises from an initial state S_0 which maps data onto I-language. Question (iii) breaks down into two parts: a "perception problem" and a "production problem." The perception problem would be dealt with by construction of a parser that incorporates the rules of the I-language along with other elements; e.g., a certain organization of memory and access (perhaps a deterministic pushdown structure with a buffer of a certain size, as in the Marcus parser; see Marcus 1980), certain heuristics, etc. A parser should not map expressions into their structures in the way that these are associated by the I-language; for example, it should fail to do so in the case of garden path sentences or sentences that overload memory for left-to-right pass, it should mirror the difficulties experienced with sentences such as (8)–(10). The production problem is considerably more obscure; we return to that.

One might ask whether it is proper to use the term "knowledge" in this context. Is it, for example, proper to say that a person who knows a language in the ordinary sense "knows the rules of the I-language" in the technical sense? In part, the answer is certainly negative, since I-language, like other technical notions of scientific approaches, is not language in the pretheoretic sense for reasons mentioned earlier. It is not clear that much is at stake here; ordinary usage in fact differs from language to language in this regard (one does not speak of "knowing a language" but rather of "speaking" or "understanding" it in languages very similar to English). It seems that knowledge of language involves (perhaps entails) paradigm examples of propositional knowledge: knowledge that in the word *pin*, /p/ is aspirated, while in *spin* it is not; that in the sentences (2), (3) (repeated here) the pronoun may be referentially dependent in one case but not the other; etc.:

> (2) I wonder who the men expected to see them
> (3) the men expected to see them

If these are not instances of knowledge, it is hard to see what is.

Suppose that our best theory asserts that speakers know these facts because the I-language they internalize (to use a more neutral term) yields certain representations and contains certain principles. Specifically, suppose that according to this theory, the I-language provides the representation (2′) for (2) and (3′) for (3), where *e* is an empty category variable bound by the quasi-quantifier *who* and PRO is a pronoun-like empty category bound by *the men*, and where brackets represent clause boundaries; and the I-language contains also the Binding Theory principle P that requires a pronoun to be free in the domain of a subject, these notions being structurally determined in an appropriate way:

> (2′) I wonder [who the men expected [e to see them]]
> (3′) the men expected [PRO to see them]

Then the interpretations of (2) and (3) are determined just as they would be in (2″), (3″), where we have overt rather than empty categories:

> (2″) I thought [the men expected [Bill to see them]]
> (3″) I expected [the men to see them]

Thus in (2′), (2″), the pronoun must be free in the domain of the embedded subject (*e*, *Bill*, respectively) and may therefore be (locally) bound by the more remote subject *the men*; but in (3'), (3'') the pronoun cannot be bound by the embedded subject and also cannot be bound by the remote subject [in (3') because that would entail that it is bound by PRO, which is bound by *the men*; and in (3'') because the remote subject is inappropriate].

There is good reason to suppose that something like this is correct. Should we then say that the person who "has" this I-language "knows the rule P"? This seems quite consistent with normal usage. If John knows English and Pierre is a speaker of French who is learning English, and John aspirates /p/ in word initial position but Pierre doesn't, we would say that John knows the rule of aspiration but Pierre does not yet know it, though he will know it when he learns more. Here the rule of aspiration is understood to be one of the rules of English, a particular I-language. The same is true for (2), (3), even if the rule P belongs to S_0 (imagine a Martian learning English). Of course, to attribute knowledge of the relevant rules to John and Pierre, *we* must know the meanings of the terms that enter into the formulation of them, just as we must know the meaning of "fusion" if we are to describe what is happening inside the sun in terms of fusion; but this is not relevant here. Note that it is irrelevant whether John or Pierre know the meanings of these terms, at least so far as ordinary usage of the terminology of rule following and knowledge of rules is concerned. In these and many other cases, it seems that to speak of knowledge of rules, following rules, etc., is reasonably in accord with normal usage, except, of course, with regard to the proviso given earlier concerning the normative-teleological aspect of the common-sense notion of language. But again, not much seems to be at stake; different terms can be invented if one is uncomfortable with what appears to conform closely to normal usage (though not various philosophical theories) in these cases.

I will continue, then, to assume that it is legitimate to say that John knows the rule R if the best theory of available evidence attributes to John a state of the mind/brain with an I-language including R; and to say that John follows the rule R in doing so-and-so [say, interpreting (2) and (3)] if the best account of this behavior invokes the rule R in a relevant way.

Facing Plato's Problem

Returning to the main theme, suppose that we tentatively accept these general proposals as to how to approach the questions (1), which more or less define the subject of generative grammar. At this point substantive questions arise as to how these proposals should be fleshed out.

The earliest ideas were roughly as follows. Suppose that UG provides a certain format for I-languages, that is, a specification of permitted types of rules and permissible interactions among them, and also an evaluation metric that assigns a value to an arbitrary I-language. This is what constitutes S_0. We may think of UG as specifying an infinite class of possible I-languages. Given data, S_0 searches the class, selecting the highest-valued I-language consistent with the data and entering the state S_1, which incorporates the rules of this I-language. Given new data, the system enters S_2, etc., until it enters a state S_s in which the procedure terminates (either because of some property of S_s or because the system has reached a state of maturation that does not permit it to proceed).

We might further suggest, as an empirical hypothesis, that order of presentation of data is irrelevant, so that learning is "as if it were instantaneous." Thus S_0 maps the data directly to S_s. We then have a certain model of language acquisition and of explanation. We explain the fact that . . . [e.g., that (2) and (3) have the range of meanings they do have] and that John knows this, by showing that these facts follow from the rules of the highest-valued I-language consistent with the data presented to John. We may say that a particular theory of UG meets the condition of *explanatory adequacy* to the extent that it yields such explanations and that the grammars it provides under the boundary conditions of given experience are *descriptively adequate* to the extent that they correctly describe the I-languages attained.[15] This is, in fact, the model of explanation generally used in linguistics, insofar as one or another approach is concerned with explanation at all. It depends crucially on the legitimacy of the idealization to instantaneous learning. If this move is empirically incorrect, there will be no explanations of the standard form; conversely, if such explanations can be produced, that counts as evidence that the empirical assumption, which is not at all an obvious one, is correct. One can imagine various intermediate positions, but as a working hypothesis, the assumption so far seems rather credible, perhaps surprisingly.

The model of acquisition and explanation assumed in this early work is essentially that of Peircean abduction: innate limitations (the "guessing instinct") yield a small class of admissible hypotheses that are submitted to "corrective action," a procedure that works because "Man's mind has a natural adaptation to imagining correct theories of some kind."[16] In the light of the facts of language acquisition, the basic problem is to construct UG so that the class of admissible hypotheses is small, perhaps single-membered. If so, UG provides a significant part of the answer to (1ii) and attains explanatory adequacy in significant respects; if not, it does not. Similar considerations apply in other domains as well, I believe (cf. Chomsky 1975a, 1980b).

As noted earlier, the basic problem is that our knowledge is richly articulated and determinate and is shared with others from the same speech community, whereas the data available seem much too impoverished to determine it by any general procedure. There is good reason to believe that children learn language from positive evidence only (corrections not being required or relevant), and they appear to have the right answers without relevant experience in a vast array of complex cases, such as those illustrated. It must be, then, that the "guessing instinct" yields very few admissible hypotheses to test.

Note that the generative capacity of UG is a matter of no obvious empirical import. What is important is a requirement of "feasibility" that has no clear relation to the scope of UG. What is required for feasibility is that given data, a fairly small collection of languages are made available for inspection and evaluation, and that accessible languages are "scattered" in value. A theory of UG might fail this condition, even if its scope were finite, and might meet this condition if it provided a grammar for every recursively enumerable E-language. Other factors concerning the structure of UG are relevant at this point, not generative capacity.[17]

There is a tension between the demands of descriptive and explanatory adequacy. To achieve the latter, it is necessary to restrict available descriptive mechanisms so that few languages are accessible (note that many might be available in principle, but this would not matter if only few are highly valued). To achieve descriptive adequacy, however, the available devices must be rich and diverse enough to deal with the phenomena exhibited in the possible human languages. We therefore face conflicting requirements. We might identify the field of generative grammar as an area of research, with the domain in which this tension remains unresolved.

The dilemma arose in a clear and sharp form as soon as the research program of generative grammar was formulated. As noted earlier, the earliest efforts to construct explicit grammars quickly uncovered a vast array of new phenomena, previously unobserved in studies that relied on the intelligence of the reader, including quite simple ones. To deal with these facts it seemed necessary to enrich the class of descriptive devices, but this could not be the correct move, given the requirement of explanatory adequacy. Let us consider now how the problem has been addressed, and the recent conceptual shift to which these efforts have led.

The format proposed in the earliest work allowed for two types of rules, phrase structure rules of the form (11) that form phrase-markers (representations of categorial structure) and transformational rules that map phrase-markers into other phrase-markers:

(11) $X \rightarrow Y / Z$—W (X is rewritten Y in the context Z—W)

Transformational rules are defined, in turn, in terms of structural descriptions (SDs) that determine their domain and structural changes (SCs) that determine what they do (substitutions, adjunctions, etc.); general principles determine the resulting phrase-marker. Both types of rules are modeled on traditional grammar; phrase structure rules were more specifically motivated by earlier work in what is now called "generative phonology." In this earlier work, phrase structure rules for syntax were permitted to be considerably more complex, with "complex symbols" containing features that could "percolate down" through derivations; such ideas were also developed in later approaches that enrich the class of possible phrase structure grammars.

The immediate task was to show that these devices suffice for descriptive adequacy. To illustrate the kind of problem that arose, consider the rules that form interrogative and relative clauses.[18] We have such examples as (12):

(12) (i)   the man [who John saw e]
      (ii) (I wonder) [who John saw e]
      (iii) the man [John saw e]
      (iv) *(I wonder) [John saw e]
      (v)   (I wonder) [what he found of yours]
      (vi) *(I wonder) [who he found of yours]
      (vii) *(I wonder) [who a picture of e is on the table]
      (viii) *the man [[to whom]$_2$ I wonder [what$_1$ he gave e$_1$ e$_2$]]
      (ix) *what$_2$ did you meet the man [who$_1$ e$_1$ saw e$_2$]

Examples (i) and (ii) are straightforward. We could describe them in the format provided as follows: phrase structure rules generate declaratives with a noun phrase (NP) or prepositional phrase (PP = P NP) in the position of e. We may think of *wh-* as a feature that appears in the surface form within a word (a noun, in this case) but is abstractly associated with the NP of which this noun is the head or the PP containing this NP. This is the "*wh*-phrase," designated "*wh-*." The NP is spelled out as *who* or *what*, depending on the category of the noun. The *wh*-phrase is moved to the left of the clause by the transformation described informally in (13), with the SD (X, *wh*, Y) and the SC "move the second term to the left" (with a convention requiring "local" movement):

$$(13) (X, wh\text{-}, Y) \rightarrow (2, 1, 3)$$

This is a simple rule, covering both relatives and interrogatives. It can readily be extended to other syntactic categories. Let us refer to it as the rule: Front-*wh*-.

Consider next (12iii, iv). As these examples illustrate, the relative *wh*-phrase can delete, but the interrogative cannot; thus, some new transformation is required applying to one construction but not the other. Turning next to (v), (vi), with such corresponding declaratives as "he found a book of yours," "he found a friend of yours," we see that some further condition must be imposed on the rules (the same is true of the corresponding relatives). Example (vii), with the corresponding declarative "a picture of John is on the table," shows that the SD of (13) must be complicated to rule out movement in this case. Examples (viii) and (ix) (with the corresponding declaratives "he gave the book to the man," "the man saw the dog"), indicate that the SDs must be further complicated.

The descriptive mechanisms provided by the format of UG did provide mechanisms that sufficed for these purposes but at a serious cost. The problem can be put in various forms: (I) why does the child not use the simple rule (13), thus deriving the wrong answers in many cases, instead of the more complex rules required for descriptive adequacy?; (II) the mechanisms are so rich that far too many languages are submitted to the evaluation metric for choice; (III) explanatory power is sacrificed, since we have no explanation for the facts as they are. Many problems of this sort arose as soon as the task of constructing explicit grammars was faced.

The obvious way to approach such problems is to seek general principles governing rule application that can be abstracted from individual rules and attributed to UG, thus leaving only the simple rule (13): Front-*wh*-. The earliest proposals appear in Chomsky (1964).[19] A principle of recoverability of deletion states that an element can be deleted only if it is determined by a phrase that is structurally related to it or if it is a "designated element," where these notions have to be made precise. In (i), the relative element *who* is determined by "the man" and can therefore be deleted, giving (iii); but in (ii) it is not determined, so that (iv) is ungrammatical. Taking the designated representative of NP to be the singular indefinite *someone, something,* so that only these elements can be replaced by a *wh*-phrase, we reduce (v)–(vi) to the fact that "I found something of yours" is grammatical but "I found someone of yours" is not.[20] The A-over-A principle states that a phrase of the category A (A arbitrary) cannot be extracted from another phrase of the category A, thus barring (vii), which requires that the NP *who* be extracted from the NP "a picture of who." Turning to (viii) and (ix), a general principle of UG states that a particular rule [say, (13)] cannot apply twice to the same clause, thus barring these examples.

With these general principles attributed to UG, we can keep to the simple rule (13) for both relatives and interrogatives. What the child has to learn is that English moves *wh*-phrases to clause-initial position; other properties of the constructions then follow by principles of S_0, expressed in UG. On this assumption, the child will know that the facts are as in (12) once (13) has been learned, and (13) can be learned from very simple data, e.g., (12i). The principles of S_0 constitute, in effect, one component of what Hume called the "parts of [our] knowledge [that] derive from the original hand of nature."

Note that if the reduction to (13) can be sustained, we no longer have rules associated with particular constructions: there is no "rule of relativization" or "interrogative rule." Rather, there are general principles such as (13) which enter into the formation of various constructions, along with other principles. Later work led to the conclusion that this "modular" character of the system of language is quite general.

Subsequent work showed that directionality need not be stipulated in (13), so that the rule can be reduced further from Front-*wh*- to Move-*wh*. Further work along these lines gave substantial support to the idea that all transformational rules can be reduced to a form similar to (13) once the general principles are correctly formulated. The study of NP movement showed that the rules for passive and raising reduce to Move-NP, so that there is no passive or raising rule but simply an interaction of principles of UG yielding various constructions, differing from language to language as a consequence of other options that the languages allow. Furthermore, the differences between Move-*wh*, Move-NP, Move-PP, etc., can be in large part (perhaps completely) explained in other terms, so that we are left with the rule Move-α, α being an arbitrary category. It would be far too strong to claim that this conclusion has been demonstrated, but it seems a reasonable hypothesis and many particular cases appear well substantiated.

Insofar as this conclusion is accurate, the transformational component of the grammar can be reduced to the rule Move-α—i.e., move anything anywhere—or perhaps even Affect-α (do anything to anything: delete, insert, move), as suggested by Lasnik and Saito (1984).

Nevertheless, there is still something to learn in connection with these rules. Thus, while in English, *wh*-phrases are moved to the left, in Chinese and Japanese they are left in place. We might say, then, that the general principle Move-α has associated with it a parameter determining the choice of α; its value must be fixed by experience. The exact nature of this parametric difference among languages has been the subject of important work, in particular that of Huang (1982) who gave strong evidence, subsequently extended by others, that even in Chinese–Japanese the *wh*-phrase is moved to the boundary of the clause, leaving an empty category as a variable. This mapping does not take place overtly, as in English, but rather in the mapping of the syntactic structure (S-structure) to a level of LF (read: "logical form," with familiar provisos) in which scope and other properties are indicated. English too has instances of LF-movement of *wh*-phrases, as in multiple-*wh*-questions such as "I wonder who gave the book to whom," first studied in something like this framework by Baker (1970). Hence the LF-representations of English, Japanese, and Chinese will be very similar, though the S-structures differ; this is what we might expect, if it is LF-representation that is the interface between syntax (in the broad sense) and the systems of language use. If this is correct, the parameter in question will have to do not with choice of α but rather with the level at which the rule Move-α applies for various choices of α.[21]

There are other complexities in the system just discussed. Thus compare (12viii) with (14):

(12viii) *the man to whom I wonder [what he gave e e]

(14) *the man whom I wonder [what he gave e to e]

With regard to (12viii), there is variation in judgments, and few speakers find it as hopelessly bad as (14). Hence something is missed when we simply mark both examples as ungrammatical. The relevant difference seems to be that in (14), the two empty categories are NPs, whereas in (12viii), one is an NP and one a PP. We might reformulate the principle that blocks multiple application of a rule to a clause as a "filter" on S-structure: a VP cannot contain two empty categories of the same type. Then (14) will be barred by a principle of UG, but (12viii) will be barred (or not) by some other principle that is subject to lower-level parametric variation among languages. This may well be the case. On the relevant parameters for (12viii), see Rizzi (1982a).[22]

Note that developments of the sort just outlined would constitute no progress at all if some other component of the grammar were enriched in descriptive power while the transformational component was restricted; in that case, the same problems would arise once again. A crucial part of this work, then, was that it did not lead to an increase in the variety of possible phrase structure grammars.

In fact, the phrase structure component poses much the same problems as those illustrated with regard to transformations: there are far too many possible systems of the permitted format available, so explanatory adequacy is sacrificed and our variant of Plato's problem is unresolved. The solution was the same: find ways to reduce the variety of phrase structure systems by abstracting general properties, assigning them to S_0. This topic too was addressed from the early 1960s. It was noticed, for example, that reference to context in such rules as (11) is restricted to rules assigning lexical items to their syntactic categories. The obvious suggestion, then, is to separate the lexicon from the syntax, as a separate component; syntactic phrase structure rules are then "context-free," so that their possible variety is radically reduced. Further studies showed that the variety of transformations could be reduced by eliminating options that were required for structures (e.g., complex nominal constructions) that should be attributed to the lexicon, which has interesting properties of its own.

The phrase structure component can be reduced still further, regarded as a kind of "projection" of lexical properties. Phrases typically consist of a "head" (noun, verb, adjective, preposition, and possibly others) and an array of "complements" determined by lexical properties of the head. The category constituted of the head and its complements is a projection of the head (e.g., NP if the head is an N). Further general properties of the system are formulated in a component of UG called "X-bar theory," with further reduction of the options for phrase structure rules. Subsequent work suggested that the order of complements can in large part be determined by other general principles of UG.

The end result of this work has been to suggest that the phrase structure component can be entirely eliminated, apart from certain parameters of X-bar theory (e.g., does the head precede its complements, as in English, or does it follow them, as in Japanese?). The exact nature of these parameters is currently under investigation, but it seems now that rules of phrase structure are not among the elements learned in the transition to the steady state; rather, values are fixed for certain of the parameters of X-bar theory.

A number of general principles have been proposed concerning well-formed structures that reduce the recourse to rule systems still further. One is the Projection Principle, which, put informally, states that lexical structure must be represented categorically at every syntactic level. Intuitively, the principle states that if some element is "understood" in a particular position, then it is *there* in syntactic representation, either as an overt category that is phonetically realized or as an empty category assigned no phonetic form (though its presence may affect phonetic form). Thus if "see" is lexically characterized as a transitive verb, there must be an object, syntactically represented as its complement is a Verb Phrase (VP), at every syntactic level. If there is no overt element in this position, there must be an empty category of the required type. The structural representation of "the man I saw," then, must be (15), where e is the NP object of "see":

(15) the man [I [$_{VP}$ saw e]]

Furthermore, the properties of empty categories, which are determined by other subsystems of UG, require that e in this case be a variable bound by an operator in clause-initial position, so that there is still another empty category in this position in (15), as in (15'), where O is an empty category operator binding e:

(15') the man [O[I [$_{VP}$ saw e]]]

Further properties of UG require that every element that appears in a well-formed structure must be "licensed" in one of a small number of available ways: an operator is licensed by binding a variable, from which it is not "too distant" in a certain abstract sense; a variable must be bound, in the special sense that it must have its range determined by an appropriate operator or its value determined by an appropriate antecedent; a predicate must have a subject [where the notions are syntactically defined; see Williams (1980) and subsequent work]; NPs of the "denoting" type (names, definite descriptions, variables, etc.) must be assigned semantic roles (thematic roles, or theta-roles) determined by their grammatical function and by lexical properties of heads, where the former are expressed in syntactic configuration, and these theta-roles can be assigned only if the NP (apart from PRO) is assigned abstract case (which is sometimes phonetically realized, depending on other properties of the language) in accordance with general principles of case theory; referential dependency must meet the conditions of Binding Theory; etc.

We might express these ideas by saying that there is a principle of Full Interpretation (FI) that requires that every element of PF (phonetic form) and LF, taken to be the interface of syntax (in the broad sense) with systems of language use, must receive an appropriate interpretation—must be licensed in the sense indicated. At the level of PF, each phonetic element must be licensed by some physical interpretation: the word *book* could not be represented/fburk/, where we simply disregard /f/ and /r/; that would be possible only if the language contained explicit rules deleting these elements. Similarly we cannot have sentences of the form "I was in England last year the man," "who John saw Bill," "every everyone was here," interpreted, respectively, as "I was in England last year," "John saw Bill," "everyone was here," simply disregarding the unlicensed elements "the man," "who," "every." This is not a logically necessary property of any possible language; it is, for example, not observed in standard notations for quantification theory that permit vacuous quantifiers in well-formed expressions. But it is a property of natural language. Given this very general property and an appropriate theory of licensing, it would be redundant—i.e., flat wrong—to include in a grammar of English rules that specifically bar examples of the sort just illustrated, e.g., rules that require that "who" must be followed by a sentence with a "gap" of a certain sort: a missing position, an empty category, or in some languages a resumptive pronoun as in the marginal English examples "who did you think that if he gets married, then everyone will be happy." Such rules simply restate in some complex way facts that follow from quite general properties of language. See Chomsky (1982).

I will not attempt to spell out these notions here, but only to indicate very informally the general idea. UG consists of various subsystems—binding theory, case theory, theta theory, etc.—each with certain principles with a limited degree of parametric variation. There are, in addition, certain overriding principles such as the Projection Principle, FI, and the principles of licensing. Certain concepts, such as the concepts of c-command and government, play a central role in each of these subsystems. The interaction of the principles of these various "modules" determines when a structure is well formed. There are no rules for particular constructions; in this respect, the example of *wh*-movement already discussed is typical.

To illustrate how such a system works, consider the sentence (16):

(16)   who was John persuaded to visit

Let us ask what specific knowledge beyond S_0 is required to understand this sentence, insofar as the language contributes to this end—i.e., what specific knowledge must be acquired by the child to assign it the structure that underlies semantic interpretation and use. We must, first of all, know the lexical properties of the words; otherwise, we cannot understand the sentence. Suppose we do. We know, then, that "visit" is a transitive verb, which, by X-bar theory, must head a VP and, by the Projection Principle, must have an NP object. The latter must be an empty category, since there is no overt NP present. One of the values of the X-bar theory parameters for English is that English is a "head-first" language, and so the object is to the right of "visit." Furthermore, to be licensed, the predicate "visit e" must have a subject, the two forming a clause (S); since the subject is not overt, it must be another empty category, a conclusion that follows in any event since case is not assigned in the position of the subject of the infinitive. Turning to "persuade," we know that it is a verb that takes an object and a clausal complement (as appear overtly in "I persuaded John that he should take part"). The order of these complements is determined by general principles of UG. Continuing in this way, we conclude that the structure of (16) must be (17), where I omit a number of categories and category labels, for simplicity:

(17)   who was [John [$_{VP}$ persuaded e_i [e_j to [$_{VP}$ visit e_k]]]]

This much of the structure is determined simply on the basis of lexical properties and the value of the head-complement parameter (not strictly relevant for the task at hand), given principles of UG. For the structure to be well formed, it is necessary that each element be licensed. The *wh*-phrase must bind a variable, and *John* and each empty category must be assigned theta-roles. For reasons determined by UG, only e_k may be a variable (the other empty categories are not in case-marked positions and therefore are not "visible" for theta-role assignment). Therefore *who* must bind e_k. *John* is the subject of a passive, a position to which no theta-role is assigned (a non-theta-position), as we can see from the fact that nondenoting expressions appear there ("it is alleged that . . . ," "advantage was taken of Bill," etc.). Therefore it must bind some element in a theta-position that can "transfer" its theta-role to *John* (by general convention regarding "chains" consisting of NPs and empty categories that they bind). Principles of Binding Theory exclude e_j as a candidate, and so *John* must bind e_i, which, though not in a case-marked position, is nevertheless "visible" for theta-marking because it is now in a chain with the case-marked element *John*. This leaves e_j, which, by general principles, must be the pronoun-like element PRO of (3'). We know that *persuade* requires that its object control such a PRO, as we see, e.g., in "John persuaded Bill [PRO to leave," where Bill, who is persuaded by John, is the one who is to leave. So in (17), PRO (namely, e_j) is controlled by e_i, the object of "persuade."

All of these connections are determined by general principles. Spelling them out, we interpret (16) roughly as "for which person x, someone persuaded John that John should visit x." To achieve this interpretation, the only information required specifically about English is knowledge of the lexical items, which of course must be learned, though there are no doubt very heavy universal constraints in this system as well. The remainder is deduced from general principles.

To take a somewhat more complex case, consider again examples (4)– (7), repeated here:

(4) John ate an apple
(5) John ate
(6) John is too stubborn to talk to Bill
(7) John is too stubborn to talk to

The problem posed by these examples is that the natural inductive procedure that accounts for (5) fails for (7), since the object in (7) is understood to be "John" rather than some arbitrary person, whereas the subject of "talk to" is understood to be some arbitrary person, not "John" as in

(6). How do we know these facts? It must be that they are largely or completely deducible from general principles, since specific relevant information is unavailable to the language learner. What, then, do we know about the structure of (7), given just UG, knowledge of the lexical entries (and, though it is not here relevant, of the parameters of X-bar theory, etc.)?

As in the case of (16), we know that "talk to" has an empty category object with which it forms a VP, and an empty category subject forming a clause with VP as predicate. Thus, the structure is, to begin with, something like (18):

(18)   John is too stubborn [$_S$ e_i to [$_{VP}$ talk to e_j]]

General principles of Binding Theory require that e_i, once again, be PRO, and that e_j cannot be PRO and cannot form a chain with *John* (which, in any event, already has a theta-role). It follows that e_j must be a variable, this being the only option left. The embedded clause, then, must have an empty operator O binding e_j. But to be licensed, the variable may not be "free" in the sense defined earlier. Since its operator, being empty, does not specify a range, the variable must be associated with an antecedent in a structurally appropriate position that assigns it a value. Only *John* is available as an antecedent, and it is in an appropriate position, as the subject of the predicate "too stubborn to talk to e_j," for general reasons. Therefore e_j takes John as its value. If PRO were bound by *John*, and hence assigned the same value as the variable, we would have a violation of the general principle of "strong crossover" which, in particular, bars the interpretation of the pronoun as a variable bound by *who* in such sentences as "who did he expect to see e" (this principle follows from the principles of Binding Theory). Since PRO cannot be bound by *John* and there is no other binder, it must be arbitrary in interpretation, as it is in such sentences as "it is illegal [$_S$ PRO to vote twice]."

The interpretation of the sentence (7), then, must be "John is so stubborn that no one will talk to him (John)," as distinct from (6). The same principles explain the interpretation of (10) as distinct from (9).[23] Again, the structure and interpretation are deducible from general principles, given knowledge of the lexical items. As noted, something of the sort must be the case, given the empirical conditions of the problem.

The analysis of (7) that is entailed by the principles of UG has many other verifiable consequences. If e_j is indeed a variable bound by an empty operator, it must observe a variety of conditions on movement to clause-initial position, such as those illustrated in (12vii–ix) above; and indeed these structures do observe these conditions. Furthermore, only variables, not other empty categories, license so-called "parasitic gaps," as in (19i), where the parasitic gap e_j is licensed by the variable e_i, bound by "which book," and (19ii), where the parasitic gap is licensed by the variable e_i; compare (19iii), in which e_i is not a variable:

(19) (i) which book did you file e_i [without reading e_j]
   (ii) John is too charming [O_i to talk to e_i [without liking e_j]]
   (iii) *the book was filed e_i [without reading e_j]

The distribution of possible gaps in these constructions is also explained on the assumption that e_j is a variable bound by an empty operator (see Chomsky (1980a). In short, there is substantial empirical evidence in support of the analysis just informally outlined. In the present context, the important point is that the interpretation of (7) is completely determined by principles of UG, given knowledge of the lexical items. We can therefore explain how it is that children know these facts without instruction or relevant evidence.

I will return in a moment to other evidence bearing on the validity of the principles of UG informally outlined here and the representations they provide. Let us first review the general picture of language and grammar that emerges. We no longer consider UG to provide a format for rule systems and an evaluation metric. Rather, UG consists of various subsystems of principles (it has the modular structure that we regularly discover in investigation of cognitive systems), many of which are associated with parameters that have to be fixed by experience. The parameters must have the property that they can be fixed by quite simple data, since this is what is available to the child; the value of the head-parameter, for example, can be determined from such sentences as "John saw Bill" (versus "John Bill saw"). Once the values of the parameters are set, the whole system is operative. Borrowing an image suggested by James Higginbotham, we may think of UG as an intricate system associated with a finite set of switches, each of which has a finite number of positions (perhaps two). Experience is required to set the switches. When they are set, the system functions. The transition from S_0 to S_s is a matter of setting the switches. There may be general principles that determine how the switches are set, e.g., the subset principle discussed by Berwick (1982). There may also be principles of markedness that determine preferred values, and principles relating various parameters, which need not be and probably are not independent.

Returning to the questions of (1), what we "know innately" are the principles of the various subsystems of S_0 and the manner of their interaction, and the parameters associated with these principles. What we learn are the values of the parameters. The language that we then know is a system of principles with parameters fixed. It is not at all clear that what we know should be regarded as a rule system. It might be, in fact, that the notion of rule, like the notion of E-language (so it seems), has no status in linguistic theory. One can, in fact, formulate algorithms that determine rule systems given a choice of values for the parameters of UG, but it is not obvious that this is a significant move or that it matters how it is done.

This conception of UG and I-language has slowly emerged over the past twenty years in the course of research aimed at resolving the tension between descriptive and explanatory adequacy. It has, in fact, only been formulated in the past few years, as various approaches to this problem have converged. This represents the second of the two major conceptual shifts that I noted at the outset. It has made possible the explanation of quite an interesting range of phenomena, such as those illustrated, in a number of languages of typologically different sorts that have been investigated from this point of view. It also opens some new questions for investigation and suggests a reformulation of others. Consider a few examples.

Note that a change in the value of a single parameter may have complex consequences, as its effects filter through the system. A single change of value may lead to a collection of consequences that appear, on the surface, to be unrelated. Thus, even languages that have separated only recently may differ in a cluster of properties, something that has been observed in comparative studies. We can use information of this sort to help determine the structure of principles and parameters of UG. Some new and intriguing questions of comparative linguistics and universal grammar are thus opened up for investigation, and quite suggestive work has been done in several language areas, particularly the Romance languages.[24] We also expect to find, and apparently do find, that a few changes in parameters yield typologically different languages, another topic now being subjected to extensive investigation. These conclusions should be qualitatively correct, given the tension between the demands of descriptive and explanatory adequacy noted above—that is, given the fact that typologically different languages can be acquired with equal ease and limited data on the basis of a fixed S_0.

Note further that investigation of the empirical effects of slight changes in parameters can have broad implications concerning UG in other ways. One new line of inquiry of this sort is opened up by Huang's work on the parameters of Move-α, noted above. Recall that *wh*-movement can take place either in the syntax, affecting S-structure, or in the LF-component, affecting LF-representation but not S-structure. English is a language of the first type; Chinese–Japanese are of the second type (though English also has LF *wh*-movement, as noted). Suppose that the range of interpretations of certain interrogatives is the same in Chinese–Japanese and in English. Then it is reasonable to conclude that these are determined by LF conditions, since it is at this level that the languages are alike. Suppose that the range of interpretations differs in Chinese–Japanese and English. Then these are presumably determined by S-structure conditions, since it is here that the languages differ. Thus, we have a research tool for determining the exact point in the system at which various conditions of UG apply. For exploration of these ideas, which has been quite productive, see Huang (1982), Lasnik and Saito (1984), among many others.[25]

This conceptual revision suggests a change in the way we view problem (1ii), the problem of language acquisition; i.e., not as a problem of acquiring rules but one of fixing parameters in a largely determined system. It also suggests rethinking of the parsing problem. Parsing programs are typically rule-based; the parser in effect mirrors a rule system and asks how these rules can assign a structure to a string that is analyzed word by word. The examples just discussed, and many others, suggest that a different approach might be pursued. Given a lexicon, structures can be projected from heads by virtue of the Projection Principle, X-bar theory, and other subsystems of UG that are involved in licensing elements, which are furthermore associated by these principles in the manner already illustrated. Perhaps parsers should not be based on rules at all but should rather be based on lexical properties and principles of UG that determine structures from them. Rule-based parsers are in many respects implausible. For one thing, complexity of parsing increases rapidly as rules proliferate; for another, since languages appear to differ substantially if viewed from the perspective of rule systems, they will require quite different parsers if the latter are rule-based, an unlikely consequence. The entire question merits substantial rethinking, so it appears.[26]

As conceived in earlier work, UG permits an infinite number of I-languages. The conception just outlined, however, permits only a finite number: there are finitely many parameters and each has a finite number of values. This is, of course, a qualitative change. Some recent work in formal learning theory by Osherson, Stob, and Weinstein (1983) suggests from an entirely independent point of view that this change may be in order. They formulate the thesis of "strong nativism," which asserts that there are only finitely many essentially different languages. According to this thesis, then, S_0 only permits finitely many essentially different realizations. They then show that the thesis of strong nativism follows from some quite plausible assumptions concerning the properties of a learning function.[27] Two languages are regarded as essentially the same if they differ only in finitely many sentences (e.g., English with n sentences of French added on) or if they differ in lexical items that do not change the syntax (thus, if L has the names *John, Bill, Tom,* and L' is identical except that is has the names *John, Bill, Mary,* then L and L' are essentially the same, but if L has the verb *persuade* and L' lacks any word with its subcategorization properties— taking an object and a clausal complement—then L and L' are essentially different). Otherwise, they are essentially different. The thesis of strong nativism then follows from the assumption that the learning function f is not disturbed by a finite amount of noise (i.e., a finite number of intrusions not from the language being learned, each of which can occur indefinitely often); that it has a certain locality property (the next conjecture is based on the current conjecture and memory of only recent sentences); and the requirement that the space of accessible hypotheses is ordered in "increasing complexity" in such a way that the learning procedure never has to take too large a "leap" in forming its next conjecture (i.e., if there is a hypothesis much more complicated that will work, there is also one that will work that is not more than some fixed distance from the current conjecture). These are natural conditions. Thus there is some independent reason to believe that the thesis of strong nativism is correct.

Osherson, Stob, and Weinstein point out that if the thesis of strong nativism is correct, the language faculty must be a "distinct" component of the mind, i.e., that language acquisition is not a matter of applying general learning mechanisms (if such exist) to the particular case of language. Certainly we cannot assume that "epistemic boundedness" is, in general, subject to this thesis.

The previous discussion has assumed the familiar Bloomfieldian idealization to a homogeneous speech community, but a further sharpening of these ideas is certainly in order. The systems called "languages" in common-sense usage tolerate exceptions to their basic system: irregular morphology, idioms, etc. These do not fall naturally under the principles-and-parameters conception of UG. Suppose we distinguish *core language* from *periphery,* where a core language is a system determined by fixing values for the parameters of UG, and the periphery is whatever is added on in the system actually represented in the mind/brain of a speaker–hearer. This distinction is a theory-internal one; it depends crucially on a formulation of UG. It goes beyond the earlier idealization, since, even under the assumption of homogeneity, a core–periphery distinction can be maintained.

The idealization to a homogeneous speech community isolates for investigation a real property of the mind/brain, namely, the property that would account for language acquisition under the conditions of the idealization and that surely underlies real-world language acquisition. The same is true of the idealization to core language. What a particular person has in the mind/brain is a kind of artifact resulting from the interplay of accidental factors, as contrasted with the more significant reality of S_0 and core language (with its core grammar), a specific selection among the options permitted in the initial state.

The distinction between core and periphery leaves us with three notions of markedness: core versus periphery, internal to the core, internal to the periphery. The second has to do with the way parameters are set in the absence of evidence. As for the third, there are no doubt significant regularities even in departures from the core principles (for example, in irregular verb morphology in English), and it may be that peripheral constructions are related to the core in systematic ways, say, by relaxing certain conditions of core grammar.

On General Features of Language

We have focused attention so far on the S-structure representations that are licensed (equivalently, generated) through the interaction of the modules of UG with values of parameters fixed, such representations as (2'), (3'), (2''), (3''), where we add here the associations determined by principles of UG (i distinct from j, k; j possibly identical to k):

(2') I wonder [who$_i$ the men$_j$ expected [e$_i$ to see them$_k$]]
(3') the men$_i$ expected [PRO$_i$ to see them$_k$]
(2'') I thought [the men$_j$ expected [Bill to see them$_k$]]
(3'') I expected [the men$_i$ to see them$_k$]

Brief mention has also been made of another level of representation, LF-representation. Here corresponding sentences of Chinese–Japanese-type languages, with slightly different values for the Move-α parameter, will have representations similar to (2') even though the *wh*-phrase is *in situ*— that is, in the position indicated by the empty category of (2')—at S-structure. Undoing the effects of Move-α in (2'), we have the underlying D-structure representation (20):

(20) I wonder [the men expected [who to see them]]

This is analogous to (2''), with *who* replacing *Bill*. D-structure representation can be defined as the level that constitutes a "pure representation" of thematically relevant grammatical relations (subject, object, etc.), the latter being configurationally defined: subject as the NP immediately dominated by S, object as the NP immediately dominated by VP, etc.[28] By this we mean that at D-structure every expression that requires a theta-role for licensing (every "argument") is in a theta-position (a position to which a theta-role is assigned by virtue of the interaction between grammatical relations and the lexical properties of heads), and every theta-position is occupied by an argument. The D-structure corresponding to (17), then, would be (21):[29]

(17) who was John [$_{VP}$ persuaded e_i [e_j to [$_{VP}$ visit e_k]]]
(21) e was [$_{VP}$ persuaded John [PRO to [$_{VP}$ visit who]]]

It then becomes an empirical hypothesis that D-structure is related to S-structure by Move-α, a rule that has certain definite properties involving the two positions related by movement (in particular, they cannot be "too far apart" in a structurally determined sense). We have been thinking of S-structure as derived from D-structure by application of Move-α. One might, alternatively, think of Move-α as in effect a relation on S-structure, so that D-structure is abstracted from S-structure by this rule. There may be empirical differences between these approaches, but if so, they are rather subtle; for present purposes, we may consider these as two equivalent formulations.[30]

In addition, there is also a level of "surface structure representation," derived from S-structure by the rules of morphology and phonology; at this level, sentences are represented in phonetic form with constituency marked.

On these assumptions, then, the modules of UG with values of parameters fixed assign to each expression a structure (D, S, PF, LF), where D is its D-structure, S its S-structure, PF its surface structure, and LF its "logical form."

Recall that the properties of LF are a matter of empirical fact, so that it may not coincide with what is called "logical form" in the tradition of philosophical logic. The term LF is used, with familiar provisos, because it seems, in fact, that LF does have many of the notational properties of familiar logical form, including the use of quantifier–variable notation. This is, of course, by no means an a priori necessity, but there are empirical reasons to believe that the assumption is correct [see, among others, Chomsky (1976), Higginbotham (1983a), Huang (1982), May (forthcoming)].

We may assume that the levels of PF and LF are the "interface" between formal structure and other components of the mind/brain which interact with the language faculty (in the sense of this discussion) in the use of language in thought, interpretation, and expression.

It must be emphasized that the choice of levels of representation and their properties is an empirical matter, to be verified by their explanatory role. The matter has been discussed above in connection with properties of S-structure—in particular, the properties determined by the Projection Principle and the licensing principles that require that empty categories appear in certain positions, as in (2'). The question of the existence and properties of empty categories lacking phonetic form is a particularly interesting one, since the language learner is presented with no direct evidence concerning them.

Some nontrivial consequences of the Projection Principle and the licensing principles concerning empty categories have been illustrated informally in connection with examples (7), (10), above. Examples (2'), (3'), as noted earlier, also provide empirical motivation for the assumption that empty categories appear where determined by these principles, with the properties entailed by UG. On these assumptions, we can explain the interpretation of (2'), (3') as a consequence of the principles required independently to account for (2''), (3''); specifically, we can explain why the surface form "the men expected to see them" has a different interpretation in (2') and (3'), with possible referential dependency in the former case but not the latter. If movement did not leave an empty category (trace)—equivalently, if empty categories were not required, as implied by the Projection Principle and the licensing principles at S-structure and LF—then these facts would remain a mystery. The hypothesis that movement leaves trace, then, is an empirical one, which is supported by evidence of the sort just illustrated.[31]

There is also fairly direct evidence concerning other empty categories required by the UG principles discussed. Consider the empty category that we have called PRO, which appears as something like a free variable in (22) and a bound pronoun in (23):[32]

> (22) it is illegal [PRO to vote twice]
> (23) John decided [PRO to vote twice]

In these cases, the D-structure, S-structure, and LF representations are identical (with an indication of referential dependency in (23), at least at LF), and the PF representation is the same except that the empty category is missing. Is it correct to assume that the "syntactic" representations are as in (22), (23), or should PRO be missing here too, as it is at the PF level? Again, the question is an empirical one, concerning the form and properties of certain mental representations.

There is considerable indirect evidence supporting (22), (23), that is, supporting the principles that require these representations. Thus, the licensing principle that requires predicates to have subjects is supported by the fact that it accounts for the distribution of the pleonastic, semantically empty elements that appear in such sentences as "it is raining," "I expect there to be rain tomorrow," "its having rained surprised me," etc. It is supported further by evidence drawn from "null subject languages" such as Spanish or Italian, which allow the subject to be missing at PF but require it, whether it is an argument or pleonastic, as an empty category at the other levels, as shown by considerations too complex to review here.[33] But there is also more direct evidence.

The Projection Principle requires that complements of heads must be represented at each syntactic level (D-structure, S-structure, LF), so that in particular objects must be represented, but it says nothing about subjects. It thus distinguishes between what Williams (1980) calls "internal" and "external" arguments, specifically, object and subject. The Projection Principle requires that the former be syntactically realized, but not the latter, though they are required as subjects of predication (in this case, whether they are arguments or pleonastic).[34] Thus, external arguments must appear as subjects of VP in clauses, as in "they destroyed the town," but not as subjects in corresponding nominalizations such as "their destruction of the town," with a subject, and "the destruction of the town," without one; the clause contains a VP predicate, the nominalization does not contain a predicate. Similarly, subjects may be pleonastic, whereas a strong version of the Predication Principle (as in Chomsky 1981) asserts that objects may not, a question currently under debate. In general, there seems to be considerable evidence supporting the idea that subjects and objects bear fundamentally different relations to the verb.[35]

For reasons deriving from Binding Theory (or, some have argued, case theory), the element PRO is restricted to subject position, in fact, to the position of subject of infinitive or gerund, where its presence is required by the licensing principle assumed earlier. The question we are asking is whether this is correct, or whether the S-structure, D-structure, and LF representations have no element at all in these positions, like the PF representation. Note that, in principle, there are three ways in which a subject may fail to appear overtly in some clausal structure: (i) it may be syntactically realized as an empty category; (ii) it may be realized as a lexical property of the V head of its VP predicate, which assigns it a theta-role; (iii) it may be missing in both syntactic and lexical representations. In fact, all three conditions are realized, and they have distinctively different properties.[36]

The three possible cases are illustrated in (24):

(24) (i) I decided [PRO to sink the boat]
      (ii) the boat was sunk e (where *e* is the trace of *the boat*)
      (iii) the boat sank

Take these to be both S-structure and LF representations.

There are a number of properties that distinguish these cases. Consider first the possibility of "spelling out" the missing agent of "sink" by an overt by-phrase. This is impossible in case (i), possible in case (ii), and impossible in case (iii), as illustrated in (25):

> (25) (i) *I decided to sink the boat by John
>   (ii) the boat was sunk by John
>   (iii) *the boat sank by John

There is no semantic reason for the status of (i), (iii); thus, (i) could mean "I decided that John should sink the boat" (analogous to "I wanted John to sink the boat") but it does not. Rather, the fact is that only a subject that is present lexically but not syntactically, as in (ii), can be overtly realized in a by-phrase.

This property distinguishes (ii) from (i), (iii). Structures (i), (ii) are distinguished from (iii) by the possibility of adding "agent-oriented" adverbs such as "voluntarily":

> (26) (i) I decided [PRO to leave voluntarily]
>   (ii) the boat was sunk voluntarily
>   (iii) *the boat sank voluntarily

These adverbs require an agent, which may be expressed syntactically as in (i) or lexically as in (ii).

Thus, the three possible cases exist and are distinguished from one another. In particular, there is evidence for the syntactic presence of PRO and the lexical presence of a "missing argument."

There are a variety of further properties that distinguish these cases. Consider the question of control (binding) of the formally missing understood subject, as illustrated in (27):

> (27) (i) they expected [PRO to give damaging testimony]
>   (ii) *they expected [damaging testimony to be given]
>   (iii) *they expected [the boat to sink]

The asterisks in (ii), (iii) refer to the interpretation analogous to (i), with the subject of the main clause controlling the "understood subject" of the embedded clause: impossible in (ii), (iii) but required in (i).[37] Thus, only a syntactically present element can be controlled by an antecedent.

Consider control by the understood subject, as in (28):

(28) (i) it is time [PRO to sink the boat [PRO to collect the insurance]]
      (ii) the boat was sunk [PRO to collect the insurance]
      (iii) *the boat sank [PRO to collect the insurance]

Only an element that is present at the syntactic or lexical level can serve as a controller.

Consider the binding of an anaphor by the understood subject, as in (29):

(29) (i) they decided (that it was about time) [PRO to hit each other]
      (ii) *damaging testimony was given about each other
      (iii) *the boats sank for each other

Examples (ii), (iii) do not mean "they gave damaging testimony about each other," "they sank the boats for each other," respectively. Apparently, only a syntactically present category can bind an anaphor. Note that in (i), it is PRO, not *they*, that binds the anaphor, as is clear from the fact that the sentence remains grammatical if "they decided" is deleted (perhaps even more clearly with "themselves" in place of "each other") and from the meaning: "they decided that it was about time that each hit the other," not "each decided that it was about time to hit the other." Similarly, in "they decided [PRO to read a book each]," *each* is associated with PRO, not *they*, as antecedent, as the meaning makes clear. The facts follow from general properties of Binding Theory, in particular the "Specified Subject Condition."[38]

There are certain adjuncts that require explicit arguments, e.g., "together" or "without reading them" (at S-structure: "without [PRO reading them]"). These can be predicated of PRO but not of a lexically represented understood subject:

(30) (i) (a) it is impossible [PRO to visit together]
           (b) it is impossible [PRO to be visited together]
           (c) it is impossible [PRO to file the articles [without reading them]]
      (ii) (a) *it is impossible [for me to be visited together]
           (b) *it is impossible [for the articles to be filed [without reading them]]
      (iii) (a) *the boat sank together
           (b) *the boat sank [without seeing it]

The examples of (i) are well formed, since there is an explicit formal subject, PRO, to serve as the subject of the predication. Note that in case (ib), the adjunct is predicated of the explicit formal subject PRO, not the understood subject of "visit." The example (iia) is excluded since the understood subject of "visit," being only lexically represented, cannot serve as the subject of the predication; and *me* cannot be the subject of the adjunct "together." The examples of (iii) are impossible, because there is no subject for the predication.[39]

Consider next the question of what can be the subject of adjectival predication, as in (31):

(31) (i)   they expected [PRO to leave the room angry]
      (ii) *the room was left angry
      (iii) *the boat sank angry

Only a syntactically present element can be the subject of the predicate "angry."[40]

Further properties are exhibited when we consider other constructions, such as nominalizations, or constructions with "missing subjects" in other languages: e.g., impersonal constructions and constructions involving causatives and perception verbs in the Romance languages. But without going into these rather complex matters, it is clear from the above that all three of the possible cases exist and that they are differentiated in their properties. In part, these properties are predictable on general grounds, but in part it is not obvious why they should distribute among the several types of understood elements as they do.

As this discussion illustrates, there is considerable empirical evidence to support the conclusion that empty categories appear where they are predicted to appear by the principles of UG discussed, and that they have quite definite and distinctive properties. A genuine explanatory theory of language that addresses the problems raised in (1) will have to come to terms with these facts. Although many questions can be raised about the specific principles discussed here and presented with more care and detail elsewhere, it seems clear that they are genuine empirical hypotheses, with considerable explanatory import, bearing on the nature of I-language and the innate structures from which it arises.

On Rule Following

We have, so far, considered the first two of the questions (1) that express the essential research program in generative grammar: (i) what constitutes knowledge of language, and (ii) how does it arise? The proposed answer to (i) is that to know an I-language is to be in a certain state of the mind/brain described in part by a core grammar consisting of principles of UG with values of parameters fixed in one of the permissible ways and a periphery of marked exceptions. This description is given at a level of abstraction from (largely unknown) mechanisms which we believe, rightly or wrongly, to be appropriate in the sense that it enables us to discover and express explanatory principles of some significance and in the sense that it will guide the search for mechanisms. The proposed answer to (ii) is that this state is attained by setting values in parameters of a fixed initial state S_0 of the language faculty, one of the subsystems of the mind/brain, and adding the periphery on the basis of specific experience in accordance with the principles of a (largely unknown) markedness theory. The result of this process of parameter determination and periphery formation is a full and richly articulated system of knowledge. Much of what is known lacks relevant grounding in experience, justification, or good reasons, and is not derived by any general reliable procedures. The same may well be true of large areas of what might be called "common-sense knowledge and understanding"; and if the model of Peircean abduction is correct, it may also be true to a significant extent of scientific knowledge as well, though in this case argument and evidence are required to justify knowledge claims.[41] Along these lines, we can develop a possible answer to our variant of "Plato's problem."

I have so far said little about question (iii), the question of how knowledge of language is put to use, apart from a few remarks about the perceptual aspect of this problem. With regard to the far more obscure production aspect, the common-sense answer is that use of language is rule-guided behavior: we have (generally tacit) knowledge of the rules of language and we use them in constructing "free expressions" (in Jespersen's sense). Some questions have been raised above about the propriety of reference to rules of language, but let us now put these aside and assume that indeed it is legitimate to project a rule system from the I-language that a person knows.[42] Let us assume, then, that the common-sense picture is more or less correct, with the modifications already discussed: in particular, the abstraction from the sociopolitical and normative-teleological elements of the common-sense notions of language and rule.

An attempt to flesh out this common-sense account runs into numerous problems, some of them classic ones. There are, in the first place, what we might call the "Cartesian problems." In the Cartesian view, the "beast—machine" is "compelled" to act in a certain way when its parts are arranged in a particular manner, but a creature with a mind is only "incited or inclined" to do so because "the Soul, despite the disposition of the body, can prevent these movements when it has the ability to reflect on its actions and when the body is able to obey" (La Forge). Human action, including the use of rules of language, is free and indeterminate. Descartes believed that these matters may surpass human understanding: we may not "have intelligence enough" to gain any real understanding of them, though "we are so conscious of the liberty and indifference which exists in us that there is nothing that we comprehend more clearly and perfectly" and "it would be absurd to doubt that of which we inwardly experience and perceive as existing within ourselves just because we do not comprehend a matter which from its nature we know to be incomprehensible." One can question various aspects of this formulation: for example, that we literally "know" the matter to be incomprehensible and that the limits are not merely those of human intelligence but rather of undifferentiated mind, not part of the biological world at all. But even so, it is difficult to avoid the conclusion that serious problems are touched on here, perhaps impenetrable mysteries for the human mind, which is, after all, a specific biological system and not a "universal instrument which can serve for all contingencies," as Descartes held in another context. There is no more reason to suppose humans to be capable of solving every problem they can formulate than to expect rats to be able to solve any maze.

A second class of problems concerning rule following are what we might call the "Wittgensteinian problems."[43] This topic has been greatly clarified by Saul Kripke's recent exegesis and analysis (Kripke 1982). I will not enter into the textual question of whether Kripke's version of Wittgenstein is the correct one but will merely assume that it is (as seems plausible), referring to Kripke's Wittgenstein henceforth as "Wittgenstein"; the quotes below are from Kripke, unless otherwise indicated. Kripke does not specifically endorse the picture he presents, but it is undoubtedly an extremely important one and one that appears to be highly relevant to the concerns of generative grammar, as Kripke stresses several times. Of the various general critiques that have been presented over the years concerning the program and conceptual framework of generative grammar, this seems to me the most interesting one.

Kripke suggests that "our understanding of the notion of 'competence' [equivalently, "knowledge of language," as used above] is dependent on our understanding of the idea of 'following a rule,'" so that Wittgenstein's skeptical paradox concerning rule following crucially bears on the central questions addressed in generative grammar. Furthermore, if we accept Wittgenstein's solution to his skeptical paradox, then

> the notion of "competence" will be seen in a light radically different from the way it implicitly is seen in much of the literature of linguis-

tics. For *if* statements attributing rule-following are neither to be regarded as stating facts, nor to be thought of as *explaining* our behavior . . . [as Wittgenstein concludes], it would seem that the *use* of the ideas of rules and of competence in linguistics needs serious reconsideration, even if these notions are not rendered "meaningless."

One aspect of the account given earlier, and of the work reviewed, is that it is presented in the framework of individual psychology: knowledge of language (competence) is taken to be a state of the individual mind/brain. Wittgenstein's solution to the skeptical paradox concerning rule following is crucially framed in terms of a community of language-users. Furthermore, the preceding account assumed that the statements of grammar and UG are not different in principle from the statements of natural science theories; they are factual, in whatever sense statements about valence or chemical structure or visual processing mechanisms, etc., are factual and involve truth claims. We can look forward to the day when these statements will be incorporated into a broader theory concerning mechanisms which will explain why they are true (or why they are not) at the level of abstraction at which they are formulated. But all of this appears to be undermined by Wittgenstein's solution to his skeptical paradox. As Kripke puts it, generative grammar "seems to give an explanation of the type Wittgenstein would not permit." Thus, "depending on one's standpoint, one might view the tension revealed here between modern linguistics and Wittgenstein's sceptical critique as casting doubt on the linguistics, or on Wittgenstein's sceptical critique—or both." He further observes that the issue has nothing to do with whether rules are explicitly stated—with whether people have access to the rules that constitute their knowledge, in our terms. Note also that the questions arise even under the abstraction from the sociopolitical and normative-teleological aspects of the common-sense notion of language, i.e., under the idealizations we have assumed.[44]

Wittgenstein's skeptical paradox, in brief, is this. Given a rule R, there is no fact about my past experience (including my conscious mental states) that justifies my belief that the next application of R does or does not conform to my intentions. There is, Wittgenstein argues, no fact about me that tells me whether I am following R or R′, which coincides with R in past cases but not future ones. Specifically, there is no way for me to know whether I am following the rule of addition or another rule (involving "quus," not "plus") which gives the answer 5 for all pairs beyond the numbers for which I have previously given sums; "there was no *fact* about me that constituted my having meant plus rather than quus," and more generally, "there can be no such thing as meaning anything by any word." Each application of a rule is "a leap in the dark." My application of a rule "is an unjustified stab in the dark. I apply the rule *blindly*." The argument is not limited to use of concepts but extends to any kind of rule application.

In short, if I follow R, I do so without reasons. I am just so constructed. So far, this is compatible with the account discussed earlier. I follow R because S_0 maps data presented into S_s, which incorporates R. There is no answer to Wittgenstein's skeptic and there need be none. My knowledge, in this instance, is ungrounded. I know that $27 + 5 = 32$, that this thing is a desk, that in a certain sentence a pronoun cannot be referentially dependent on a certain noun phrase, etc., as a consequence of knowing rules, which I follow (or I may not, for some reason, perhaps by choice, thus giving wrong answers). But I have no grounds for my knowledge in any useful general sense of the term and no reasons for following the rules: I just do it. If I had been differently constituted, with a different structure of mind/brain (S_0' instead of S_0), I would have come to know and follow different rules (or none) on the basis of the same experience, or I might have constructed different experience from the same stimuli.

The apparent problem for our account arises when we consider a different question: how can I tell whether you are following R or R'? Under what circumstances does it make sense for me to attribute rule following to you; when is this attribution correct or justified? Here we may distinguish two cases: my doing so as a person, and my doing so as a scientist. The first case raises a question of description: when do I, in fact, attribute to you a particular instance of rule following? Both cases raise questions of justification: when am I entitled, as a scientist or as a person in ordinary life, to say that you are following a rule?

Consider the first case: ascription of rule following in ordinary life. Wittgenstein holds that I am entitled to say that you are following R if you give the responses I am inclined to give, if you interact with my community, and if the practice of attributing the rule R to you has a role and utility in our communal life. Then I "take you into the community" to which I belong. The community attributes a concept (rule) to an individual as long as he/she conforms to the behavior of the community, its "form of life." Since deviant behavior is rare as a matter of brute fact, this practice of attributing concepts and rules is a useful one. Since attribution of rule following requires reference to the practices of a community, there can be no "private language." There is no substance or sense to the idea of a person following a rule privately. It seems that the "individual psychology" framework for generative grammar is undermined.

Wittgenstein holds, then, that "if we confine ourselves to looking at one person alone, his psychological states and his external behavior, this is as far as we can go. We can say that he acts confidently at each application of a rule . . . there can be no facts about him in virtue of which he accords with his intentions or not." "If one person is considered in isolation, the notion of a rule as guiding the person who adopts it can have *no* substantive content," so that the statements of a generative grammar, which appear to consider a person in isolation, can have no substantive content. But "the situation is very different if we widen our gaze from consideration of the rule follower alone and allow ourselves to consider him as interacting with a wider community. Others will then have justification conditions for attribution correct or incorrect rule following to the subject . . . ," namely, if his responses coincide with theirs. There are no truth conditions for "Jones is following rule R," because there is no fact of the matter (and in general, we should not seek truth conditions but rather assertability conditions).

As for the justification conditions, Jones is entitled to say "I mean addition by 'plus,'" subject to various provisos, "whenever he has the feeling of confidence . . . that he can give 'correct' responses in new cases." His inclination to go on in a certain way is to be regarded as "primitive." Smith is entitled to say that Jones means addition by "plus" if he judges that Jones is inclined to give the answers to addition problems that he, Smith, is inclined to give; and since, as a matter of "brute fact," the community is roughly uniform in its practices, this "game" of attributing rule following has a role and utility in our lives. Smith's behavior, too, is "a primitive part of the language game."

Recall that Wittgenstein's solution is not intended to reform language use but to describe it, to show why it is fine as it is. It must therefore be descriptively adequate. But this account is very far from descriptively adequate; it simply does not work for standard cases of rule following. Possibly the discussion is obscured by concentrating on cases that are felt to be deep in their character and implications and that certainly are deeply embedded in the philosophical tradition: specifically, attribution of concepts. These are, furthermore, cases where there is understood to be some normative standard of correctness. Let us consider, however, typical cases of attribution of rule following that are less "loaded" in this sense.

At a certain stage of language growth, children characteristically overgeneralize: they say "sleeped" instead of "slept," etc. We have no difficulty in attributing to them rules for formation of past tense or plurals, rules that we recognize to be different from our own. In this case, we will say that their rules are "incorrect," that is, different from that of the adult community. Here we invoke the normative-teleological aspect of the common-sense notion of language. If all adults were to die from some sudden disease, the language would "change" so that these irregularities would be erased and the child's rule would now be "correct" for the new language. In accordance with the move suggested earlier, we may, then, say that the child is following a rule of his/her language at the time, one of the possible human languages but not exactly ours.

To avoid the issue of the normative-teleological aspect of the common-sense notion, consider a different case. Suppose that we have visitors from a dialect area different from ours where lax and tense /i/ are merged before /g/, so that the words "regal" and "wriggle" are pronounced the same way, with an intermediate vowel; or where people say "I want for to do it myself" or "he went to symphony" instead of "I want to do it myself" and "he went to the symphony." Again, we would say that they are following rules, even though their responses are not those we are inclined to give and we do not take them into our linguistic community in these respects. They do not share our "form of life" or "interact" with our community in the relevant sense. In such cases as these, there is no question of "correctness" any more than in the choice between English and French. Furthermore, our conclusion that they are following rules different from our own has no obvious role or utility in our "form of life." In fact, such questions are commonly ignored. It might even be that the usual case of attribution of rule following is when the responses do not accord with ours, when they are unexpected and unfamiliar. Few people other than linguists would be inclined to say that Jones is following the rule of Disjoint Reference when he understands *him* to be free in reference, not dependent on *John*, in "John expected to like him." This case, though unusual in practice, does follow the Wittgensteinian paradigm; normal cases do not.

The same applies to attribution of concepts. Like many people, I learned the word "livid" from the phrase "livid with rage" and in my language at the time, it meant something like "flushed" or "red." Later, my linguistic knowledge and practice changed and in my current language it means something like "pale." I have no difficulty in attributing a different rule (my earlier one) to someone who I see follows it. Similarly, it is standard to attribute concepts different from ours to children and foreigners, or speakers of other languages. In the "plus"–"quus" case we would, as players of the normal language game, attribute one or the other concept to a person by inspecting his behavior, though in one case his responses would not accord with our own. There may be a question as to how we do it, but there seems little doubt that we do do it. Furthermore, none of this seems to have much if any role or utility in our lives.

Note that in standard cases of attribution of rule following such as those mentioned, the rules in question may or may not be followed in behavior; the child who overgeneralizes, for example, may choose not to apply his/her rule for forming the past tense of *sleep* in some particular case, or for some other reason might not follow the rule (and might, perversely, even say "slept," violating the rule); our visitors might pronounce "regal" and "wriggle" with a tense–lax vowel distinction (as we do), possibly by choice, thus violating what is their rule at the time (but keeping this rule, though violating it), etc. Thus, even when we drop any of the various normative considerations, the rules are not descriptions of behavior or of regularities in behavior (in principle, our visitors might choose to violate their rule most or all of the time, for one or another reason). The problem of determining when the rule is being followed, and when not, may be a difficult empirical one, but there seems little doubt that it does arise in the manner just indicated.

One of the centerpieces of Kripke's discussion is par. 202 of the *Philosophical Investigations*:

> ... to *think* one is obeying a rule is not to obey a rule. Hence it is not possible to obey a rule "privately"; otherwise thinking one was obeying a rule would be the same thing as obeying it.

This passage misconstrues our attribution of rule following in ordinary usage or science. We say (in both cases) that a person is following rules even if he does not think he is, either because he does not think about rules at all, or because his self-analysis is wrong for one or another reason (in general, the account that people give for their behavior is highly unreliable, even when they feel that they can offer one). Jones can be said to obey a rule "privately"—that is just the way we play the game—even if he thinks he is obeying a different rule or has no idea about rule following (and is responding differently than we would). The premise of the paragraph is correct, but the conclusion does not follow from it. Perhaps Wittgenstein is tacitly assuming here some notion of "accessibility to consciousness" with regard to mental states and their contents. This seems inconsistent with the way we use the relevant concepts in normal discourse, however deeply rooted the assumption may be in philosophical theories of various sorts.

At the very end of his discussion (p. 110), Kripke brings up a case that might be construed as being of the kind discussed above, where attribution of rule following violates the Wittgensteinian paradigm: namely, the case of Robinson Crusoe, not part of any community. Kripke asks whether the Wittgensteinian argument against the possibility of a "private language" entails "that Robinson Crusoe, isolated on an island, cannot be said to follow any rules, no matter what he does," referring to a passage where Wittgenstein discusses the "somewhat similar question" of a person playing a familiar game translated by some rule into a different modality. If Robinson Crusoe's responses are those we would be inclined to give, then this case raises no new questions. It is essentially the same as the case of our meeting someone whose responses agree with our own, so that we attribute rule following to him in accordance with the Wittgensteinian paradigm, which as Kripke outlines it does not ask whether the person is part of a community but rather whether we can take him into our community. The case becomes interesting, however, if Robinson Crusoe gives responses different from ours, that is, speaks a language of his own, shared by no community, in particular not our community. If the case is understood this way, it does serve as a (rather exotic) example of the type discussed earlier. Let us interpret Kripke's discussion so as to include this case—noting however that this may not be what was intended—and ask how his account, so construed, applies to the cases discussed earlier (in fact, quite normal cases, so it seems).

Kripke argues that we can still attribute rule following to Robinson Crusoe along the lines of the Wittgensteinian solution. Namely, we regard him as a *person* who acquires rules under certain experiences, though not ours, because we had different experiences. Then we can take him into the broader community of persons, who share our "form of life" in a broader sense. "Our community can assert of any individual that he follows a rule if he passes the tests for rule following applied to any member of the community," that is, he acts in the manner of a rule follower though he does not give our responses. This would include the cases discussed earlier but at the cost of abandoning any consequences of the "private language argument" that bear on the attribution of rules within the framework of individual psychology. Furthermore, though we may now regard Robinson Crusoe as a rule follower, we still have no way to determine what rules he is following, within this extension of the Wittgensteinian paradigm.

There seems to be an equivocation in the concept "form of life," which plays a central role in Wittgenstein's argument. The term is defined (by Kripke) as referring to "the set of responses in which we agree, and the way they interweave with our activities" (p. 96). In this sense, I take you into the community sharing my "form of life" if your responses are like mine, in accordance with the Wittgensteinian paradigm for attribution of rule following. But in this sense, Robinson Crusoe does not share our "form of life," and the solution collapses if intended to capture normal usage; we cannot attribute rule following to Robinson Crusoe, or to standard cases of the sort mentioned earlier. But Kripke also suggests a metaphorical usage of the phrase "form of life." In this extended sense, "form of life" (he gives the term in quotes, indicating that it is a metaphorical extension) refers to the "highly species-specific constraints" that "lead a child to project, on the basis of exposure to a limited corpus of sentences, a variety of new sentences for new situations" (p. 97n). Here, "form of life" refers to characteristic species behavior. It is this sense that is relevant to attribution of rule following or possession of a concept when the behavior does not match our own; Robinson Crusoe shares our "form of life" in this extended sense.

In the terms of the earlier discussion, the distinction is one of level of description: the technical usage of "form of life" is at the level of particular grammar (the attained I-language); in the extended sense it is at the level of UG (S_0). We might modify the Wittgensteinian solution to incorporate this distinction explicitly, so that it would cover normal usage. If we do, however, we derive a very different analysis of the "practice" of attributing concepts and rule-governed behavior, one that undermines the private language argument and the consequences drawn from it, since a member of the species might well have unique (or simply different) experience that yields a unique rule system, a private language, though we could "take him into our community" in the broader sense of "form of life." Indeed, this is the normal case, if we investigate a person's I-language in sufficient detail, and, as noted, this is a standard case (maybe *the* standard case) of attributing rule-governed behavior.

Returning to the statement that "if one person is considered in isolation, the notion of a rule as guiding the person who adopts it can have *no* substantive content" (p. 89), the conclusion that seemed to undermine the individual psychology framework of generative grammar, we see that this must be understood as we have interpreted Kripke's account in the context of the Robinson Crusoe example (p. 110): it does not refer to an individual whose behavior is unique but to someone "considered in isolation" in the sense that he is not considered as a person, like us. But now, the argument is defanged. Robinson Crusoe has a private language with its own rules, which we discover and attribute to him by some means other than those allowed in the solution to the skeptical paradox—exactly as we do in the normal cases discussed earlier.

Note that we might also say that if a sample of water is "considered in isolation," not regarded as water, then we can say nothing about its chemical constitution, etc.; and we can say nothing about a fruit fly in a genetics experiment if we do not consider it as a member of the class of fruit flies. An entity becomes an object of inquiry (scientific or common sense) only insofar as it is assigned to a particular natural kind. But there are no interesting conclusions to be drawn from this, beyond those that hold of descriptive commentary (scientific or otherwise) quite generally and hence are not relevant here.

We may ask how, in ordinary life, we assign Robinson Crusoe to the category of persons and what is the sense of this attribution; and whether, as scientists, we are entitled to say that this attribution amounts to a factual claim that Robinson Crusoe shares with other persons some actual property—specifically, the initial state S_0 of the language faculty—so that given his experience he follows the rules of the attained state $S_{L'}$, not our rules. The answer to the first question seems to be an intuitive and vague version of the scientist's answer: to be a person is to be an entity of a certain kind, with certain properties. We decide that Robinson Crusoe is an entity of this type, with these properties of personhood, by investigating what he does under various conditions. The status of these judgments becomes clearer when we consider the second question, to which we turn directly.

Keeping to the first question, we are led back, I think, to something like the Cartesian conception of "other minds." According to this view, I attribute to you a mind like mine if you pass tests that indicate that your behavior exhibits intelligence,[45] where to "exhibit intelligence" is to exceed the limits of mechanism in the sense of Cartesian contact mechanics. If a variety of such experiments succeed in showing this, then "I would not be reasonable if I did not conclude that [the subjects] are like me," possessing a mind (Cordemoy). The major tests outlined by the Cartesians, including Descartes himself, involve what I have called elsewhere "the creative aspect of language use," the use of language that is unbounded, stimulus free, appropriate to situations, coherent, evoking appropriate thoughts in me, etc. Or if your behavior reflects understanding and the exercise of will and choice as distinct from mechanical response, by a variety of tests, I attribute to you possession of mind, a power that exceeds the bounds of Cartesian contact mechanics (as does, in fact, the motion of the heavenly bodies as Newton subsequently showed, thus undermining the body–mind problem as Descartes formulated it since there is no longer any clear content to the notion of body). By various tests, I try to determine whether your "cognoscitive power" is "properly called mind," that is, whether it is not "purely passive" but rather "forms new ideas in the fancy or attends to those already formed," not completely under the control of sense or imagination or memory (*Rules for the Direction of the Mind*). If so, I "take you into my community" in the broader sense; I take you to be a person, sharing my "form of life" in the extended sense (at the level of UG), and I assume that you follow rules as I would under similar past–present conditions. However, the rules I attribute to you are not mine—our responses disagree, and we do not share a "form of life" in the technical sense. There is no issue of "utility" in all of this. I just make these determinations, without reasons, just as I follow rules, without reasons, as a reflection of my nature.

The Kripke–Wittgenstein dismissal of the Cartesian position is based on Humean arguments (namely, that we have no impression of self) that do not seem to me to bear on the relevant aspects of Cartesian thought, since they fail to take into account the respects in which attribution of mind is a theoretical move, part of a pattern of explanation based on assumptions with regard to the limitations of mechanism. We surely need not accept Cartesian mechanics or metaphysics or the beast–machine conclusions, nor need we accept the model of conscious testing and theory construction for normal usage. But the kernel of thinking seems plausible enough, and it is not unlike the proposed extension of the Wittgensteinian paradigm to the cases of normal usage that clearly violate it as it is formulated. I attribute rules to you (though perhaps not mine), rules that I would have followed if I had had your experience. I do this because you seem to be a person, exhibiting characteristic features of will and choice, the creative aspect of language use, and other indications of intelligence (and for Cordemoy, looking like me), though further analysis is required to explain how I attribute *particular* rules to you.

Summarizing, Kripke's Wittgenstein holds that (I) "to judge whether an individual is indeed following a given rule in particular applications" is to determine "whether his responses agree with their own." (II) We therefore reject the "'private model' of rule following," according to which "the notion of a person following a given rule is to be analyzed simply in terms of facts about the rule follower and the rule follower alone, without reference to his membership in a wider community." And (III) "our community can assert of any individual that he follows a rule if he passes the tests for rule following applied to any member of the community."

As for (I), it is not true in standard cases. We regularly judge that people are following rules when their responses differ from our own. As for (III), it is tenable if we understand it as meaning that whether or not an individual's "responses agree with [our] own," we may assert of him that he follows a rule if he passes the tests for rule following, not with respect to particular rules, or with reference to any particular community of rule users, but more generally: he acts as a person, passing the tests for "other minds" in roughly the Cartesian sense (with the provisos noted). By virtue of such facts about the individual (which are not facts about his experience and mental life), we "take him into the community" of persons and assume him to be following rules like ours, though perhaps not ours. It remains to determine what these rules are by observation, applying our own intuitive criteria. All of this is done without reasons, just as we follow rules ourselves without having reasons ("*blindly*"). Contrary to (II), there seems nothing objectionable about the "private model" of rule following nor is any serious alternative proposed to it, at least in any sense relevant to the explanations and concepts involving "competence" or "knowledge of language" in generative grammar; reference to a community of users of a language seems beside the point.

All of this has to do with the way, as persons, we attribute rule following without much if any reflection to others we take to be persons (and also, probably, to nonpersons in some cases). But it does not yet deal with the objection that there is no fact of the matter. This issue arises when we consider the second question raised earlier: What about our conclusion, as scientists, that Jones is following the rule R? Here we need reasons and justification. Can they be given?

The approach sketched earlier holds that we should proceed as follows. We amass evidence about Jones, his behavior, his judgments, his history, his physiology, or whatever else may bear on the matter. We also consider comparable evidence about others, which is relevant on the plausible empirical assumption that their genetic endowment is in relevant respects the same as his, just as we regard a particular sample of water as water and a particular fruit fly as a fruit fly (in our case, with the specific assumption of uniformity of the language faculty across the species). We then try (in principle) to construct a complete theory, the best one we can, of relevant aspects of how Jones is constructed—of the kind of "machine" he is, if one likes.

One heavy empirical condition is that this theory must incorporate a theory of the initial state that suffices to yield both the account of Jones's I-language (given relevant experience) and the account of the state attained by others (given their different experience). This theory is about Jones's capacities and how they are realized, these being facts about Jones, and at the same time it is a theory about persons, the category to which we take Jones to belong, as an empirical assumption.

Suppose that our best theory takes the initial state to incorporate as one component the initial state S_0 of the language faculty (a distinct component of the mind/brain), certain processing mechanisms, a certain organization and size of memory, a theory of random errors and malfunctions (parts wearing out or whatever), etc.: all of this as a species characteristic. This theory provides an account of the current state of the person as incorporating a particular I-language L, which is a particular realization of S_0 with values of parameters fixed. Then we conclude that the person follows the rules projected from L,[46] which determine what expressions mean for him, their correct forms for him, etc. This approach is not immune to standard skeptical arguments, e.g., inductive uncertainty, Putnam's antirealist arguments, etc. But these are not relevant here, since they bear on science more generally. It is not clear that there are any further skeptical arguments that apply. A particular theory of this sort may certainly be wrong and may be shown to be wrong, for example, if the theory UG of S_0 proposed to account for Jones's I-language (and thus to explain facts about Jones's judgments and behavior, in the explanatory model discussed earlier) fails with respect to someone else, say a speaker of Japanese. In fact, this has repeatedly been the case, and is surely the case with regard to current theories. It seems, then, that these theories are empirical ones, which could also be right.

Kripke argues against a "dispositional" account of rule following and concludes that the account must be "normative," not "descriptive" (p. 37). As he notes, the preceding account is not dispositional (it says little about what a person is disposed to say under particular circumstances), and it is also not "causal (neurophysiological)." Furthermore, the account is not "functionalist"; it does not "regard psychology as given by a set of causal connections, analogous to the *causal* operations of a machine" (p. 36n), though it has causal aspects, namely, with regard to the mapping of experience to S_s by S_0 and the operations of a parser that uses the I-language.[47] But the account of "competence" is descriptive: it deals with the configuration and structure of the mind/brain and takes one element of it, the component L, to be an instantiation of a certain general system that is one part of the human biological endowment. We could regard this instantiation as a particular program (machine), though guarding against implications that it determines behavior. Thus, an account can be descriptive though it is neither dispositional nor causal (neurophysiological or functional), in Kripke's sense.

Kripke argues, however, that what program a machine is following is not an objective fact about the machine and that we can distinguish between machine malfunction and following its program only in terms of the intention of the designer: "Whether a machine ever malfunctions and, if so, when, is not a property of the machine itself as a physical object but is well defined only in terms of its program, as stipulated by its designer." If a machine fell from the sky, there would be no answer to the question: "What program is it following?" In our case, there is no designer, but nevertheless we do assert that the machine incorporates a particular program. This assertion is part of a more general account of the properties of the mind/brain, an account that defines "malfunction" and "intrusion of extraneous factors" and is answerable to a wide range of empirical evidence, including evidence concerning the person's history and concerning speakers of other languages, and in principle much more: physiology, psychological experiment, brain damage, biochemistry, etc. Our assumption is that the person before us has a language which incorporates particular rules and principles along with other systems that interact with it as a matter of mental/physiological fact, and which we might think of as a particular machine program with a particular data structure, etc. There may be empirical problems in sorting out the effects of these interacting systems, but these seem to be problems of natural science, and in this world, with its regularities, the problems do not seem hopelessly difficult. Indeed, they have been addressed with some success.

It should furthermore be noted that there is no necessary restriction to human behavior here. It might be appropriate to describe the way a sheep dog collects the flock, or the way a spider spins a web, or the way a cricket walks, in terms of rule following, with reference to an underlying "competence" consisting of a system of rules of some sort, a faculty that might be intact though unusable, or misused for some reason, and that underlies abilities that might be impaired, lost, recovered, etc.

Though the matter is not relevant here, it seems to me that Kripke's comments about machines are too strong. Suppose that a machine fell from the sky, say, an IBM PC with a particular operating system and a particular program stored in machine memory. Could we distinguish hardware, operating system, particular program? It seems that we could learn something about the matter by investigating input–output properties. For example, we might ask what aspects of the functioning of the machine can be changed just by using the keyboard and what can be changed by inserting a new board, or by going inside the microprocessor and manipulating the circuitry, etc. We could distinguish properties of this specific device from those that hold of any device made up of such components (some properties of random behavior). We could develop a theory of the machine, distinguishing hardware, memory, operation system, program, perhaps more. It is hard to see in what sense this would be crucially different from a theory of other physical systems, say the interior of the sun, or an internal combustion engine, or the organization of neurobehavioral units (reflexes, oscillators, and so on) that explain how a cricket walks, and so on.

Wittgenstein's skeptic goes beyond this argument when he concludes that there are no facts of the matter. What he has shown is that the facts concerning Jones's past behavior and conscious mental states are not sufficient to establish that Jones is following the rule R, but it does not follow that "there can be no facts about him in virtue of which he accords with his intentions or not," i.e., in virtue of which he can be said to follow the rule R. Kripke notes that there might be a neurophysiological theory that would explain a person's behavior, but this would not be to the point, because it does not have the required prescriptive force: it does not provide justification and thus does not answer the skeptic; and furthermore such theories would not be relevant to ascription of rule following by others who know nothing of these matters but do ascribe rule following. It does not follow, however, that we must accept the skeptical conclusion that there is no fact as to whether Jones means plus or quus, or whether he follows the rule of Disjoint Reference, or the rule that merges tense and lax /i/ before /g/. The approach just outlined leads to confirmable theories as to whether indeed Jones follows these rules.

Wittgenstein holds that there is a crucial difference between the case of Robinson Crusoe and the case of a molecule of water or benzene. In the latter case, we regard a particular entity as a sample of water or benzene and then determine its properties, which are real properties of that sample. In the case of Robinson Crusoe, we regard him as a person and thus consider him a rule follower who behaves as we would had we had his experiences; and somehow, though not by the Wittgensteinian paradigm, we identify particular rules that he follows, perhaps not ours. In our terms, we assume that he has a language faculty that shares with ours the state S_0 and attains a state S_L different from ours, on the basis of which we can develop an account for his current perceptions and actions. But, Wittgenstein holds, we are not entitled to go on to assert that the initial state S_0 or the attained state of knowledge S_L are real properties of this individual, that statements about them are true or false. There is no fact of the matter about Robinson Crusoe, or about persons in general, apart from the facts about communities. But his arguments fall far short of establishing this conclusion except insofar as they reduce to standard skeptical doubts concerning scientific procedure and hence are not relevant here. And his account leaves as a complete mystery our practice of assigning rules to Robinson Crusoe, an exotic instance of what is in fact a standard case, as noted.

We should stress again that there are differences among these examples. The structure of a molecule of water or benzene determines how they will behave in a chemical experiment, but the structure of Jones's language does not determine what he will say, though it does determine (fairly closely) how he understands what he hears; and the structure of his initial state S_0 determines (again, fairly closely) what his language will be, given experience. Our theory of Jones—a grammar G of his language, a theory UG of the initial state of his language faculty—is a descriptive theory of his attained or initial competence, his knowledge system and its origins. It is not a causal or dispositional theory concerning his behavior.

Here, I think an observation of Paul Horwich's is to the point. We may take Wittgenstein's skeptic to have undermined the "naive" claim "that there *must* exist inner states of understanding which explain our behavior. But that is not to question that there could be good a posteriori grounds for accepting such a picture. Nor is it to deny that, in either case, facts about meaning are as fully-fledged as facts ever manage to be" (Horwich 1984); and similarly for rule following over a broader domain.

This seems to me correct, though I should add again that reference to a community seems to add nothing substantive to the discussion, except under something like the Cartesian interpretation, moving to the level at which "form of life" corresponds to UG, i.e., to attribution of "personhood," a move that does not impugn the private model of rule following (and that is probably too narrow, as a matter of descriptive fact concerning normal usage and possibly potential science).

As persons, we attribute rule following to Jones on the basis of facts about him, though perhaps without having reasons that justify this move; one might, but need not, adopt the intellectualized Cartesian account in this case. And as scientists, we do attempt to develop a rather complex account in terms of postulated mental/physical states, though not ones accessible to conscious introspection. The classical problems about rule following remain unanswered; we have nothing like a "causal" account of behavior or any reason to believe that one exists. It also may be that the best theory will depart from the model of rule following altogether, both for the receptive and productive side of linguistic behavior, perhaps on the grounds already discussed, perhaps others.

Returning to the three original questions of (1), there have been interesting and fruitful developments bearing on the first and second, the nature of language (meaning, I-language) and knowledge of language, and the basis for its acquisition. Fundamental questions concerning the use of language remain unanswered, perhaps unanswerable. In the area that seems open to inquiry, a major conceptual shift has been proposed which provides interesting answers to many questions about the form and interpretation of linguistic expressions and their mental representations, language typology, and much else. If this shift proves to be in the right direction, as I believe it is, it also suggests that other questions may well merit rethinking.

Notes

This is an edited and slightly expanded version of a paper submitted for discussion at the Sloan Conference on Philosophy and Cognitive Science held at MIT, May 1984, not originally intended for publication. An extended version of this material will appear in a forthcoming book: *Knowledge of Language: Its Nature, Origins, and Use* (Harper and Row). I am indebted to James Higginbotham for helpful comment on an earlier draft of this paper.

1. A number of different current approaches share properties of the sort discussed here and may be intertranslatable to a considerable extent. I will not consider this topic here, nor will I make an effort to survey the range of ideas, often conflicting, that fall within the particular tendency that I will discuss, what is now sometimes called "Government-Binding (GB) theory"—not strictly speaking a "theory" but rather a range of related ideas within a common general point of view.

2. Quine, of course, argued that there was a very severe, in fact insuperable, problem of indeterminacy affecting all aspects of language and grammar, and much of psychology more generally (Quine 1960, 1972). I do not think that Quine succeeded in showing that some novel form of indeterminacy affects the study of language beyond the normal underdetermination of theory by evidence; his own formulations of the thesis furthermore involve internal inconsistency (see

Chomsky 1975a, 1980b). There seems no reason on these grounds, then, to distinguish linguistics or psychology in principle from the natural sciences in accordance with what Hockney (1975) calls Quine's "bifurcation thesis." Essentially the same conclusion is reached by Putnam (1981) in his abandonment of metaphysical realism on Quinean grounds. His step also abandons the bifurcation thesis, though in the opposite direction.

3. See Crain and Nakayama (1984) for empirical study of this question with 3- to 5-year-old children.

4. The reaction to such phenomena, also unnoticed until recently, again illustrates the difference of outlook of structuralist-descriptive and generative grammar. For many practitioners of the former, the statement of the facts, which is straightforward enough, is the answer—nothing else is necessary; for the latter, the statement of the facts poses the problem to be solved. Cf. Ney (1983), particularly his puzzlement about the "peculiar view of grammar [that] unnecessarily complicates the whole matter" by seeking an explanation for the facts. Note that there is no question of right or wrong here, but rather of topic of inquiry.

5. On structures of this type, and problems of Binding Theory more generally, see Higginbotham (1983a), among much other work.

6. See Fodor (1983). But it is too narrow to regard the "language module" as an input system in Fodor's sense, if only because it is used in speaking and thought. Furthermore, even regarded as an input system, the language module does not appear to have the property of rapidity of access that he discusses, as indicated by (8)–(10). Note also that even if Fodor is right in believing that there is a sharp distinction between modules in his sense and "the rest," which is holistic in various respects, it does not follow that the residue is unstructured in respects that do not involve strict information encapsulation. In fact, this seems highly unlikely, if only because of the "epistemic boundedness" that he notes. Many other questions arise concerning Fodor's very intriguing discussion of these issues, which I will not pursue here.

7. There were, however, exceptions: for example, the theory of "overall patterns," of which each English dialect was held to be a subsystem. Note that the question of "variable rules," as discussed by some sociolinguists, is not relevant here.

8. One might also note some unintentionally comical objections, such as the charge by Oxford professor of linguistics Roy Harris (1983) that the Saussurean–Bloomfieldian idealization reflects "a fascist concept of language if ever there was one," since it takes the "ideal" speech community to be "totally homogeneous."

9. One might question this move; we speak of a person as knowing American history without assuming that there is an entity, American history, to which the person stands in a cognitive relation. Let us, however, assume the move to be legitimate.

10. For a related but somewhat different way of viewing these questions, see Higginbotham (1983b).

11. Weaker assumptions than strict identity would suffice, but since this stronger assumption seems a reasonable one, to a very good approximation, I will keep to it here.

12. For some discussion of this matter, see Marr (1982). Obviously, different questions arise in the study of vision and the study of the questions (1) above. See note 6. Note that the question of the legitimacy or sense of a realist interpretation of science in general is not at issue here; rather, nothing new in principle seems to arise in the case of the study of I-language and its origins. If one wants to consider the question of realism, psychology and linguistics seem poor choices; the question should be raised with regard to the more advanced sciences, where there is much better hope of gaining insight into the matter.

13. I have not discussed here Saussurean and other notions of language that use these images, because they face other problems. Saussurean structuralism, for example, does not accommodate the notion of "free expression" in Jespersen's sense; the notion "sentence" is left in limbo, with an indeterminated status, perhaps belonging to the theory of performance in some manner but not part of "language" in the sense of any of the Saussurean concepts.

14. As for the latter, the earliest publications on generative grammar were presented in a framework suggested by certain topics in automata theory (e.g., my *Syntactic Structures*, actually notes for an undergraduate course at MIT and hence presented from a point of view related to the interests of these students). Specifically linguistic work, such as my *Logical Structure of Linguistic Theory* (1955–56; published in part in 1975), was not publishable at the time. In the latter, considerations of weak generative capacity, finite automata, and the like were completely absent, and the emphasis was on I-language, though the term was not used.

15. Henceforth, by "language" I will mean I-language unless the contrary is indicated.

16. Cf. Tomas (1957). Peirce's invocation of natural selection as a *deus ex machina* to account for theory construction in science will not do, however, though there is, I think, good reason to believe that what Fodor calls "epistemic boundedness" (Fodor 1983) is crucial in this domain as well; see Chomsky (1968, 1975a).

17. See Chomsky (1965), pp. 61–62, for further discussion. In fact, it is not even clear that the question is properly formulable, in the light of the unclear status of E-language (cf. Chomsky 1980b).

18. Anachronistically, I will give examples with an empty category *e* indicating the position of the variable, the position occupied by a full noun phrase in the corresponding declarative. Asterisk indicates an ungrammatical expression.

19. This actually appeared in two earlier published versions; I will collapse the three here, though they made somewhat different proposals as to the relevant principles.

20. We might take *wh-* to be a determiner in the category of *some, any, every,* with phonological rules spelling out *wh-one* as *who,* etc. There are interesting questions here, which I will ignore, concerning "relational" nouns like *friend* as distinct from nonrelational ones like *book.* Many of these questions remain open.

21. On how the parameter might be formulated, and other variants beyond those mentioned here, see Lasnik and Saito (1984).

22. It appears to be widely believed that the attempt to reduce the richness and variety of transformational rules was motivated by concern over generative capacity; see, e.g., Johnson-Laird (1983), who asserts that this "reappraisal of transfor-

mational grammar" began in the late 1970s as a consequence of the observation by S. Peters and R. Ritchie that an unconstrained grammar of this sort could generate every r.e. set (more interestingly, they showed that a simple formal property sufficed to reduce generative capacity to recursive sets). This is doubly wrong: the work began 15 years earlier for others reasons and was unaffected by this observation; moreover, it had been pointed out years before the result was enunciated that it would have no empirical import (see above). Johnson-Laird also believes that the Peters–Ritchie result had other "embarrassing consequences," specifically, in undermining "Chomsky's 'universal base' hypothesis." Such a hypothesis had indeed been proposed, but I had never accepted it; furthermore, the hypothesis would be unaffected by this observation, for essentially the reasons already noted.

23. See Chomsky (1981, 1982) for a detailed analysis that makes these informal comments precise, in this and other cases discussed here.

24. See, for example, Rizzi (1982a), based on the pioneering work of Kayne (1975). See also Kayne (1984) for many important ideas concerning UG.

25. It should be noted that this is a very lively area of current research and many alternative approaches are being actively pursued. See, among many others, Kayne (1984), Aoun (1982, forthcoming), Pesetsky (1983), Longobardi (1983).

26. On this topic, see Berwick (1982) and Barton (1984). See also Fodor, Bever, and Garrett (1974) for a similar conception.

27. See Osherson, Stob, and Weinstein (1983). One must be cautious in relating their very interesting results to our concerns here. They are considering E-language, not I-language, and are restricting their attention to weak rather than strong generative capacity of grammars (i.e., to the class of sentences enumerated by a grammar). They take a learning function f of "identify" (i.e., to learn) a language L if it converges on a grammar for any text, a text being an infinite sequence of sentences drawn from L and exhausting L, with no "uniformity condition" requiring that f converge on the same grammar for L for all texts. The results are, however, very suggestive and rather surprising. On this matter, see also Wexler and Culicover (1980) and Baker and McCarthy (1981).

28. The idea that these grammatical relations are configurationally defined is controversial. There is, I think, considerable evidence to support it. See, for example, Whitman (1982) and Saito (1984), who present evidence that in Japanese, which had been argued to be a nonconfigurational language lacking VP (so that a configurational definition would be impossible), there is in fact a VP and more generally a highly configurational structure at D- and S-structure and LF. Other work suggests that this may be true more generally, possibly universally.

29. We abstract here from the effects of the application of Move-α that determines the position of the auxiliary at S-structure.

30. On this matter, see Chomsky (1981, 1982), Rizzi (1982b), and Sportiche (1983), among others.

31. Certain theories of UG assume that there is no trace in such structures, e.g., earlier theories of transformational grammar, or theories that complicate and extend the variety of phrase structure grammars, as discussed in Johnson-Laird (1983). Evidence of the sort just mentioned indicates that these theories are mistaken. Johnson-Laird regards it as an advantage of the theory he describes, follow-

ing Stanley Peters, that it does not employ the rule Move-α. Even in isolation from the neglected empirical facts, the argument lacks merit. The UG properties of Move-α (e.g., locality, etc.) will have to be stated somewhere; even apart from this, it is difficult to see why the complication of phrase structure rules is "simpler" or provides fewer possible grammars than the rule-free system incorporating Move-α as a principle—if anything, the opposite seems true. As noted earlier, questions of generative capacity appear to be beside the point, even if we do not adopt the thesis of "strong nativism."

32. On the structural conditions that determine the choice of these options, see Manzini (1983).

33. See, among others, Burzio (forthcoming), and the review of some results of his and others in Chomsky (1981).

34. This property is called the "Extended Projection Principle" in Chomsky (1981). Zagona (1982) and Rothstein (1983) suggest that it can be derived from a version of Williams's predication theory, essentially in the manner informally indicated here, as one of the licensing principles.

35. In addition to the references cited above, see also Marantz (1984), among others.

36. On this matter, see particularly Roeper (1983).

37. The point is illustrated as well in null subject languages such as Italian, in which the analogue of "e [$_{VP}$ sank the boat]," with "the boat" remaining in its theta-position, is a permissible variant to "the boat sank"; the empty category here is pleonastic, not PRO, analogous to English "there" in "there arrived three men." See Burzio (forthcoming).

38. The difference between cases (28) and (29) raises some questions about the reduction of control theory to binding theory. There are also questions about the nature of PRO with arbitrary (free) interpretation [is it, in fact, controlled by a lexically represented "understood argument," an assumption that would explain the absence of this interpretation in (28iii), as Roeper notes, as well as other facts?]. Questions also arise about verbs of "subject control" such as "promise." Compare *"John was promised to leave" with (28ii).

39. Case (iib) is perhaps problematic, since some poorly understood element of modality may be involved; compare "the articles can be filed without reading them."

40. Roeper notes such examples as "the game was played barefoot (nude)," which seem to violate the paradigm illustrated. Luigi Rizzi observes that in Italian the corresponding form is adverbial, not adjectival, suggesting that perhaps this is the case here as well despite the morphology, though many questions remain; see Roeper (1983).

41. See Chomsky (1968, 1975a, 1980b).

42. Some analyses of rule following would appear to exclude the standard cases of common-sense usage, for example, Dennett's proposal (1983) that we can speak of rule following only if there is a "very strong resemblance" to the case where we actually refer to an explicit representation of the rule in a formula (say, on a page, or as a "physically structured object, a *formula* or *string* or *tokening* . . . ," somewhere in the brain. As he seems to interpret "resemblance," this account would rule

out virtually all standard cases of rule following, linguistic or other, since they are not accompanied by recourse to such objects on a page, or written in the brain. If Dennett has something weaker in mind, it is not clear how it bears on the questions he is addressing, including those under consideration here (as he holds it does). His further observation that rule systems might be only "tacitly represented" in the sense in which addition is represented in a hand-calculator is correct but uninformative. Such possibilities cannot be excluded a priori. The question is one of best theory, and here it is of no interest to observe, e.g., that for every account that explains "input–output" relations in terms of rules, there is another with the same input–output properties that does not involve rules. Presumably this is so, e.g., an account in terms of brain cells, but the question, as always, is whether in these terms we can formulate the applicable explanatory principles, provide explanations for a variety of facts within and across languages, or even state facts about words, phrases, repetitions, and so on; surely facts, if anything is.

43. I will discuss these only insofar as they bear on the production problem, without implying that a variant does not arise in the case of the perception problem.

44. Note that one must not assimilate Kripke's notion of "normative" in this discussion to the "normative-teleological" notion discussed above.

45. What is now sometimes called the "Turing test," understanding this to provide evidence for possession of higher intelligence.

46. If this is the right approach; it may not be, as discussed earlier.

47. On the significance of these points, see Kirsh (1983).

Bibliography

Aoun, J. 1982. *The formal nature of anaphoric relations.* Ph.D. diss., MIT.

_____. Forthcoming. *Generalized binding: The syntax and interpretation of WH interrogative construction.*

Baker, C.L. 1970. "Notes on the description of English questions." *Foundations of Language* 6:197–219.

Baker, C.L. and J. McCarthy, eds. 1981. *The logical problem of language acquisition.* Cambridge: MIT Press.

Barton, E. 1984. Toward a principle-based parser. MIT.

Berwick, R. 1982. *Locality principles and the acquisition of syntactic knowledge.* Ph.D. diss., MIT.

Bloomfield, L. 1928. A set of postulates for the science of language. *Language* 2:153–164. Reprinted in *Readings in linguistics,* ed. M. Joos, pp. 26–31, 1957. Washington, D.C.: American Council of Learned Societies.

Burzio, L. Forthcoming. *Italian syntax: A government-binding approach.*

Chomsky, N. 1964. *Current issues in linguistic theory.* The Hague: Mouton.
———. 1965. *Aspects of the theory of syntax.* Cambridge: MIT Press.
———. 1968. *Language and mind.* New York: Harcourt, Brace and World.
———. 1975a. *Logical structure of linguistic theory.* New York: Plenum.
———. 1975b. *Reflections on language.* New York: Pantheon.
———. 1976. Conditions on rules of grammar. *Linguistic Analysis* 2:4. Reprinted in *Essays on form and interpretation*, Amsterdam: North Holland, 1977.
———. 1980a. On binding. *Linguistic Inquiry* 11:1.
———. 1980b. *Rules and representations.* New York: Columbia Univ. Press.
———. 1981. *Lectures on government and binding.* Dordrecht: Foris.
———. 1982. *Some concepts and consequences of the theory of government and binding.* Cambridge: MIT Press.

Crain, S., and M. Nakayama. 1984. Structure dependence in grammar formation. Univ. of Connecticut.

Dennett, D. 1983. Styles of mental representation. *Proceedings of the Aristotelian Society* 83:213–226.

Fodor, J. 1983. *The modularity of mind.* Cambridge: MIT Press.

Fodor, J., T. Bever, and M. Garrett. 1974. *The psychology of language.* New York: McGraw–Hill.

Harris, R. 1983. Theoretical ideas. *Times Literary Supplement*, October 14.

Higginbotham, J. 1983a. LF, binding and nominals. *Linguistic Inquiry* 14:3.
———. 1983b. Is grammar psychological? in *How many questions?*, ed. L.S. Cauman, I. Levi, C. Parsons, and R. Schwartz. Indianapolis: Hackett.

Hockney, D. 1975. The bifurcation of scientific theories and indeterminacy of translation. *Philosophy of Science* 42:4.

Horwich, P. 1984. Critical notice: Saul Kripke: Wittgenstein on rules and private language. *Philosophy of Science* 51:1.

Huang, C.-T. J. 1982. *Logical relations in Chinese and the theory of grammar.* Ph.D. diss., MIT.

Jespersen, O. 1924. *The philosophy of grammar.* London: Allen and Unwin.

Johnson-Laird, P. 1983. *Mental models.* Cambridge: Harvard Univ. Press.

Joos, M., ed. 1957. *Readings in linguistics.* Washington, D.C.: American Council of Learned Societies.

Kayne, R. 1975. *French syntax.* Cambridge: MIT Press.
———. 1984. *Connectedness and binary branching.* Dordrecht: Foris.

Kirsh, D. 1983. *Representation and rationality: Foundations of cognitive science.* Ph.D. diss., Oxford Univ.

Kripke, S. 1982. *Wittgenstein on rules and private language.* Cambridge: Harvard Univ. Press.

Lasnik, H., and M. Saito. 1984. On the nature of proper government. *Linguistic Inquiry* 15:2.

Lewis, D. 1975. Languages and language. In *Language, mind, and knowledge*, ed. K. Gunderson. Minneapolis: Univ. of Minnesota Press.

Longobardi, G. 1983. Connectedness, scope, and C-command. Scuola Normale Superiore.

Manzini, M.-R. 1983. On control and control theory. *Linguistic Inquiry* 14:3.

Marantz, A. 1984. *On the nature of grammatical relations*. Cambridge: MIT Press.

Marcus, M. 1980. *A theory of syntactic recognition for natural language*. Cambridge: MIT Press.

Marr, D. 1982. *Vision*. San Francisco: Freeman.

May, R. Forthcoming. *Logical form*. Cambridge: MIT Press.

Ney, J. 1983. Review [of Chomsky 1982]. *Language Sciences* 5:2.

Osherson, D., M. Stob, and S. Weinstein. 1983. Learning theory and natural language. MIT.

Peirce, C. S. 1957. The logic of abduction. In *Peirce's essays in the philosophy of science*, ed. V. Tomas. New York: Liberal Arts Press. (Originally pub. in Collected papers of Charles Sanders Peirce, ed. C. Hartshorne and P. Weiss, Cambridge: Harvard Univ. Press, 1931–1935.)

Pesetsky, D. 1983. *Paths and categories*, Ph.D. diss., MIT.

Putnam, H. 1981. *Reason, truth, and history*. Cambridge: Cambridge Univ. Press.

Quine, W.V. 1960. *Word and object*. Cambridge: MIT Press.

————. 1972. Methodological reflections on current linguistic theory. In *Semantics of natural language*, ed. G. Harman and D. Davidson. New York: Humanities Press.

Rizzi, L. 1982a. *Issues in Italian syntax*. Dordrecht: Foria.

————. 1982b. On chain formation. Universita della Calabria.

Roeper, T. 1983. Implicit semantic roles in the lexicon and syntax. Univ. of Massachusetts.

Rothstein, S. 1983. *The syntactic form of predication*. Ph.D. diss., MIT.

Saito, M. 1984. *Some asymmetries in Japanese and their theoretical implications*. Ph.D. diss., MIT.

Sapir, E. 1921. *Language*. New York: Harcourt, Brace.

Sportiche, D. 1983. *Structural invariance and symmetry in syntax*. Ph.D. diss., MIT.

Tomas, V., ed. 1957. *Peirce's essays in the philosophy of science*. New York: Liberal Arts Press.

Wexler, K., and P. Culicover. 1980. *Formal principles of language acquisition*. Cambridge: MIT Press.

Whitman, J. 1982. Configurationality parameters. Harvard Univ.

Williams, E. 1980. Predication. *Linguistic inquiry* 11:1.

Zagona, K. 1982. *Government and proper government of verbal projections*. Ph.D. diss., Univ. of Washington.

DANIEL C. DENNETT

The Logical Geography of Computational Approaches: A View from the East Pole

Westward the course of empire takes its way.
—*BERKELEY*

With many different people claiming to be explaining the mind in "computational" terms, and almost as many denying that this is possible, empirical research and ideological combat are currently proceeding on many fronts, and it is not easy to get one's bearings. But some themes are emerging from the cacophony, and they tempt me to try to sketch the logical geography of some of the best-known views, with an eye to diminishing the disagreements and misrepresentations that sometimes attend them.

There are still dualists and other mystics in the world who assert (and hope and pray, apparently) that the mind will forever elude science, but they are off the map for me. A goal that unites all participants in the conflict area I will explore is the explanation of the aboutness or intentionality of mental events in terms of systems or organizations of what in the end must be brain processes. That is, I take it as agreed by all parties to the discussion that what we want, in the end, is a materialistic theory of the mind as the brain. Our departure point is the mind, meaning roughly the set of phenomena characterized in the everyday terms of "folk psychology" as *thinking about* this and that, *having beliefs about* this and that, *perceiving* this and that, and so forth. Our destination is the brain, meaning roughly the set of cerebral phenomena characterized in the *non*intentional, *non*symbolic, *non*-information-theoretic terms of neuroanatomy and neurophysiology. Or we can switch destination with departure and construe the task as building from what is known of the plumbing and electrochemistry of the brain toward a theory that can explain—or explain away—the phenomena celebrated in folk psychology. There has been a surfeit of debate on the strategic question of which direction of travel is superior, top-down or bottom-up, but that is now largely behind us and well understood: obviously both directions can work in principle, both have peculiar pitfalls and opportunities, and no one with an ounce of sense would advocate ignoring as a matter of principle the lessons to be learned from the people moving from the opposite end.

A much more interesting clash concerns what to look for in the way of interstitial theory. It is here that manifestos about "computation" vie with each other, and it is this issue I will attempt to clarify. Consider the extreme positions in their purest forms.

First, there is what I shall call *High Church Computationalism*, which maintains that intervening between folk psychology and brain science will be at least one level of theory quite "close" to the high level of folk psychology that is both "cognitive" and computational." The defining dogmas of High Church Computationalism (HCC) are a trinity:

(1) *Thinking is information processing.* That is, the terms of folk psychology are to be spruced up by the theorist and recast more rigorously: "thinking" will be analyzed into an amalgam of processes ("inference" and "problem solving" and "search" and so forth); "seeing" and "hearing" will be analyzed in terms of "perceptual analysis" which itself will involve inference, hypothesis-testing strategies, and the like.

(2) *Information processing is computation (which is symbol manipulation).* The information-processing systems and operations will themselves be analyzed in terms of processes of "computation," and since, as Fodor says, "no computation without representation," a medium of representation is posited, consisting of *symbols* belonging to a *system* which has a *syntax* (formation rules) and *formal rules of symbol manipulation* for deriving new symbolic complexes from old.

(3) the semantics of these symbols connects thinking to the external world. For instance, some brain-thingamabob (brain state, brain event, complex property of brain tissue) will be the symbol for MIT, and some other brain-thingamabob will be the symbol for budget. Then we will be able to determine that another, composite brain-thingamabob refers to the MIT budget, since the symbolic structures composable within the repre-

sentational medium have interpretations that are a systematic function of the semantic interpretations of their elements. In other words, there is a language of thought, and many of the terms of this language (many of the symbols manipulated during computation) can be said to *refer* to things in the world such as Chicago, whales, and the day after tomorrow.

At the other extreme from the High Church Computationalists are those who flatly deny all of its creed: there is no formal, rule-governed, computational level of description intervening between folk psychology and brain science. Thinking is something going on in the brain all right, but is not computation at all; thinking is something holistic and emergent—and organic and fuzzy and warm and cuddly and mysterious. I shall call this extreme version Zen Holism.[1]

In between these extremes are all manner of intermediate compromise positions, most of them still rather dimly envisaged at this inchoate stage of inquiry. It would be handy to have a geographical metaphor for organizing and describing this theory-space, and happily one is at hand, thanks to Fodor.

In a heated discussion at MIT about rival theories of language comprehension, Fodor characterized the views of a well-known theoretician as "West Coast"—a weighty indictment in the corridors of MIT. When reminded that this maligned theoretician resided in Pennsylvania, Fodor was undaunted. He was equally ready, it turned out, to brand people at Brandeis or Sussex as West Coast. He explained that just as when you are at the North Pole, moving away from the Pole in any direction is moving south, so moving away from MIT in any direction is moving West. MIT is the East Pole, and from a vantage point at the East Pole, the inhabitants of Chicago, Pennsylvania, Sussex, and even Brandeis University in Waltham are all distinctly Western in their appearance and manners. Boston has long considered itself the Hub of the Universe; what Fodor has seen is that in cognitive science the true center of the universe is across the Charles, but not so far upriver as the wild and woolly ranchland of Harvard Square. (To a proper East Pole native, my outpost farther afield at Tufts is probably imagined in terms of crashing surf and ukuleles.)

Since MIT is the Vatican of High Church Computationalism, and since the best-known spokesmen of Zen Holism hold forth from various podia in the Bay area, I propose to organize the chaos with an idealized map: positions about computational models of mental phenomena can be usefully located in a logical space with the East Pole at the center and the West coast as its horizon. (This is not, of course, just what Fodor had in mind when he discovered the East Pole. I am adapting his vision to my own purposes.) In between the extremes there are many positions that

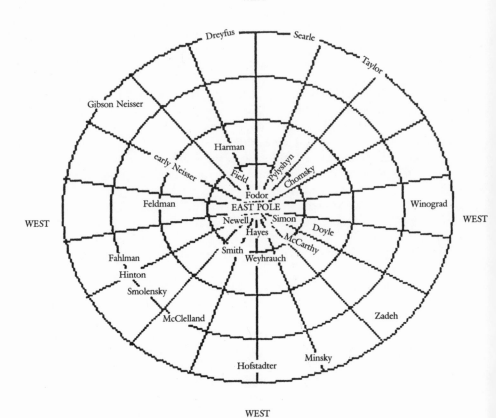

Fig. 1. A view from the East Pole.

disagree sharply over many matters (they are, as one says, "diametrically opposed"), but can nevertheless all be seen to be more or less Western, depending on which denials or modifications of High Church Computationalism they defend. As in any attempt at cartography, this is just one of many possible projections, claiming no essential rightness but inviting your consideration as a useful organizer.[2]

These warring doctrines, High Church Computationalism and its many heresies, are not themselves theories; they are ideologies.[3] They are ideologies about what the true theory of the mind will or must be like, when we eventually divine it. Various attempts to create genuine theories—various research programs—*seem* to be committed to various ideologies arrayed in our space, but as we shall see, the bond between research program and ideology is rather loose. In particular, the fact that great progress is (or is not) being made on a research program might tell us next to nothing about the ultimate soundness of its inspiring ideology.

And vice versa: refutation of an ideology sometimes bodes not very much at all for the research done under its banner. Ideologies are important and even unavoidable; they affect how we imagine the issues, and how we express the questions. A false ideology will typically tempt us to frame the wrong questions and thereby waste time and effort on low-grade research and avoidable artifactual puzzles. But sometimes one can make progress even while asking awkward and misguided questions, and sometimes (quite often, in fact, I think) researchers half-consciously know better than actually to ask the questions their ideology holds to be the right questions. Instead, they ask questions they can see how to answer and hardly notice that these inquiries are rather remotely related to the official questions of their school of thought.

Not surprisingly, it is philosophers who have been the most active formulators and guardians of the ideologies. Jerry Fodor, in *The Language of Thought* (1975) and *RePresentations* (1981), has for some time been the theologian in residence at the East Pole [his more recent heresy in *The Modularity of Mind* (1983) will be discussed in due course]. Hubert Dreyfus and John Searle at Berkeley are the gurus of West Coast Zen Holism. Hartry Field (1978) is another East Polar apologist, and so is Gilbert Harman (1973), though he is not entirely Orthodox.

Joining Dreyfus and Searle on the West Coast is Charles Taylor.[4] Other philosophers range in between: Stephen Stich, Robert Cummins, John Haugeland, and Margaret Boden, to name a few.[5] (For my part, I have always considered myself bi-coastal.[6]) Philosophers are not the only major participants in this ideological conflict however. Allen Newell,[7] Noam Chomsky,[8] and Zenon Pylyshyn[9] have staunchly represented the East, while Terry Winograd,[10] Lotfi Zadeh, and Douglas Hofstadter are nonphilosophers in the West who have contributed more than passingly to the formulation of doctrine.[11] And in psychology we have for instance the Apostate Ulric Neisser, whose book, *Cognitive Psychology* (1963), was a founding document of High Church Computationalism, but who, under the influence of J. J. Gibson, renounced the faith in his book, *Cognition and Reality* (1975), and helped to turn Ithaca into something of a West Coast colony.[12]

Real-world geography is obviously only an intermittent clue to logical geography. The San Diego school of Norman, Rumelhart, and McClelland is appropriately Western in its attitude, but now that McClelland is joining the rather Middlewestern group of Hinton and Fahlman at Carnegie–Mellon, Pittsburgh (given the Dreyfusian and hence Coastal sympathies of John Haugeland) would begin to look like another Western colony were it not for the counterbalancing Eastern voices of Newell and Simon (and Jon Doyle). Jerry Feldman at Rochester is a founding member of the distinctly Western school of New Connectionists (of which more later), but his colleague Patrick Hayes (who once told me he was quite sure the brain conducts its business in the predicate calculus) is about as East Pole as you can get. John McCarthy at Stanford is also an East Pole missionary, of course, as are Richard Weyhrauch and Brian Smith, in spite of their real-world locations.

All that should ruffle a few feathers. I doubt that the points of agreement between, say, Searle and Hofstadter, or Winograd and Feldman, loom very large in their minds, nor do I suppose Chomsky and Fodor are all that comfortable being lumped with McCarthy and Simon and vice versa. And rightly so, for the defining issues that place these people in the same "latitudes" are less integral to their widely differing research programs and methodological principles than they have acknowledged. So my cartography is indeed in some regards superficial. The dependence of some researchers on the dogmas of High Church Computationalism can be made to loom large at first glance, but I hope to show that it dissolves under scrutiny.

Over the years there has been an intermittent but intense focus on Fodor's and Chomsky's grounds for taking High Church Computationalism (HCC) seriously in their research programs in linguistics, psycholinguistics, and cognitive psychology, and I consider the issues raised in that focus to be sufficiently well known and analyzed that I need not review them here. Instead I will draw attention to how some other research programs in cognitive science *apparently* broaden the support for—or reveal the breadth of the dependence on—HCC.

Consider John McCarthy's quest for a *formal representation* of the knowledge an agent requires in order to *prove* that various courses of action are best (or just acceptable) under various circumstances.[13] This is, as McCarthy says, an epistemological question, and the formality constraint McCarthy imposes on the answer *apparently* has the same rationale as Fodor's formality constraint:[14] the brain, as a mechanism, can respond only to the formal (not semantical) properties of its states.

Or consider Newell and Simon's quest for the *rules* of problem-solving strategies adopted by self-conscious, deliberate human problem solvers, and their characterization of the phenomenon of problem solving as a transition between one (formally explicit) representation of the problem and another (formally explicit) representation of the solution.[15] Doesn't their empirical exploration of problem solving cast in these terms presuppose a commitment to the hypothesis that problem solving in human beings is a computational process taking explicit, formal symbol structures into other explicit, formal symbol structures? They often say as much, and when they do, they express what is in any case the common understanding about the whole point of their research program.

In fact, from one vantage point all AI seems unproblematically committed to HCC. If your models are written in LISP and are actually designed to run on computers, how can you take yourself seriously as a theorist or modeler of mental processes without taking yourself to be presupposing the thesis—or at least playing the hunch—that mental processes are analogous to the constituent computer processes of your model at least to the extent of being formal, computational processes of symbol manipulation?

Many cognitivist theorists have been content to avow just such an ideology. After all, what's wrong with it? This is the question that has thrown down the gauntlet to the ideological foes of HCC, who have been so concerned to demonstrate the shortcomings of HCC doctrines *as ideology* that they have seldom cared to ask whether the research programs of the proponents are as deeply committed to the doctrines as the proponents have maintained. (Mightn't the manifestos be more a matter of fancy advertising jingles than enabling assumptions? Your true-blue ideologue doesn't care; all that matters is under what conditions the advertising is *defensible*.)

Thus a recurrent and powerful line of criticism of High Church Computationalism points out that such computational models as have actually been proposed by workers in AI or cognitive psychology are ludicrously underdetermined by the available data, even when they are quite plausible, as they often are.[16] This criticism usefully reveals how far from being demonstrated the central claims of High Church Computationalism are, but otherwise it strikes a glancing blow, since if there happen to be deep methodological reasons for hoping for a winning computational model, the prospect that early exploratory models will be drastically undetermined by the data should be viewed as a tolerable (and entirely anticipated) phase of the research program.

And Fodor has provided us with a candidate for a deep methodological reason for throwing our lot with HCC: it is the only remotely explicit positive idea anyone has.[17] Fodor's challenge ("What else?") has very effectively embarrassed the opposition for years, since Zen Holism itself is not a positive alternative but only a brute denial. Saying that thinking is holistic and emergent only announces the flavor of your skepticism and gestures in the direction of an alternative.

In the absence of plausible, explicit alternatives and faced with the drastic underdetermination of any HCC theory, ideologues and critics have been lured into a startlingly premature debate on what *would be* good evidence for one brand or another of computational theory. I'm all for thought experiments, but in this instance it seems to me that things have gotten out of hand. While scarcely measurable progress is being made on garnering real evidence for any particular computational theory or model,[18] tremendous effort has been expended on reaching and defending verdicts on imagined future evidential circumstances. (I have played this game as exuberantly as others—I do not exempt myself from these second thoughts.)

But we can ask the challenging question again: what is the alternative? That is, what else ought the troubled skeptic do, faced with an implausible and underdetermined ideology that defends itself with the challenge: what is the alternative? Dreyfus and the other West Coast philosophers have taken the extreme course: they have attempted to find a priori arguments showing that HCC *couldn't possibly* be true—without notable success. They have formulated their arguments but won few converts with them, and the verdict of many onlookers is that the debate conducted in those terms is a standoff at best.

If the a priori gambit has been overdone, there is a more modest Western tactic that has seldom been adopted by philosophers but has been quite influential in some AI circles: trying to explain not why HCC is impossible, but why, even if it is both possible (for all one can tell) and the only articulated possibility to date, it is so unlikely.

High Church Computationalism does seem to me (and to many others) to be highly implausible, for reasons that are hard to express but that hover around the charge that a computational, symbol-manipulating brain seems profoundly unbiological.[19] This unelaborated suspicion should not be trusted, for one's intuitions about what is biological and what is not are (for most of us, surely) an undisciplined crew. What could seem more unbiological (from one intuitive vantage point) than the clockworky mechanisms of DNA replication, for instance? So if this is to be more than just another way of saying Nay to NCC, we need to say something more explicit about why we think an HCC-style brain would not be Nature's Way.

Douglas Hofstadter has recently found a way of expressing this misgiving that strikes me as being on the right track.[20] HCC systems, designed as they are "through a 100% top-down approach" (p.284), are *too efficient* in their utilization of machinery. As we work our way down through the nested black boxes, "functions calling subfunctions calling subfunctions," decomposing larger homunculi into committees of smaller, dumber homunculi, we provide for no waste motion, no nonfunctional or dysfunctional clutter, no featherbedding homunculi or supernumeraries. But that is not Nature's Way; designing systems or organizations with that sort of efficiency requires genuine foresight, a *detailed* anticipation of the problem spaces to be encountered, the tasks the system will be called upon to perform. Another way of saying it is that such systems, by being designed *all the way down*, have too much intelligence implicated in their design at the lower levels.

Nature's Way of providing flexibility and good design involves a different kind of efficiency, the sort of efficiency that can emerge opportunistically out of prodigious amounts of "wasteful" and locally uninterpretable activity—activity that isn't from the outset "for" anything, but is enlisted to play some very modest role (or many roles on many different occasions) in some highly distributed process.

This is a theme to counterbalance the themes of HCC that have so dominated imagination, but is it just a theme? Until very recently, Fodor's challenge stood unanswered: no one had any explicit proposals for how such bottom-up systems could do any recognizable cognitive work. The only suggestions forthcoming from the philosophers (and neuroscientists as well) were metaphorical and mysterious.[21]

But now from out of the West something better is coming. Explicit proposals, and even working, testable models are emerging from a variety of workers clustered around the so-called New Connectionism. (I am still only beginning my attempt to map out the relations between these kindred spirits and no doubt will leave out, misinclude, and misrepresent some people in the course of providing my introductory list, but since this paper cannot wait for a year, I will have to present my half-formed reflections.)

The most compelling *first* impression of the New Connectionists (and the point of their name) is that they are looking closely at neural architecture and trying to model much closer to the brain than the mind. That is, if East Pole AI programs appear to be attempts to *model the mind*, New Connectionist AI programs appear to be attempts to *model the brain*. And some of the purer or more extreme approaches feature explicit commentary on the parallels between neurons or neuron assemblies and the functional units of their models.[22] But it is a mistake, I think, to read the movement as "neurophysiology carried on by other means."[23] Nor is the distinctive difference simply or mainly a matter of being much more bottom-up than top-down.[24] For whereas specifically brainish-looking bits and pieces and assemblies do often appear in these new models, what is more important is that at a more abstract level the systems and elements—whether or not they resemble any known brainware—are of recognizable biological types.

The most obvious and familiar abstract feature shared by most of these models is a high degree of parallel processing, either simulated or based on actual parallel hardware.[25] Although the point has been brought home to everybody by now that the brain is a massively parallel processor and that this is important in understanding how the mind's work is done by the brain, there is less interest among the New Connectionists in the question of just what kind of parallel processor the brain is than in what the powers of massively parallel processors in general are. Hence some of the parallel-processing models are almost willfully "unrealistic" as models of brain organization. For instance, one of the guiding analogies of Hofstadter's Jumbo architecture is the constructing of molecules by enzymes floating freely within the cytoplasm of a cell—but of course Hofstadter doesn't think the cognitive tasks the Jumbo architecture is designed to perform (the example exploited in the exposition and testing of the architecture is solving anagrams) are performed within the cell bodies of people's brain cells![26]

Another widely and diversely used New Connectionist idea derives from statistical mechanics: "simulated annealing."[27] Computational analogues of alternatively "warming" and "cooling" structures to get them to settle into the best combinations have proven to be powerful new methods in several different domains.[28]

Although there is a lot of diversity and disagreement among the people in my Western cluster around the New Connectionists, a few characteristics—family resemblances—are worth noting. In these models, typically there is:

(1) "distributed" memory and processing, in which units play multiple, drastically equivocal roles, and in which disambiguation occurs only "globally." In short, some of these models are what you might call computational holograms. For instance, Pentti Kanerva's distributed recognition memory[29] has a strictly limited capacity for high-quality memory, but when it is overloaded, the effect is not to create a simple overflow in which no new information can be input. Rather, the input of too much information leads to the partial degradation of information previously stored; the superimposition of the excess information smudges or obscures the information already in memory.[30]

(2) no central control but rather a partially anarchic system of rather competitive elements. (See, e.g., the discussion in Feldman and Ballard of "winner take all" or WTA networks. Many of these ideas can be seen to be new versions of much older ideas in AI—e.g., Selfridge's Pandemonium, and of course perceptrons.)

(3) no complex message-passing between modules or subsystems. [For instance, no discursive messages "about the outside world." "The fundamental premise of connectionism is that individual neurons *do not transmit large amounts of symbolic information*. Instead they compute by being *appro-*

priately connected to large numbers of similar units" (Feldman and Ballard 1982, p.208).]

(4) a reliance on statistical properties of ensembles to achieve effects.

(5) the relatively mindless and inefficient making and unmaking of many partial pathways or solutions, until the system settles down after a while not on the (predesignated or predesignatable) "right" solution, but only with whatever "solution" or "solutions" "feel right" to the system. This combines the idea of simulated annealing (or a close kin of it) with the idea that in nature not all "problems" have "solutions" and there is a difference between a process stopping and a process being turned off.

The models being explored are still computational, but the level at which the modeling is computational is much closer to neuroscience than to psychology, What is computed is not (for instance) an implication of some predicate-calculus proposition *about Chicago*, or a formal description *of a grammatical transformation*, but (for instance) the new value of some threshold-like parameter of some element *which all by itself has no univocal external-world semantic role*. At such a low level of description, the semantics of the symbolic medium of computation refers only (at most) to events, processes, states, addresses within the brain—within the computational system itself. In short, on this view the only formal, *computational* "language of thought" is *rather* like a machine language for a computer, and you can't say "it's raining in Chicago" in machine language; all you can express are imperatives about what to do to what contents of what address and the like.

How then do we ever get anything happening in such a system that is properly *about Chicago*? On these views there must indeed be higher levels of description at which we can attribute external-semantical properties to brain-thingamabobs (this brain-thingamabob refers to Chicago, and that one refers to MIT), but at such a level the interactions and relationships between elements will not be computational but (and here we lapse back into metaphor and handwaving) statistical, emergent, holistic. The "virtual machine" that is recognizably psychological in its activity will not be a *machine* in the sense that its behavior is not formally specifiable (using the psychological-level vocabulary) as the computation of some high-level algorithm. Thus in this vision the low, computational level is importantly *un*like a normal machine language in that there is no supposition of a direct translation or implementation relation between the high-level phenomena that do have an external-world semantics and the phenomena at the low level. If there were, the usual methodological precept of computer science would be in order: ignore the hardware since the idiosyncracies of its particular style of implementation *add nothing* to the phenomenon, provided the phenomenon is rigorously described at the higher level. (Implementation details do add constraints of time and space, of course, which are critical to the assessment of particular models, but these details are not normally supposed to affect *what information processing is executed*, which is just what makes this Western proposal a break with tradition.)

My favorite metaphor for this proposal is meteorology. (What would you expect from the author of *Brainstorms*? But the analogy is developed in detail in Hofstadter's *Gödel, Escher, Bach*, pp.302–309.) Think of meteorology and its relation to physics. Clouds go scudding by, rain falls, snowflakes pile up in drifts, rainbows emerge; this is the language of *folk meteorology*. Modern day folk meterorologists—that is, all of us—know perfectly well that *somehow or other* all those individual clouds and rainbows and snowflakes and gusts of wind are just the emergent saliencies (saliencies relative to *our* perceptual apparatus) of vast distributions of physical energy, water droplets, and the like.

There is a gap between folk meteorology and physics but not a very large and mysterious one. Moving back and forth between the two domains takes us on familiar paths, traversed many times a day on the TV news. It is important to note that the meteorologist's instruments are barometers, hygrometers, and thermometers, not cloudometers, rainbometers, and snowflakometers. The regularities of which the science of meteorology is composed concern pressure, temperature, and relative humidity, not the folk-meteorological categories.

There is not, today, any field of computational cloudology. Is this because meteorology is in its infancy, or is such an imagined science as out of place as astrology? Note that there are patterns, regularities, large scale effects, and, in particular, reactive effects between items in folk-meteorological categories and other things. For instance, many plants and animals are designed to discriminate folk-meteorological categories for one purpose or another. We can grant all this without having to suppose that there is a formal system governing those patterns and regularities, or the reactions to them. Similarly—and this is the moral of the meteorological metaphor—it does not follow from the fact that the folk-psychological level of explanation is the "right" level for many purposes that there must be a computational theory at or near that level. The alternative to HCC is that it is the clouds and rainbows in the brain that have intentionality— that refer to Chicago and grandmother—but that the rigorous computational theory that must account for the passage and transformation of these clouds and rainbows will be at a lower level, where the only semantics is internal and somewhat strained as semantics (in the same way the "semantics" of machine language is a far cry from the semantics of a natural language).

But how are we to move beyond the metaphors and develop these new low-level hunches into explicit theory at the "higher," or more "central," cognitive levels? The bits of theory that are getting explicit in the New Connectionist movement are relatively close to the "hardware" level of description, and the cognitive work they so far can do is often characterized as either relatively peripheral or relatively subordinate. For instance, pattern recognition appears (to many theorists) to be a relatively early or peripheral component in perception, and memory appears (to many theorists) to be a rather subordinate ("merely clerical" one might say) component in the higher intellectual processes of planning or problem solving. To the ideologues of the West, however, these appearances have misled. All thinking, no matter how intellectual or central or (even) rule-governed, will turn out to make essential use of fundamentally *perceptual* operations such as versatile pattern recognition; it is no accident that we often say "I see" when we come to understand. And, according to the Western view, the apportionment of responsibility and power between memory and intelligent processing will be unlike the underlying (and ineluctably influential) division of labor in von Neumann machines, in which the memory is inert, and cold storage and all the action happens in the central processing unit; a proper memory will do a great deal of the intelligent work itself.

So far as I know, no one has yet come up with a way of sorting out these competing hunches in a medium of expression that is uniform, clear, and widely understood (even if not formal). What we need is a level of description that is to these bits of theory *roughly* as software talk is to hardware talk in conventional computer science. That is, it should abstract from as many low-level processing details as possible while remaining in the spirit of the new architectures.

The problem is that we do not yet have many clear ideas about what the functions of such systems must be—what they must be able to do. This setting of the problem has been forcefully developed by David Marr in his methodological reflections on his work on vision.[31] He distinguishes three levels of analysis. The highest level, which he rather misleadingly calls computational, is in fact not at all concerned with computational processes, but strictly (and more abstractly) with the question of what function the system in question is serving—or, more formally, with what function *in the mathematical sense* it must (somehow or other) "compute." Recalling Chomsky's earlier version of the same division of labor, we can say that Marr's computational level is supposed to yield a formal and rigorous specification of a system's *competence*—"given an element in the set of x's it yields an element in the set of y's according to the following rules"—while remaining silent or neutral about implementation or *perfor-*

mance. Marr's second level down is the *algorithmic* level, which does specify the computational processes but remains neutral (as neutral as possible) about the *hardware*, which is described at the bottom level.

Marr's claim is that until we ge a clear and precise understanding of the activity of a system at the highest, "computational" level, we cannot properly address detailed questions at the lower levels, or interpret such data as we may already have about processes implementing those lower levels. Moreover, he insists, if you have a seriously mistaken view about what the computational-level description of your system is (as all earlier theorists of vision did, in his view), your attempts to theorize at lower levels will be confounded by spurious artifactual problems. [It is interesting to note that this is also the claim of J. J. Gibson, who viewed all cognitivistic, information-processing models of vision as hopelessly entangled in unnecessarily complex Rube Goldberg mechanisms posited because the theorists had failed to see that a fundamental reparsing of the inputs and outputs was required. Once we get the right way of characterizing what vision receives from the light, he thought, and what it must yield ("affordances"), the theory of vision would be a snap.]

Now Marr claims to have gotten the computational level right for vision, and his claim is not obviously too optimistic. But vision, like any peripheral system, is apparently much more tractable at Marr's computational level than are the central systems of thought, planning, problem solving, and the like that figure so centrally in AI explorations. Fodor argues in *The Modularity of Mind* (1983) that while there has been dramatic progress on the peripheral perceptual "modules" that "present the world to thought," "there is no serious psychology of central cognitive processes."

> We have, to put it bluntly, no computational formalisms that show us how to do this, and we have no idea how such formalisms might be developed. . . . If someone—a Dreyfus, for example—were to ask us why we should even suppose that the digital computer is a plausible mechanism for the simulation of global cognitive processes, the answering silence would be deafening. (p. 129)

But what is this? One would have thought that never the twain would meet, but here is Fodor, Archbishop of the East Pole, agreeing with Dreyfus, Guru of the West Coast, that High Church Computationalism has made no progress on "central cognitive processes." If Fodor is right in his pessimism—and I think for the most part he is—what might a reasonable theoretician do?

My proposal: go right on doing the sort of AI that has traditionally been associated with High Church Computationalism but abandon the computationalist ideology altogether and reinterpret the programs of these AI practitioners as *thought experiments*, not *models*.

Here is what I mean. If Marr is right to insist that progress must first be made on the problems at the computational level, then the first task confronting us if we want a theory of "central cognitive processes" is just to say what those processes are supposed to be able to accomplish. What is the nature of those central faculties? Forget for the moment *how* they do what they do. Just what is it that they (are supposed to) do? What is the competence the theorist should try to explain? As Fodor insists, no one has a clear, crisp explicit account of this. But several researchers are trying. Allen Newell, for instance, calls this level of description the Knowledge Level. It is, in effect, Marr's computational level as applied to the central arena. McCarthy draws a similar level distinction.[32] What these and many other theorists in AI have been doing is not proposing HCC models of human cognition or testing theories with empirical experiments, but casting about, in a *thought*-experimental way, for constraints and relationships that might inform the description (at Marr's "computational" level) of the mysterious "central cognitive processes." And at least this much progress has been made: we have enlarged and refined our vision of what powers human minds actually have. And we now know quite a few ways *not* to try to capture the basic competence—let alone the implementation—of the central cognitive systems. The process of elimination looms large in AI research; virtually every model seriously considered has been eliminated as far too simple for one reason or another. But that is progress. Until the models are seriously considered and eliminated they lurk as serious possibilities to tempt the theorist.

Thus McCarthy's formality constraint is not a commitment to High Church Computationalism (or need not be). It might be nothing more than the demand for enough rigor and precision to set the problem for the next level down, Marr's algorithmic level, except that this would probably not be a good term for the highest level at which the processes (as contrasted with the products) of the New Connectionist sort were described.

And Newell and Simon's search for "rules" of "thinking" need not commit them or their admirers to the HCC doctrine that thinking is rule-*governed* computation. The rules they discover (supposing they succeed) may instead be interpreted as regularities in patterns in the emergent phenomena—the cognitive "clouds" and "rainbows"—but not "mere" regularities. The well-known distinction (in philosophy) between rule-following behavior and rule-described behavior is often illustrated by pointing out that the planets do not compute their orbits, even though *we* can, following rules that describe their motions. The "rules" of planetary motion are law-like regularities, not "followed" rules. This is true, but it ignores a variety of regularity intermediate between the regularities of planets (or ordinary cloud formations) and the regularities of rule-following (that is, rule-*consulting*) systems. These are the regularities that are preserved under selective pressure: the regularities dictated by principles of good design and hence homed in on by self-designing systems. That is, a "rule of thought" may be much more than a mere regularity; it may be a *wise* rule, a rule one would design a system by if one were a system designer, and hence a rule one would expect self-designing systems to "discover" in the course of settling into their patterns of activity. Such rules no more need to be explicitly represented than do the principles of aerodynamics honored in the design of birds' wings.

For example, Marr discovered that the visual system operates with a tacit assumption that moving shapes are articulated in rigid linkages and that sharp light-intensity boundaries indicate physical edges. These assumptions are not "coded" in the visual system; the visual system is designed to work well only in environments where the assumptions are (by and large) true. Such rules and principles should be very precisely formulated at the computational level—not so they can then be "coded" at the algorithmic level but so that the (algorithmic) processes can be designed to honor them (but maybe only with a high degree of regularity).

Are there "rules" of (good) problem solving that must be (and are) tacit in the regularities that emerge in the information processing of mature thinkers? One might discover them by attempting to *codify* such rules in a rule-following system whose behavior exhibited those regularities because those were the regularities it was "told" to follow. Such systems can be put through their paces to test the adequacy of the rules under consideration.[33] It is this testing that has led to the (often informative) elimination of so many tempting models in AI.

In sum, there is no reason I can see for AI or cognitive science to take on the rather unlikely burden of defending HCC. It seems to me that all the valuable AI research that has been done can be viewed as attempts to sketch competences. (Marr, of course, went far beyond that.) As such it is best viewed as consisting of (preliminary) thought experiments, not as more "mature" genuinely experimental science. But its thought experiments are subject to a modicum of control. One can *test* such a sketch of a competence by test driving an unbiologically produced Rube Goldberg device with that competence (the actual "computational" AI program) to see how it would perform.

This leaves us with an almost embarrassingly ecumenical conclusion. Everyone is right about something. Dreyfus and the Zen Holists are right that we need not commit ourselves to the defining dogmas of High

Church Computationalism, but the people engaged in devising computational models of cognitive processes are right that their methodology is probably the best way to make headway on the mysteries of the mind. Everybody agrees that something or other in the brain must be capable of having the semantic property of referring to Chicago and that it is the task of *some* sort of computational theory to explain and ground this power. Residual disagreements are either based on unmotivated allegiances to bits of outworn creed or are substantive disagreements on just which brand of interstitial computational theory is apt to be most promising. There is only one way to settle these latter disagreements: roll up our sleeves and devise and test the theories.[34]

Notes

This paper was prepared for the Conference on Philosophy and Cognitive Science at MIT, May 17–20, 1984, sponsored by the Sloan Foundation. Written under a deadline for the purpose of providing a glimpse of the state of the art in mid-1984, it will no doubt have a short shelf life. So read it now, or if now is later than 1986, read it as a quaint reflection on how some people thought back in 1984.

1. Richard Dawkins speaks of those who are "holistier than thou" in *The Extended Phenotype* (1982, p.113).

2. For another attempt at a systematic spatial ordering of views on a closely related issue, see John Haugeland's paper, "The Intentionality All-Stars," (still unpublished, alas) which identifies various positions on intentionality with baseball positions, and in the process creates some striking and illuminating juxtapositions. For instance, Fodor, Kant, and Husserl are all on first; Wittgenstein, Quine, and Ryle are shortstops; Searle is out in right field with Derrida. (Nagel is at the plate, of course, wondering what it's like to be at bat.)

3. Allen Newell would call them intellectual issues. See Newell 1983.

4. See, e.g., Taylor 1983.

5. Stich 1983; Cummins 1983; Haugeland 1978, 1981; Boden 1984.

6. See, e.g., Dennett 1982, 1983a, 1984a (my review of Fodor's *Modularity of Mind*).

7. Newell 1980.

8. See, e.g., Chomsky 1980a, 1980b.

9. See, e.g., Pylyshyn 1978, 1980, 1984.

10. In the someday-forthcoming 8th edition of *The Philosophical Lexicon*, "winograd" (n. sometimes pronounced "wino-grad") is defined as the degree of intoxication occasioned by moving to the West Coast.

11. Hofstadter, on reading an earlier draft of this paper, suggested that Zadeh's fuzzy set theory is actually better seen as an attempt, entirely within the Eastern

Orthodoxy, to achieve West Coast ends with East Pole means. I am inclined to agree; this is one of the fine points of interpretation in need of further work.

12. A forthcoming collaborative effort by psychologist Steven Kosslyn and philosopher Gary Hatfield, "Representation without Symbols" in *Journal of Social Research*, expresses Western views similar to those developed by Boden and by me in "Styles of Mental Representation."

13. See, e.g., McCarthy 1980.

14. Fodor 1980.

15. See, e.g., Newell and Simon 1972, 1976.

16. See, for instance, Edward Stabler 1983, pp. 391–422, and especially the commentaries. See also Chomsky 1980b, and the commentaries.

17. Newell and Simon rely on the same challenge in "Computer Science as Empirical Enquiry: Symbols and Search." See (in Haugeland reprinting) p.50: "The principal body of evidence for the symbol-system hypothesis that we have not considered is negative evidence: the absence of specific competing hypotheses as to how intelligent activity might be accomplished—whether by man or by machine."

18. Simon has objected (in conversation) that his work with Newell is replete with solid empirical evidence in favor of their "production system" models of human problem solving. But even if I were to grant that *something very like* Newell and Simon's productions have been shown empirically to be involved in—even the basis of—human problem solving, there would still be no empirical evidence as yet showing that the *computational implementation* of production systems in computers realistically models any level of the neural implementation of the production-like processes in human thinking. For a related argument see Stabler (1983) and my commentary on Stabler (1983b, p.406–407).

19. See Dennett 1984b.

20. Hofstadter 1983b. Hofstadter calls High Church Computationalism the Boolean Dream.

21. In "Cognitive Wheels" (1984b) I call this dodge the declaration that "the brain is wonder tissue."

22. See Feldman and Ballard 1982.

23. Clark Glymour, in "Android Epistemology," (forthcoming) declares that AI—and here he is surely referring to East Pole AI—is actually "logical positivism carried on by other means."

24. See, e.g., McClelland, unpubl. manuscript.

25. Hillis 1981; Fahlman, Hinton, and Sejnowski 1983.

26. Hofstadter 1983a.

27. Kirkpatrick, Gelatt, and Vecchi 1983.

28. Smolensky 1983.

29. Kanerva 1983.

30. John Haugeland, in "The Nature and Plausibility of Cognitivism," held out bravely for some sort of hologram-like alternative to a computationalist language of thought. Now there are some actual models to examine—and not just the (perhaps visionary but) metaphorical suggestions of Pribram and Arbib.

31. Marr 1982.

32. Newell 1982; McCarthy 1980.

33. I think it *may* be helpful to compare this interpretation of AI strategy with the simulations explored by evolutionary theorists such as John Maynard Smith and Richard Dawkins, who ask questions about whether certain behavioral "strategies" are evolutionarily stable by explicitly codifying the strategies in the behavior of imaginary organisms, and then pitting them against alternative (explicit, rule-governed) strategies embodied in rival imaginary organisms, to see which (pure, idealized) strategy would win in Nature under various conditions. See Dawkins (1976, 1982) for good introductory discussions. See also George Axelrod (1984) on prisoners' dilemma competitions between simulations for a similarly motivated research effort.

34. Douglas Hofstadter has had an even greater role than usual in shaping my thinking on these issues, so if I am all wrong about this, he *is* responsible, and will have to share the blame. But he is not responsible for my failures to understand or do justice to the various efforts I discuss here. Others who have commented on earlier drafts of this paper, including Robert Cummins, Jerry Feldman, John Haugeland, Hilary Putnam, and Herbert Simon, are hereby thanked and absolved in the usual manner.

Bibliography

Axelrod, G. 1984. *The evolution of cooperation*. New York: Basic Books.

Boden, M. 1984. What is computational psychology? *Proceedings of the Aristotelian Society* 58 (suppl.):17–53.

Chomsky, N. 1980a. *Rules and representations*. New York: Columbia Univ. Press.

———. 1980b. Rules and representations. *Behavioral and Brain Sciences* 3:1–61.

Cummins, R. 1983. *The nature of psychological explanation*. Cambridge: MIT Press, Bradford Books.

Dawkins, R. 1976. *The selfish gene*. Oxford: Oxford Univ. Press.

———. 1982. *The extended phenotype*. Oxford and San Francisco: Freeman.

Dennett, D. 1978. *Brainstorms: Philosophical essays on mind and psychology*. Cambridge: MIT Press, Bradford Books.

———. 1982. Beyond belief. In *Thought and object*. ed. Andrew Woodfield, pp. 1–95. Oxford: Clarendon Press.

———. 1983a. Styles of mental representation. *Proceedings of the Aristotelian Society* 83:213–226.

———. 1983b. When do representations explain? *Behavioral and Brain Sciences* 6:406–7.

———. 1984a. Carving the mind at its joints. *Contemporary Psychology* 29:285–286.

———. 1984b. Cognitive wheels: The frame problem of AI. In *Minds, machines and evolution,* ed. C. Hookway, pp. 129–151. Cambridge: Cambridge Univ. Press.

Fahlman, S. E., G. Hinton, and T. J. Sejnowski. 1983. Massively parallel architectures for AI: NETL, Thistle and Boltzmann machines. *Proceedings of the American Association of Artificial Intelligence* 83:109–113.

Feldman, J. and D. H. Ballard. 1982. Connectionist models and their properties. *Cognitive Science* 6:205–254.

Field, H. 1978. Mental representation. *Erkenntnis* 13:9–61.

Fodor, J. 1975. *The language of thought*. New York: Crowell.

_____. 1980. Methodological solipsism considered as a research strategy in cognitive psychology. *Behavioral and Brain Sciences* 3:63–110. [Also published in Fodor (1981, pp. 225–253).]

_____. 1981. *RePresentations: Philosophical essays on the foundations of cognitive science*. Cambridge: MIT Press, Bradford Books.

_____. 1983. *The modularity of mind*. Cambridge: MIT Press, Bradford Books.

Gibson, J.J. 1975. *Cognition and reality*. San Francisco: Freeman.

Glymour, C. Forthcoming. Android epistemology.

Harman, G. 1973. *Thought*. Princeton: Princeton Univ. Press.

Haugeland, J. 1978. The nature and plausibility of cognitivism. *Behavioral and Brain Sciences* 1:215–260. [Also published in Haugeland (1981, pp. 243–281).]

_____, ed. 1981. *Mind design: Philosophy, psychology, artificial intelligence*. Cambridge: MIT Press, Bradford Books.

_____. The intentionality all-stars. Unpublished.

Hillis, D. 1981. *The connection machine (computer architecture for the new wave)*. AI Memo 646 MIT, September.

Hofstadter, D. 1979. *Gödel, Escher, Bach: An eternal golden braid*. New York: Basic Books.

_____. 1983a. The architecture of Jumbo. In *Proceedings of the Second International Machine Learning Workshop*, 161–170. Urbana, Ill.: Univ. of Illinois.

_____. 1983b. Artificial intelligence: Subcognition as computation. In *The study of information: Interdisciplinary messages,* ed. F. Machlup and U. Mansfield, pp. 263–285. New York: Wiley.

Kanerva, P. 1983. *Self-propagating search: A unified theory of memory.* Techn. rept. Center for the Study of Language and Information, Palo Alto.

Kirkpatrick, S., C. D. Gelatt, Jr., and M.P. Vecchi. 1983. Optimization by simulated annealing. *Science*, 13 May 1983, 671–680.

Kosslyn, S. and G. Hatfield. Forthcoming. Representation without symbols. *Journal of Social Research*.

Marr, D. 1982. *Vision*. New York: Freeman.

McCarthy, J. 1980. Circumscription—a form of non-monotonic reasoning. Stanford AI Lab memo AIM-334, February. (Also pub. in *Artificial Intelligence* 13:27–39.)

McClelland, J. L. Models of perception and memory based on principles of natural organization. UC San Diego. Unpublished.

Neisser, U. 1963. *Cognitive psychology*. New York: Appleton–Century–Crofts.
———. 1975. *Cognition and reality*. San Francisco: Freeman.

Newell, A. 1980. Physical symbol systems. *Cognitive Science* 4:135–183.
———. 1982. The knowledge level. *Artificial Intelligence* 18:87-127.
———. 1983. Intellectual issues in the history of artificial intelligence. In *The study of information: Interdisciplinary messages,* ed. F. Machlup and U. Mansfield, pp. 187–227. New York: Wiley.

Newell, A., and H. Simon. 1972. *Human problem solving*. Englewood Cliffs, N.J.: Prentice-Hall.
———. 1976. Computer science as empirical inquiry: Symbols and search. *Communications of the Association for Computing Machinery* 19:113–126. (Also published in Haugeland. 1981. 35-66.)

Pylyshyn, Z. 1978. Computational models and empirical constraints. *Behavioral and Brain Sciences* 1:93–127.
———. 1980. Computation and cognition: Issues in the foundations of cognitive science. *Behavioral and Brain Sciences* 3:111–169.
———. 1984. *Computation and cognition: Toward a foundation for cognitive science.* Cambridge: MIT Press, Bradford Books.

Smolensky, P. 1983. Harmony theory: A mathematical framework for learning and parallel computation. *Proceedings of the American Association of Artificial Intelligence* 83:114–132.

Stabler, E. 1983. How are grammars represented? *Behavioral and Brain Sciences* 6:391–422.

Stich, S. 1983. *From folk psychology to cognitive science*. Cambridge: MIT Press, Bradford Books.

Taylor, C. 1983. The significance of significance: The case of cognitive psychology. In *The need for interpretation,* ed. S. Mitchell and M. Rosen, pp. 141–169. London: Athlone. New York: Humanities.

· Information and Association

Here's what happened. I started out to write something about the use of associative networks as models of mental processes, but it kept turning into a paper about what notion of information is the right one to use in cognitive psychology. So I thought: Very well then, I shall write something about what notion of information is the right one to use in cognitive psychology. When I set to work on that, however, it kept turning into a paper about the use of associative networks as models of mental processes.

It began to dawn upon me that perhaps there is some connection between questions about the use of associative networks as models of mental processes and questions about what notion of information is the right one to use in cognitive psychology. This idea rather surprised me since I don't remember ever having heard these two sorts of questions discussed together. (Indeed, the people who have recently had interesting things to say about the first are mostly psychologists and the people who have recently had interesting things to say about the second are mostly philosophers-cum-semanticists. For all I know, cognitive science being what it is, these two groups of researchers have never heard of one another.) So it occurred to me that perhaps I should write a paper about information and association and how views about the one are related to views about the other.

What follows is thus cartography. I want to see how some ideas that are current in cognitive science fit together to comprise a landscape. The main thesis is that two markedly distinguishable prototheories at present occupy the field, and that these express very different—perhaps irreconcilable—construals of the doctrine that minds are information processors. I have (this will become abundantly evident) my preference as between these views, but my present purposes are only partly polemical. I'm also interested in getting clear what the options are and how they are assembled from their parts.

By way of prospectus, then, the views I have in mind are typified by the following galaxies of claims:

type 1 theories

mental processes are largely associative
mental computations are "executive free"
mental processing is massively parallel
the information transmitted is the basic notion in cognitive theory
information is "in the world"
intentionality is a nuisance
the typical explanatory constructs of cognitive psychology are semantic

type 2 theories

mental processes are largely computational
mental processes are executive driven
mental processing is typically serial
the information encoded is the basic notion in cognitive theory
information is a by-product of representation
intentionality is the key to the mental
the typical explanatory constructs of cognitive psychology are proof-theoretic.

As must be apparent, none of these slogans attains the highest degree of perspicuousness. Nor, I take it, is it transparently obvious why I have them grouped the way they are. Getting all that sorted out will be the burden of the following.

Let's begin with the simplest sort of case. Suppose we have a "Boolean Network" set up as follows. (Information flows "up"—from higher- to lower-numbered nodes—unless otherwise specified. It may be assumed, though I shan't generally stress this, that the routes through this network are probabilistic.)

N1:   1 (P v Q)
                               .
                               .
                               .

                             2 (P v Q)
                          .   .
                       .   .
                    .   .
                  3 (P)   4 (Q)

I have, arbitrarily, labeled the nodes of this network with propositional constants. Propositons can be either true or false; therefore the network is interpreted as exhibiting relations among the truth values of a certain set of abstract objects. But, in fact, the network might be interpreted in any way at all so long as the kinds of entities (objects, events, whatever) that are assigned to the nodes are (a) capable of assuming (at least) two "distinguished" states (on and off; T and F; 0 and 1; instantiated and uninstantiated; etc.), and (b) the distinguished states of each of the entities depends, in the ways that the diagram specifies, on the distinguished states of the others.

So, for example, you might interpret N1 as specifying a "neural network": To effect this interpretation, (a) a collection of neurons is assigned to each node; (b) we distinguish between two states of each of the collections (excitation and quiescence, as it might be); and (c) paths along the network are identified with routes of causation, so that the state of excitation of the objects at node 2 depends, in the ways specified, upon the states of excitation of the objects at nodes 3 and 4.

But, equally, we might imagine that the nodes of N1 represent four *people,* each of whom can be in either of two states (hands up or hands down, for example). There might be a convention that these people follow: person 2 puts his hands up just in case either person 3 does or person 4 does. My point in stressing the plurality of possible interpretations of N1 is to make clear that there is nothing peculiarly *mental* (or even biological, or even physical) about the pattern of dependencies among distinguished states that N1 specifies. More generally, if a notion of the "information" in a system can be defined in terms of such relations, then that notion will exhibit a desirable sort of ontological neutrality: since it depends only upon *patterns of relations* of distinguished states it is ipso facto *in*dependent of the ontological status of the entites that are in those states. This is important for psychologists because notions like information seem to be crucial in the explication of the mental and we would like our psychology not to assume that the properties of minds are *sui generis*. One way to achieve the *naturalization* of the mental would be to show that, in the sense of information in which minds are information processors, so too are a lot of other things.

Suppose, for example, that there is some sense of information in which information is transmitted from node to node in realizations of network N1. In some (*NB: but not in all*) such realizations, the mechanism for the transmission of that information may itself include the occurrence of mentation. Thus, in the case where the nodes are people who raise and lower their hands, part of the story about why the guy at node 2 raises his hands may involve reference to thoughts he has about what the guys at nodes 3 and 4 are up to. It might be that 2 says to himself: "3 has raised his hands, and the convention is that I raise my hands if 3 or 4 does, so I must raise my hands." But, though this gives a characteristically mental tone to the account of how information is transmitted through *that* instantiation of N1, the conditions for *being* an instantiation of N1 (hence, *ex hypothesi*, sufficient conditions for being an information-processing system) do not depend upon the occurrence of any mental processes. These conditions require (to repeat) only that certain dependencies obtain among the distinguished states of the objects at the nodes *however those dependencies are achieved*.

Well, as everybody knows, there *is* a notion of information—which I'll call the *Standard* notion of information—that does satisfy the condition that the transmission of information through a network depends solely on the existence of patterns of relations among distinguished states of the objects that constitute the network. Since everybody knows about the Standard notion of information, I won't bother even to sketch it here. [People who want to see a version of the Standard notion that is worked out with an eye specifically to its application to the mental should read Dretske (1981).] Suffice it that, according to the Standard notion of information, x transmits information about y just in case (and, just to the extent that) the distinguished states of x are correlated with the distinguished states of y. Correlation makes information, according to the Standard view.

Corollaries of the Standard view:

1. Information is cheap (because lots of things are correlated).
2. Information is "in the world" (because lots of things in the world are correlated).
3. If information about the world is "in the head" (if, for example, the belief that it is raining contains information about whether it is raining) that must be because states of the head are correlated with states of the world.

Well, then, just what notion of an *information processor* does one arrive at if one starts from the Standard notion of information? And is it the notion of information processor that we want for our cognitive psychology? I propose to sneak up on this by slow stages. First, I want to build some intuitions; to suggest that there are aspects of what one might pre-theoretically take the informational situation in N1 to be that are *not* reconstructed by the Standard notion of "information transmitted." I'll then propose some arguments to show that these neglected informational notions are ones we actually need for our account of minds.

Here's an easy question to begin with: According to the Standard notion, what information is transmitted from 2 to 1 in N1? Standard answer: the information that P v Q. (If N1 is a neural net rather than a network of propositions, the excitation of 2 transmits the information that either 3 is excited or 4 is excited; and the quiescence of 2 transmits the information that both 3 and 4 are quiescent.) Why, according to the Standard view, is that the right answer? Because, by assumption, the true description of the state of affairs in N1 is that the distinguished states of 2 are correlated in a certain way with the distinguished states of 3 and 4 (e.g., 2 fires if 3 fires or 4 fires) and, we're assuming, correlation makes information. Notice that, while this much is uncontentious, that's only because it's stipulative; it follows from the definition of the Standard notion of information together with the specification of N1.

Well, by stipulation then, the activation of 2 transmits information about the activity of 3 and 4; and it does so because the state of activity of 2 depends on the state of activity of 3 and 4. But, of course, the activation of 2 doesn't transmit the information *that* the state of activity of 2 depends on the states of activity of 3 and 4. That information isn't represented *anywhere* in the network (except in the labels; a point that I'll return to.) A graphic way of seeing this is to imagine yourself "in" the network at node 1. This is what the rest of the network looks like from that perspective:

2

Node 1 can't, as it were, "see" the network beyond node 2. So that, for example, from the point of view of node 1, network N2 looks just like network N1.

N2:   1 (P & Q)
                               .
                               .
                               .

                             2 (P & Q)
                            .   .
                          .   .

                   .   .
              3 (P)   4 (Q)

We—standing outside the networks, so to speak—can see what node 1 cannot: that, whereas the situation in N1 is that the activation of 2 is effected by the *dis*junction of 3 and 4, the situation in N2 is that the activation of 2 is effected by the *con*junction of 3 and 4. Hence, standing outside the networks, we can see that the information transmitted by the activation of 2 in N1 is different from the information transmitted by the activation of 2 in N2. But node 1 can't see this; all that node 1 can see, in either network, is node 2 going on and off.

One might put it, as friends of the Standard notion often do, that this conception makes information an "objective" quantity—that it makes information *perspective free* or *observer neutral*. The basic idea is that what information is transmitted through the network to 1 is independent of what 1 can "see" (a fortiori, it is independent of what, if anything, 1 knows or believes). For, absolutely *all* that matters in determining what information is transmitted through the network is what situation objectively obtains in the network. Similarly, the only thing about 1 that matters in determining whether 1 *receives* the information that 2 transmits is that the designated states of 1 really do correlate with the designated states of 2. The information that 1 receives isn't, one might say, in 1. If it's anywhere, it's in the correlation between the designated states of 1 and 2; i.e., its *in the network*. And if—as might be the case—the network is in the world, then the information is in the world too.

Of course one buys this objectivity at a price. A way to see this is to distinguish between the information *transmitted* by the activation of 2 and the information *displayed* by the activation of 2. (Unlike "the information transmitted," "the information displayed" does not, alas, readily admit of quantification. It isn't even well defined. I am not, however, building a theory. I'm just building intuitions in aid of making clear why the account of information that the Standard notion offers isn't the one that our cognitive science needs.) In the present case, then, we can identify the information that is *displayed* at 2 with the information that is visible from 1: i.e., information about the designated states of 2 (information that 2 is active or quiescent, if we stick to the neural network interpretation). Notice that access to the information displayed at 2 does not, in and of itself, allow you to distinguish N1 from N2. To tell which network you are in, you need to know not just what information is displayed at 2 but also how the information displayed at 2 covaries with the information displayed at 3 and 4.

The distinction between the information transmitted and the information displayed is easily obscured when you label the diagrams of a Boolean network. For each label, given its intended interpretation, actually *displays* the information that is transmitted by the activation of the corresponding node. The label of a node says how the activation of that node depends upon the activation of the rest of the network. It is thus of primary importance to understand that, in Boolean networks (and other executive-free information-processing systems) *the labels are for us, not for the machine.* This is not a philosophical gloss; it's *strictly* true. There is nothing in the operation of a Boolean network, qua Boolean network, that is sensitive to the character of the labels. Qua Boolean network, all that matters is the connectivity of the nodes and their instantaneous states of excitation. To put it slightly differently, each node can "see" the states of excitation of its neighbors; but it can't see their labels.

One reason that this is so hard to keep in one's head is that one tends to be misled by features that some *but not all* instantiations of Boolean networks have in common (hence, features that the notion of a Boolean network per se *fails* to reconstruct.) So, for instance, it's possible to think of instantiations of a Boolean network where the information at a node *is* displayed as well as transmitted; cases where the labels *do* matter for the operation of the network.

Consider an instantiation of N1 where the nodes are people and they exchange information by displaying flashcards on which formulas ("P", "Q", and "P v Q", as it might be) are inscribed. So, when 2 is activated (when guy 2 holds up the flashcard that reads "P v Q"), he not only transmits, but also displays, the information that P v Q. When (and only when) an event displays the information that is transmits, we can say that the event *encodes* that information. Intuitively speaking, the fact that the information is encoded, and not just transmitted, has striking consequences. For, though the guy at 1 still can't see the network beyond 2, *he nevertheless can tell what the network is like beyond 2 assuming that he can "read" the display.* In short: once we introduce a notion of information encoded (to contrast with the Standard notion of information transmitted) we see that there is room for a corresponding notion of a display being read (to contrast with the Standard notion of information being received.) And, just as information can be transmitted even when no information is encoded, so information can be received without any display being read (think of N1 as instantiated in a neural net.) All that receiving information requires is correlation between designated states of the receiver and designated states of the source. God knows what reading a display requires; the least you need is access to a code.

I have been nagging about the distinction between the information transmitted and the information displayed, and about the heuristic status of the labels in diagrams of Boolean networks, because it's only when one keeps these points in mind that one sees the profound inappropriateness of the Standard notion of information for reconstructing the cognitive scientist's notion of an information processor. I suppose that the fundamental intuition about information processors is this: they are systems whose behavior in a given situation is determined *by the character of the information that is available to them* in that situation. We want a notion of information that will let us hang on to that intuition, and I'm claiming that we can't get one by identifying the pretheoretical notion of the information available with the Standard notion of the information received.

The basic reason is what we have already seen: while the (distinguished) state of a node in a network depends only on the states of the nodes it can "see" (i.e., the local nodes to which it is connected), the information received by a node depends upon the state of the entire network, "visible" or otherwise. It is thus perfectly possible to have two networks which display the same information to a given node while transmitting different information to that node, as, indeed, we saw that networks N1 and N2 display the same information to node 1 (viz. information about the state of activation of node 2) although the information that gets transmitted through the networks is that P v Q in one case and that P & Q in the other. Well, to put it in a nutshell, what determines what information is (intuitively) *available* at a position in a network depends on what information is *displayed* at that position, not on what information is *transmitted* at that position.[1]

The best way to see this—this still being all just intuitive and pretheoretical—is by thinking about examples. So, here's Johnny walking down Elm Street past the open windows of his neighbors, through which the morning news is audible. As he passes the window of number 7, he hears the announcer say, "It's raining here"; as he passes the window of number 9 he hears the announcer say, "It's raining here." Let us suppose, however, that the radio in number 7 is tuned to a station in Chicago and the radio in number 9 is tuned to a station in Tulsa. Then: (a) the information *displayed* is the same at number 7 and at number 9; but (b) the information *transmitted* is different since, presumably, the signal at number 7 is correlated with the weather in Chicago (but not with the weather in Tulsa) and the signal at number 9 is correlated with the weather in Tulsa (but not with the weather in Chicago). Question: what is the information available to Johnny-qua-information-processor, such that his behavior in the current situation is determined by the availability of that information? Answer: surely it is the information displayed, not the information transmitted. Ceteris paribus, it would be a *miracle* if the information *transmitted* determined Johnny's behavior because, to put the point crudely, there's nothing in the situation to tell Johnny what information *is* being transmitted. (Remember: the signal at number 7 transmits the information that it is raining in Chicago. But it does not transmit the information that it transmits the information that it is raining in Chicago. Compare the case where what the announcer says is: "It's raining here in Chicago."

Here the information that it is raining in Chicago is *encoded* as well as transmitted. Since it is encoded it follows that it is displayed. And since it is displayed, it is available to modulate Johnny's behavior.)

I don't want to say that the information available *is* the information displayed. But I do want to say something like this: the information available is the information displayed plus whatever the receiver can figure out from the display. The information that is (in the Standard sense) *transmitted* becomes (in the pretheoretical sense) *available* only when an information processor can infer the information transmitted from the information displayed.[2]

Roughly, there will be two kinds of cases where the information that is transmitted becomes available to a receiver: when the transmitted information is encoded (hence displayed) and the receiver knows the code; and when the receiver knows how the character of the display depends upon the state of the rest of the network and is thus able to infer from the display what information it transmits. It is terribly important to understand that both these conditions constrain the receiver in ways that merely being a recipient of information transmitted does not; that is, they require more of the receiver than covariance of its designated states with designated states of the source.

THE MORAL: The notion of available information, unlike the Standard notions of information transmitted and information received, is intentional, perspectival, and receiver relative. What information is available depends upon one "objective" factor (viz., what information is on display) and one "subjective" factor (viz., what the receiver is able to infer). This is too sad for words, but it is nevertheless true.

Moreover, deep down, everybody knows that it is true. Suppose you have a correlation between A and B and a correlation between B and C. Then, to a first approximation, you have a sufficient condition for the transmission of information from A to C given the Standard notion of information transmission. ("Transmits information to" is, approximately, transitive since it's just a way of spelling "is correlated with." That "makes information available to" is *not* transitive is a way of putting the point that I've been struggling to make.) If you then ask a friend of the Standard notion how the *mere* existence of two such correlations could, in and of itself, be sufficient for the *availability* of information about A at C, what he is likely to say is this: Well, what information is *available* at C is a matter not just of what information is objectively there, but also of what information C is "attuned" to.

For example: "There is a lawlike relation between smoke and fire. Situations where there is smoke are, by and large, close to situations where there is fire. And it is attunement to this relation that enables us to learn

about [particular occasions of] fires from [particular occasions of] smoke."
(Barwise and Perry 1983, p. 12). It's not clear, however, what this "attunement" comes to, not even as a metaphor. It's one thing for a device to be "attuned" to a class of particulars (as, indeed, smoke detectors might be said to be attuned to smoke); presumably, to be attuned to a class of particulars is to be disposed to respond selectively to things that are in that class. But it's quite another matter to make sense of a device to being attuned to a *generalization* (e.g., to the generalization that if there's smoke there's fire). Barwise and Perry don't give us much help in understanding what tuning to a generalization might amount to. Here's what they say (1983, p.12): "Being attuned to . . . [the] relation . . . [between smoke and fire presupposes] only the ability to detect smoke, to respond in some way appropriate to fire, and to do the latter on the occasion of the former." This, however, is an old and unconvincing story, one which age has not improved. (See, for example, Mowrer 1960; Osgood 1963).

To begin with—as people have endlessly pointed out—you can't rely on formulas like "a response in some way appropriate to fire" to pick out a class of behaviors, since whether behavior *is* appropriate depends not just on the fire but also on the utilities of the behavior. (See, for example, "Norma," act 2, part 2: "Vanne al rogo ed il tuo scempio/ Purghi l'ara e lavi il tempio," and so forth). There is thus more subjectivity—not to say intentionality—built into talk about attunement than the unwary may at first suppose. But pass that; there is worse to come. Look, to respond to *smoke* in a way that is actually appropriate to *fire* would not give evidence of attunement to a relation between them; at best it suggests that you have mistaken the one for the other. And at worst it suggests a sort of craziness since, quite generally, forms of behavior that are "appropriate to" smoke are ipso facto not appropriate to fire and vice versa. Thus, one says, "Oh dear, I fear that there may be a fire" in the presence of clear cases of smoke, but *not* in the presence of clear cases of fire; one throws a bucket of water on clear cases of fire but *not* on clear cases of smoke; show me a man who tries to roast his hotdogs in smoke and I'll show you a man who ends up with bloodshot eyes and a raw weiner. Etcetera. You can't, in short, take this story about "attunement to relations" literally; and that you can't is *very* old news.[3]

But probably you're not supposed to. Probably it's a euphemism. What the Real Story is, is something like this: to be attuned to the relation between smoke and fire is to *know that* "situations where there is smoke are, by and large, close to situations where there is fire"; and to use what you know for spotting fires is to come to *expect* fire when you detect smoke. It's behavior appropriate to the *expectation* of fire that you produce if you have detected smoke and are "attuned to" the fact that smoke means fire. It is, however, not allowed for friends of the Standard notion to tell the Real Story since the Real Story makes it painfully clear that you need intentional apparatus (believing; expecting; Lord knows what all else) to bridge the gap between the information that is in the world and the "available" information, the information out of which an organism acts.

That philosophers of Barwise and Perry's sophistication should be caught flirting with behaviorism suggests that something has gone very badly wrong indeed.[4] It is thus worth emphasizing that the passage just quoted isn't merely a slip of the pen. Here's another one: "The school bell rings and the students learn that it is time for class to end. A certain type of sound, one they hear on different days, is systematically related to a certain type of situation, the end of class. It is this relation between different types of situations that the students become attuned to, and thereby learn that the sound of the bell means that it is time for class to end. Thus the sound of the bell, on any particular occasion, conveys the information about the end of class" (Barwise and Perry 1983, p.13).

It pays to attend closely to what "conveys" conveys when it's used in the way that Barwise and Perry use it here. To begin with, on the reading of "conveys the information" that the authors are most clearly entitled to, the remark that the "sound of the bell, on any particular occasion, conveys the information about the end of class," though it comes at the end of the passage, is not the *conclusion* of the argument; it's one of the premises. For, given the "objective" notion of information that Barwise and Perry adhere to, that the sound of the bell conveys the information about the end of class—i.e., that it Standardly *transmits* that information—is *equivalent to* the assumption that "a certain type of situation. . . ." What *doesn't* follow from this assumed correlation, however, is that the ringing of the bell "conveys the information" in the pretheoretical sense of "making the information available" to the students. It is, of course, this second, stronger sense of "conveying the information" that we need to explain why the students start to gather their papers together when they hear the bell. To get it, we need to assume the attunement of the students to the information that the ringing of the bell transmits. But what on earth could this attunement come to except that the students have (somehow) learned that when the bell rings the class is over and that, on each occasion when the bell rings they (somehow) use what they have learned to infer that they have come to the end of the class. Notice, once again, that (a) you must have "the information available"—not just the information transmitted—if you are to predict the behavior that ensues; (b) "the information transmitted" does not determine the information available; and (c) what information is available, unlike what information is transmitted, is receiver relative.

Here, then, is the bad news in brief: you can have an objective notion of information—one that puts the information "in the world"— but it will not do the work of the pretheoretic notion of "the information available" to an information processor. Alternatively, you can have a notion of "the information available," but it will not be receiver neutral *and it will not be naturalistic either* because it will depend on what the receiver knows and is able to infer. What we don't have—what, for all we now know, we *can't* have—is a notion of information that is both "objective" and appropriate to behavioral explanation. Would that this were other, but it is not and loose talk about attunement won't make it go away: the notion of attunement is either blatantly behavioristic (and therefore hopeless) or implicitly intentionalistic (and therefore useless). In short, as things now stand, the notion of information that is required for cognitive science is *nonnaturalistic, unreduced, and intentional through and through.* A fortiori, the "objective" notion of information does not reconstruct the intentional one. For all we now know, nothing like it ever will.

On the other hand, it is one thing to argue, as I've just finished doing, that the Standard notion of information isn't the one you need for cognitive science when the information processor under analysis is a *whole organism* chock full—as whole organisms are wont to be—with beliefs, desires, and other such prima facie irreducibly intentional states. It is quite another to argue, as I now propose to do, that the *"subpersonal"* information processors—whose operations, according to psychologists, underlie and account for the cognitive capacities of whole organisms—aren't plausibly construed according to the Standard notion either. That the project of reconstructing the intentional apparatus of belief/desire psychology in terms of an "objective" concept of information should fail is not, perhaps, surprising. Beliefs and desires, after all, *do* seem to be in the head; in the head is *exactly* the right place to cause behavior from. But it might nevertheless be possible to reconcile the objectivity of Standard information with the subjectivity of the propositional attitudes by taking a rather different tack. It might be possible to construe beliefs and desires as "emergents" out of the acitivity of subpersonal (presumably neural) information processors, and perhaps the Standard notion of information—with its correlative apparatus of associative networks—will find a home in the analysis of these subpersonal mechanisms. Certainly nothing that has been said so far would deny that this is so.

In fact, the view that mental processes are performed by networks of associated elements is currently quite fashionable in cognitive science. The connection between this idea and the correlational account of information should be clear from the previous discussion. Since the nodes in a network interconnect, activating some of them is causally sufficient for activating others. The pattern of causal determination implicit in the structure of a network in turn implies patterns of correlation among the designated states of its nodes. Correlation makes Standard information, so the flow of activation from node to node can be interpreted as the flow of Standard information through the network. Endless variations of this basic proposal are possible; thank goodness the details don't matter much for what follows.

There are a number of arguments that are supposed to show that associative networks are prima facie plausible candidates for modeling subpersonal cognitive processes. For one thing, because they are massively parallel such networks can be very fast: in principle, the only limiting conditions are the size of the network and the speed with which excitation can be transmitted from node to node. Then again, stress is sometimes placed on the *physiological* plausibility of the view that subpersonal information processes are associative. Neurons, to a first approximation, go on and off; and they do so in consequence of excitation that flows through the brain from one cell to another. So perhaps the brain is a congeries of associative networks. (Much of the discipline known as "cognitive neuroscience" consists of speculations at about this level of sophistication.)

Slightly more convincing is the a posteriori demonstration that some rather detailed properties of mental processes involving list search can be modeled by associative nets. Lexical access, specifically the perceptual identification of printed letters and words, has provided most of the parade cases. A number of the phenomena of lexical access suggest connections among items in the internal lexicon. The "priming" of words by their synonyms, the "word superiority" effect in letter recognition, and the fact that certian sorts of input distortion (such as the misspelling of "certain" earlier in this sentence) are usually tolerated effortlessly, all suggest that the lexicon is some sort of a network with the nodes connected by both "vertical" relations (like constituency) and "horizontal" relations (like synonymy). The basic idea is that if the lexicon is indeed a network, then these lexical access phenomena can perhaps be explained by appeal to the spread of activation horizontally and vertically from node to node. A good deal of detailed attention has been paid this possibility, and it turns out that— with sufficient parametric tinkering—many of the more robust chronometric properties of lexical access can be accomodated (see, for example, Anderson 1983). Whether this is because the lexicon really is a network or only because the available models provide enough degrees of freedom to accomodate damn near anything I leave it to the reader to decide. In what follows I'll have nothing at all to say about the use of networks as models of subpersonal processes of list search. I do, however, have a few unsympathetic remarks to make about the use of networks as models of subpersonal *inference*; and these points are quite closely related to ones that turned up earlier in the discussion.

Even quite simple networks, like N1 and N2, can be viewed as devices for making inferences. So, when activation spreads from node 3 or node 4 to node 2 in N1, the network can be thought of as computing the inference from P or Q to P v Q; when activation spreads from nodes 3 and 4 to node 2 in N2, the network can be thought of as computing the inference from P and Q to P & Q; and when activation in N2 spreads "downwards" from node 2 to node 3 or 4, the network can be thought of as computing the inference from P & Q to P or Q. Given some ingenuity and enough nodes, *any* inference that is valid in propositional logic can be computed by a network essentially similar to these. So, perhaps one's ability to perform such inferences reduces to the activation of associative networks available at the neural level. This proposal is not irrational, but I believe it to be profoundly misguided.

To begin with, though it is true that for any propositional inference there exists a network which computes it, it is also true that there is considerable indeterminacy—there is, if you like, no matter of fact—about which inference a given network is computing. Thus we said that N1 computes the inference from P or Q to (P v Q). But it would have been equally right to say that it computes the inference from, say, (P v (R & −R)) or Q to ((P v (R & −R)) v Q); or, indeed, that it computes any inference generable from "P or Q → P v Q" by substituting logical equivalents in the premise or the conclusion. This is just to say that the only constraint that the structure of the network places upon its interpretation is that if activation flows from the set of nodes {A} to the set of nodes {B}, then the inference from the propositions assigned to A to the propositions assigned to B must be valid. There are, in general, lots of ways—indeed, an infinity of ways—of assigning propositions to nodes consonant with this condition. Of course, the *labels* assigned to the nodes in a network *do* tell us which inferences the network computes. But (have I mentioned this before?) *the labels are for us, not for the machine;* nothing in the behavior of the network qua network depends on how we label it. Or, to put it the other way around, if there is an indeterminacy about what inference a network is computing, then there is, of course, the same indeterminacy about what labels are the right ones for its nodes.

Why does this matter? Well, the proposal under consideration was that our capacity to make propositional inferences reduces to (or is modeled by, or is explained by—talk any way you want to here) the postulated associative networks. But this suggests that, from the psychological point of view, it's all one whether one is inferring from P or Q to (P v Q) or from, as it might be, $(P \lor (R \& -R))$ or Q to $(P \lor Q)$. Whereas, of course, it's precisely from the psychological point of view that it's *not* all one which inference one is drawing. It is entirely conceivable, for example, that someone for whom the former inference is fast and obvious might find the latter inference obscure and slow. This is, as must be evident, a paradigmatic intentionality problem. Networks don't slice mental states and processes "thin enough": Whereas networks distinguish inferences up to logical equivalence, it appears that what is in one's head sorts them out with finer grain. [Not surprisingly, precisely the same point holds for "the information transmitted." It doesn't distinguish between logical equivalents either, so that if " . . . transmits the information that P" is true, so too is whatever you get by substituting for P a logically equivalent formula. As Fred Dretske once put it (personal communication), information in the Standard sense is "propositional" rather than "sentential." This is exactly right assuming that logically equivalent sentences express the same proposition. The present point is that mental processes, like drawing inferences, appear to be sentential rather than propositional. That is bad news for networks and bad news for the Standard notion of information.]

The argument just walked through is precisely the sort that leaves psychologists dry eyed. So here's another, less philosophical sounding but deriving—as we'll see—from much the same considerations. Pick an inference that N1 can compute, say P or Q to $(P \lor Q)$. Imagine that Baby has learned to draw that inference, and that his learning to do so reduces to his having—as it were—"grown" a neural instantiation of N1. Question: what does he have to grow to learn the inference from P or Q or R to $(P \lor Q \lor R)$. Answer: *he has to grow a whole new network*, e.g., N3.

N3:

$$1 \quad (P \lor Q \lor R)$$

$$2 \ (P) \quad 3 \ (Q) \quad 4 \ (R)$$

And, indeed, this will be true whenever we want to add a new class of inferences to Baby's repertoire; it will be true even when the new inferences are, intuitively speaking, of the same "form" as ones that Baby has already mastered. Why is this so? Because the notion of the form of an inference can get no grip in an associative net. But why is *that* so? Because the nodes in a network *have* no form (if you prefer, the network treats all logically equivalent formulas as having the same form). But don't the *labels* have form? Yes, indeed, but (I'm *sure* I've mentioned this before) the labels are for us, not for the machine.

The point, then, is that we know about some (indeed, we know about infinitely many) arguments that they are valid in virtue of their form. But networks don't know this. So there is something about our inferences that networks don't reconstruct. Notice that this is *not* just a "performance/competence" argument. My point isn't that, since you need to grow a new network for each new form of valid argument, and since there are infinitely many valid forms of argument, it follows that networks cannot reconstruct our logical competence. That is, I think, quite a good argument, but it too is of a kind that leaves psychologists unmoved (excepting, perhaps, very sophisticated psychologists). "For," they say, "after all, there is nobody who can actually recognize the validity of more than a finite number of arguments. Especially *babies!* Babies *never* recognize the validity of more than a finite number of arguments, so it doesn't *matter* whether our theories about Baby represent his logical competence as finite . . . and so on, and so forth, blah, blah, blah." I think that I am growing old. I no longer wish to discuss performance/competence arguments.

However, the present argument isn't one of them. Rather, it's that there is something I know about inferences, something that I use routinely in validity checking, that network models can't know and can't use: viz., that arguments of the form A or B . . . $\rightarrow$ A v B . . . are valid in virtue of their form, and that the argument P or Q $\rightarrow$ P v Q, and the argument P or Q or R $\rightarrow$ P v Q v R both reduce to the form A or B . . . $\rightarrow$ A v B. Networks can't know this and can't use it because there is no sense to the question "what is the form of the argument that this network computes?" And there's no sense to that question because networks are (exhaustively) arrangements of nodes and paths, and there is no sense to the question "What is the form of this node/path?" There is, of course, sense to the question "What is the form of this node *label*?" But—to put the point minutely differently from the last time—the labels aren't part of the network.[5]

And while we're blocking misunderstandings, here is another one that ought to be avoided. The present argument is *not* that networks suffer from some computational incapacity as compared to machines with other kinds of architectures. Specifically, it's not that there are arguments of the form P to P v Q that you can't compute with a network. On the contrary, since there is a network that arbitrarily approximates any given deterministic Turing machine, you can use a network to compute *any* computable function. The interesting psychological question isn't, therefore, about the generative capacity of network models; in fact, mere generative capacity is rarely what chooses among computational models in psychology. What's crucial is usually the ability of the model to capture important generalizations about how we think. In the present case, the issue is whether networks have access to information about arguments that apparently *is* available to us, information about the *form* of the arguments. And the answer appears to be that they do not; for, on the one hand, in a network the form of the argument being computed is represented only in the node labels, and on the other hand, networks have no access to the labels on their nodes.

This paper is beginning to turn back upon itself, which suggests that it is getting to be time to stop. I hope the general pattern is now clear: The idea that information processors process information-as-Standardly-construed comports with the idea that information processors are typically associative networks. These ideas exhibit interlocked inadequacies: What's wrong with networks is that they transmit information without encoding it; what's wrong with the Standard notion of information is that whereas what we need is "the information encoded," what it gives us is only " the information transmitted."

To allow ourselves a notion of "information encoded" is to admit a new degree of freedom into our theory since we can now distinguish between various ways of encoding what is, from the Standard point of view, the same information transmitted. There is every reason to think we need this extra degree of freedom because there is every reason to think that psychological processes are sensitive to the character of the encoding of the information that organisms receive. Indeed—as I have argued elsewhere—there is every reason to think that psychological processes are sensitive *only* to the character of the encoding of the information that organisms receive; this is a way of putting the claim that psychological processes are sensitive to *syntactic* variables (like form) but not to *semantic* variables (like the information-objectively-transmitted). The appeal to "attunement" is best viewed as an attempt to explain how mental processes *could* be sensitive to the information transmitted without regard to how—indeed, whether— the information is encoded. But as we saw, the appeal to attunement, closely scrutinized, comes to rather less than nothing very much.

It is sometimes said in praise of networks that they finally do get the ghost out of the machine. Unlike other computational models that cognitive scientists have been attracted by, networks require no executive, no little man in the head whose job it is to assess the stimulus and plan the response. And, though Turing taught us that there is no *principled* objection to executive-driven computers, the practical fact is that the hardest problems of cognitive theory tend to be problems of executive control. Maybe the reason that the homunculus has seemed so intractable is that, in point of fact, he isn't there.

This may, for all I know, be right. One of the functions executives perform in machines that have them is solving coordination problems, determining the order in which the computational capacities of the machine will be exploited. Nothing I have said here shows that good simulations of people have to have executives in *that* sense. For all that I have argued, the mechanisms of coordination may be "distributed;" for all that I have argued, problems of coordination may all be solved "architecturally," i.e., at the level of the fixed structure of the machine.

But there is another thing that executives do; roughly and metaphorically—but close enough for our purposes—they're there to read the labels on the nodes, to insure that the computational consequences of exciting a node are specific to the information that the node displays. It's been the burden of my plaint thay you need the labels because information has its behavioral effects only qua encoded; transmission isn't good enough. But if you need the labels, then you also need a guy to read them.

Is there, then, *no* use for the Standard notion of information transmission? Yes, do not despair. There must be an internal code for the sorts of reasons we have just reviewed. And that code must be semantically interpreted because beliefs and desires have contents and truth values. If, however, internal formulas have a semantic interpretation, there must be something that determines what their semantic interpretation is. It may be, it *just* may be, that what fixes the interpretation of formulas in the internal code is the covariance of their tokenings with tokenings of situations in the world. That is: it may be that what fixes their interpretation is the information about the world that they Standardly transmit. This is a dim hope, but, as things now stand, it is our best hope.[6] Is it, then, excessive optimism to suppose that progress will lead in the direction of a unified theory—a theory which, on the one hand, does justice to the richness and profundity of intentional phenomena, and on the other, unites the previously disparate (and sometimes apparently opposed) insights garnered from research in psychology, semantics, and computation theory? And, if you are prepared to buy that, could I maybe show you something in a nice preowned car?

Notes

This article will also appear in *The Notre Dame Journal of Formal Logic* 27(2), special issue on situation semantics.

1. The patient reader has earned a review of the terminology. Currently in play

are the following notions: the information *transmitted*, the information *received*, the information *displayed*, the information *encoded*, and the information *available*. For expository purposes, I assume that all except the last of these are to be applied to information processes in *networks*. Well then:

—Node i transmits information to node j iff the distinguished states of i and j are (let's say, causally) correlated (with the causation running from i to j).

—Node j receives information from node i iff node i transmits information to node j.

—Node i displays information to node j iff node i is "visible" to node j (that is, iff i and j are intransitively connected).

—Node i encodes the information that it transmits to node j iff it displays the information it transmits to j. (There is the following degenerate case: a node both displays and transmits the information that it is in one or another of its distinguished states. It follows that it encodes the information that it is in that state. The interesting case, by contrast, is the one where a node transmits and displays—hence encodes—information about the states of nodes *other than itself*).

—Finally, information is available to a system just in case the system is in a position to act on (or out of) that information. In the most familiar cases, the system is intentional and the information that it acts on is the object of one or other of its propositional attitudes: Psmith brings his umbrella because he knows (thinks/ expects/ fears . . . etc.) that it will rain.

2. Notice that no information can be available from the display unless it is transmitted by the display. In this sense (as Dretske has correctly insisted) information transmission places constraints on any other notion of information exchange. Alas, these constraints are, from the point of view of defining "information processor," not very revealing.

3. By the way, Barwise and Perry's account of attunement to a relation fails in the other direction too. For example, I am sometimes disposed to respond to my kept potato plant in a way that would be appropriate to a fire: viz., I pour water on it. This does *not* imply—or even indicate—that I am attuned to a relation between fires and potato plants, or that I am trying to put my kept potato plant out.

I am prepared to stop beating this dead horse, but only if Barwise and Perry are prepared to stop trying to ride it.

4. I should emphasize, however, that Barwise and Perry are clearly not comfortable with this behavioristic account of attunement, nor are they consistent in their allegiance to it. Thus they say, on p. 268, that "an organism . . . is attuned to the constraint [that a certain kind of plant is edible for that kind or organism] provided it eats the plant if it sees it, under certain circumstances—say when it is hungry . . . ." But we are also told that ". . . an organism is attuned to C if, under certain circumstances, its cognitive conditions 'follow' C" (ibid) and it turns out, on p. 269, that "'following' is nothing but a very general type of inference, where [or-

ganism] *a* infers from the presence of a situation of type S that there is a situation of type S.'" This is perfectly reasonable as far as it goes, but it makes attunement an inherently mentalistic notion, thus undermining the project of constructing an account of intentionality that relies solely upon an "objective" conception of information. "What the percept means to the organism" is now a matter of what the organism can infer from the percept; this is a long way from "smoke means fire," and it's about as far as you can get from the "Ecological Realism" of Gibson and Reid (cf. Barwise and Perry's Preface, p. x). It is, indeed, a way of putting the moral of this paper that the only consistent form of Ecological (or informational) Realism is behaviorism.

5. It will have occurred to you that we don't, strictly speaking, need the labels to recover the notion of validity in virtue of form; we could use the form of the networks themselves and define validity in terms of congruences among families of networks. For example, any network derivable from N1 by daughter adjoining a node to 2 will be "valid" so long as 2 has the firing characteristics of an "or-gate" (i.e., so long as it is activated by the activation of any of its daughters). This, however, doesn't help with the main problem; for, as we mentioned above, none of the nodes in the network can "see" the network—all a node can see is its neighbors. In short: just as you can't use the form of the labels to define validity unless there is somebody in the system who can read the labels, so you can't use the overall form of the network to define validity unless there is somebody in the system who can look at the overall form of the network. Neither condition is met by "executive free" systems; that, indeed, is part of what it is for them to be executive free.

6. By the way, this sort of correlational theory of meaning is *far* more plausible for mental representations than for expressions of a natural language since the tokenings of the latter (but not, presumably, of the former) are contingent upon the motivations, linguistic competences, and communicative intentions of the speaker who utters them—in fact, on a whole grab bag of "pragmatic" variables. Thus, for example: Suppose Psmith notices that Mary's hair is on fire, and hence, perforce, thinks: *Mary's hair is on fire* (thereby tokening the Mentalese expression whose truth condition is that Mary's hair is on fire). Whether he then *says* "Mary's hair is on fire" (thereby tokening the English expression whose truth condition is that Mary's hair is on fire) depends, *inter alia*, on whether he thinks that Mary (or some other suitably situated auditor) would be interested to know that Mary's hair is on fire. (See Grice, 1969 for an indication of how complex these sorts of pragmatic considerations can become.)

In short, the correlation between mental representations and semantically relevant situations in the world is typically better—more reliable—than the correlation between English sentences and semantically relevant situations in the world. This is because the causal chain that connects the tokenings of mental representations to events which satisfy their truth conditions is typically *shorter than* (indeed, is typically a proper part of) the causal chain which connects the tokenings of English sentences to events which satisfy *their* truth conditions. That is the principle reason why it is mental representations, not English sentences, that are the natural candidates for being the primitive bearers of semantic properties.

Bibliography

Anderson, J. 1983. *The architecture of cognition*. Cambridge: Harvard Univ. Press.

Barwise, J., and J. Perry. 1983. *Situations and attitudes*. Cambridge: MIT Press.

Dretske, F. 1981. *Knowledge and the flow of information*. Cambridge: MIT Press.

Grice, H. P. 1969. Utterer's meaning and intentions. *Philosophical Review* 78:147–177.

Mowrer, O. H. 1960. *Learning theory and the symbolic processes*. New York: Wiley.

Osgood, C. 1963. On creating and understanding sentences. *American Psychologist* 18:735–751.

FRED DRETSKE

Aspects of Cognitive Representation

A cognitive system is a control mechanism whose function it is to initiate, adjust, and, if necessary, suppress behavior in the service of need and desire satisfaction. In order to perform this function the control mechanism must have direct and continuing access to intelligence about the circumstances *in* which activity is to be carried out. Hence, the cognitive system is that part of the executive mechanism whose contributions to control are themselves under the control of (or at least sensitive to) whatever information is (or has been) available about the theater in which operations are to be performed. It is an information-driven control system.

Our ordinary attributions of perception, knowledge, and belief reflect this general picture of cognitive processes. To say what someone sees, knows, or believes is to identify particular control states by means of their representational properties—in terms of the *kind* of information (or putative information) they are themselves under the control of. Such, at least, is the representational theory of cognitive processes as we find it (or as *I* find it) embodied in ordinary descriptions and explanations of animal and human behavior. What I want to do here is to explore this way of looking at cognitive systems in order to see how much weight it can bear. Is the general idea of a representational control system fertile enough to support the enormously rich and variegated attributions of semantic content characteristic of our ordinary descriptions of what we see, know, and believe? Can it, furthermore, provide us with a way of understanding how such attributions figure, as they are ordinarily thought to do, in explanations of behavior?

By a representational system I shall mean any system whose function it is to indicate, by its various states, how things stand with respect to some other object, condition, or magnitude. This, obviously, is not to require much of a representational system. A variety of simple devices qualify. A tachometer, the sort of instrument found on the dashboard of many automobiles, is a representational system according to this characterization. Its various states indicate, and have the function of indicating, something about the rate at which the engine is rotating. Hence, it represents the angular velocity of the crankshaft. A doorbell, in virtue of indicating the condition of the doorbutton (depressed or not), thereby represents the position of the button. And the firing of a neural cell, by indicating the presence and orientation of a certain energy gradient on the surface of a photoreceptor, represents the whereabouts and orientation of an "edge" in the optical input.

In speaking of a representational system I shall continue to speak of the information the system carries about the quantities, conditions, and objects it represents. I intend nothing subversive in this way of speaking—nothing, I hope, that begs the questions which it is my project to explore. For by information I mean nothing more, and certainly nothing less, than what, in virtue of certain nomic correlations, the particular states of a representational system indicate to be so. And X can indicate that Y obtains *whether or not* any conscious (or otherwise cognitive) interpreter is *aware* of this fact.[1] Thus the tachometer's registration of "1,000 rpm" indicates, and thereby carries the information that, the engine is running at 1,000 revolutions per minute, and it indicates this even if the driver mistakes it for the speedometer (or ignores it altogether). The ringing doorbell carries the information that the doorbutton is being depressed (and therefore the information that someone is at the door) because, presumably, this is what it indicates. Representational systems and information processing systems are, on this way of thinking, two sides of the same coin. Information is what representational systems need in order to represent, and representation is what information processing systems do for the things about which they carry information.

In thinking of a cognitive system as an information-driven control mechanism, therefore, we are thinking of it in representational terms. This may not be *all* we have to say about a cognitive system in order to distinguish it from other control mechanisms (e.g., those associated with the autonomic nervous system), but it will do as a start. The project is to see how large an oak we can tease out of this tiny acorn, how far one can go in understanding perception, knowledge, and belief with these semantically meager resources. If they prove *too* meager, it will at least tell us something about the special character of cognitive processes.

When functioning normally, then, a cognitive system both controls output and indicates something about external conditions. To the extent that this is true, the output is not *merely* output. It can be viewed as a *response to* the conditions its control states represent. By classifying control states in terms of their representational properties, in terms of what they indicate, a unique form of causal explanation is made available: an explanation of output by reference to *the content* of the control states producing it. So, for example, the wolf's relentless pursuit of the sick caribou can be explained in terms of what the wolf *knows* or *believes* about its prey—that it is sick, slower, easier to catch, or more defenseless than the hundreds of other nearby animals. Such explanations are, I submit, explanations of pursuit movements by a control state with a content, a content determined by what the control state indicates about the condition and movements of the fleeing caribou. Just how we think of this internal representation, what we take it to indicate about the caribou (that it is weak, crippled, sick, easy to catch, or whatever), determines the content of the wolf's cognitive state—*what* it knows about its prey.

In thinking about a representational system, there are at least two questions one can ask about its representational capacity. And when the representational system is, in addition, a control system, there are at least three questions that should be asked. One can ask, first, *what* it is, what quantity, property, object, person, or condition, the system is representing. A thermometer represents the temperature, a fuel gauge the amount of gasoline in the tank, a photograph the objects (persons, building, foliage) that the picture was taken of. Secondly, one can ask *how* what is represented is represented. What does the representation *say* or indicate about what it represents? That it is 95° (in the case of the thermometer)? That the gas tank is almost empty (fuel gauge)? That your niece has let her hair grow long (photograph)? The first question is a question about the *reference* or *denotation* of the representation. The second question is about the *content* of the representation. Topic and Comment.

There are, in other words, pictures *of* black horses and what Nelson Goodman (1976, p. 29) has called black-horse pictures. Unless the picture of a black horse is a black-horse picture, it will not represent the black horse *as* a black horse. Imagine, for example, a picture of a black horse in which the horse is photographed at a great distance in bad light with the camera slightly out of focus. The horse appears as a blurry spot in the distance. This is a picture of a black horse but not what Goodman calls a black-horse picture. When invited to see pictures of your friend's black horse, you expect to see, not only pictures of a black horse, but black-horse pictures—pictures in which the denotation of the picture is *identifiably* a black horse, pictures in which the black horse is represented *as* a black horse.

Of course, not all representations are pictorial. Many representations are not expected, even under optimal conditions, to *resemble* the objects they represent. Ringing doorbells do not resemble doorbuttons, and fuel gauges (at least the old-fashioned ones) do not resemble tanks full of gasoline. And, presumably, the wolf's neural representation of the caribou's condition, position, and movements do not actually resemble a terrified reindeer. Pictures, though, are merely one kind of representation, a representation in which information about the referent is carried by means of elements that resemble the properties they indicate the referent to have. But nonpictorial representations exhibit the same dimensions: a reference and a content, a topic and a comment. My fuel gauge is not only a representation *of* a half-full tank of gasoline, it is also (when things are working right) a half-full-tank-of-gasoline representation. This is what it indicates about my half-full tank of gasoline, the comment it makes, the information it carries, about that topic. My gas tank is also very rusty. My fuel gauge doesn't comment on this feature of its reference.

Similarly, the wolf's internal representation of the sick caribou may or may not be a sick-fleeing-caribou representation. But it certainly is a representation *of* a sick fleeing caribou. *How* it represents the animal is, to some degree, a matter of speculation, but unless it has *some* means of representing defenseless caribou, a way of commenting on these creatures which is, for practical wolfish purposes, extensionally equivalent to *being a defenseless caribou*, its relentless and unerring pursuit of these particular animals is inexplicable. It would be like trying to explain the behavior of a thermostat in controlling the furnace if it had no means of representing the room temperature as above or below the desired setting. There has to be something in there that "tells" the thermostat what it needs to know for it to carry out its function. The same is true of the wolf.

Of course, some black-horse pictures are not pictures of any (existing) black horse. I can draw a black-horse picture without the picture I produce being a picture *of* any black horse. Or I can have a black-horse picture which is, in fact, a picture of a white cow (carefully camouflaged to look like a black horse). A miscalibrated (or malfunctioning) gauge can be a representation of a half-full tank without its being a half-full-tank representation, without indicating *that* the tank is half-full.[2] The analogy, only I don't think it is *merely* an analogy, to hallucination and illusion is obvious.

I rehearse these familiar facts about representations only to emphasize that in thinking about a cognitive system as a representational control mechanism, the *same* questions can be asked about our cognitive states:

what do they represent and *how* do they represent it. What are they getting information about and what information are they getting. But I said that there were *three* questions that can be asked about a representational system when it functions as a control mechanism. We can ask not only about its topic (*what* it represents) and the comments it makes about that topic (the *way* it represents what it represents) but about which of these comments, if any, has a control function. *Which* elements of the representation play a causal role in the determination of behavior? A representation may be ever so rich in the comments it makes about what it represents, but if none of this information is, or can be, *used* to control and direct movements, it is causally inert and hence functionally irrelevant. Therefore the representation, *qua* representation, plays no role in the system's *cognitive* economy. A black-horse picture of a black horse can be used to paper over a hole in my wall. In this case, the representationally significant aspects of the picture, those that make it a black-horse picture rather than (say) a white-cow picture, are irrelevant to the way it is functioning (concealing the hole). I could as well have used a picture of a white cow or a picture of nothing at all. And if our internal representations are to qualify as cognitive, they must (potentially at least) make some contribution to the way that mechanism functions in controlling and directing behavior. They must do so, moreover, by means of their representationally significant properties. Only by so doing will the classification of cognitive states in terms of their content figure in the explanation of the behavior they produce.

This third aspect of representations raises some controversial issues that are best postponed.[3] So let me return to the first two aspects of a representation, those having to do with its semantics: its topic and comment. I will return later to the *functional* significance of these semantic aspects for the overall performance of a cognitive system.

Our ordinary attributions of sensory and cognitive states reflect the kind of distinctions just discussed. And this, to my mind at least, supports the idea that our familiar, folk-psychological picture of cognition *is* a picture of a kind of representational control mechanism. We say, for example, that Clyde can see a black horse (in the distance) without (for various reasons having to do either with the great distance, the camouflage, the lighting, or the fact that he doesn't have his glasses on) its looking *like* a black horse, without its presenting a black-horse appearance. This merely reflects the fact that in describing what Clyde sees, we are describing what his sensory representation is a representation *of*. We are ignoring the kind of comment his perceptual system is making about that topic in order to specify the topic itself about which a comment is being made.

Compare this to our descriptions of a simple gauge. The state of your fuel gauge (registering "half-full") doesn't specify or indicate *which tank* it represents as being half-full. It carries information about your tank, but not the information that it is your tank about which it is making this comment. Normally, of course, such gauges are connected to the (only) gasoline tank in the car, but there is no reason we couldn't have auxiliary tanks (with a single gauge systematically accessing the different tanks). Or we could connect your gauge to *my* tank (by radio control, say). In this case the representation would have a different referent, a different topic. But the *same* content. It would say, not that *your* tank was half-full, but that *my* tank was half-full. Of course, the fact that it was saying this, rather than something else, would not be evident from the representation itself. But neither is it evident, from the representation itself, what I am saying (or thinking) when I say (or think), "*This* is only half-full." To know what I am saying, in the sense of knowing what I am saying it *about*, you have to know, just as in the case of the gauge, to what I am connected in the appropriate way. Examining the representation itself won't tell you what condition in the world satisfies the representation, what condition would (were it to obtain) make the representation an *accurate* representation. For that you have to look at the wiring.

The job of a fuel gauge is to carry information about the tank to which it is connected, *not* information about which tank it is connected to. And so it is with pictures and most other forms of representations. Clyde can see a black horse, thereby getting information about a black horse (that it is near the barn, for instance) without getting the information that it is a black horse (because the animal is too far away to identify). Without, in other words, seeing *what* it is. Our internal perceptual representations are often as silent as gauges about *what* it is they represent—on what topic it is on which they comment.

Thinking of the cognitive system as a representational mechanism gives us, therefore, the resources for understanding not only the propositional attitudes, those attitudes (like knowledge and belief) that take (in their verbal expression) sentential clauses as complement of the verb, but also those attitudes (like seeing and hearing) that take concrete nominals as objects of the verb. S sees a bush, mistakes it for an animal crouching beside the path, and flees in panic. The description of what S sees is an expression of what his internal representation is a representation of—in this case a bush. What he sees it *as*, what he takes it to be, or (under optimal conditions) what he can see that it is, is an expression of the way he represents the bush. In this case he has a crouching-animal representation of a bush—the analogue, I submit, of a white-cow picture of a black horse.

There is then, as I see it, no real question about the validity of our ordinary descriptive apparatus for assigning perceptual-cognitive states to organisms. For in describing a creature as seeing, knowing, or believing something, we may be (and, I would urge, certainly are) doing no more than what we are *already* doing with such simple representational devices as gauges, instruments, and detectors. We are saying *what* and *how* things are being represented. The mind, at least that much of it having to do with *cognitive* processes, is the brain in its representational-control mode. The only *real* question about the representational model (aside from the causal efficacy of these representations—a point I will get to later) is whether our ordinary descriptions of what a creature sees, knows, and believes are semantically *too rich* to be supported by the actual physical representational resources of the organism. Are our ordinary assignments of reference and content to an organism's internal representations compatible with—and, if so, are they realizable *in*—the actual neural machinery available for generating these representations? There may be no real dispute in assigning the reference *my gas tank* and the content *half-full* to my gauge's representations, for the actual physical construction of the device and the laws governing its operation clearly reveal that this is what the device indicates and what it indicates it about. But in saying that the wolf saw a sick caribou on the edge of the herd, recognized it *as* sick and, therefore, *as* easy prey and, because of this, pursued the animal while ignoring the thousands of healthy ones nearby, are we assigning reference and content that exceed the representational resources of the animal we are describing? If not, what about our descriptions of Jimmy as seeing his uncle and recognizing him as the man who promised to fix his bicycle? Does Jimmy, like the gauge, have an internal "neural needle" capable of registering all this? If so, this is, truly, an extraordinary instrument. I can understand how to build a device that responds accurately to the level of fluid in a tank, but how does one build something sensitive to promises to repair a bicycle?

If I knew the answer to this question, I would be at home with my soldering iron, not here asking the question. But, as always in philosophy, one doesn't need *all* (indeed *any*) of the answers to point vaguely in directions in which answers might be found. So let me take a few more minutes to suggest that a representational system, of the primitive variety we are now considering, has a good deal more in the way of representational potential than might be supposed.

I have so far confined myself to what philosophers might call *de re* representational contents: representations *of* a tank as being half-full, *of* an animal as being crippled, *of* a doorbutton as being depressed. These might be called *de re* representations because the representation assigns the content to, makes a comment about, an object which is picked out in some nonrepresentational way. If causal theorists are right, the reference is determined by causal considerations: that object, condition, or situation which is causally responsible for the varied indications of the representation. But we needn't suppose that all representations are of this *de re* variety. We can have something corresponding to *de dicto* representations: representations in which the topic (reference) is determined by the comment (representational content).

Imagine a detector whose function it is to keep track of the ordinal position and color of articles passing it on an assembly line. It represents the fourth one as red. At the time it is registering the color and ordinal position of *delta* (the fourth article on the assembly line) it can be said that it provides a *de re* representation of *delta* as red and as the fourth one to pass by. Or, alternatively, we can view this as a *de dicto* representation having the content: the fourth item is red. Nothing, I suppose, forces either reading of the representational content at the time the object's position and color is being registered, but the *de dicto* version certainly seems the most plausible reading at a later time—a time when the causal connection that supported the *de re* reading has vanished. At this later time *delta*'s color is relevant to the determination of the accuracy of the representation *only in so far* as *delta* was the fourth item on the assembly line. This seems like a genuine attributive use of the description "the fourth item"—comparable to my belief, one day later, that the fourth person to enter the room was wearing a funny hat. If I retain, in memory, no other description capable of picking out who I believe to have been wearing a funny hat (as is the case with our imagined detector), then this is a *de dicto* belief about *whoever* was the fourth person to enter the room.

We can go further in this direction by equipping our representational system with projectional facilities, some means of extrapolating or interpolating indicated patterns. Rather than provide details about how this might go, consider a simple example. It is the third day of the month. Clyde, whose birthday is on the 23d, wants to know on which day of the week his birthday will occur. Instead of going through the necessary computations, Clyde merely dials his calendar watch ahead 20 days and observes its representation of the 23d as a Thursday. This example is probably too simple to capture what I want, but it is meant to suggest the idea that, if a system has the capacity for representing relations between elements to which it is causally related, then it can, by projection, represent elements to which it is not causally related—those (if any) which bear the relationship in question to elements the system directly represents.

Let me leave the issue of topic or reference, however, and return to the question of content. Indicators, and thereby representational systems, are what I shall call *property specific*. By this I mean that a system can represent something as being F without representing it as being G even if, in point of fact, all Fs are G. An electric eye in an elevator door will indicate someone's (or *something*'s) presence in the door opening. It will *not* represent the sex of this object even if *only* males ever enter or leave the elevator. So, despite the fact that everyone (or everything) it responds to is male, it does not indicate *that* they are male. I think this is obvious on intuitive grounds. A system isn't indicating that x is a male if it would, in the very same circumstances, respond identically to a female. What a system represents something to be is limited by its discriminatory powers, and system S may be able to discriminate between Fs and non-Fs without being able to discriminate between Gs and non-Gs even though, as chance would have it, all and only the Fs are G.

This is, I think, a bit too strong. We do not demand infallibility from our indicators. A fuel gauge will respond identically to water in the gas tank. This does not prevent it functioning as a *fuel gauge*—as an indicator that there is still some gas left.[4] What a system represents is determined by its function and by the set of regularities that dominate the environment in which it normally operates. That is to say, an indicator indicates what it can reliably discriminate (when functioning normally) *in its natural habitat*. Remove a cricket from the swamp (or invade that habitat with unusual gimmickry) and the creature may no longer be a reliable discriminator and detector of other crickets. Those precisely tuned, and astonishingly sensitive, neural detectors that indicate whether a complex sequence of chirps and trills is the song of a fellow (i.e., same species) cricket *can* be "fooled" by a tape recording or a synthesized pattern that mimics the call of a conspecific. But such fallibility (or foolability) is irrelevant to determining what the various states of this detector indicate (and thereby represent) about the cricket's surroundings. The relevant question to ask is what these detector states indicate (what they are correlated with) in the cricket's normal surroundings, the kind of surroundings *in which* this indicator evolved to service the cricket's biological needs (Bentley and Hay 1974, p. 34).[5] And (a better known example) the fact that frogs will flick at appropriately contrived shadows in the laboratory does not show that the neural mechanisms responsible for this response are not *bug* detectors.[6]

What the *property-specific* character of indicators reveals is that we cannot automatically infer that because a representational system functions (in its natural habitat) infallibly in the detection of Gs, that it thereby represents them *as* G—that this is its representational *content*. For it may be that it represents these Gs *as F* in an environment in which all Fs are G. That is, its representational successes (in identifying Gs) may be explained by its capacity to represent something as F and the additional fact that in the relevant operational environment, only Gs are F. We are, of course, familiar with this phenomenon from a variety of studies of animal cognition and, closer to home, in our own identificatory efforts. You will have no trouble picking out my uncle, more or less infallibly, if my uncle is eight feet tall and always wears an evening dress. You may not recognize him *as* my uncle, but that shouldn't prevent you from always being right in pointing out my uncle. And so it is in nature. Stickleback fish unerringly identify other male sticklebacks in their natural habitat. They do so by means of their red underside. This quickly becomes obvious from the fact that these fish will exhibit the same patterned response to appropriately colored pieces of wood and even red vehicles visible through the window in the laboratory. Nature has designed an economical system of representation since this was all that was necessary in the fish's natural habitat—there being no colored pieces of wood, pillar boxes, or fire engines in the waters inhabited by the fish. Being able to represent something as having a certain characteristic red underside was good enough to enable the fish to direct mating (in the case of females) and aggressive (in the case of other males) behavior toward the right things--other male sticklebacks.

So it isn't enough to know that the timber wolf infallibly identifies the sick, lame, or young caribou in its predatory behavior. This only tells us that the wolf represents sick, lame, and young caribou in some distinctive way, but it doesn't tell us *how*. It doesn't tell us what the content of this representational system is. If the wolf always prefers a caribou to a moose (when both are available), this tells us that the wolf can discriminate between a caribou and a moose, but it certainly doesn't tell us that it has some neural mechanism indicating that yonder animal is a caribou rather than a moose. It doesn't tell us anything about the representational *content* of the wolf's cognitive state—hence, nothing about what it believes or knows about its prey, nothing about *how* it represents what it represents. To determine this we would have to conduct an empirical study (as was done in the case of the stickleback fish) of the wolf's discriminatory capacity in its natural environment. We would also have to get clearer about how such facts determine the content of a representation.[7]

There is much about the semantics of representational systems, both their reference and their content, that remains to be said—especially if one thinks (as I do) that an organism's cognitive states, including our own rich and diversified corpus of beliefs and knowledge, can be illuminated by this representational model. But instead of pursuing this project here, I want to turn to the third aspect of representational systems—the causal or explanatory efficacy of these representational contents in the cognitive life of an organism. That is, assuming that there *is* some representation in the wolf of the caribou as F, where F is roughly co-extensional with "young, sick, or lame," of what explanatory value is this content in accounting for the wolf's pursuit of the caribou?

As remarked earlier, a representation may be ever so rich in content without this content playing any role in the way the system having this content responds to the object it represents. A black-horse picture of a black horse (i.e., a picture that indicates of the black horse that it is a black horse) can function, or be used, in a way in which this fact is totally irrelevant—to cover a hole in the wall, to start a fire, or as a book mark. But some representations are integrated into a larger system in such a way that those properties of the representation in virtue of which it is, say, a black-horse representation (rather than, say, a white-cow representation) figure crucially in the determination of how the system behaves, in how it responds to what it is a representation *of.* To oversimplify considerably, if the color of pigment in the picture, and the manner in which this pigment is formed, exercise some control over subsequent activities of the system itself, then it becomes plausible to say that it *does* make a difference, a causal difference, that the internal representation is a black-horse representation rather that a white-cow representation. Had it been a white-cow representation, the system would have behaved differently. Hence, we can explain, *causally,* why the organism did what it did by appealing to the representational properties of the control state. The system responded the way it did when it saw the black horse because it recognized it *as* a black horse and could see *that* it was a black horse, because, in other words, its internal representation had one content rather than another. Herein, I submit, lies the explanatory efficacy of our ordinary notions of belief and knowledge. They are ways of picking out which properties of the internal representations are (potentially at least) influencing the continuing operations of the system. The ascription of content to our control states is a way of identifying the causally efficacious properties of these control states—not in terms of their shape or physical structure (neurological details about which we are generally ignorant), but in terms of what these shapes and structures (whatever they are) represent about the organism's surroundings (something which we often *do* know).

This threefold distinction between reference, content, and efficacy is neatly reflected in our ordinary attributions of perception, belief, and knowledge. The organism sees a black horse but it is too far away to identify it as a black horse. This is a representation *of* a black horse that, because of distance, has not yet achieved the status of a black-horse representation. The horse approaches and it is seen under optimal conditions. The picture of a black horse has now become a black-horse picture. The sensory representation of the horse has been informationally enhanced to the point that we can now speak of it as indicating *of* its reference that it is a black horse. It now (in some phenomenal sense of "looks") *looks like* a black horse to the perceiving organism. But what does the organism *take it to be?* What does it know or believe about what it sees? That it is a black horse? A four-legged animal? A large animal? Or what? What we describe the creature as knowing or believing about what it sees, what it sees the horse *as* or sees it *to be*, is, I submit, merely our folksy way of describing what properties of the internal black-horse representation are functioning in a control-relevant way—which properties of the representation have their hand on the steering wheel. If those properties of the representation which indicate merely that it is a four-legged animal of some unspecified sort are the only ones that are control relevant, then the perceiving organism sees a black horse but recognizes it only as a four-legged creature of some sort. The details of the sensory representation, those indicating that the creature is, in particular, a black horse, are playing no causal role in the perceiving organism's response to the black horse. Perhaps, though it sees a black horse, it doesn't understand what a horse is, doesn't have the *concept* of a horse. Having the concept of a horse, on this account of things, is merely being representationally developed enough to have those features of the representation that represent the horse *as* a black horse able to play some causal role in one's responses to black horses.

Of course we all know that a system being "driven" by a black-horse representation is really being driven by physical characteristics of the representation itself. The representational *content*, the state of affairs that these characteristics indicate or represent, are not themselves pulling the control levers. Some philosophers, hostile toward, or merely suspicious of, our folk psychological advertence to content (i.e., beliefs and desires) in the explanation of behavior, are fond of insisting that the semantic dimensions of a representation are causally inert.[8] Whether there is a black horse being represented, or indeed any black horses in the world at all, makes no difference to the causal efficacy of a black-horse representation. Hence, it isn't its being a representation of a black horse, or even its being a black-horse representation, that carries the explanatory weight. It is the *syntax*, not the *semantics*, of our internal representations that make the muscles twitch and, therefore, causally explain why we do what we do.

If all this means is that there is not (causal) action at a distance, it is correct, but, for the same reason, wholly irrelevant to a representational theory of cognitive processes. It is as irrelevant as would be a similar point about a thermostat which started the furnace because it sensed a drop in the room temperature. To describe a thermostat in this way is, I suggest, merely to describe what is being indicated by that internal configuration which closed the circuit to the furnace. It is, in other words, to describe the operation of a representational control system—to explain why it is doing what it is doing in terms of representationally specified internal states. If you don't know that it is the degree of curvature of a bi-metal strip that controls the ciruit to the furnace, it is convenient, not to mention perfectly accurate, to explain its behavior by referring to this control state—the curvature of the bi-metal strip—in terms of what it represents about the temperature of the room.[9]

I think, therefore, that our ordinary cognitive vocabulary is not only appropriate to the systems to which we apply it, but it has the explanatory force we ordinarily attribute to it. Our cognitive mechanism *is* a representational control system and our descriptions of what we see, hear, smell, believe, and know are attempts to describe the various aspects of this control system. What isn't so clear is that we *have* to invoke this ordinary descriptive apparatus in our *scientific* studies of cognition, and, if we do, whether the kind of content we so easily attribute to both humans and animals in our attempts at explanation reflect any real potential of the representational systems we are talking about. I, personally, think we *will* have to use this descriptive machinery in any adequate study of human and animal cognition, but the argument for this is complex and controversial—involving, if I am right, understanding the way an animal's capacity for *learning* forces one into this level of information-theoretical or representational abstractness. But to the second question, the question about the kinds of representational contents we may be forced to use in articulating this approach to cognition, I remain skeptical. It is, as I see it, an empirical question, and I have some real doubts about whether the empirical questions will be answered in such a way as to confirm our everyday views about what we know and believe.

Notes

1. For a more extended treatment, and defense, of this objective notion of information see Dretske (1981).

2. This remark suppresses a very difficult problem—the problem, namely, of saying in what sense a representational system (e.g., our fuel gauge) can represent something which is *not* the case (e.g., that the tank is empty). I have said that a system represents what it indicates. Since nothing can indicate that the tank is empty when it is not empty, at least not on any naturalized reading of "indicate," I owe an explanation of how misrepresentation is possible on my interpretation of representation. I have tried to supply this in "Misrepresentation" (forthcoming). Also see Jerry Fodor, "Psychosemantics or: Where Do Truth-Conditions Come From," mimeo.

3. The issues associated with what has come to be called methodological solipsism; see Jerry Fodor (1980).

4. One gets into tricky contrastive effects in trying to say what the indicator indicates. It would be wrong, of course, to say that the gauge indicates that there is

some gasoline in the tank. With this contrastive stress one implies that the gauge is capable of distinguishing between gasoline and other sorts of liquid in the tank. This is not true. It would be better to say that the gauge indicates that there is some gasoline *in the tank*—or, perhaps, indicates of gasoline that there is some in the tank. The fact that a doorbell is not designed to tell you that *some person* is at the door (not a mischievous squirrel or a woodpecker) doesn't mean it can't indicate that someone is at the door (minus the contrastive emphasis). For more on this see Dretske (1972).

5. If there is, in an animal's natural surroundings, items which would trigger the same response, then this *is* relevant to determining what is indicated by the detector states. For example, parasite birds place their eggs in the nests of host birds. Natural selection has supported this form of parasitism by making the parasite young virtually indistinguishable from the host's own young. The elaborate color markings are virtually identical. In this case, though we have a neural indicator (in the host bird) that evolved to enable it to recognize members of its own species, the development of parasite birds has altered the representational (indicator) status of this mechanism. See Nicolai (1974, p. 93).

6. Whether or not they are bug detectors depends, in part, on what the biological *function* of this detector is and this, in turn, depends (as I argue in "Misrepresentation") on the kind of resources the organism has for processing information about bugs and whether it is capable of expanding these resources by some kind of associative learning.

7. See "Misrepresentation" (Dretske, forthcoming).

8. Besides Fodor, I have in mind such people as Steve Stich (1983) and Paul Churchland (1981).

9. When writing this (late 1983) I thought this was the best that could be done in vindicating the explanatory role of content characteristic of folk psychology. It says, in effect, that though a structure's having a content doesn't cause anything, we can identify the structure that does have causal efficacy (in virtue of its "formal" properties) by mentioning its content. Advertence to content, therefore, becomes a useful bookkeeping device in specifying those structures that are causally efficacious in virtue of quite different properties. As I read him, this is close to Brian Loar's notion that sentential contents are merely indices of functional states (see Loar 1981). I now (late 1984) believe that a much more "realistic" account can be given of the explanatory, indeed *causal*, role of propositional contents, but this is a story that must be given elsewhere.

Bibliography

Bentley, D. and R. R. Hoy. 1974. The neurobiology of cricket song. *Scientific American* 231:34–44.

Churchland, P. 1981. Eliminative materialism and the propositional attitude. *Journal of Philosophy* 78:67–90.

Dretske, F. 1972. Contrastive statements. *Philosophical Review* 81:411–437.

———. 1981. *Knowledge and the flow of information.* Cambridge: MIT Press, Bradford Books.

———. Forthcoming. Misrepresentation. In *Belief,* ed. Radu Bogdan. Oxford: Oxford Univ. Press.

Fodor, J. 1980. Methodological solipsism considered as a research strategy in cognitive psychology. *Behavioral and Brain Sciences* 3:63–110.

———. Forthcoming. Psychosemantics or: Where do truth-conditions come from?

Goodman, N. 1976. *Languages of art.* Indianapolis: Hackett.

Loar, B. 1981. *Mind and meaning.* Cambridge: Cambridge Univ. Press.

Nicolai, J. 1974. Mimicry in parasitic birds. *Scientific American* 231:92–98.

Stich, S. 1983. *From folk psychology to cognitive science.* Cambridge: MIT Press, Bradford Books.

Inexplicit Information

Introduction

In a recent conversation with the designer of a chess playing program I heard the following criticism of a rival program: "It thinks it should get its queen out early." This ascribes a propositional attitude to the program in a very useful and predictive way, for as the designer went on to say, one can usually count on chasing that queen around the board. But for all the many levels of explicit representation to be found in that program, nowhere is anything roughly synonymous with "I should get my queen out early" explicitly tokened. The level of analysis to which the designer's remark belongs describes features of the program that are, in an entirely innocent way, emergent properties of the computational processes that have "engineering reality."
—Daniel Dennett

Before discussing the issue raised by this passage, we need to do a little house-cleaning. We are not interested, or shouldn't be, in what representations exist in (are tokened in) the program. Our interest is rather in what representations exist in the system as the result of executing the program, i.e., with representations constructed by the system or that exist in one of its data bases at run time. Thus, although the program Dennett is discussing might contain nothing explicitly about queen deployment, the system might well construct such a representation at run time. For example, the system—call it CHESS—might begin by executing a rule that says, in effect,

(1) Whenever circumstance C obtains, construct the goal DEPLOY THE CURRENTLY HIGHEST RATED PIECE.

Given the way CHESS typically opens, C regularly obtains early in the game, when the Queen is the highest rated piece. Hence, it typically happens early in the game that the system constructs the goal DEPLOY THE QUEEN.

It is all too easy to write programs that do unintended things like this, so it is all too likely that the case Dennett is actually discussing is like this. But if it is, it is boring. To keep things interesting, I will assume that the system never constructs or uses a representation having the content DEPLOY THE QUEEN. Surely that is the case Dennett intended.

Given that the system never constructs the goal to deploy the queen, what are we to make of the characterization "It thinks it should get its queen out early"? What kind of characterization is that? Dennett's point might be simply that the device behaves *as if* it were executing a program with the explicit goal of early queen deployment. A more interesting interpretation, however, is that information to the effect that the queen should be deployed early is in the system in some sense relevant to the explanation of its performance, but is not explicitly represented. It is this interpretation I want to pursue, so I'll assume it's what Dennett meant.[1]

What's interesting about this interpretation, of course, is that it assumes the propriety of a kind of intentional characterization—a characterization in terms of propositional content—in the absence of any token in the system having the content in question. I agree with Dennett that it is common and useful to intentionally characterize a system even though the system nowhere explicitly represents the propositional content figuring in the characterization. I have doubts, however, about Dennett's "intentional systems theory" that would have us indulge in such characterization without worrying about *how* the intentional characterizations in question relate to characterizations based on explicit representation. How does "The queen should be deployed early" relate to what is explicitly represented by the system? What determines the content of an intentional characterization at this level of analysis?

In what follows, I will try to distinguish and clarify various distinct types of what I will call *inexplicit information*, i.e., information that exists in a system without benefit of any symbolic structure having the content in question. "Untokened" might be a better term than "inexplicit" for what I have in mind, but it just doesn't sound right. I also have qualms about "information." As Dretske (1981) uses the term, a system cannot have the information that p unless p is the case. I see much merit in this usage, but in the present case it won't do. As I use the term below, information may be false information.

Types of Inexplicit Information

Control-implicit Information

There are many cases in which the natural thing to say is that some piece of information is implicit in the "logic" or "structure" of the flow of control. Imagine a circuit fault diagnosis system so organized that it checks capacitors, if any, only after verifying the power supply, and suppose that it is now executing an instruction like this:

(2) CHECK THE CAPACITORS.

Given the way the program is structured, the system now has the information that the power supply is OK. It has this information because it cannot execute instruction (2) unless it has verified the power supply. There may be no explicit representation of this fact anywhere in memory—no token having the content, "The power supply is OK"—but the fact that control has passed to rule (2) means that the system is in a state that, as Dretske would say, carries the information that the power supply is OK. Programmers, of course, constantly rely on this sort of fact. The system doesn't need to explicitly represent the power supply as being OK because this fact is implicit in the current state of control. This type of implicit information is ubiquitous in almost every computer program.

It isn't difficult to imagine how early queen deployment could be at least partly control implicit in CHESS. The easiest way to see this is to consider how one might exploit control structure to prevent early deployment of the queen. To imagine a trivial illustration—this would be a very bad way to build a chess system—suppose use of the pieces is considered in order, lowest rated pieces being considererd first. Only if no acceptable move is found involving a lower rated piece does the system consider moving a higher rated piece. In this way, it might seem, we will avoid queen deployment except when it's really needed. But now suppose that the move evaluation routine was designed with the middle and end game primarily in mind, parts of the game where one might want to rate "aggressiveness" fairly heavily. As a consequence, very few moves in the early part of the game score high, since it is more difficult to make aggressive moves early on. A side effect will be that control will be passed to consideration of queen moves in circumstances that we assumed would occur only in the middle game but which in fact regularly occur earlier. Passing control to a consideration of queen moves amounts to assuming that other moves are insufficiently aggressive, and this assumption will be made much too early in the game.

This sort of possibility comes close to fitting Dennett's original description. Although, in the case imagined, we don't have "Deploy the queen early," we do have the system deciding that only a queen move will do, and doing this early in the game, and doing it without explicitly representing anything like early queen deployment as a goal.

Domain-implicit Information

With a few degenerate exceptions, the information we think of a system as having is always to some extent lodged in the environment. Suppose I write a program, execution of which will get you from your house to mine. Now, in some sense, the program represents me as living in a certain place, perhaps correctly, perhaps not. Where does it say I live? Well, nothing like the proposition

(3) Cummins lives at location L.

need be explicitly represented; the program may *fix* the location in question in that execution of it will get you to my house from yours. But nowhere need there be anything remotely like (3), either in the program itself or constructed at run time.

It is easy to get confused about this and suppose that the location in question must be *inferrable* somehow from the location of your house, together with information given in the program. But this is seriously mistaken. I could give you a perfectly precise program for getting to my house from yours, and another for getting from your house to Paul's, and you could not, without executing them, determine so much as whether Paul and I live in the same place. I could do this by, for example, relying exclusively on LEFT, RIGHT, counting intersections, and counting houses. In such a case, the location of my house just isn't going to be a consequence, in any sense, of premises supplied explicitly. The only way you could use the program to figure out where my house is would be to execute it, either in real space or using a sufficiently detailed map. The information in question is as much in the map or geography as it is in the program; the program is completely domain dependent for its success.

Nevertheless, given the terrain, the program does carry the information that my house is at a certain place: if you follow it and wind up at the bus depot, you have every right to complain that I gave you the wrong information.

The phenomenon Dennett describes could be like this. Imagine a set of tactics designed to achieve early control of the center. Suppose they aren't very good; most good opponents can frustrate them, and really good opponents can exploit the situation to draw out the queen, queen deployment being, in the situation that develops, the only way CHESS can protect its knights. Here, the analogue of the geography is the opponent's play. It shifts from game to game, but given the way CHESS plays, good opponents are going to respond in similar ways. The resulting interactions typically result in CHESS deploying its queen early. The analogy becomes closer if we imagine that I used *parked cars* as landmarks in my directions. Given that you seldom leave for my house before seven and that most people are home from work by six-thirty and typically park in front of their houses, the result will be that you typically get to my house. But sometimes you will get to the bus depot, or the deli, or somewhere else.

If the phenomenon Dennett describes *is* like this, then it is misleadingly described. If early queen deployment is domain implicit in CHESS, then neither the programmer nor the device executing the program thinks in general, or momentarily, that the queen should be deployed early. Early queen deployment is rather an unintended, unexpected, and perhaps even unnoticed artifact of a variety of factors in the system that have nothing to do with the queen interacting with factors in the "environment" that do. Intuitively, the goal is "in the environment"—i.e., in the opponent's play. Indeed, it's the opponent's goal! Nevertheless, the flaw—early queen deployment—is a flaw in the program; it's in the program in just the way that information about the location of my house is in the program consisting of "Two lefts, a right, opposite the blue Chevy station wagon."

Rules, Instructions, and Procedural Knowledge

Once upon a time, there was something called the procedural-declarative controversy in Artificial Intelligence. This controversy had to do with whether it is better to represent knowledge as a procedure—i.e., as a program applying it—or as a set of declarative propositions. What everyone decided was that it all depends on what's convenient for the programming purposes at hand. In short, the controversy died for want of an issue. In a well-known article (*Artificial Intelligence Meets Natural Stupidity*), Drew McDermott (1976) enjoined us never to talk about it again. Nevertheless,

I intend to follow a long philosophical tradition of ignoring the injunctions of such courts and prod these dead issues a little bit anyway.

Let's begin with an example. Suppose we set out to build a system called FIXIT that diagnoses faults in appliances. Expert system programs—programs designed to duplicate the performance of an expert in some domain such as appliance failure diagnosis—are written as sets of *productions*. A production is a rule of the form IF C THEN A, where C is some condition and A is some action. Whenever something in working memory matches C, A is performed. In the simplest case, the rules are unordered; the flow of control is determined solely by which conditions happen to be matched, together with some simple conflict resolution routines that determine what happens when more than one condition is matched.

The rules of an expert system are supposed to formulate the knowledge of humans who are expert at the task the system is to perform. FIXIT, for example, would probably have a rule like this:

(R) IF APPLIANCE DOESN'T START THEN FIND OUT IF IT IS PLUGGED IN.[2]

Most of *us*, on the other hand, probably begin with the goal to start the appliance, together with a belief like this:

(B) If the appliance isn't plugged in, then it won't start.

If the appliance doesn't start, we use (B) and some inference procedures to construct a subgoal: find out if the appliance is plugged in. Experts, unlike the rest of us, seem to have "proceduralized" this business: they just execute (R). The difference is that novices must remember that an appliance won't start if it is unplugged and then reason from this to the conclusion that the plug should be checked. Experts don't have to figure out what to do: they simply check the plug when the thing won't start.

There are two ways in which a system can "have" a rule like (R): (R) might be a rule that is represented in the system's memory, or (R) might be an *instruction*, i.e., a rule in the program that the system executes. These are quite different matters. Let's take them in order.[3]

First, then, suppose that FIXIT has rule (R) represented in memory. (R), then, is one of the rules it "knows." But having access to (R) is evidently quite a different matter from having access to (B). A system that has access to (R) knows what to do if the appliance won't start. A system with access to (B) must *infer* what to do and hence must have some capacity for means–ends analysis. This is why a system operating on the basis of (R) can be expected to make different sorts of errors than a system operating on the basis (B), and why a system operating on the basis of (B) can be expected to be slower than one operating on the basis of (R). It is precisely because a system with access to (R) doesn't need to infer what to do that it is a mistake to suppose its access to (R) amounts to knowing the same thing it would know if it had access to (B) instead. A system with access to (R) knows what to do, and a system with access to (B) instead does not: it must figure out what to do.[4]

So much, then, for the case in which (R) is represented in memory—a genuine rule. What about the case in which (R) is a rule in the program that the system executes—i.e., an instruction? Let's move back to the original example derived from Dennett. Suppose the *program* executed by the *device* CHESS contains the following rule:

IF IT IS EARLY IN THE GAME THEN DEPLOY THE QUEEN.

Does CHESS—the *device* executing the program—believe that it should deploy its queen early? The programmer certainly believed it. And CHESS will behave as if it believed it too: hence the characterization Dennett reports. But CHESS (as we are now imagining it) simply executes the rule without representing it at all, except in the degenerate sense in which rubber bands represent the rule IF PULLED THEN STRETCH, and masses represent the rule COALESCE WITH OTHER MASSES. Like the rubber band, CHESS simply executes its rule, and executing that rule amounts to having a behavioral disposition to deploy the queen early.[5] By contrast, it *does* represent the state of the game—e.g., the positions of the pieces and the fact that it is early in the game—and it does that by executing a set of instructions that say, in effect, REPRESENT THE CURRENT STATE OF THE GAME. Moreover, the system not only represents facts about the game, but its representations of these facts play something like the role that functionally distinguishes belief from other intentional states, viz., availability as premises in reasoning and susceptibility to evidential evaluation (if CHESS is a learner). But CHESS (as we are now imagining it) does not represent the rule requiring early queen deployment, nor is anything with a comparable content available for reasoning or epistemic assessment. Consequently, I think we should resist the claim that CHESS thinks or believes or knows that it should deploy the queen early. The rules CHESS executes—what I've been calling its instructions—are quite different and have a very different explanatory role from the rules CHESS knows.[6]

A frequent reply to this point is that our system has *procedural knowledge* to the effect that the queen should be deployed early in virtue of executing a program containing the rule. Ordinary usage condones this line to some extent by allowing us to describe the capacities of cognitive systems as knowing how to do something even though there is no explicit tokening of the rules executed. Notice, however, that we aren't allowed this license when speaking of noncognitive systems: rubber bands don't know how to stretch when pulled. I think talk of procedural knowledge has its place— it's the case we discussed a moment ago in which we have (R) explicitly tokened in memory—but a system's procedural knowledge is not knowledge of the rules it executes. The rules a system executes—the ones making up its program—are not available for reasoning or evidential assessment for the simple reason that they are not represented to the system at all.[7]

Of course, if CHESS is implemented on a general purpose computer, rather than hardwired, the program itself will also be represented "in" the system: it may be on a disk, for example. But these are not representations to CHESS, they are representations to the system that implements CHESS, typically an interpreter and operating system. The interpreter "reads" these rules, not CHESS. The program file is not a data base for CHESS, it is a data base for the interpreter. CHESS doesn't represent its program, it executes it, and this is made possible by the fact that a quite different system *does* represent CHESS's program. If we hardwire CHESS, the program is no longer represented at all; it is merely "embodied." There is all the difference in the world between writing a program that has *access* to a rule codified in one of its data structures and a program that *contains* that rule as an instruction.[8]

The presence of our rule in CHESS's program, therefore, indicates something about the programmer's knowledge but nothing one way or the other about CHESS's representational states. Contrast a case that *does* tell us something about CHESS's representational states:

IF OPPONENT HAS MOVED THEN UPDATE CURRENT POSITION.

When this instruction is executed, CHESS will create a representation of the current position and store it for future access.

Once we are clear about the distinction between representing a rule and executing it, we are forced to realize that production systems demonstrate that a system can have a cognitive skill or ability—e.g., the ability to diagnose appliance failure or to play chess—without knowing the sorts of things appliance fixers or chess players typically know. When knowledge is "proceduralized," it ceases to be knowledge, if by "proceduralization" we mean that the rules in question become instructions in the program the system executes. Nevertheless, and here is the main point at last, even though the system doesn't represent such rules, the fact that it executes them amounts to the presence in the system of some propositionally formulatable information, information that is not explicitly represented but is inexplicit in the system in virtue of the physical structure upon which program execution supervenes.

If we turn back to Dennett's parable now, we find something of a muddle. Evidently, the case in which we have a rule explicitly tokened in memory is not the one at issue. In the case lately imagined, however, although we do have an instruction *in the program*, nothing like DEPLOY THE QUEEN EARLY is tokened *by the system*. This is the case we are interested in, but here it seems plainly incorrect to say that the system thinks or believes that it should deploy the queen early, though this does apply to the programmer. Instead, the correct description seems to be that in the system there is a kind of inexplicit information, information lodged, as it were, in whatever physical facts underwrite the capacity to execute the program. Explanatory appeals to this sort of information evidently differ radically from explanatory appeals to the system's representations—e.g., representations of current position. Moreover, it is plain that it is the appeal to rules *executed*—i.e., to instructions—that is the basic explanatory appeal of cognitive science. It is only in virtue of the instructions a system executes that the knowledge it has can issue in behavior. Indeed, it is only because of the instructions executed that it has any representational states at all.

Conclusion

We have now seen several ways in which it makes a kind of sense to describe a chess system in terms of informational contents that are not explicitly represented. Moreover, each type of inexplicit representation appears to have a bona fide—indeed essential—explanatory role, and, though the details want spelling out, each seems to supervene in conceptually straight-forward ways on ontologically kosher features of program-executing systems. In general, once we realize that a system can have all kinds of information that isn't in its memory, information that *it* does not represent at all, we see that intentional characterization—characterization in terms of informational content—is not all of a piece and that the different pieces have radically different explanatory roles. Explanation by appeal to any of the three kinds of inexplicit information I have been discussing is always explanation by appeal to rules executed and hence is quite different from explanation by appeal to knowledge structures. Everyone realizes that what you can do is a function of what information you have, but not everyone in cognitive science seems to realize the importance of information that is not explicitly represented or stored in memory.

I've been making much of the distinction between representing a rule and executing it. Executing a rule, I've been urging, isn't knowing or believing it. And conversely, there is ample evidence that knowing a rule isn't sufficient for being able to execute it. Explicit information—knowledge and belief properly so-called—is a matter of which representations are created or exist in the system at run time and of how these are used by the system. If a representation of the world exists in the system, is available as a premise in reasoning, and is subject to evidential assessment, we have at least the salient *necessary* conditions for intentional characterization as knowledge or belief. *Inexplicit* information, on the other hand, is a matter of which rules or instructions the system executes—a matter of its program—and the environment the system operates in. A system can have much information that is *not represented by the system at all* and that doesn't function anything like knowledge or belief, even tacit knowledge or belief. When we formulate the content of this information and attribute it to the system, we intentionally characterize that system, and rightly so, even though the propositional contents of our characterizations are not represented by the system we characterize. But we are not characterizing what it knows or believes.

Current cognitive science, with its emphasis—nay, fixation—on "knowledge representation," has neglected (officially, if not in practice) the ubiquitous and critical information that isn't represented[9] (not represented by the cognitive system anyway). It *is* represented by the programmer, of course, and one of the important insights of the cognitive science movement is that a program is a theory. When we write a program, we are theorizing about our human subjects, representing to each other the rules we suppose they execute. When we do this, what we are doing to a great extent is specifying the inexplicit information that drives human as well as computer cognitive processes. Everyone recognizes the importance of what is represented; I've been urging the importance of what isn't.

Notes

1. Perhaps Dennett doesn't distinguish these two interpretations, being an instrumentalist about goals. But he should, as the sequel will show, I think.

2. Something must be done, of course, to prevent the left-hand side of this rule matching forever. The completed rule might read: IF A DOESN'T START AND

NOT (PLUG CHECKED) THEN CHECK PLUG AND WRITE (PLUG CHECKED).

3. The literature on expert systems treats this distinction with a benign neglect. It only matters if we want the system to be able to alter its own productions, in which case they must be rules, not instructions.

4. The received view is that we have the *same knowledge* represented in each case, but represented in different forms—a declarative form and a procedural form—and this difference is held to account for the characteristic differences in performance. But is this right? Is the difference only a difference in how the same thing is represented? It seems clear the difference is a difference in *what is known* rather than simply a difference in how what is known is represented. To make the point once again: the system with (R) knows what to do, whereas the other must figure it out.

5. We might mark the distinction by saying that instructions are "embodied" in the device that executes them. Cf. the notion of E-representation in Cummins 1977, 1983.

6. For more on the explanatory role of appeals to instructions executed see Cummins 1977, 1983.

7. When inference-dependent propositions like (B) are replaced by rules like (R) *in memory*, we have a kind of proceduralization that does yield knowledge but not the *same* knowledge.

8. From an AI perspective, this is trivial, of course: simply putting a rule in memory is not going to get it executed; we must somehow pass control to it.

9. "Knowledge representation" seems a misnomer: What we are interested in is how a cognitive system represents (or should represent) the world, not how to represent knowledge. "How does *S* represent the world?" = "How is *S*'s knowledge *encoded*?"

Cognitive science might be interested in knowledge representation in the following sense: how should we, as theorists, represent in our theoritical notation the knowledge a cognitive system has of, say, chess. This is a legitimate issue but not the one generally meant by "knowledge representation."

Bibliography

Cummins, R. 1977. Programs in the explanation of behavior. *Philosophy of Science* 44:269–287.

———. 1983. *The nature of psychological explanation*. Cambridge: MIT Press, Bradford Books.

Dennett, D. 1978. *Brainstorms*. Cambridge: MIT Press, Bradford Books.

Dretske, F. 1981. *Knowledge and the flow of information*. Cambridge: MIT Press, Bradford Books.

McDermott, D. 1976. Artificial intelligence meets natural stupidity. In *Mind design*, ed. J. Haugeland. Cambridge: MIT Press, Bradford Books, 1981.

Functionalism and Belief

Introduction

There are three mind/body problems.

The first concerns the nature of *minds*, things satisfying open sentences like

[1] x is in pain.
[2] x believes that God is good.

The *dualist* with respect to minds joins with Descartes in claiming that no mind satisfies any physical predicate which, like "x weighs 117 pounds," entails being an occupier of space. One way of being an *anti-dualist* with respect to minds is by being an eliminativist with respect to the mental and thus to claim that, as nothing satisfies mental predicates like [1] and [2], there are no minds. The more common way of being an anti-dualist is to claim that minds are also occupiers of space.

The second mind/body problem concerns the nature of *mental state* (event, process) *tokens*, datable occurrences satisfying open sentences like

[3] x is a pain.
[4] x is a belief that God is good.

The dualist with respect to pains, beliefs, desires, and all other mental state-tokens claims that no mental state-token is identical to any other kind of state-token; in particular, not identical to any physical state-token, to something which satisfies an open sentence like

x is an instance of blah-blah pattern of neural activity.

The anti-dualist with respect to mental state-tokens who is not an eliminativist about them will insist that mental state-tokens are physical state-tokens and that in human beings, at least, pains and beliefs are states of the nervous system.

The third mind/body problem concerns the nature of *mental properties*, properties expressed by open sentences like [1]–[4] (the properties expressed by [3] and [4] are mental state-*types*). The dualist here claims that these properties are irreducibly mental and thus not identifiable with properties expressed by predicates devoid of mental terms. This is precisely what is denied by the noneliminativist anti-dualist about properties. Forty years ago this anti-dualist argued that mental properties were identical to certain kinds of behavioral properties, viz., dispositions to behave in certain ways; but it proved difficult to say in behavioral terms what those ways were. Twenty years ago he argued that mental properties were physical properties, or, what comes to the same, that mental state-types were physical state-types. But this "type–type identity theory" was thought to founder on the phenomenon of multiple realization: surely we must not, by an identification of belief-properties with neurophysiological properties, preclude machines from having beliefs, and it is not, we know, very plausible to suppose that the physical property that realizes pain in a person also realizes pain in a rat. Nowadays a noneliminativist anti-dualist about mental properties is most likely to claim that they are properties of a kind that I shall now call *functional properties*, using that expression in the broadest possible way.[1]

The notion of a functional property is to derive from that of a functional role.

A *functional role* is simply *any* second-order property of first-order state-types possession of which entails that the state-type possessing it is causally or counterfactually related in a certain way to other state-types, to ouputs, to inputs, or to distal objects and their properties. Thus, the property expressed by the following open sentence is a functional role:

x is a first-order state-type such that one's being kicked causes x to be tokened in one, which in turn causes one to wince.

More apposite examples are much more difficult to give, for they will take the form

$$Tx,$$

where substituends for "x" will produce very complex *theories* about the behavior of very complex systems, such as computers, or even persons. Still, the very simple example illustrates two important features of all functional roles:

(1) A given physical state-type can, and invariably will, have indefinitely many functional roles. That is, a state-type can stand in numerous distinct causal (or transitional) relations to numerous other states, or to outputs, etc.

(2) Two distinct physical state-types can have the same functional role: a state-type that figures in the etiology of my behavior can have a causal property that is also had by a different state-type that figures in the etiology of the behavior of a computer.

Now, each functional role determines a unique *functional property*, viz., the property of having some property which has that functional role; since the properties which have functional roles are state-types, the functional property determined by a functional role is the property of being a token of a state-type which has that functional role. In other words, if F is a functional role, then the property expressed by the open sentence

x is a token of some state-type which has F

is a functional property.

A few comments should prove useful.

(a) A first-order physical state-type may be said *to realize a functional property* just in case it has the functional role determinative of that functional property. Then it follows that a functional property can be *multiply realized*: many different physical properties can realize the same functional property.

(b) One reason why it is important clearly to distinguish functional properties and functional roles is that, as belief-properties such as *being a belief that snow is white* are properties of state-tokens, they could not coherently be identified with functional roles, but only with functional properties.

(c) I began this excursion into functional properties with the claim that contemporary noneliminativist anti-dualists about belief-properties would identify them with functional properties, in the sense just explained. But of course this needs qualification, as it could only apply to those belief-properties, like the one expressed by [4], that are state-types, and not to those, like the one expressed by [2], that are properties of persons. However, the latter can be defined in terms of the former in the style of

x believes that such and such iff x has a belief that such and such.

The more cautiously worded statement of the contemporary view is, then, that each belief state-type is identical to some functional property,[2] whereas for each belief-property of persons there is some functional property such that the belief-property is identical to the property of having some state-token which has that functional property. This is how I should be understood when I write without qualification of the view that belief-properties are functional properties.

(d) Functional roles are properties of state-types, but this should be understood as relativized to organisms and times: state-type N has functional role F in x at t—thus leaving open the possibility that N might not have F in y at t'. Suppose, for example, that neural state-type H realizes hunger in both Al and Bob and that only in Al is it the case that the smell of pizza always causes a tokening of H. This would be a theoretically uninteresting example of H's having a functional role in Al which it did not have in Bob; the possibility of theoretically interesting examples of this phenomenon is discussed below in connection with "Twin Earth" counterexamples to functionalism.

(e) The nebulous label "functionalism" will nowadays support nearly any antimentalist, physicalistically creditable theory of belief-properties, but I nevertheless decline to apply the label "functionalism" to the position that belief-properties are functional properties. For any theorist who claims that each belief-property is identical to some functional property owes an account of what it is that determines *which* functional property a given belief-property is identical with. As will later be apparent, there is more than one way in which a theorist might seek to discharge this debt. One of them is to claim that there is some psychological theory such that the identification of each belief-property with a given functional property is determined by the role that the notion of belief plays in that theory, and I think that, given the history of our subject, "functionalism" finds its most felicitous application here—as a label not just for the thesis that belief-properties are functional properties, but for that thesis *together with* a certain thesis about the way in which the pairing of belief-properties with functional properties is determined. I do not, however, pretend that this is anything more than a terminological point.

One can be an anti-dualist about minds and a dualist about mental states, or an anti-dualist about mental states and a dualist about mental properties. The most thoroughgoing anti-dualism, or physicalism, is one that is anti-dualistic with respect to all three kinds of mental entities. It will not countenance anything of any ontological category that is irreducibly mental, neither minds nor mental states nor mental properties.

The theorist who interests me in this article is a noneliminativist physicalist of the highest degree, who holds that belief-properties, and propositional attitude-properties generally, are functional properties in the sense explained. He holds, in other words, that

For each proposition p there is some functional role F such that being a belief that p = being a token of a state-type that has F.[3]

If this is true, then there must be *some* principled way of correlating propositions with functional roles that determines an identification of each belief-property with some functional property. This article is mostly about functionalist ways this might be done. But before getting down to that, and as a preliminary to it, it will be helpful to introduce the notion of a *functional theory* and to discuss the way propositions might enter into them.

Functional Theories and Propositions

We might have a *black-box problem*: we are given an input/output system (the black box) whose outputs are a function of its inputs and its internal, physical states; although we have access to the inputs and outputs, we know nothing about the nature of the internal states nor of the causal laws governing them. Nevertheless, we seek a theory that will be explanatory and predictive of the outputs. To provide such a theory is to solve the black-box problem.

We might be able to solve the black-box problem by devising a correct *functional theory* of the system: we might theorize that there are so-and-so many internal state-types the system might be in which are related to one another, to inputs, and to ouputs in such-and-such causal or transitional ways. If this theory is correct and detailed enough it could enable us to predict its outputs on the basis of its inputs, just as knowledge of a computer's program may provide us with the ability to predict its outputs even though we know next to nothing about its internal hardware. (So it ought to be clear that there is a big difference between function*al* theories and functional*ist* theories: the former are empirical theories about the behavior of I/O systems, whereas the latter are philosophical theories about the identification of mental properties and functional properties. There are an enormous number of true, although perhaps unformulated, functional theories, but I doubt that there is even one true functionalist theory.) What form will a functional theory take? If it needs only to quantify over a relatively small number n of internal state-types, it can take the form of a straightforward existential generalization over them:

[i] $(ES_1), \ldots, (ES_n)(T(S_1, \ldots, S_n))$.

Here the open sentence

[ii] $T(S_1, \ldots, S_n)$

expresses an n-ary relation among state-types and will relate them to one another and to possible inputs and outputs. The theory [i] will be true, of course, provided that there is an n-tuple of physical state-types that satisfies [ii]. Each member of this n-tuple will have the *functional role* determined for it by the open sentence (i.e., it will be, for some i, the ith member of an n-tuple of physical state-types that satisfies a certain complex causal or transitional relation). These physical state-types that realize the theory will be the ones that enter into the causal laws whose unavailability defined the black-box problem. We are about to see that a functional theory might not be able to take the simple, straightforward form of a quantification over the causally operative, internal, physical state-types of the system. In other words, [i] is not the only form that an explicitly functional theory might take.[4]

How might *propositions* enter into a functional theory providing the solution to a black-box problem?

Suppose that in order to solve a given black-box problem we needed, somehow, to ascribe functional roles to indefinitely many internal, physical state-types. This would preclude our functional theory from taking the form [i], where we quantify directly over the physical states to which functional roles are being ascribed. How, then, are we to devise a theory that ascribes functional roles to each of indefinitely many physical state-types?

Well, as a first step, we might hypothesize that the causal, or transitional, relations that obtain among the system's internal states *mirror* certain logical (or other) relations that obtain among propositions. Then we might hope to ascribe functional roles to internal state-types via a quantification over functions that map propositions onto state-types whose causal relations to one another, to inputs, and to outputs mirror the relevant logical (or other) relations in which their correlated propositions stand to other propositions. This is what we would be doing if our speculation were to take a form such as this:

> $(Ef)(Eg)(p)(q)(r)(s)$(if p is true and condition C_1 obtains, then one is in $f(p)$; if one is in f(q only if r) and in $g(q)$, then one is in $g(r)$; if one is in $g(s)$ and condition C_2 obtains, then s becomes true.)

(The resemblance between this and a rudimentary belief (f)/desire (g) theory, with C_1 a perceptual input condition and C_2 an output condition, is not accidental but is inessential to the illustration.) This theory says that there is a pair of functions from propositions to internal states having the functional roles dictated by the theory's content. In a functional theory of this sort propositions are exploited as *external indices* of the functional roles one wishes to ascribe to possible physical states of the system in question. So this, as Loar has made clear, is how propositions might enter into a functional theory: as objects wholly external to the system and its workings to which we refer in order to enable us to ascribe functional roles to unknown physical state-types of the system—i.e., unavailable state-types that enter into unavailable causal laws that are explanatory of the system's behavior at a deeper level than that to which the functional theory aspires.

It will help to solidify the intuitive idea just invoked by remarking on the analogous way in which physical properties can be indexed by numbers. The analogy has been well expressed by Robert Stalnaker:

> What is it about such physical properties as having a certain height or weight that makes it correct to represent them as relations between the thing to which the property is ascribed and a number? The reason we can understand such properties—physical quantities—in this way is that they belong to families of properties which have a structure in common with the real numbers. Because the family of properties which are *weights* of physical objects has this structure, we can . . . use a number to pick a particular one of the properties out of the family.

Stalnaker then suggests an analogous explanation of how a person can be related to a proposition:

> The analogy suggests that to define a relation between a person or physical object and a proposition is to define a class of properties with a structure that makes it possible to pick one of the properties out of the class by specifying a proposition.[5]

What we have learned from Brian Loar is that an explicitly functional theory which exploits propositions in the way just adumbrated will take the form

$$[\text{iii}] \quad (Ef_1), \ldots, (Ef_n)(T(f_1, \ldots, f_n)),$$

where the quantified variables (the f_i's) range over functions that map propositions onto physcial state-types of the system which, if the theory is true, will have the functional roles it determines.

Theories of types [i] and [iii] are functional theories.[6] *Functional* theories are empirical theories about the causal (or transitional) organization of the internal states of I/O systems; they are not philosophical theories and imply nothing whatever about the nature of propositional attitudes. *Functionalism* is a philosophical theory about the nature of propositional attitudes, and it will be convenient to reserve the rubric "functionalist theories of propositional attitudes" for philosophical theories of belief and desire that are of that persuasion. What makes a functionalist a functionalist is the way he explicates propositional attitudes in terms of functional theories.

The functionalist with whom we are presently concerned holds that

Some psychological theory determines a correlation of each proposition p with a functional role indexed by p in that theory in such a way that being a belief that p = the functional property of being a token of some (first-order, physical) state-type that has that functional role.

This raises two questions: (1) *What* psychological theory does this? (2) *How* does it do it? That is, given that we have a psychological theory which we know "defines" belief, how should we go about constructing that "definition"? (The scare-quotes indicate that a "definition" which determined the identification of each belief-property with a given functional property need not give the *meaning* of "believes," the importance of this to be manifested in the later discussion of "Psychofunctionalism.")

Brian Loar, improving on the work of F. P. Ramsey and David Lewis, has proposed an answer to (2) that, I hazard, would have to be the right sort of answer, if functionalism were true.[7] The issues here are actually many, subtle, and technical, but I hope that for our purposes the following will suffice.

Suppose that one has a psychological theory T involving the theoretical constructs belief and desire and that, for simplicity, there is no question of the theory's reducing, or defining, any other notions in tandem with them.

Now, to form the Loar-style "definition" of belief with respect to T, write out T as a single sentence replacing all occurrences of the "theoretical" predicates "x believes p" and "x desires p" with functional (in the set-theoretic sense) expressions of the form

x is in (a member of the set of first-order state-types) Bel(p),

thus yielding as our representation of T,

[1] T(Bel, Des),

wherein, if [1] is true, "Bel" and "Des" are names of functions that map propositions onto sets of neurophysiological state-types having functional roles determined by the roles of "Bel" and "Des" in [1].[8] By two applications of existential generalization [1] yields its Ramsey sentence,

$$(Ef)(Eg)T(f, g),$$

which is an explicitly functional theory of form [iii]. This we get trivially whether or not [1] defines Bel and Des. But *if* [1] does define them, then the idea, roughly speaking, is that [1] is *equivalent* to

There are functions f and g that uniquely are such that T(f, g),

and that one gives the desired functionalist reduction of Bel and Des thus:

Bel = $_{df}$ the first member of the unique ordered pair of functions that satisfies "T(f, g)".
Des = $_{df}$ the second member, etc.[9]

For *any* theory T containing the constructs *belief* and *desire* (and any others, such as *intention*, which we think should be co-defined with them—a qualification I shall continue to ignore), we can form *the Loar-style definition of Bel and Des with respect to T*—i.e., the definitions those functions would have *if* they were correctly defined by T. [Bel and Des, it should be kept in mind, are simply believing and desiring construed as functions from propositions to (sets of) internal state-types.] Each such definition may be construed as the *stipulative* definition of the function Bel_T, with respect to which one can always ask: Is it the case that Bel = Bel_T?

Now, for each proposition p in the domain of Bel_T, there is a functional role F such that it *follows from the definition of Bel_T* that

$Bel_T(p)$ = (the set of first-order, physical state-types) S iff every member of S has F.

Then we may say that F is *the T-correlated functional role of $Bel_T(p)$* (intuitively, the functional role determined by the role of the belief that p in the generalizations of T) and know that

Bel = Bel_T iff, for each p, one believes p just in case one is in a token of a state-type which has the T-correlated functional role of $Bel_T(p)$.

In other words, if Bel = Bel_T, then *the criterion* for a state-token n's being a belief that p is that n be a token of a state-type that has the functional role that the definition of Bel_T correlates with p.

In light of this resolution of question (2), the claim of the functionalist with respect to belief is just this:

For some theory T, Bel = Bel_T.

Question (1) is then: What theory is that?

Common-Sense Functionalism

Functionalism is the theory that, for some T, Bel = Bel_T; functionalists may differ on what they take that theory to be. *Common-sense* functionalism (CSF) is the theory that Bel = Bel_{T*}, $T*$ being folk psychology, that common-sense psychological theory that embeds our concepts of belief and desire and is common knowledge among those who have them.

Perhaps no one today is a common-sense functionalist, but that (if one will overlook the anachronism of my Loarian formulation) was not so a few years ago, most thoroughgoing materialists then being functionalists and CSF the dominant functionalism. And David Lewis taught us the reason for this.[10]

Scientists, in articulating new theories, often do so using new terms that are not explicitly defined by them but just show up working in the statement of the theory. It is convenient to think of terms like "electron," "mass," "gravity," "quark," "gene," "id," "phlogiston," and others as having been given life in this way. If so, then it is plausible to suppose that these "theoretical terms" derive their meanings from their roles in the theories which introduce them. But how? David Lewis, furthering work of Ramsey's,[11] offered a theory which purported to show how we could derive explicit definitions of a theory's theoretical terms in terms of the roles they play in the theory. It was then tempting to conjecture that psychological terms such as "believes" and "desires" were theoretical terms of our common-sense psychological theory, defined by their roles in it. CSF was then simply a consequence of this, the Loar-style definition now viewed as an improved suggestion about the style of theoretical definition involved.

Of course, if propositional attitude verbs have their *meanings* determined by theoretical roles they play, then the theory in which they play those roles must be one available to those who understand those terms, and that could only be the folk theory. An advantage, therefore, of CSF vis-à-vis alternative functionalist theories, is that it is the only one that can offer an account of the meanings of psychological terms and thus of our *concepts* of belief and desire. I am inclined to think that this is an important point and will later use it to the disadvantage of both CSF and its functionalist competitor.

In any event, CSF is false; there simply is no common-sense belief/desire psychological theory with the wherewithal to define those notions. The reasons for this are, by and large, known, but I think worth rehearsing.

1. It is in the first place not entirely clear that there *is* a folk psychological theory. The common-sense psychological theory is supposed to be that system of law-like generalizations using the notions *belief* and *desire* that is known, or "used," by plain folk who possess those concepts. *But can anyone state so much as a single generalization that fills that bill?* Certainly, the *raison d'être* of our common concepts of belief and desire is their interlocking role in the explanation of behavior, a role exemplified when John explains that Mary raised her arm because she wanted the waiter's attention and believed that that was a good way of getting it. What is far from obvious, however, is that to explain John's explanatory ability we must credit him with implicit knowledge of, or see him as somehow employing, a system of generalizations involving the constructs *belief* and *desire* which, when conjoined with circumstantial facts, yields explanations of behavior. When we explain a person's behavior in terms of his beliefs and desires we do not advert to psychological laws; we simply ascribe to him particular beliefs and desires. David Lewis noticed this, and asked: "How can my behavior be explained by an explanans consisting of nothing but particular-fact premises about my present state of mind? Where are the covering laws?"[12] Thinking that there had to be some, he answered his own question with the claim that the covering laws were implied by ascriptions of particular beliefs and desires, the mechanism of this implication revealed by the definitions of belief and desire with respect to folk psychology. But if we cannot find these "covering laws"—and I am about to suggest that we cannot—then we should wonder whether the covering law model of ex-

planation is the correct model for common-sense, belief/desire explanations of behavior. It *might* just be a fact about our internal processing that we ascribe beliefs and desires under certain conditions and draw behavioral conclusions from those ascriptions under certain other conditions, even when none of this allows us to recover anything that looks like a law-like generalization. In a forthcoming book, *Remnants of Meaning*, I try to show how our propositional attitude concepts can function in an explanatory and predictive way even if no folk *theory* embeds them; now I want to consider the less-than-conclusive reasons for doubting the availability of folk psychological generalizations.

The folk theory is commonly thought to contain at least three kinds of generalizations: those determinative of what might be called *internal functional roles*, which describe how beliefs determine, or constrain, beliefs, and how beliefs and desires generate further desires; *perceptual input conditions*, which take us from certain observable states of affairs to beliefs that they obtain; and *output conditions*, generalizations that take us from beliefs and desires, or intentions, to basic acts.

As regards *internal functional roles*, I am unaware that anyone has ever revealed a true, common-sense law that shows how beliefs and desires determine further desires. One wants to say

If x believes (p only if q) and desires p and . . . , then x desires q.

But how is this to be completed, especially without recourse to anything better than very rough ways of capturing *degrees* of belief and desire? [I trust that it is clear that the inserted sentence would be false without the dots. One may very much desire to be rich, believe that one will be rich only if one murders one's parents, and yet not desire to murder one's parents. Or, to take another kind of exception, if a person believes that (she will gorge herself on chocolate only if she craves chocolate) and desires to gorge herself on chocolate, it does not follow that she desires to crave chocolate. Her desire to gorge may be an unwilling capitulation to a craving she desires not to have.] Turning to rationality constraints among beliefs, one naturally thinks of generalizations such as

If x believes (p and q), then x believes p;
If x believes ((if p, q) and p), then x believes q;
If x believes p, then x does not believe not p.[13]

Yet it is doubtful that any of these are either true or part of the folk lore. Perhaps the last of these is the most conservative; but it cannot be part of the folk psychology, because that is defined by what the folk believe, I am one of the folk, and do not believe it: the generalization fails in the light of unconscious belief, self-deception, and compartmentalized, irrational thought.

Perceptual input conditions may well be in the worst shape. Surely, if any belong to a folk theory, then that theory ought to dish up some sort of completion, probabilistic or otherwise, of this:

[P] If there is a red block directly in front of x and . . . , then x will believe that there is a red block in front of x.

If a completion of [P] is to be common knowledge, it will have to fill the gap with conditions that entail that x is "well enough" sighted, not color-blind, has his eyes open with the block in his line of vision, is attentive to color and shape, has experienced red and square things, is a human being above a certain age, normal to a certain extent, sober and undrugged, in circumstances that satisfy such and such lighting conditions, and not possessed of any beliefs that would defeat the prima facie evidence of his sense experience. It is not obvious to me that *I* could ever succeed in completing this in a way that would yield a truth, nor, if I could, that it would not be of a complexity that defied its being commonly believed and thus of the folk theory.

Similar remarks are in order for attempts to state true and interesting output conditions and input conditions for desires that are not derived from beliefs and other desires.

2. Suppose we understand the notion of *a* folk psychology as *any* untaught belief/desire *theory* implicitly held by *any* ordinary people. Then I have just argued that there is reason to doubt that there is *any* folk psychology. A different point is this: even if there are folk psychological theories, there is none that is held by all the folk, and therefore none that can *define* belief.

If the *meaning* of "believes" is determined by a folk psychology expressed by its use, then that theory must be one implicitly held by everyone who has the concept *belief*. But there cannot be such a commonly held theory for this reason: if a belief/desire theory is to have any chance of defining our concept of belief, it will have perceptual input conditions; but it is clear on reflection that no such condition is common knowledge, however implicitly, among all who have the concept *belief*. Consider in this regard the mooted completion of [P], as good a candidate for a folk psychological input condition as one can hope to find. It is simply obvious that there could be humans, blind or sighted—not to mention extraterrestrials and machines—who have the concept of belief, yet fail to know or use any theory to which a completion of [P] belongs. At the same time we must notice that (a) the perceptual input conditions (if any) that belong to the "common sense" belief/desire theory (if any) that most sighted people know seem to consist almost exclusively of *visual* input conditions, and that (b) insofar as we have perceptual input conditions for nonvisual sensory modes, the point made with respect to [P] can be made with respect to them: there can be people who have the concept *belief*, but, owing to their own sensory deprivations (they are deaf, have no sense of smell or touch, etc.), are ignorant of perceptual conditions satisfied by those who have the sensory capacities they lack.

It is not just that sighted people rely mostly on sight for their worldly knowledge, but also that most sighted people are extemely ignorant about the perceptual input conditions appropriate to blind people, let alone people like Helen Keller. It might of course be suggested that no one who was ignorant of the perceptual input conditions that we know could have the same concept of belief that we have. However, to mention just one problem with this suggestion, it seems clear to me that, when Ray Charles says, "I believe that Count Basie is dead," he means just what I mean when I say, "Ray Charles believes that Count Basie is dead," even if Ray Charles knows no completion of [P].

The dilemma for CSF is thus apparent. On the one hand, the *point* of being a *common-sense* functionalist is that it allows one to say that folk psychology *defines* "belief" (as opposed merely to determining its extension). On the other hand, if folk psychology contains [P], then it cannot *define* "belief" (for there will be people with our concept of belief who know no theory containing [P]); and if it does not contain [P], then it will contain very few and meager perceptual input conditions, and so, once again, cannot define "belief."

Notice that the problem just generated derives from the fact that there can be those who have our concept of belief while being *ignorant* of our folk theory (assuming that there is such a theory); the fact that our folk theory *fails* relevantly *to apply* to those people is the basis for a different objection, to be made shortly.

3. Now let us assume that there is a folk psychology, a common-sense belief/desire psychological theory, that it is suitably regimented, fully stated, and as rich as one might reasonably hope it to be; let T^* be that folk theory. T^* defines belief only if $Bel = Bel_{T^*}$, and $Bel = Bel_{T^*}$ only if, for each p, the T^*-correlated functional role of $Bel_{T^*}(p)$ provides a *sufficient* condition for believing p, i.e., only if a sufficient condition for believing p is that one is in a state having the T^*-correlated functional role of $Bel_{T^*}(p)$. But the T^*-correlated functional role of $Bel_{T^*}(p)$ will not in general provide a sufficient condition for believing p, and one reason

(there are others) that this is so is that T* will often determine the same T*-correlated functional roles for distinct beliefs; it will sometimes follow from the definition of Bel_{T*} that $Bel_{T*}(p) = Bel_{T*}(q)$, when believing p and believing q are in no sense equivalent.[14]

Consider the "theory"

[T#] (p)(q)(x)(if x believes p and x believes q, then x believes (p and q)).

Even without having a settled format for specifying the functional defini-tion of "believes" with respect to a given theory, it ought to be intuitively clear that one reason why T# cannot define "believes" is that it determines the same functional role for all nonconjunctive beliefs: in the relevant sense, it distinguishes no role for the belief that snow is white that it does not also distinguish for the belief that grass is green. Certainly with the Loarian format it can be shown that it follows from the definition of $Bel_{T}#$ that $Bel_{T#}$ (that snow is white) = $Bel_{T#}$ (that grass is green), i.e., that both $belief_{T#}s$ have the same T#-correlated functional roles. The moral, then, is this. If T* is to define belief, then for each p the T*-correlated functional role of $Bel_{T*}(p)$ must be *unique*, in this sense: there is no q such that both (i) the belief that p and the belief that q are nonequivalent beliefs and (ii) $Bel_{T*}(p)$ and $Bel_{T*}(q)$ have the same T*-correlated functional roles. But how is T* to satisfy this uniqueness constraint?[15]

(a) If there is a folk theory, it will contain generalizations determinative of internal functional roles; but they will fare no better with respect to the uniqueness constraint than T#: as propositional variables occur in these generalizations only within belief contexts, and not outside of them, these generalizations will assign the same functional roles to all beliefs of the same logical form.

(b) Since we are allowing optimism to run unbridled, we may suppose that the folk theory has an output component that takes us from beliefs and desires to intentions to perform basic acts, and from them to basic acts. Perhaps the final output condition will be a completion of this:

[O] If x intends to do A now, A is a basic act-type and . . . , then x does A now.

As the act-type variable "A" occurs here both within *and without* content clauses, it is reasonable to suppose that unique T*-correlated functional roles are assigned to at least some beliefs whose contents are specifiable using substituends of "A". However, [O] together with the generaliza-tions determinative of internal functional roles will at best still only assign unique functional roles to some beliefs about basic act-types. If T^* consisted only of these two components, the T^*-correlated functional role of Bel_{T^*}(that snow is white) would be the same as that of Bel_{T^*}(that grass is green), and thus it would not be the case that $Bel = Bel_{T^*}$.

(c) If T^* is to define belief, it must *at the least* have a fairly vast array of perceptual input conditions, and if there are any such conditions, some completion of [P] would certainly be among them. If a proposition p occurs in the antecedent of an input condition, then Bel_{T^*}(p) will have a unique T^*-correlated functional role. However, only a very restricted range of propositions will enter into the perceptual input conditions. If T^* consists only of the foregoing constraints on internal functional roles, ouput conditions, and perceptual input conditions, it cannot possibly satisfy the uniqueness constraint—that tripartite theory will determine no functional role for the belief that dinosaurs are extinct that it does not also determine for the belief that fleas are mortal.

Might T^* reasonably be thought to include generalizations that are not of the three sorts reviewed and that would assure unique functional roles for beliefs not affected by the output or perceptual input conditions? It seems unlikely that such generalizations would take the form of nonperceptual input conditions; for even if we could find a few, it seems unlikely that we could find enough to make any appreciable headway.

Loar has suggested that T^* will contain generalizations, reminiscent of Carnap's "meaning postulates,"[16] that are partially constitutive of inter-belief content relations. He calls them *M-constraints* and gives as an example:

If x believes that y is north of z and that u is north of y, then x believes that u is north of z.

The thought occurs that T^* could satisfy the uniqueness constraint if the M-constraints linked each proposition not occurring in an input condition to a proposition occurring in one in a unique way. But the folk theory, *ex hypothesi*, is one available to all the folk, and it seems obvious to me that no such theory contains nearly enough M-constraints to do the job in question. One needs only to consider the proposition that the government of New Zealand is a dictatorship and to ask what "observation proposition" that proposition is related to in a way that no other propostion is related to. Nor can I think of what else the folk theory might include to secure satisfaction of the uniqueness constraint. I am therefore inclined to suppose that folk psychology cannot provide the functionalist reduction of belief.

4. The preceding objection was that, because T^* could not satisfy the

uniqueness constraint, there would be some p such that the T^*-correlated functional role of $Bel_{T^*}(p)$ did not provide a sufficient condition for believing p. The present objection offers a different reason why T^*-correlated functional roles will not in general yield sufficient conditions for being in the belief states associated with them. The argument is very familiar, so I may be very brief: CSF is false because one can always construct a Twin Earth or Burge-type example in which, for some p, (a) someone does not believe p even though (b) he is in a state which has the T^*-correlated functional role of $Bel_{T^*}(p)$. Well, perhaps I should not be quite *that* brief.

Twin Earth is *exactly* like Earth except for the following difference and whatever it entails: although the things they call "cats" on Twin Earth look and behave exactly like cats, they are not cats but have a radically different genetic make-up and comprise a wholly disparate biological species. Anyway, Earthling Ralph utters "There are cats" and, in doing so, expresses his belief that there are cats. That belief is realized in Ralph by a token of the neural state-type N which has the T^*-correlated functional role of Bel_{T^*}(that there are cats), F^c. Twin-Ralph is a molecule-for-molecule duplicate of Ralph, and so he, too, utters "There are cats," and he, too, is in a token of N. The problem for CSF is that its falsity is evidently entailed by these two truths:

(1) Since N in Ralph has F^c, so, too, does N in Twin-Ralph;

but, notwithstanding this,

(2) Twin-Ralph does not believe that there are cats.

The truth of (1) is not really debatable. Although a specification of F^c might conceivably require a reference to cats (and not to their Twin Earth lookalikes, tcats), the *counterfactual* nature of F^c would secure that it was satisfied by N in Twin-Ralph. Perhaps the point here can be most clearly made by changing the example slightly. Suppose that the T^*-correlated functional role of Bel_{T^*}(that one is looking at a cat) is such that a state-type has that functional role only if the presence of a cat in one's line of vision would under such and such conditions cause that state-type to be tokened in one. If that functional role is possessed by the neural state-type N' that realizes Ralph's belief that he is looking at a cat, then it is clearly also possessed by N' in Twin-Ralph; for if there *were* a cat in his line of vision (etc.), then N' *would* be tokened in him. (*Ex hypothesi*, cats and tcats are distinguishable only at the chromosomal level, a level we may assume to be unavailable to ordinary people.) The general point, then, is that T^*-correlated functional roles will invariably by counterfactual in a way that entails their possession by Twin-Ralph's states, assuming their possession by Ralph's states.

It is important, however, to be clear that the truth of (1) does not follow from a truth about *functional roles* but from a truth about *T*-correlated* functional roles. It is, we know, perfectly possible for a neural state-type to have a functional role in Ralph that it does not have in Twin-Ralph. For example, the functional role expressed by

Every token of x in y is caused by y's looking at a cat.

might well be satisfied by the pair <N, Ralph>, but not by the pair <N, Twin-Ralph>. The reason that Twin Earth is a problem for CSF is that the functional role determined for the belief that there are cats by the folk theory will, by virtue of its counterfactual nature, be satisfiable in a world in which there are no cats.[17]

There are two ways in which one might think to deny (2). (a) One might claim that the creatures on Twin Earth really are cats, there then being no reason to deny that Twin-Ralph believes that there are cats; or (b) one might hold that he has that belief even though there are not cats, but only tcats, on Twin Earth.

It is difficult to take either of these responses seriously. What would the proponent of (a) say about the bizarre mutant offspring of two turtles that ended up looking and behaving exactly like a cat though it was genetically a turtle? If he should insist that it is a cat, then we shall have to agree to disagree; if he agrees that it is not a cat, then he owes a reason for supposing that the creatures on Twin Earth are cats. As regards (b) it is just absurd to suppose that in using "cat" Twin-Ralph is not talking and expressing beliefs about the tcats he thinks he is talking and thinking about but is really talking and thinking about cats, none of which he has ever encountered or even heard of. Twin-Ralph, by parity of reason, has as much right as Ralph does to be said to be expressing a true belief about the thing he is looking at when he says, "I'm looking at a cat," in which case we cannot say that he believes that he is looking at a cat, since *that* belief, unlike the one he expresses, is false.

There is an inclination even among philosophers, who ought to know better, to disparage Twin Earth arguments because of their science fiction flavor. That really is to miss the point. Twin Earth is simply a very fanciful way of making a very plain point: in order to have beliefs with contents ascribable with sentences containing "cat," one must have had some sort of contact, direct or indirect, with cats; but that evident platitude would be a falsehood if CSF were true.

There is one reply that the common-sense functionalist might make to the Twin Earth counterexample that we should very briefly consider before turning to the similar, but interestingly different, counterexample of Tyler Burge's.

The common-sense functionalist might try to hold a *description theory* of natural kind concepts and argue that the truth of (1) and (2) does not refute his functionalism.

He will first of all point out that, in presenting a simplified account of his position, we have oversimplified. The Bel function should not be represented as a unary function but, at the minimum, as a dyadic function of the form

$$Bel(x, p),$$

which maps a person x and a proposition p onto states of x's having the functional role indexed by p in the folk theory. Without this minor refinement, CSF would be all too easily refutable: the neural state-type which realizes my belief that *I* am phlegmatic has exactly the same T^*-correlated functional role as your belief that *you* are phlegmatic, and if belief were simply represented as the unary function, that common functional role would, on the simplified characterization of CSF, entail that we believed the same proposition (which, of course, we do not, as your belief is true iff *you* are phlegmatic, mine iff *I* am phlegmatic). When belief is correctly represented as the dyadic function, then we may see the definition of Bel_{T^*} as yielding, for some F,

x is in Bel_{T^*}(x, that x is phlegmatic) iff x is in a state having functional role F,

from which we would get the right result.

His theory aligned, the functionalist may then try to explain the truth of (1) and (2) thus:

> The concept *cat* is the same on Earth and Twin Earth—roughly, the concept expressed by "those creatures which are conspecific with the such-and-such looking creatures I have encountered." As such, *cat* would refer to cats on Earth, to tcats on Twin Earth. When Ralph says "That's a cat" he is expressing his belief that the creature before him is conspecific with such-and-such creatures in *his* environment, and when Twin-Ralph says "That's a cat" he is expressing his belief that . . . in *his* environment. These are different though analogous beliefs, each determined by the T^*-correlated functional role shared by the same neural state-type which realizes both their beliefs, all this in accord with its being the case that $Bel = Bel_{T^*}$.

The trouble with this reply, as I show elsewhere,[18] is that the implicit description theoretic account of natural kind concepts is as demonstrably false as philosophical theories of that status can be.

So much for the Twin Earth counterexample. Burgian counterexamples to CSF are more interesting than Twin Earth ones; for although they share the same intuitive force, they differ in these two important respects:

(i) They also constitue a very strong *prima facie* objection to Gricean accounts of meaning, which seek to define semantic notions in terms of the potential beliefs and intentions of language users, as the Burgian examples appear to show that the content of one's belief is sometimes a function of the meanings of words in one's linguistic community.

(ii) Let us say that a functional role F is *environment restricted* if, like the one expressed by "Every token of x is caused in so-and-so by his looking at a cat," we cannot know whether a system is in a state of a type that has F without knowing details about the physical environment in which that system is located. The Twin Earth objection to CSF works because T^*-correlated functional roles are *not* environment restricted, and this might engender a non-common-sense functionalist hope that $Bel = Bel_T$, for some T whose T-correlated functional roles *are* environment restricted. The second reason Burgian examples are of interest is that they seem to show that *no* functional role can determine what one believes.

The now-classic example unfolds as follows.[19] Alfred's use of "arthritis" encompasses more than the correct use of that term, which is limited to inflammation of the joints; Alfred also applies the word to rheumatoid ailments not in the joints. So it is not surprising that, noticing an ailment in his thigh which seems to him symptomatically like the disease in his hands and ankles, Alfred says to his doctor, "I have arthritis in the thigh." Here Burge claims, and I think rightly, that Alfred has the false belief that he has arthritis in the thigh. Calling the world we have in mind "w", we may therefore say

In w Alfred has the belief that he has arthritis in his thigh.

We next consider a possible world w′ which differs from w in just one respect (and whatever it entails): in w′ Alfred's use of "arthritis" is the *correct* use; it is the accepted usage of that term in Alfred's linguistic com-community. *Ex hypothesi*, all other facts about Alfred are the same; his physical environment and functional organization are unchanged. Since Alfred's use of "arthritis" in w′ is entirely correct, it seems clear that the belief Alfred expresses in w′ when he says "I have arthritis in the thigh" is *true*. But then

In w' Alfred does *not* have the belief that he has arthritis in his thigh,

for that belief is false (arthritis being, by definition, an inflammation of the joints), whereas the one he has is true.

Now, by construction, Alfred in w' is in exactly the same T*-correlated functional states as Alfred in w. Therefore, if CSF were correct, he would be expressing the same belief by his two utterances; he is not; therefore, CSF is false.[20]

But also, by construction, Alfred in w' is in *all respects* functionally equivalent to himself in w, and that was the point made in (ii).[21]

But also, since (a) Alfred believes that he has arthritis in his thigh only in w, and not in w', and since (b) the only difference between w and w' is in the meaning of "arthritis" in Alfred's linguistic community, then (c)— and this was the point made in (i)—the contents of one's beliefs must, in contradiction with Gricean semantics, sometimes be partly a function of the meanings of one's words in one's linguistic community.

5. If Bel = Bel_{T*}, then, for each p, the T*-correlated functional role of $Bel_{T*}(p)$ must provide a *necessary condition* for believing p; it must be a necessary condition for one's believing p that one be in a token of a state-type that has the T*-correlated functional role of $Bel_{T*}(p)$. But it is doubtful that such necessary conditions are provided by the folk theory.

If there is a folk theory that defines my use of "believes," then it is one that I know. If there is such a theory and it is to have any chance of defining anything, it must have perceptual input conditions. These perceptual input conditions will partly determine T*-correlated functional roles for the beliefs that enter into them. But there will be people who have those beliefs but who are not in states with those T*-correlated functional roles. Therefore, those functional roles do not provide necessary conditions for having the beliefs they are correlated with and CSF is false.

The dilemma for CSF—for that is one way of seeing this objection— may be put thus. Consider my belief that there is an apple in my hand. Either there is an input condition applicable to this belief, or there is not. If there is not, CSF cannot begin to get off the ground: there simply will not be a folk theory rich enough to define anyone's concept of belief. If there is a perceptual input condition for my belief, it will be visual, of the form:

If there is an apple in x's hand and x is sighted and . . . , then x will believe that there is an apple in x's hand.

For that is the only input condition, if any, that *I* know, and CSF is supposed to tell me how to explicate *my* concept of belief. But my concept of belief allows me to say of a blind person that she believes that there is an apple in her hand, and I assume that such ascriptions can be literally true. I assume, too, that many blind people can discern by touch and smell that they are holding an apple, but I do not know how they do this and certainly do not know any perceptual input condition applicable to them for such beliefs.

Now let F^a be the T^*-correlated functional role of Bel_{T^*} (that there is an apple in x's hand), T^* being the folk theory that I know. Suppose that Sally is a blind person who presently believes that there is an apple in her hand, and let N be the neural state-type that realizes her present belief that she is holding an apple. *Must we suppose that N has the functional role F^a?* To say that N has F^a is to say that, if Sally *were* sighted, and there were an apple in her hand, and . . . , then N would be tokened in her. However, it seems to me absurd to suppose that this must be the case, and doubtful that it is the case. Quite likely, if Sally were sighted, some *other* neural state-type would realize her belief that she is holding an apple. But CSF is true only if the possession by N of F^a is a necessary condition for its being a belief that Sally has an apple in her hand. Therefore, CSF, once again, is false.

The moral of this last objection is really this: if CSF is true, then there is a folk theory with perceptual input conditions applicable to all believers. But there is obviously no such theory.

Psychofunctionalism

The functionalist says that, for some theory T, $Bel = Bel_T$. T is not, we know, any common-sense psychological theory; but perhaps it is a *scientific* psychological theory, cognitive psychology the science. Block has called the philosophical theory which affirms this "Psychofunctionalism,"[22] and we may turn straightway to some reasons for doubting it.

1. If, as Psychofunctionalism claims, there is a scientific psychological theory that determines the identity of each belief-property with some functional property, then that theory is neither known, formulated, nor conceived. Evidently, the position must be that there is some true but yet-unthought-of scientific psychological theory T^s such that $Bel = Bel_{T^s}$. T^s, it would have to be conceded, could not *define* "believes," but the idea would be that it does determine that term's reference. The idea would be that, for each p,

being a belief that p = being a token of a state-type that had the T^s-correlated functional role of $Bel_{T^s}(p)$ (i.e., the functional role indexed by p in T^s), where this would be a necessary truth, but one that is only knowable a posteriori after scientific investigation had unearthed T[s].

Now how on earth can the reference, or extension, of "a belief that bedbugs are mortal" in my mouth be determined by a theory that no one knows? I know that some will want to respond: in just the same way that scientists can discover that being a dog = being of such-and-such genotype. But this response is not altogether unproblematic.

First of all, *scientists* cannot discover that being a dog = being of a certain genotype. Scientists can perhaps discover that all and only past, present, and future *actual* dogs are of that genotype and that properties of that genotype account for the phenotypical and behavioral features by which we identify dogs as dogs; but to deduce the property identity we should need a *philosophical* theory that (a) entailed a completion of

Being a dog = being of such and such a genotype if . . . ,

and that (b) in conjunction with the scientific discovery entailed that

Being a dog = being of such and such genotype.

If there is a philosophical theory with this power, I am ignorant of it.

If there were such a philosophical theory, it could take the form of a theory of the meaning or reference of "dog," and some will look here to the seminal work of Kripke, Putnam, and others.[23] That work is indeed suggestive, although it is not obvious what philosophical theory of the sort needed it suggests. In any event—and I suppose this is the most important point apropos of Psychofunctionalism—the intuitive picture suggested by the Kripke/Putnam line on natural kind terms seems inapplicable to belief-predicates.

"The original concept of [dog]," Kripke has written, "is *that kind of thing*, where the kind can be identified by paradigmatic instances."[24] It is as if the word "dog" got introduced by our coming across certain hitherto unknown creatures, which we assumed to belong to a single biological species, and saying, "Let's call something a 'dog' if it belongs to the species of those creatures—whatever that species turns out to be"; scientists then prepared ultimately to reveal, in genetic terms, what this species is. But what analogous caricature is there that is both helpful to the Psychofunctionalist and possessed of a shred of plausibility? In ascribing to someone a belief that most Rolls Royces are stolen by morally bankrupt logicians it seems not to be one's intention to ascribe to that person whatever functional state is enjoyed by paradigm holders of the same belief, since one is apt not to think that anyone else has that belief.

I should summarize my first doubt thus: (a) Psychofunctionalism has no greater plausibility than the plausibility of there being a correct semantic theory of belief-predicates which in conjunction with a scientific psychological theory T^s entails that $Bel = Bel_{T^s}$, but (b) no one has given us the slightest reason to think that this semantic theory exists.

2. This is merely to remind the reader of a couple of points that I shall not take the space properly to develop but which are forcefully argued for in the literature.

(a) It is by no means to be assumed that the forthcoming, correct, and suitably powerful theories of cognitive psychology will employ any construct that is co-extensive with our notion of belief. The functional architecture postulated by such an information-processing theory might simply be too rich and fine-grained to enable one to identify beliefs with functional states invoked by the theory.[25]

(b) Even if a scientific functional theory will need to quantify over belief-states, there remains reason to doubt that it would need *to assign content to those states*, clearly a condition for that theory's providing the functionalist reduction of our contentful belief-properties. In fact, it would seem that, in this regard, we are in a position to say something fairly strong: to the extent that it is clear to us what theories in cognitive psychology should be theories of, it is clear that the objects of belief need be nothing more than uninterpreted sentences. The essential point has been well expressed by Hartry Field:

> If the task of psychology is to state (i) the laws by which an organism's beliefs and desires evolve as he is subjected to sensory stimulations, and (ii) the laws by which those beliefs and desires affect his bodily movements, then semantic characterizations of beliefs and desires are irrelevant to psychology: one can state the laws without saying anything at all about what the believed or desired sentences mean, or about what their truth-conditions are or what their subject matter is.[26]

That is the essential point, but it might be well to work our way back to it along a route of mostly familiar points.

The one thing we clearly want from cognitive psychology is a functional theory that solves the black-box problem we humans pose: a theory that, by specifying functional properties of inner states, is explanatory and predictive of bodily movements in the light of sensory stimulations and other inputs. Given the complexity of our internal structure, this theory will entail a quantification over functions from external indices of functional roles to physical state-types having them. Propositions, we have seen, might be those external indices, but *they need not be*. What is now generally appreciated is that *uninterpreted formulae can fulfill that function just as well*. In using propositions to index functional roles we would be exploiting logical relations among them, but we could use uninterpreted formulae to index the same functional roles by exploiting formal, or syntactic, relations among those formulae. Instead of a law of the form

$$\text{If } x \text{ is in } f(p \text{ and } q), \text{ then } x \text{ is in } f(p),$$

we could have a law of the form

$$\text{If } x \text{ is in } f(\ulcorner \sigma \& \sigma \urcorner), \text{ then } x \text{ is in } f(\sigma),$$

the utility of this last in no way requiring that the values of these sentential variables be semantically interpreted.

If we want to make sense of there being an *unformulated* theory, it is useful to identify it with the equivalence class of sentences that would formulate it. If the theory is a functional theory of us, one of these formulations will contain no propositional attitude terms but will simply be an existential quantification over functions from external indices of functional roles to state-types to which those roles are being ascribed. To say that a yet-unthought-of scientific theory will need to invoke notions of belief and desire is just to say that a formulation of the theory using the Loarian "Bel" and "Des" will belong to the equivalence class of formulations of that theory; by existential generalization on these functors we get that other member of the class which explicitly quantifies over functions of the sort described. Combining the points just made, we can see how a functional theory of us might be formulated using "Bel" and "Des," convenient technical reconstructions of our "belief" and "desire," but in which the functions expressed by those terms had in their domain uninterpreted formulae rather than propositions.

The foregoing is a partial vindication of the claim that, to the extent that it is clear to us what theories in cognitive psychology should be theories of, it is clear that objects of belief need be nothing more than uninterpreted sentences. For we have seen that one sort of theory we clearly expect from cognitive psychology can get along with meaningless symbols as the objects of propositional attitudes. But a full vindication would need to show that *no* strictly legitimate theory of cognitive psychology will need to assign content to belief-states, and I have no idea how one would hope to show that. At the same time, it is true, I think, that—*pace* Jerry Fodor and Tyler Burge—we cannot yet say clearly (or perhaps even unclearly) what sort of scientific theory would need contentful objects of belief.[27]

3. It is absurd to a degree to suppose that there could be a single be-lief/desire scientific psychology that was both applicable to all possible believers and powerful enough to determine a functional property for each belief-property to be identical with. If there were such a theory it would have to include *perceptual input conditions* applicable not just to fully nor-mal university graduates but to very young children, Helen Keller, the most primitive and culturally remote tribesman, extraterrestrials with un-dreamt-of perceptual faculties, and certain machines. Nothing could be such a theory; anything that purported to be would at best be a motley disjunction of distinct theories each applicable to a limited range of believ-ers. If this is right, then there is no scientific psychological theory T^s such that $Bel = Bel_{T^s}$; for $Bel = Bel_{T^s}$ only if, for each p, the T^s-correlated func-tional role of $Bel_{T^s}(p)$ provided a necessary condition for believing p, and that would require the applicability of T^s to all possible believers.

4. $Bel = Bel_{T^s}$ only if, for each p, the T^s-correlated functional role of $Bel_{T^s}(p)$ provides a sufficient condition for believing p. For T^s to satisfy this "sufficiency constraint" its T^s-correlated functional roles would have to be possessed by Alfred's inner state-types but not by Twin-Alfred's, and not by Alfred's in the possible world in which his use of "arthritis" is correct. The claim that $Bel = Bel_{T^s}$ must, in other words, be immune to Twin Earth and Burge-type counterexamples, and who can give any ground for confidence on this score?

Functionalism Extended

"Funtionalism," I have stipulated, is to be our label for the philosophical thesis that

> Some psychological theory determines a correlation of each proposi-tion p with a functional role indexed by p in that theory in such a way that being a belief that p = the functional property of being a token of some state-type that has that functional role.

This is then perspicuously, but I think harmlessly, recast as the thesis that

> For some psychological theory T, $Bel = Bel_T$.

But it is, for the reasons just rehearsed, doubtful that there is such a the-ory; doubtful, therefore, that functionalism is true.

There are two positions in logical space either of which the erstwhile functionalist might next seek to occupy, without ceasing to hold that belief is a relation to propositions and without just surfacing listlessly to the Sargasso Sea of mentalism.[28] The first is very close to what we have been considering. It concedes that there is no *single* psychological theory that determines the functionalist reduction of belief-properties, but supposes that there is one for each thing capable of having beliefs. That is:

> For each possible believer x there is some psychological theory T such that, for each proposition p, x believes p iff x is in $Bel_T(p)$.

Now this would be an exceedingly puzzling and unhelpful suggestion in the absence of some proposal as to the conditions which a psychological theory of a thing would have to satisfy in order to determine that thing's belief-properties. So a fuller characterization of the proposal would be that

> For each possible believer x there is some psychological theory T which satisfies _____ condition, such that, etc.

The filling for the blank would then, in effect, provide a necessary and sufficient *metacondition* for a psychological theory's "defining" belief for a particular believer. The challenge, of course, would be to produce a persuasive metacondition, one immune to the objections already leveled against mundane functionalism.

Brian Loar has proposed a theory along the foregoing lines, but I find it unconvincing, in part for the following reasons:

1. Loar does not give a fully general proposal. The only metacondition he considers is one provided by a common-sense theory that is applicable only to perceptually normal adults in our society, and I can see no obvious way of generalizing Loar's proposal to yield a metacondition applicable to all believers. Moreover, it is a consequence of Loar's theory that the predicate "believes that the *The New Yorker* publishes Ved Mehta" in my idiolect is partially defined by a common-sense theory that is false of each blind person, and that, consequently, as I use that predicate, the sentence

Ved Mehta believes that *The New Yorker* publishes Ved Mehta

cannot be true, as Ved Mehta is blind. This I cannot support.

2. Loar's theory is not immune to Twin Earth and Burge-type counterexamples, and although he is aware of their threat, I find inadequate his description theoretic way of countering it.

There are, I think, other problems with the Loarian proposal, but, as I cannot consider it properly here, I urge anyone interested in functionalism to give it careful study and to decide for himself or herself if it offers the propositionalist a viable form of materialism.

The second position in logical space to which the frustrated functionalist might move offers a more radical departure from functionalism. The theorist occupying this position concedes that no psychological theory will in itself provide any sort of definition, or reduction, of predicates such as

> x believes that some dogs have fleas,

but he does think that a functionalist definition is available for the predicate

> x is a belief

He therefore proposes the following strategy:

First, find a psychological theory with respect to which one can functionally define the *monadic predicate* "x is a belief."

Second, determine a functional property for each composite belief-property via a *nonfunctional*, explicit definition of the form

> [R] x believes p iff (Es) (s is a belief; x is in s; and sRp),

for a given specified relation R.

Robert Stalnaker sees hope in this approach; adapting an idea of Dennis Stampe's, he has in effect suggested that a promising approach to completing [R] would be via a refinement of the idea that

> [FG] x believes p iff x is in a belief-state which, under optimal conditions, x would not be in unless it were the case that p.[29]

We might call the intuitive idea expressed by [FG] the "fuel gauge model of mental representation."[30] If a neural state-token n is a belief that it is raining, then n represents the proposition, or possible state of affairs, that it is raining. Now, representation is not just a feature of mental states: the position of a needle on the dashboard of your car can represent your gas tank as being three-fourths full. How is it that the position of the needle has this representational power? Because of the capacity of the fuel gauge to be a reliable indicator of the amount of fuel in the gas tank, surely; because, under optimal conditions, the needle is where it is (viz., pointing at "$\frac{3}{4}$") only when the tank is three-fourths full of gasoline. The idea, then, is that representation *in general* derives from the capacity of a system to be a reliable indicator of its context. What accounts for the gas gauge's representational features also accounts for those of my belief that it is raining: under optimal conditions, I would not be in that belief-state unless it were raining. It is because being in that belief state is in that way a reliable indicator of the weather that it is a belief *that it is raining*.

However promising the strategy of [R], and however promising the fuel gauge model, [FG] can be no more than a first stab. Among other problems, it implies that, under optimal conditions, one has no false beliefs. That may be, but then one wonders what these never-satisfied "optimal conditions" are, and, especially, how they might be specified without rendering [FG] viciously circular by presupposing the very intentionality it is supposed to explicate.

In any event, [FG] is merely one suggested way of completing [R]; and [R], and the strategy which is supposed to culminate in a completion of it, must await its refutation for another occasion.[31]

Notes

1. David Lewis is a notable exception; although Lewis defines mental terms in terms of functional properties, he identifies mental properties with the physical properties that realize those functional properties. He has, not surprisingly, some pretty fancy maneuvering to do in order to try to accommodate multiple realization. See Lewis 1970, 1971, 1980a, and 1980b.

2. Functional properties are also functional state-types; but I prefer the former locution because it keeps clearly in mind the fact that the bearers of those properties are physical state-tokens. Talk of functional states, although perfectly acceptable, is apt to create the confusion that functional state-tokens are something other than physical state-tokens; cf. Boyd 1980.

3. For the purposes of this article, "propositions" are whatever the objects of belief turn out to be; i.e., the values of the objectual variable "p" in the schema "x believes p." Although I will not argue it here, it is essential to functionalism that believing be a relation in the foregoing sense. Whether or not believing (and, of course, every other propositional attitude) really is a relation in that sense is another matter.

4. This was first made clear in Loar (1981); all references to Loar, unless otherwise noted, are implicitly references to this work.

5. Stalnaker 1984; the first quote occurs on p. 9, the second on p. 11.

6. But not all functional theories are of these two types (or at least they need not

be *formulated* as such). First, there may, as functionalists suppose, be psychological theories that are logically equivalent to theories of types [i] and [iii], although they are not formulated as existential generalizations. In the case of such *implicit* functional theories we obtain *explicit* functional theories by existential generalizations on the implicit theory's "theoretical" psychological terms. Second, as we shall presently note, there are functional theories which utilize uninterpreted formulae rather than "propositions" as external indices of functional roles.

7. Ramsey 1978; Lewis 1970, 1980a; Loar 1981.

8. The values of Bel are *sets* of state-types in order to accommodate multiple realization; see Loar 1981, pp. 59–63, for the complete, unsimplified account.

9. Properly spelled out, of course, these "definitions" would contain no metalinguistic references; see Loar 1981, pp. 61–62.

10. Lewis 1970, 1980a.

11. Ramsey 1978.

12. Lewis 1980a, p. 213.

13. "Rationality constraint" is Loar's expression, and he claims that the last of these generalizations belongs to that folk theory that is common knowledge among adults in our society. Paul Churchland is also quite adamant about folk psychology being a theory and asserts that both explanations and the making of predictions presuppose laws. He also offers the following as a law of folk psychology (1981, p. 69):

$(x)(p)(q)[((x \text{ believes that } p) \& (x \text{ believes that } (\text{if } p \text{ then } q))) > (\text{barring}$ confusion, distraction, etc., x believes that q)].

However, this is not a law, but, at best, a partial specification of one; one wonders how Churchland would replace "etc."

14. Loar makes this point when he says that the common-sense theory fails to imply something unique about each belief, i.e., something about each belief that it implies about no other belief.

15. It should be noted that the uniqueness constraint is a very weak constraint and that satisfaction of it would not imply that T-correlated functional roles provided sufficient conditions in the sense in question. The following "theory," for example, satisfies the uniqueness constraint, but its T'-correlated functional roles do not begin to provide sufficient conditions for being in the belief-states associated with them:

[T'] If p is true, then one believes p.

Because of the way in which "p" occurs both within *and without* of belief contexts, T' will imply something unique about each belief. This can be seen from the way in which it follows from the definition of $\text{Bel}_{T'}$ that $\text{Bel}_{T'}$ (that snow is white) = N only if N is tokened in one if snow is white.

16. Carnap 1947.

17. Cf. Owens 1983. But might not one of folk psychology's platitudes be that beliefs about cats are typically caused by cats? No doubt *some* such beliefs (e.g., that

one is looking at a cat) are highly reliable indicators of the truth of the propositions believed, at least among normal adults in our society; but this can hardly be elevated into a necessary condition for a state's being such a belief. Besides, Twin Earth and Burge-type counterexamples can be constructed for beliefs that are typically unreliable indicators of their truth.

18. Schiffer, forthcoming.

19. Burge 1979; see also Burge 1981 and 1982.

20. As before, and with no greater chance of success (see Schiffer, forthcoming), the functionalist might try to rebut this argument with a description theoretic construal of the content of Alfred's belief, suggesting that the content of the belief expressed by Alfred's utterance of "I've arthritis in my thigh" is that he has in his thigh the disease called "arthritis" in his linguistic community.

21. One might worry that Alfred in w' is not in all respects functionally equivalent to himself in w, as there will be environment-restricted functional differences owing to the way in which Alfred's use of "arthritis" was acquired in w'. However, as Burge himself painstakingly shows, the example is easily set up so that there really are no functional differences whatever.

22. Block 1980.

23. Kripke 1980; Putnam 1975; Devitt 1981; and Salmon 1981.

24. Kripke 1980, p. 122.

25. Churchland 1981; Stich 1983; Dennett, this volume.

26. Field 1980, p. 102; Field's point is that to state these psychological laws, believing need only be construed as a relation to uninterpreted formulae. See also Field 1984; Fodor 1981; Loar 1981; Schiffer 1980; and Stich 1983.

27. Sometimes the fact that a given person has a certain belief is good evidence that that belief is true. A "reliability theory" of x is a theory that would tell us the ways in which x's beliefs were or were not reliable indicators of external states of affairs, and it has been suggested that semantically characterized beliefs are needed to formulate such theories (see Field 1980; Loar 1981; Schiffer 1980; and Stich 1983). The relevance of reliability considerations to the theory of belief content is discussed in my forthcoming book, *Remnants of Meaning*; here it may simply be noted that (a) it is doubtful that reliability theories fall within the province of cognitive psychology and that (b) "reliability theory" (such as it is) will turn out to need semantically characterized beliefs only in a highly Pickwickian sense that is of no use to the functionalist. Of course I am not saying, and will not say, that beliefs do not have semantic content: my present belief that Nixon is retired is indeed true, and true iff Nixon is retired.

The "*pace*" allusions are to Burge (1984) and Fodor [forthcoming (b), (c)], where a central role for content in cognitive psychology is plumped for.

28. The metaphor is Quine's (1975, p. 91).

29. Stalnaker 1984. See also Dretske, this volume; Fodor, forthcoming (a); Stampe 1979.

30. The fuel gauge example and the attendant claim about mental representation are taken from Dretske (this volume).

31. I am indebted to Stewart Cohen, Brian Loar, Keith Quillen, and Richard Warner for their very helpful comments on an earlier draft of this article.

Bibliography

Block, N. 1980. Troubles with functionalism. In *Readings in philosophy of psychology*. Vol. 1, ed. N. Block. Cambridge: Harvard Univ. Press.

Boyd, R. 1980. Materialism without reductionism: What physicalism does not entail. In *Readings in philosophy of psychology*. Vol. 1, ed. N. Block. Cambridge: Harvard Univ. Press.

Burge, T. 1979. Individualism and the mental. In *Midwest studies in philosophy*. Vol. IV; *Studies in metaphysics,* ed. P. A. French, T. E. Uehling, and H. D. Wettstein. Minneapolis: Univ. of Minnesota Press.

———. 1981. Other bodies. In *Thought and object*, ed. A. Woodfield. Oxford: Oxford Univ. Press.

———. 1982. Two thought experiments reviewed. *Notre Dame Journal of Formal Logic* 23:284–293.

———. 1984. Individualism and psychology. Paper presented at the Sloan Conference. MIT.

Carnap, R. 1947. *Meaning and necessity*. Chicago: Univ. of Chicago Press.

Churchland, P. M. 1981. Eliminative materialism and propositional attitudes. *Journal of Philosophy* 78:67–89.

Devitt, M. 1981. *Designation*. New York: Columbia Univ. Press.

Field, H. 1980. Mental representation. In *Readings in philosophy of psychology*. Vol. 2, ed. N. Block. Cambridge: Harvard Univ. Press.

———. 1984. Thought without content. Paper presented at the Sloan Conference. MIT.

Fodor, J. A. 1981. Methodological solipsism considered as a research strategy in cognitive psychology. In *RePresentations*. Cambridge: MIT Press, Bradford.

———. Forthcoming (a). Psychosemantics—or where do truth conditions come from?

———. Forthcoming (b). Narrow content.

———. Forthcoming (c). Banish disContent.

Kripke, S. A. 1980. *Naming and necessity*. Cambridge: Harvard Univ. Press.

Lewis, D. 1970. How to define theoretical terms. *Journal of Philosophy* 67:427–446.

———. 1971. An argument for the identity theory. In *Materialism and the mind–body problem*, ed. D. Rosenthal. Englewood Cliffs, N.J.: Prentice–Hall.

———. 1980a. Psychophysical and theoretical identifications. In *Readings in philosophy of psychology*. Vol. 1, ed. N. Block. Cambridge: Harvard Univ. Press.

———. 1980b. Mad pain and martian pain. In *Readings in philosophy of psychology*. Vol. 1, ed. N. Block. Cambridge: Harvard Univ. Press.

Loar, B. 1981. *Mind and meaning*. Cambridge: Cambridge Univ. Press.

Owens, J. 1983. Functionalism and propositional attitudes. *Nous* 17:529–549.

Putnam, H. 1975. The meaning of "meaning." *Philosophical papers*. Vol. II, *Mind, language, and reality*. Cambridge: Cambridge Univ. Press.

Quine, W. V. O. 1975. Mind and verbal dispositions. In *Mind and language, Wolfson College lectures, 1974*. Oxford: Oxford Univ. Press.

Ramsey, F. P. 1978. Theories. In *Foundations*, ed. D. H. Mellor. London: Routledge and Kegan Paul.

Salmon, N. U. 1981. *Reference and essence*. Princeton, N.J.: Princeton Univ. Press.

Schiffer, S. 1980. Truth and the theory of content. In *Meaning and understanding*, ed. H. Parrot and J. Bouveresse. Berlin/New York: de Gruyter.

———. Forthcoming. The real trouble with propositions. In *Belief*, ed. R. Bogdan. Oxford: Oxford Univ. Press.

Stalnaker, R. 1984. *Inquiry*. Cambridge: MIT Press, Bradford.

Stampe, D. W. 1979. Toward a causal theory of linguistic representation. In *Contemporary perspectives in the philosophy of language*, ed. P. A. French, T. E. Uehling, Jr., and H. K. Wettstein. Minneapolis: Univ. of Minnesota Press.

Stich, S. P. 1983. *From folk psychology to cognitive science: The case against belief*. Cambridge: MIT Press, Bradford.

Thoughts about Things

For years and years, philosophers took thoughts and *beliefs* to be modifications of incorporeal Cartesian egos. Happily, since early in the present century, it has become clearer that believers are complex organisms embedded in natural, physical environments and nothing (metaphysically) more than that; materialism in one form or another has prevailed ever since. Yet the mere rejection of spookstuff has done little or nothing to illuminate the positive nature of thought and belief. We have heard it said (in effect) that to believe that P is to act or be disposed to act as if one believed that P (that was in the 1940s), or perhaps to have one's B_P-fibers firing (1950s), or to be in some state or other that instantiates square B_P of whatever Turing Machine table applies (1960s), or for the belief that P to be predictively attributable to one (1970s). Only with the comparatively recent resurgence of interest in intentionality itself and with the attending of philosophy to "cognitive science" have we begun to see where to look for a more substantive idea of what a belief might be and to detail the ontological anatomy of believing.

This paper is a modest contribution to the anatomical project. I want to distinguish several kinds of doxastic *aboutness* and in the process to explicate the traditional notion of "belief *de re*" in terms of the psychological model of believing that I have been defending of late.[1] Then, after clearing up a few misconceptions about belief *de re*, I shall note the impact of Putnam and Fodor's "methodological solipsism" on that notion and gesture towards the usefulness of *de re* belief-ascriptions for psychology despite their violation of the solipsistic constraint.

In case anyone is not already vividly aware of the fact, I should mention that philosophers' treatment of belief *de re* over the past decade is a disgusting mess. I doubt that any two contributors to the literature have used the expression "*de re*" in just the same way; between terminological confusion and substantive divergence of theoretical goals and interests, writers on this topic have spent most of their time and ink talking past each other. For this reason one might want to urge a total moratorium on the use of the term "*de re*" and its apparent antonym, "*de dicto*," the moratorium perhaps backed by the death penalty or at least mutilation followed by transportation to Yazoo City, Mississippi. I have great sympathy with this proposal myself. Yet I cannot resist one last attempt (*just* before the moratorium goes into effect) at showing that the phenomena which have occasioned talk of *de re* belief are manifestations of something about believers that is worth tracking down and taking seriously. If I fail, I will try for a fast getaway.

I fall in with the view that to believe (occurrently[2]) that P is to harbor a representation-that-P. That is in turn to be in an inner state which falls under each of two classifications: The state is a *belief* that P in virtue of the type of functional role it plays, the type of job it performs within its subject's internal bureaucracy. (What makes a state a belief as opposed to a desire or an intention is that the state is a form of storage and/or is part of a map that serves its subject as a guide to action, chiefly by affording predictions as to outcomes.) The state is a belief *that P*—it is of the "that-P" type or, as Wilfrid Sellars would put it, the state is a ·P·—in that it has a certain internal structure, in virtue of which it bears certain inferential relations to other actual and possible belief states and certain causal and/or teleological relations to things out in the world. A representation is an inner state of an organism that has both a distinctive causal surface, responsible for the inferential relations aforementioned, and semantical content, determined by the relations to things in the world. I think of representations as formulas in their host's "language of thought," though this way of speaking has led some people grotesquely to overstate the commitments of the representationalist theory and to advance accordingly misguided objections.[3]

A plausible theory of belief-ascriptions fits nicely with the ontological account of beliefs that I have just sketched. Sellars, Donald Davidson,[4] and others have argued that the sentential complement of a belief sentence is profferred as an *exemplar* of the belief content being ascribed and is demonstrated by the complementizer "that"; thus,

(1) Kate believes that there are no black swans in America.

is to be understood as something like

(2) Kate believes *that*. → THERE ARE NO BLACK
SWANS IN AMERICA

or better, as

(3) Kate believes one of *those*. → | There are no black swans in America |

A sentence of another natural language such as French or Kwakiutl could count as "one of those," and so, Sellars maintains, could a formula of one's language-of-thought, i.e., a brain state having the right sort of internal structure. Therefore if Chantal is in a position to bear the "belief" relation to such an item in French or in her language-of-thought, she can believe *that* there are no black swans in America despite her total unacquaintance with English. An English speaker who ascribes this belief to Chantal uses a (complement-)sentence of his or her own tongue to classify or "index" Chantal's inner belief state.

But what allows either a linguistic token or a brain state to count as "one of those"? Answers vary among proponents of the Sellarsian theory. Sellars himself goes for sameness of *inferential* role, where "inference" is understood broadly enough to include "language-entry" and "language-exit" moves. Davidson invokes an unexplained relation of "samesaying," though given his well-known ideas about meaning we might expect him to cash this in terms of sameness of truth-condition or sameness of truth-condition plus some stronger sort of intensional isomorphism. Subsequent theorists line up on either side. My own view[5] is that there is no single answer and that in fact two quite different classificatory schemes are used by belief-ascribers depending on their interests and conversational purposes of the moment. One scheme types belief-tokens according to inferential, causal, or computational roles, the other according to truth-condition. That these two are *different* ways of classifying beliefs I take to be the minimal lesson of Putnam and Fodor's arguments for methodological solipsism; surprisingly, perhaps (until one thinks about it), beliefs' causal roles do not determine their truth-conditions nor their truth-conditions their causal roles. (The best quick illustration of this two-way failure is the case of indexical beliefs, more on which shortly.) Thus, I predict a systematic ambiguity in belief-ascriptions, and I have argued that this prediction is confirmed in a way that allows us to resolve such anomalies as "Kripke's Puzzle."[6] However, for purposes of this paper, I shall focus my attention on the truth-conditional individuation scheme, for it is appeal to that scheme rather than to the inferential or computational scheme that creates issues about *de re* belief.

Now that I have sketched a theory of believing and a companion theory of belief-ascription, what can we say about the *aboutness* of beliefs? A great advantage of the representationalist theory is that in assimilating belief-states to linguistic items it allows us to understand their aboutness as being of a piece with that of sentences. Sentences are about objects and states of affairs by containing referring terms that denote those objects and states of affairs; thus, if belief-states have quasi-syntactic and -semantic structures of the sort I have suggested, it is natural to suppose that their aboutness too consists in their having referring terms as elements, that denote things in the world (though the referential relations here are admittedly problematic in that they are unmediated by the sorts of convention that do and must figure in public linguistic reference).

As a first pass, then, let us say that a thought or belief is about an object X if and only if it is a case of its subject's hosting (in the appropriate way) a representation containing a "singular term" or individual concept that semantically denotes X, "denote" here being interpreted as broadly as Frege might have intended it. Thus, if I say to myself, "There are black swans in Western Australia," this thought is about Western Australia, and if Kate says to herself, "The first baby born in the Northern Territory must have had a hard life," her thought is about whichever person was that baby (I do not know if anyone knows who it was) and is true or false according to whether that person did in fact have a hard life.

So far, so good. But readers of Quine's "Quantifiers and Propositional Attitudes"[7] will know that the matter of aboutness only begins here, even if we accept representationalism and all its abundant benefits and advantages. For there seems to be at least one stronger notion of aboutness which is not captured by the fairly liberal criterion I have just formulated. Indeed, that there is such a notion is suggested just by the fact that "believe that" functions surface-grammatically as a sentence operator, for sentence operators have scope and so can give rise to scope distinctions when mixed either with singular terms or with quantifiers:

(4) a. Kate believes that the first baby born in the Northern Territory had a hard life.
  b. The first baby born in the Northern Territory is such that Kate believes it to have had a hard life.
(5) a. Kate believes that there are black swans in Brisbane.

    b. There are things which Kate believes { are / to be} black swans in Brisbane.

    c. There are black swans which Kate believes { are / to be } in Brisbane.

(4a) and (4b) differ in meaning, as do (5a), (5b), and (5c). Notoriously, Quine offered the following *Ur*-examples:

$$(6) \text{ I want a sloop}$$

is ambiguous as between there being a particular sloop that I want and my seeking "mere relief from slooplessness":

    (6r) (Ex) (x is a sloop and I wish that I have x)
    (6d) I wish (Ex) (x is a sloop and I have x)

Suppose too that (the now world-famous character) Ralph is aware that espionage is prevalent and also thinks that no two people are of exactly the same height. Then, being a competent logician and a bit of a pedant, Ralph idly forms the redundant belief that the shortest spy is a spy, having no idea which person that might be. As Quine puts it, Ralph has no suspect; there is not one in particular whom Ralph believes to be a spy. That is, although

    (7d) Ralph believes that ($\imath x$) (x is the shortest spy) is a spy

is unexcitingly true,

    (7r) ($\imath x$) (x is the shortest spy) is a y such that Ralph believes that y is a spy

is false. Note that the singular term in (7r) occurs transparently; if the shortest spy *were* suspected or believed in particular by Ralph to be a spy and Tatiana is in fact the shortest spy, then Tatiana is Ralph's suspect whether he knows her name or not. I would claim also, though this is at least mildly controversial, that (7d) would be true whether or not there were any spies at all (much less a shortest spy), while (7r) entails the actual existence of a shortest spy and expresses a relation between Ralph and that person.

    The relevance of all this to our proposed criterion of aboutness is that although according to that criterion Ralph has a belief about Tatiana, there is an important sense in which his belief is not *about* Tatiana in particular at all. Intuitively speaking, it is a fully *general* belief, tautologously inferred from the bare existence of espionage and the claim that any two people differ in height. Tatiana herself is related to Ralph by his belief *only* in that by sheer coincidence she uniquely satisfies the matrix of the description occurring in his representation. The representation seems a perfect instance of Russell's Theory of Descriptions: it is equivalent to the bare thesis that there exists a spy shorter than every other spy. Thus Ralph's belief could be true *whether or not Tatiana even existed,* so long as there were other spies and one of them was shorter than all the others; to put the point in possible-worlds jargon, Ralph's belief is true at any world containing *a* shortest spy, whether or not Tatiana herself inhabits that world. And it is at least in that sense that his belief is not *about* her.

Quine speaks of *relational* as opposed to merely "notional" belief and assimilates this difference to the medieval distinction between modalities *de re* and modalities *de dicto.* Just as

(8d) Necessarily, all tall spies are tall

fails to imply

(8r) All tall spies are necessarily tall

(since any actual tall spy you mention might have been short instead of tall)

(9d) Ralph believes that all tall spies are tall

fails to imply

(9r) All tall spies are {believed by Ralph to be / such that Ralph believes that they are} tall,

since none of the actual tall spies is an object of Ralph's attention; he has never heard of any of them. These data seem both hard and significant. The problem is to say what is needed for the *"de re"* formulations such as (4b), (5b), (5c), (6r), (7r), (8r), and (9r) to be true in addition to their bland *de dicto* counterparts.[8]

It should be noted that one recent philosophical tradition, inaugurated by Ernest Sosa and Mark Pastin among others[9] and called "latitudinarianism," repudiates the stronger sort of aboutness illustrated here and emphasizes the weaker sort that we have already granted. Indeed, latitudinarians have spent a good deal of energy defending aboutness of the weaker sort *as* aboutness, unnecessarily from my point of view. What is more distinctive and remarkable about their position is that they want to deny the falsity of our *de re* formulations in the circumstances imagined. If they are to make this denial convincing they must somehow explain away the appearances, i.e., they must show why the *de re* formulations seem false and would be expected to seem false even though in reality they are true. The most obvious way of doing this is to appeal to independently justified principles of conversation *a la* Grice, but I have seen no very convincing instance of this strategy. Note too that

> (10) Ralph believes that espionage is prevalent, but he does not suspect anyone in particular

is noncontradictory, so there must be *some* stronger belief relation than the latitudinarian is willing to grant.[10] For these reasons I shall presume the falsity of latitudinarianism for the purposes of this paper.

Investigators have supposed that some one factor or complex of factors is required for *de re* belief over and above minimal aboutness, though they have admitted both that no such factor stands uncontroversially in view and that the correct one, whatever it is, may well turn out to be messy and perhaps highly interest-relative. I think instead that there is a sequence of discriminable *grades* of aboutness, beginning with our bare *de dicto* or latitudinarian aboutness and terminating in a paradigm case of aboutness, a sort of arch-aboutness. Let me enumerate them.

Our initial complaint about Ralph's purely general belief and its effete relation to Tatiana is that Tatiana herself did not figure in its truth-condition. Ralph's description "the shortest spy" disappears on analysis in Russell's way, leaving no *genuine* singular term behind; indeed, if we think of Ralph's language-of-thought as a fully disambiguated logical idiom admitting no further analysis, *it* contains no Russellian descriptions at all but only the corresponding quantifiers and general terms. This underscores the anemia of the "relation" between Ralph's belief-state and the living, breathing Tatiana. As a first step in the direction of full *de re*-ness, let us require that Tatiana herself figure in the truth-condition of any belief that is (more) strongly about her—that such a belief cannot be true at a possible world unless Tatiana herself exists at that world and, more specifically, that even if there is a shortest spy at that world who is other than Tatiana, that spy's spyhood is irrelevant to the truth of (7r). The belief reported by (7r) is true at a world if and only if Tatiana is a spy at that world. If we recast this description back into the vernacular of "propositions," the proposition believed by Ralph according to (7r) is a "singular proposition,"[11] a proposition containing Tatiana herself as a constituent rather than any description of her.

But there are at least two different ways in which Tatiana might "figure in" a belief's truth-condition. (In some of my earlier writings on this topic[12] I did not distinguish them.) We think of *de re* belief as involving *contact* of some sort between the believer and the subject of his belief, but this need not hold of our current grade of aboutness as defined, for we have ways of dragging particular individuals into the truth-conditions of inner and outer utterances both, without "contact" of any sort having occurred. As David Kaplan has pointed out,[13] expressions like "actual" and "in fact" serve to tie the truth-conditions of sentences in which they occur to this-wordly referents even when the sentences are being evaluated relative to other worlds. Ralph's belief that *the actual* winner of the 1980 election is nice but subnormal is true at a world w if and only if Ronald Reagan is nice but subnormal at w, regardless of the personality or intelligence of whoever won the 1980 election at w. (Alvin Plantinga has pointed out[14] that the same rigidifying effect can be achieved by "world-indexing" one's descriptions, as in "the winner of the 1980 election *at our world / in the real world*.") In this way I can have a belief *about* the person who will be the first woman President—a belief in whose truth-condition *she* figures regardless of her presidency or even of her womanhood—despite the total lack of contact between her and me, and needless to say without my having the slightest idea who she will be. This second-grade aboutness answers to the latter key intuition regarding *de re* belief, but it falls short of full-fledgedness in at least two respects: (i) the lack of contact itself, and (ii) the fact that the relevant "singular term" appearing in the believer's representation achieves its reference only by exploiting its descriptive content—Reagan "figures in" Ralph's belief about the actual winner only in virtue of satisfying the description "wins the 1980 election at the actual world," and the first woman President figures in my belief about "the first woman President" only in virtue of her actually being President (which is not—*n.b.*—to deny that the belief's truth-value is determined at another world by *that* woman's properties rather than by those of whomever is woman-President first at that world). If we accept Plantinga's formulation and allow his world-indexed descriptions to be Russellized away (as he does), we see that the only genuine singular term left in my representation is some name of the actual world, our world, itself. This encourages the idea that there is some still more intimate way in which a belief could be about someone: though I believe about her that she will be both lucky and intelligent, she is not such that I believe her *in particular* to be lucky and intelligent; I imagine she will not so much as be born until after my death. (The use of the apparently scope-specifying phrase "in particular" is beginning to seem relative to grade-of-aboutness; this needs investigation.)

Thus it seems there is still a further grade of aboutness yet to be captured, one which involves "contact" and which is not essentially mediated by purely descriptive Russellian denotation. The idea of "contact" more than suggests causality, and this suggestion comes as no surprise to any fan of *de re* belief. Some theorists, such as Kaplan,[15] have proposed outright that a believer's representation (-token) must contain a singular term *causally grounded in* Tatiana if it is to be genuinely *de* Tatiana. Others have proposed epistemic requirements, such as that the beliver "know who" Tatiana is, have her somehow "in his ken,"[16] be "acquainted" or "*en rapport*" with her, or at least know some key things about her. The epistemic requirements seem to presuppose the initial causal condition, since (on my view) one could not bear any such relation to Tatiana unless one were causally connected to her—unless she had brought herself or been brought to one's attention. A further motivation for the minimal causal requirement is that one feels *de re* belief of the third grade to be a *real relation,* so to speak, a real relation in nature between the believer and the subject of the belief. Cognate with this is the idea that my believing *de re* of someone that she is F suffices for its being a *real property* of that person that she is believed by me to be F. It is in no way natural to say, on the basis of (7d) alone, that Tatiana is suspected by Ralph of being a spy, or even believed by Ralph to be a spy [just as (8d) attributes no property to any individual, whereas (8r) says that every tall spy has not only the property of being tall but that of being necessarily-tall]. Thus, let us say that a belief has third-grade aboutness if and only if the believer's representation contains a singular term the occurrence of which is causally grounded in[17] the object which figures appropriately in the representation's truth-condition. It is this requirement that is unsatisfied by my belief about the first woman President, and it is nicely underwritten by causal theories of *genuine reference* for natural languages.

Even here, dramatic distinctions are available. For causal contact can be made under what are epistemically the most discouraging of circumstances. Recall a justly famous case of Keith Donnellan's,[18] in which we come upon the horribly savaged body of Smith and judge on the spot that Smith's murderer is insane. I maintain that this judgment is so far ambiguous: we could (and probably would) mean that *whoever* murdered Smith is insane. But we could also mean that whoever *actually* murdered Smith is insane, so that our belief would be true if Tatiana (the real murderer) is insane even though we have never heard of her and even though we might even have someone else—Yuri, say— tentatively in mind at the same time. Note that Tatiana does here satisfy our causal requirement for third-grade aboutness, since our belief that Smith's murderer is insane is the last member of a causal chain whose earlier links include the perceptual state that produced it, the hideous condition of Smith's body which produced the perceptual state, and Tatiana, who produced the hideous condition. Yet this is still not a case in which we feel Tatiana herself is believed by us to be insane. Why not?

Several answers come to mind. Perhaps the most popular would be (a) that we lack the proper sort of *epistemic* contact with Tatiana, mentioned above, even though the bare minimal causal condition is satisfied. By the same token, (b) the causal chain is too indirect; Tatiana's getaway, disguise, prepared alibi, etc., serve as a screen that prevents us from *following* the causal chain backwards in pursuit of the culprit, at least without extraordinary detective skill and effort on our part. (c) The description under which we think of Tatiana (insofar as we are thinking *of* her at all) still feels too official, *even though it is rigidified.* It seems—almost as if it were not rigid—to specify a role rather than an occupant; we know it denotes the same individual at any world (and so does in that sense specify an occupant), but we still have to add "whoever that may be."

This last point, or feeling, can be spelled out a little more precisely as follows. How is the valuation function for our language-of-thought computed when it takes our mental token of "Smith's murderer" as argument? That is, how is the referent of that token determined? Clearly, by reference to the property of having murdered Smith; our token has conceptual content that is contingently true of Tatiana and denotes her by exploiting that content even though on our rigidified interpretation the description as a whole is necessarily true of her. Note that although an appropriate causal chain exists, it plays no role in the determination of reference: if we had tokened the rigidified description "Smith's murder" even *without* having seen the grisly evidence, the token would have denoted Tatiana just as surely and in just the way it does now. In this sense, it does not *designate* or *refer to* Tatiana even though it denotes her *and* is causally grounded in her.

We have (at least) two choices: to give our causal-chain requirement more prominence in the determination of reference, or to revert to an epistemic requirement that subsumes the causal chain. For reasons which will become clear later on, I prefer the former option, and at this point I shall re-emphasize the causal chain by tying it to Kaplan's notion of "direct reference."

In a public natural language, ordinary proper names refer without expressing contingent properties of their bearers, or so Kripke, Kaplan, and others[19] have persuasively argued. *Contra* Russell, names are not semantically equivalent to descriptions of the form "whoever or whatever is the so-and-so." Semantically speaking, they refer directly, and their referents are determined *solely* by the (appropriately shaped) causal chains that ground them in their referents. (N.B., this is not to say that a speaker's use of such a name is unaided by what Frege called a "mode of presentation," as a matter of psychology; it is only to deny that the name *semantically expresses* the content of that mode of presentation.) Now, I suggest that direct reference of this sort occurs in languages-of-thought as well: mental tokens are causally grounded in objects and thereby refer to those objects without expressing contingent information about them. A mental utterance containing a referring term of this sort expresses a "singular proposition," i.e., one which has the referent itself as a constituent rather than any conceptual representation of that referent. Now we may define a fourth grade of aboutness: A thought is about a thing in this fourth sense just in case some element of the thought *directly* refers to that thing. This condition is unsatisfied by us vis-à-vis Tatiana as we view all that is mortal of Smith.

Objection: The referent *itself* is supposed to figure in the content of a thought if that thought is to count as *about* it in the fourth sense. But this is absurd. The referent itself is not inside my head, nor does a bit of brain extend itself from my eyeball and touch upon the referent ever so lightly. (If one did, Tatiana would doubtless be surprised.)[20] What is *in my head* is at best a representation of Tatiana, and one that is directed toward her from a point of view; it seems undeniable that I can think of her only under some mode of presentation or other. Does this not deep-six the "direct reference" theory at one blow?

No, it does not, though it is plainly true. When I said that a mental token could refer without *expressing* any contingent property of its referent, I meant that no such property *figured in the truth-condition* of the containing judgment, even though the mental name is of course associated at any given time with one or more perspectival modes of presentation that account for the name's own causal powers and computational role within the believer's psychology. The key point here is the nature of this "association." Traditionally it has been taken to be a semantical matter; the name has been thought to incorporate the mode of presentation as part of its meaning. But this is a mistake, born of failure to distinguish our two schemes for individuating belief contents. Indeed, it is born of uncritical use of words like "content." As is easily shown by indexical examples such as those discussed by John Perry,[21] there is no single notion of "content" that will accommodate all our intuitions concerning sameness-of-belief. The traditional notion must be cracked in two. I maintain[22] that it splits into *proposition-expressed* in the truth-conditional sense and *inferential/ computational role*, an innercausal notion.[23]. Beliefs can differ in proposition-expressed despite their sameness of inferential role ("I am in danger"), and vice versa ("Yes, you are in danger"). This, I contend, is what happens in the case of direct reference. The mode of presentation exists, and indisputably, but figures in inferential role *rather than* truth-condition. As I put it in "The Paradox of Naming," mental names do not abbreviate descriptions (nor are they equivalent to them in any other semantical way); they merely share their inner functional roles from time to time. And this defuses the objection; our fourth mode of aboutness is secure.[24]

Even fourth-grade aboutness does not always live up to our *paradigm* of *de re* belief, for a believer may make direct reference to something even under epistemically impoverished circumstances. I can refer directly to Tully, in speech or thought, without knowing anything about him other than that he is said by Quine to be identical with the Roman orator Cicero. For some people that would be insufficient to warrant a heartfelt ascription of *de re* belief. They want a tighter causal connection that (as David Lewis puts it[25]) carries important *information* about Tully; they want epistemic contact, *intimate* contact—perceptual contact if they can get it. Thus we might define a fifth grade of aboutness, characterized by direct reference *plus* some "ken"-relation, an epistemic intimacy requirement. (This is one way of understanding Kaplan's proposal in "Quantifying In" (1969); Lewis and others have since defended such a view of the *de re*.) Here things get fuzzy, in part because no clear "ken"-relation has ever been settled on by fans of fifth-grade aboutness and in part because the intimacy requirement seemingly carried by the *de re* locutions of ordinary language are themselves interest-relative and controlled by social and other features of conversational context;[26] but there are some uncontroversially clear cases. Direct visual contact is one; direct visual contact plus manual grabbing accompanied by shouts of "*This* guy! THIS VERY PERSON!!" is perhaps the clearest.

I suppose there is in principle a *sixth* grade of aboutness: that which Russell himself had in mind throughout his discussions of the present topic. This grade requires direct *and epistemically unmediated* acquaintance with one's referent, so diaphanous that one cannot be thus acquainted with one object in two ways at the same time, at least without being aware that the two acquaintings have the same object. (Failure of the latter condition would entail the existence of an interposed representation of the object.) Thus, we cannot be acquainted with ordinary physical objects in this Russellian way; with physical objects there is always the possibility that I might bear each of two perceptual relations to one, no matter how intimate, without realizing that the objects of these relations are one and the same. The only sort of entity which I could think about in our sixth way would be a sense-datum. If like Russell we believe in sense-data, we have a truly *ultimate* grade of *de re*-ness, 100% and not just 99 $^{44}/_{100}$% pure, and can regard fifth-grade aboutness as a cheap imitation (Russell himeslf did not countenance aboutness of any but the first and sixth kinds). If, on the other hand, we reject sense-data as we rejected spookstuff, fifth-grade aboutness is the nearest fuzzy approximation.[27].

Is there, now, a single distinction between attitudes *de dicto* and attitudes *de re*? Or has that distinction shattered into fragments corresponding to our various grades of aboutness? We introduced the notion of *de re* in terms of a logical scope distinction and the permissibility of "exportation" or "quantifying in." But logical properties alone will not help us mark anything like the traditional distinction, for intuitively, existential generalization is valid whenever an extensional relation holds between thought and object, and even our first grade of aboutness establishes *an* extensional relation between believer and semantic denotatum (this is the latitudinarian's initial insight). To mark the traditional distinction in a well-motivated way we must look for a natural break in the series of grades of aboutness. And such a break is there: between grades three and four. We saw that despite the causal connection that obtains in a case of type three ("Smith's murderer" rigidly understood), the *mechanism* of reference in that case involves descriptive material and role-filling *rather than* the causal chain. Moreover, as we saw, a thought of type three expresses a singular proposition only insofar as it may refer to *the actual world,* @, itself, not a singular proposition involving the thought's denotatum as a constituent. For these reasons, third-grade aboutness differs in no theoretically significant way from second-grade aboutness.

It might be argued that the fourth-grade/fifth-grade distinction is more salient and important than the third-grade/fourth-grade distinction. Indeed, this would have been the dominant view until direct-reference theories came into vogue a decade ago. But I do not think it can be sustained, for the fourth-grade/fifth-grade distinction is *in*distinct, fuzzy, and interest-relative, while the third-grade/fourth-grade distinction is clear as a bell. Moreover, fourth-grade thoughts express "singular propositions" just as fifth-grade ones do; and it is hard to think of a case of direct mental reference that intuitively falls on the *de dicto* side of the traditional distinction.[28] I conclude that our natural break is between the third and fourth grades; if so, it is best to identify *de re*-ness with aboutness of the fourth grade or higher.[29]

What, then, of scope? That is a question about belief-*ascription*, not about belief itself.[30] Yet we can say this: *De re* belief in our sense is paradigmatically well reported by existential, universal, or individual quantification into a doxastic context, such as (4b), (5b), (5c), (7r), or (9r), since the referent of the belief appears *in propria persona* in the belief's truth-condition, rather than being represented by a descriptive proxy. Belief in a singular proposition *relates* the believer to the individual constituent of the proposition precisely for that reason, and the relation is nicely explicable in terms of the believer's hosting a representation that refers directly to that constituent.

As the latitudinarians argue, this excellent basis for quantifying in is not the only possible basis; as I pointed out earlier, one *may* perform existential generalization any time a belief relates an object extensionally to the believer. So (to take the most extreme case) there is *a* sense in which even the first grade of aboutness licenses quantifying in, a sense in which Tatiana is believed by Ralph to be a spy even though he has never heard of her and could not conceivably suspect her. But this sense is uninteresting, for the *relation* between Ralph and Tatiana in virtue of which existential generalization holds is uninteresting. (i) The relation is not secured by Ralph's proposition alone; an extraneous contingent fact about Tatiana is needed to complete the connection. (ii) Though genuine and extensional, the relation is not a "real relation in nature"—this, I think, lies behind our feelings about "contact"—but a composite relation one element of which is semantical (Tatiana's satisfying the matrix of Ralph's description). This is why latitudinarian quantification is unnatural even though it is interpretable.[31]

With all this in place, I shall pause to note a few features of my view in relation to the standard literature and to correct what I consider misconceptions that are harmful and widespread.[32]

1. Though aboutness of the fifth kind requires epistemic activity of some sort, belief *de re* has little if anything to do with *knowing who*, despite one's odd tendency to express intuitions of *de re*-ness or non-*de re*-ness by mobilizing indirect-question clauses. The notion of "knowing who" is as highly context dependent as is whatever epistemic notion figures in the analysis of fifth-grade aboutness, and this may encourage identification of the two. But in fact the interest-relativity of knowing-who far outruns that of fifth-grade aboutness, and its parameters are controlled in quite different ways.[33] Steven Boër and I argued this at stupefying length in "Knowing Who" (1975), but there are also quickie examples that illustrate the point: (A) Perry White has Clark Kent by the throat and is berating him for his timidity in chasing down stories. "Useless chicken ✱✱✱✱ milquetoast!!" he screams. That is a clear case of fifth-grade aboutness, and certainly White believes *of* Kent that he is a milquetoast; but he does not thereby *know who Kent is* for any but the most obvious and crude immediate purposes such as that of backhanding him. He has a belief *de* Kent, period, but knows who Kent is and knows of Kent who he is, only for some purposes and not others. (B) Jones is a rich man of great worldly power, who happens to enjoy slumming. He has a beat-up old Maverick

and likes to drive around seedy neighborhoods. One day, in the very worst of these neighborhoods, he runs over Gonzo's foot. Enraged (and hopping on his other foot), Gonzo chases after Jones' car and manages to catch it. He drags Jones from behind the wheel, looks at him long and carefully, and says, "Now I know what you look like. If I catch you in this neighborhood again I'll rip your ****ing lungs out." Then he slaps Jones around a bit and lets him go. Here Gonzo certainly has some attitudes *de* Jones. But Zonker, standing by, observes sardonically and correctly that Gonzo does not know who it is that he has been slapping around. (C) You are a police detective, investigating a murder and talking flaccidly or attributively about "the murderer." You prove that whoever did the murder is (again attributively) the person who lives at such-and-such an address. Then for present purposes (that of laying hands on the culprit and throwing him in jail), you do know who the murderer is; but we may suppose you have no attitudes *de* him in the sense of fifth-grade aboutness, since you have not yet tracked him down at the address in question. Thus, in some contexts there is knowing-who without *de re* belief. The moral is again that the parameters of "knowing who" are far less tightly circumscribed than are those of fifth-grade aboutness.

2. It is currently fashionable to deny that *de re/de dicto* is a distinction between *beliefs*: "There aren't two kinds of belief, but only, two kinds of belief-*ascription*."[34] I applaud this as an attempt to separate thoughts from their ascription, but it is not quite right as it stands. What is true is that (a) there are not two *mutually exclusive* kinds of belief, since on my view the *de re* is but a special case of the *de dicto*; and certainly that (b) the word "believe" is not ambiguous as between "relational" and "notional" *senses;*[35] and that (c) (in Dennett's words) there are not "two different sorts of mental phenomena," if by that he means psychologically different sorts. But there are (nevertheless) two kinds of belief: *de dicto* beliefs that are also *de re,* and *de dicto* beliefs that are not. The difference lies in the different sorts of truth-condition they have, and as we shall see, in the differential impact of "methodological solipsism" on them respectively.

3. I explicate the *de re* as a special case of the *de dicto*.[36] This is sharply at variance with the view presented by Tyler Burge in his paper, "Belief *De Re*."[37] He insists both that the *de dicto* and the *de re* are mutually exclusive and that the *de re* is psychologically if not conceptually prior to the *de dicto*.

I find Burge's initial conception of the traditional distinction very peculiar (no doubt he will find mine reciprocally peculiar). For him the root idea of the *de dicto* is that of a *fully general* belief whose truth-value is entirely context independent. Accordingly, he defines *de re* belief simply as *deictic* belief, where what is believed is in effect an open rather than a closed sentence or proposition. I agree that a deictic belief will most likely be *de re* in my sense as well, since all the indexical pronouns, etc., that make for deixis are devices of direct reference and create fourth-grade aboutness (though tense may be an exception if it does not involve reference at all). But it does not follow that a *de re* belief is not also *de dicto*; a deictic belief is a belief *de* an indexical dictum. (If there were no indexicals in the language of thought there would be no problem about indexical attitudes, and no solutions to those problems either.) Nor does it follow, by the same token, that the *de re* is irreducible to *or* conceptually prior to the *de dicto,* though it remains true as Burge says that if we did not begin with *de re* beliefs we would almost certainly never acquire any *de dicto* beliefs.

(The reason I find Burge's initial conception peculiar is that it is not directly suggested either by Quine's original data (6) through (7r) or by the medieval distinction applying to the alethic modalities. Burge shows himself well aware of these historical antecedents and argues that his own distinction is philosophically more crucial than the traditional one, but his argument seems to me flawed.[38])

4. It follows from my view that one cannot have a *de re* attitude toward a nonexistent. This is as it should be, or so I have argued independently elsewhere;[39] nonexistents can be known only by description. But some theories of believing allow beliefs *de* nonexistents,[40] and if I am right, they are wrong—or at least, their proponents' initial conceptions of the *de re* must be carefully distinguished from mine.

Let us turn at last to methodological solipsism. Putnam and Fodor[41] are concerned with enforcing the distinction between what is "in the head" and what is not; Twin-Earth and indexical examples are now familiar. Only what is "autonomously" in the head can be a direct cause of behavior, and no property that I do not share with a molecular duplicate of myself can play an indispensable role in the explanation of my behavior, if my behavior is construed as brute physical motion. Now, there could be no clearer case of a nonautonomous, nonsolipsistic notion than that of *de re* belief as I have defined it. The *de re*-ness of a belief matters nothing to the believer's internal organization but is only an etiological property. Mode of presentation is what matters to behavior; the worldly *object* of the belief does not. In the case of indexical beliefs, sameness of behavior goes with sameness of inner indexical and its computational role, not with sameness of truth-condition. Moreover, as Dennett notes,[42] the truth of a *de re* ascription affords no brute-behavioral predictions: Knowing that I believe *of* the hatchet-murderer of my mother, wife, and daughter that I am now shaking hands with him, what can you predict I will do (even given trite, normal desires and emotions and so on)? Our question, then, is since *de re* belief per se plays no role in the explanation of bodily motions, of what value is it to psychology?

A number of possible answers are suggested by the recent literature on methodological solipsism and the explanatory utility of semantical concepts. Some do not work. I shall close this paper by offering four that I think do work or will when suitably fleshed out. Each takes the predictable form of arguing that a purely solipsistic or "narrow" psychology would miss some useful generalizations about behavior or about something closely related.

Lest anyone think this odd—that a *complete* narrow psychology could miss important generalizations even though it could predict the smallest nods and twitches (are the generalizations upheld by something extraneous to the physical levers and pulleys? Are the predictions made by magic?)—let us recall that the same thing is rife even in (here) noncontroversial sciences such as biology. Useful, important, even lawlike generalizations hold at higher levels of nature without being statable, at least before the heat-death of the universe, in terms of quarks and gluons, and the higher-level theories that capture these generalizations afford predictions that could not be made in "real time" even by a superhuman LaPlacean intelligence if it knew only the microphysical laws that govern the motions of quarks and gluons through the void. (A LaPlacean demon would be frustrated and out-of-place in the macroscopic world we live in.[43]) So we should not be surprised if the same thing holds of psychology that holds of biology, automotive engineering, computer science, and economics. On to the answers.

(I) Nonsolipsistic mental concepts are expendable in the explanation of behavior described as brute physical motion. But most of the behavior we want explained is not described in terms of brute physical motion (and if it were so described, our desire to explain it would vanish). Zenon Pylyshyn has noted[44] that much of it is described rather in *semantical* or at least intentional terms, as in "said *that P*," "tried *to do A*." In order to explain behavior under these descriptions, we have to "carry the intentional interpretation inward" and attribute contentful states to the subject; a person would not say that P if he did not believe that P (unless he had intervening desires), nor try to do A if he did not want to do A.[45]

Even so: one might say (as Stitch does) that even if ordinary people have need of attributing reference and truth to the inner states of others, it does not follow that psychologists do, where "psychologist" is spelled with a capital "ψ". Psychologists may have refined and gerrymandered their data-base, entirely away from the taxonomy that common sense and ordinary language impose on behavior. Indeed, since the language of brute physical motion is far less theory-laden than is everyday action-language, this is methodologically a good thing. On the other hand, it is not, or not commonly, done. I do not know of many experiments actually performed on humans in psychology laboratories that have restricted themselves to the explanation of brute physical motion couched in syntactic machine language. We can if we like make it true by definition that *de re* belief is useless to the Psychologist, but only by also making it true that there are very few actual Psychologists in the real world in 1984.

In appealing to behavior intentionally described rather than physically described, I have begged the question against the fiercest sort of methodological solipsist, who is skeptical about *the whole semantical/intentional package deal* and about intentional description of anything whatever. Such a skeptic would never grant that bits of behavior intentionally described can stand as data to be taken for granted by philosophers, even if they are taken for granted (and unavoidably so) by ordinary people. The intentional description of behavior is laden with precisely the theory (folk psychology) that the skeptic finds so far groundless. Thus, argument (I) has no force at all.

This reply raises a puzzle. That intentional description is folk-theoretical explanation of behavior is a commonplace of current philosophy of mind. As we have seen, however, what it explains is behavior intentionally rather than brutely described; and so the skeptic concludes that its claim to fame is fraudulent, since the intentional description of behavior is as theoretical as is propositional-attitude ascription, and in the same way. Yet, this is not quite right, for as Sellars originally saw, public (particularly linguistic) behavior still precedes intentional psychology in the order of explanation; the notion of public speech is prior to that of private speech or thought and is only later explained by it. In real life, public speech episodes serve as data, in their semantical *rather than* their brute-behavioral guises; people learn semantical descriptions of verbal episodes long before they learn brute-behavioral descriptions, if they *ever* learn brute-behavioral descriptions of oral speech. The point is parallel to one that is commonly urged against sense-datum theories in epistemology: that sense-datum vocabulary is arcane and highly sophisticated in comparison to ordinary talk of public middle-sized objects and is indeed derivative from it. I do not make the corresponding derivativeness claim for the case of brute-behavioral description, but it does seem that speech episodes and other behavior action-theoretically described count as *data* in any ordinary sense of "data" and in at least one technical epistemological sense,[46] despite the fact that in some way or other they presuppose the availability of propositional-attitude explanations. The exact structure of the cycle or circularity here is very unclear to me, but I am loath to think it is vicious. The matter needs much further investigation. Fortunately there are further reasons why the semantical properties of beliefs are not expendable.

(II) Learning and informing seem to require semantics. Chantal says to me, "Il pleut," a sentence I know to be true in her language if and only if it is raining. My best explanation of her saying this is that she believes it is raining and wants me to believe it too. From the additional premises that she is unlikely to be mistaken about the weather (she is looking out the window as she speaks) and that she is unlikely to want to deceive me, I infer that it is raining and thereby learn that it is.[47] I could not have made this inference without relying on the lemma that Chantal's belief is *true*. And in general, if the beliefs people express in speech had no common referents out in the world, we would be forever doomed to talk past each other.

Here too it may be urged that *learning* and *informing* are intentional acts and indeed are most naturally defined precisely in terms of *beliefs* "widely" construed; so the argument is almost explicitly circular. But subjects' ability to use other subjects as authorities, however described, is a highly distinctive and robust phenomenon, an appearance that surely must be saved somehow even if one eschews intentional description. The question then becomes, is there an adequate solipsist account of this phenomenon, that makes no appeal to semantical properties of subjects' inner states? Since solipsist explanations of "behavior" explain only *brute* behavior, as we have seen, and since instances of what we would ordinarily call learning from authority per se have nothing brute-behavioral in common, it is hard to think of any solipsist explanation that has any chance of generalizing across all cases of learning from authority. Such cases seem to form a natural kind in psychology, but intentional characterization seems needed to frame the generalizations whose nexus constitutes this kind.

(III) As Putnam and Richard Boyd have maintained,[48] the truth of beliefs is needed to explain why subjects are so successful in achieving their goals; they are generally successful because their beliefs are usually true and so guide them reliably in action. N.B., truth is not needed to explain *any one* instance of success; any one instance could as well be explained by a narrow, solipsistic functional diagram put together with facts about the subject's immediate environment.[49] But such "divide and conquer" explanations[50] do not generalize across an open-ended history of successful actions.[51] Moreover, we want to generalize across *groups* of people as well. Groups are successful in part because of their propensities for true beliefs and in part because of their intercommunicative abilities [cf. answer (II)], for which semantical notions are also needed.

(IV) We do not know, and probably will never know, any human being's "syntactic code" or uninterpreted machine language. Thus, the assignment of referents (and consequently truth-values) to a subject's thoughts is needed as a way of indexing his internal states. Without cutting him open (and in my case even after cutting him open), we know nothing of his inside; we can describe it only by reference to the outside. The same is true of computers;[52] we speak of some one computer as "computing Robin Roberts' batting average," even though internally it is running exactly in parallel with an identical machine next door whose operator describes *it* as "computing the GNP of Pitcairn," because we do not know what it is doing described in machine code. And (N.B.) both descriptions are *correct*, even though nothing strictly inside either machine suffices for their correctness.

Obviously none of arguments (I)-(IV) is fully convincing as it stands. But I think that together the arguments point in the right direction. At any rate I hope I have shed some light on doxastic aboutness and its uses.[53]

Notes

Some of the material in this paper overlaps, though in considerably different form, parts of chapter 5 of Steven E. Boër and William G. Lycan, *Knowing Who* (1985). There it is set in the context of a rigorous formal theory of belief sentences.

1. See Lycan, 1981c, 1981b, 1984

2. I begin with a theory of *judgment*, rather than of belief *tout court*. I have attacked the problem of nonoccurrent belief, with fairly dismal results, in "Tacit Belief" [forthcoming(b)].

3. See Lycan 1981c, 1984 for rebuttals of a few of these.

4. Sellars 1963, 1967, 1973, and elsewhere.

5. Elaborately defended in Lycan 1981c, 1984.

6. See Lycan 1984. I also contend that my "two-scheme" theory removes any mystery that may linger over attitudes "*de se*," which I take to be only harmlessly special cases of the *de re*; see Lycan 1981a, pp. 148ff.

7. Quine 1966.

8. Recently, in "Intensions Revisited" (1979), Quine has renounced the objectivity of this distinction and proclaimed it radically interest-relative—on which renunciation, see note 33 below.

9. Sosa 1970; Pastin 1974; and Sosa and Pastin 1981. I believe the term "latitudinarian" as it is used here is due to Roderick Chisholm (1976).

10. Latitudinarianism is further embarrassed by the following consequence [I adapt an example from Stephen Schiffer (1978, pp. 203–204)]: Suppose Ralph

believes, falsely, that he holds the world's record for eating the most spaghetti at a single sitting. In fact, Sister Angelica holds that record. Ralph also believes that his wife is completely faithful to him, and so, due to his false belief about the world record, he believes that the holder of the record is the only person who has ever slept with his wife. According to latitudinarianism, it follows from this last fact that Sister Angelica is believed by Ralph to be the only person who has ever slept with his wife. But of course Ralph himself is also believed by himself to be the only person who has done that, even though Ralph knows perfectly well that he and Sister Angelica are distinct. So we have two people, not only distinct but known by Ralph to be distinct, both of whom are believed by Ralph to be the only person who has ever slept with his wife. Though far from fatal, this is very peculiar.

11. See Kaplan 1975.

12. Particularly Boër and Lycan 1975, 1980.

13. Kaplan 1977.

14. Plantinga 1978.

15. Kaplan 1969.

16. As I recall, this term is due to Robert Sleigh.

17. Cf. Devitt 1981.

18. Donnellan 1966, p. 285.

19. Kripke 1972; Kaplan 1977.

20. In this same vein, John Wallace writes, "Our beliefs are a map; but a map of France which had Paris and Vezelay and Mont Blanc [*themselves*, not their names or dots] on it would *be* France (1975, p. 427).

21. Perry 1977, 1979.

22. Lycan 1981c.

23. Brian Loar (1981) speaks of distinguishing "vertical" from "horizontal" aspects of belief.

24. Donnellan (1966) maintains that given suitable contextual clues, one can refer using a description to something that does not in fact satisfy that description. As a claim about speaker-reference this is obvious, but as a claim about sentential semantics it is pretty clearly false; if I token a sentence containing a description, then even if the description is used rigidly, the *sentence* is a true sentence only if the item that satisfies the matrix of the description also satisfies the predicate attaching to the description (see Kripke 1979). However, this truth-value determination is psychologically irrelevant; the speaker's description plays its characteristic computational role, regardless of its semantical mishap.

On the other hand, if "near miss" descriptions of Donnellan's sort can after all lose their normal sentential meanings and semantically denote their utterers' referents rather than the objects which satisfy their matrices, this is an even more dramatic example of fourth-grade aboutness than are the standard cases of proper names and indexical pronouns.

25. Lewis 1983. Cf. Lewis 1979.

26. See Sosa 1970; Morton 1975.

27. Perhaps it is time I recapitulated all six grades of aboutness in one spot. First grade: The believer's representation contains a singular term (of any sort) that

semantically denotes X. Second: X itself figures in the representation's truth-condition; the relevant singular term designates X rigidly. Third: X figures in the representation's truth-condition, and the relevant singular term is causally grounded in X in addition to being rigid. Fourth: The representation directly refers to X, by way of an appropriate causal chain. Fifth: There is direct reference to X and there is also a "ken" relation between the believer and X. Sixth: In holding his belief, the believer is directly acquainted with X without benefit of mediation by any *representation* at all.

28. The possibility of direct reference to and belief *de* an object in the absence of any interesting knowledge about one's referent is well illustrated by some examples of Igal Kvart's (1982, pp. 300–301).

29. Although I do tend to think reality has a joint here, I am by no means convinced that there is a fact of the matter as to which (if any) of my grades of aboutness is required for *real de re* belief. Myles Brand and Kent Bach have both complained to me that they still think some epistemic condition is needed to capture *their* respective conceptions of the *de re*; but I am quite happy to write off this apparent disagreement as terminological. My main aim in this paper is to provide a useful taxonomy of the relevant conditions that sometimes obtain in the real world, in such a way that as much remaining disagreement as possible *can* be written off as verbal.

In "Thoughts and Their Ascription" (1984), Michael Devitt complains very justly that although distinctions of the sort I have drawn are real and important, one should not try to impose the labels "*de re*" and "*de dicto*" at any point unless a strict parallel can be drawn between this usage and the traditional alethic usage. He notes a *prima facie* disanalogy between necessity *de re* and *any* relevant notion of "belief *de re*": a believing involves a representation and its referential properties, whereas—unless a metalinguistic theory of modality should turn out to be right—a case of necessity does not; a *de re* belief involves a designational token of someone's language-of-thought, whereas an ordinary thing's having a property essentially does not (necessity is ostensibly subjectless, after all). This seems quite right, though perhaps it ought to make us consider more carefully the virtues of metalinguistic theories of modality. But there remain very significant parallels between what I am calling fourth-grade aboutness and traditional *de re* necessity: The singular-proposition/general-proposition distinction fits both cases nicely and works out formally; there is a clear sense in which a fourth-grade belief is about a particular thing while a belief of lesser grade is not, just as a *de re* modality is about a particular thing while a general alethic fact is not; and in both cases the *res de* which belief or necessity obtains is intuitively felt to have a genuine property (being suspected-by-Ralph, or being necessarily-human) that objects "involved" in merely first-grade beliefs or *de dicto* necessities do not.

30. That thoughts and their ascription must be very firmly and systematically distinguished is emphasized to excellent effect by Devitt in "Thoughts and Their Ascription" (1984).

31. Two qualifications here. First, there are certain sorts of cases in which latitudinarian quantification does sound quite natural. For example (cf. Sosa 1970, pp.

894–895), suppose I am a successful arsonist. The police know that an arsonist is at work in the community, but I am so discreet that they have no clue whatever as to my identity. Nevertheless, they speculate that whoever set the fires is from out of town, since they do not suppose that any local boy would be clever enough to get away with it, and this conjecture is reported in the newspapers. My wife reads her paper and says to me, "They think you are from out of town." This utterance of my wife's does seem appropriate even though the police have no beliefs that are about me in higher than the first way (let us suppose that the police have not read Kaplan or Plantinga and so have not rigidified their description). I am not sure what it is about this case and a few others like it that licenses the ascriber's use of a directly referential pronoun, when in standard cases the pronominal reference is quite out of place (try "Tatiana, every rational person who knows that there are spies is aware that you are a spy"). But notice that the plausibility of even my wife's ascription here evaporates if the speaker stresses the pronoun in a distinctively *de re*-ish way, as in "They believe *of you* that you're from out of town," or "It is *you* they think is from out of town," or "They suspect you, William G. Lycan, of being from out of town."

Second, it may seem that in granting the interpretability of latitudinarian quantification I have posited an ambiguity in the quantificational construction or in the term "believe," for the quantifier characteristic of genuine *de re* belief is forbidden in the absence of an appropriate causal chain. I think that what is denied is rather the standard *de re voicing* and/or lexicalization of the bound variable—in particular, one may not preface the latitudinarian variable by the Quinean "of," as in "is an *x* such that . . . believes *of x*," and one may not use words like "suspect" and "candidate" which presuppose genuine *de re*-ness. Thus, it seems that "quantifying in" is not per se the fundamental issue after all. [For a somewhat different defense of this last thesis, see Robert Kraut (1983)].

32. Some standard misconceptions have already been laid to rest by D. C. Dennett (1982) and Kent Bach (1982).

33. Quine's reason for abandoning an objective *de re/de dicto* distinction in "Intensions Revisited" (1979; cf. note 8 above) seems to be just that knowing-who is interest-relative. If my impending argument is correct, this reason is inadequate, though I continue to agree that the propriety of quantifying in *is* interest-relative in its own narrower way.

34. E.g., see Dennett (1982, sec. V); John Searle (1979); and S. Stich (1983, chap. 6).

35. Several recent writers seem to have the idea that this *lexical* ambiguity claim is a popular view or at least that it has been held by some respectable philosopher or another. So far as I am aware, it has never been held by anyone at all. It is briefly mentioned, but immediately and rightly dismissed, by Quine on p. 186 of "Quantifiers and Propositional Attitudes" (1966).

36. As Searle remarks in *Intentionality* (1983, p. 209), the phrase "*de dicto* belief" is redundant on this view.

37. Burge 1977.

38. If I understand him correctly (p. 340), he argues that "the grammatical

distinction" is insufficient to capture "the intuitive *de re/de dicto* distinction" because even singular propositions are propositions and hence *dicta*. This begs the question of whether the *de re* is a special case of the *de dicto*, for one who claims it is will of course respond that a singular proposition is a special proposition in that it relates one who believes it directly to a thing in the world.

39. Lycan 1979, p. 313.

40. E.g., Lewis 1983; and John Pollock 1980, though it is clear that Pollock's initial conception *is* quite different from mine.

41. Putnam 1975; Fodor 1980.

42. Dennett 1982, pp. 86–87.

43. For graphic illustrations of the demon's plight, see Dennett (1981, pp. 64–67) and Sober (1984, chap. 4).

44. Pylyshyn 1980. I have stressed the point also, though for a different reason (Lycan 1981a, pp. 44ff.).

45. Psychological behaviorists used to make their view plausible by restricting their experimental subjects' environments in such a way that a desire, purpose, or intention could be manifested in only one brute-physically described way (such as by pressing a bar), thus masking the intentionality of action. It seems to me that Stich is indulging in a similar ploy when he relies on his paradigm of deductive reasoning in chap. 8ff (1983), and when he votes for a retaxonomizing of behavior (see below).

46. I have in mind a pragmatist rather than a positivist notion of a datum. I formulate and defend one in some detail, in "Conservatism and the Data Base" [forthcoming (a)].

47. Note that someone who did not know the truth-condition of Chantal's utterance would not gain this information, intuitively because he or she did not know what the utterance meant. This sort of case has been emphasized by Ernest LePore and Barry Loewer in various writings, notably "Translational Semantics" (1981). See also LePore 1982, 1983; Loewer 1982. However, Kim Sterelny notes (1983) that their account does not easily extrapolate to propositional attitudes other than belief; hope, gladness, and fear do not afford inferences by authority in LePore and Loewer's way, even though they are expressed by utterances of the appropriate sorts.

48. Putnam 1978. Boyd's argument has been glossed and widely misinterpreted; for his (more or less) current views, which differ from the argument presented here, see Boyd (1981, forthcoming).

49. See Devitt, forthcoming, sec. 6.7.

50. Stephen Stich exploits this same strategy against an anticipated objection to methodological solipsism (1983, pp. 168ff.).

51. I owe this point to Kim Sterelny. See Sterelny 1983.

52. Cf. Lycan 1984, pp. 81–102.

53. For helpful discussion of these issues I am particularly indebted to David Austin, Lynne Rudder Baker, D. C. Dennett, Jerry Fodor, Murray Kiteley, Robert Kraut, Stephen Schiffer, Ernest Sosa, Kim Sterelny, Stephen Stich, the late Herbert Heidelberger, and especially Michael Devitt.

Bibliography

Bach, K. 1982. *De re* belief and methodological solipsism. In *Thought and object*, ed. A. Woodfield, pp. 121–152. Oxford: Clarendon Press.

Boër, S. E., and W. G. Lycan. 1975. Knowing who. *Philosophical Studies* 28:299–344.

———. 1980. Who me? *Philosophical Review* 89:427–466.

———. 1985. *Knowing who*. Cambridge: MIT Press, Bradford Books.

Boyd, R. 1981. Scientific realism and naturalistic epistemology. In *Philosophy of Science Association 1980*. Vol. 2, ed. P. D. Asquith and R. N. Giere. East Lansing: Philosophy of Science Assoc.

———. 1984. The current status of scientific realism. In *Essays on scientific realism*, ed. J. Leplin. Univ. of Calif. Press.

Burge, T. 1977. Belief *de re*. *Journal of Philosophy* 74:338–362.

Chisholm, R. 1976. Knowledge and belief: "De dicto" and "de re." *Philosophical Studies* 29:1–20.

Davidson, D. 1969. On saying that. In *Words and objections: Essays on the work of W. V. Quine*, ed. D. Davidson and J. Hintikka, pp. 158–174. Dordrecht: Reidel.

Dennett, D. C. 1981. True believers: The intentional strategy and why it works. In *Scientific explanation*, ed. A. F. Heath, pp. 53–75. Oxford: Clarendon Press.

———. 1982. Beyond belief. In *Thought and object*, ed. A. Woodfield, pp. 1–95. Oxford: Clarendon Press.

Devitt, M. 1981. *Designation*. New York: Columbia Univ. Press.

———. 1984. Thoughts and their ascription. In *Midwest Studies in Philosophy* 9, ed. P. A. French, T. E. Uehling, Jr., and H. K. Wettstein. Minneapolis: Univ. of Minnesota Press.

———. Forthcoming. *Realism and truth*. Princeton, N. J.: Princeton Univ. Press.

Donnellan, K. 1966. Reference and definite descriptions. *Philosophical Review* 75:281–304.

Fodor, J. 1980. Methodological solipsism considered as a research strategy in cognitive psychology. *Behavioral and Brain Sciences* 3:63–110. (Also published in Jerry Fodor, 1981. *RePresentations: Philosophical essays on the foundations of cognitive science*, pp. 225–253. Cambridge: MIT Press, Bradford Books.

Kaplan, D. 1969. Quantifying in. In *Words and objections: Essays on the work of W. V. Quine*, ed. D. Davidson and J. Hintikka. Dordrecht: Reidel.

———. 1975. How to Russell a Frege-Church. *Journal of Philosophy* 72:716–729.

———. 1977. Demonstratives. Unpublished.

Kraut, R. 1983. There are not *de dicto* attitudes. *Synthese* 54:275–294.

Kripke, S. 1972. Naming and necessity. In *Semantics of natural language*, ed. D. Davidson and G. Harman, pp. 253–355. Dordrecht: Reidel.

———. 1979. Speaker's reference and semantic reference. In *Contemporary perspec-*

tives in the philosophy of language, ed. P. A. French, T. E. Uehling, Jr., and H. K. Wettstein, pp. 3–27. Minneapolis: Univ. of Minnesota Press.

Kvart, I. 1982. Quine and modalities *de re*: A way out? *Journal of Philosophy* 79:295–328.

LePore, E. 1982. Truth and Inference. *Erkenntnis* 19:379–395.

——. 1983. What model-theoretic semantics cannot do? *Synthese* 54:167–187.

LePore,E., and B. Loewer. 1981. Translational semantics. *Synthese* 48:121–133.

Lewis, D. 1979. Attitudes *de dicto* and *de se*. *Philosophical Review* 88:513–543.

——. 1983. Individuation by acquaintance and by stipulation. *Philosophical Review* 92:3–32.

Loar, B. 1981. *Mind and meaning*. Cambridge: Cambridge Univ. Press.

Loewer, B. 1982. The role of "conceptual role semantics". *Notre Dame Journal of Formal Logic* 23:305–315.

Lycan, W. G. 1979. The trouble with possible worlds. In *The possible and the actual*, ed. M. Loux, pp. 274–316. Ithaca: Cornell Univ. Press.

——. 1981a. Form, function and feel. *Journal of Philosophy* 78:24–50.

——. 1981b. Psychological laws. *Philosophical Topics* 12:9–38.

——. 1981c. Toward a homuncular theory of believing. *Cognition and Brain Theory* 4:139–159.

——. 1985. The paradox of naming. In *Analytical philosophy in comparative perspective*, ed. J. L. Shaw, pp. 81–102. Dordrecht: Reidel.

——. Forthcoming (a). Conservatism and the data base. In *Reason and rationality in natural science*, ed. N. Rescher. Univ. of Pittsburgh Philosophy of Science Series.

——. Forthcoming (b) Tacit belief. In *Belief*, ed. R. J. Bogdan. Oxford: Oxford Univ. Press.

Morton, A. 1975. Because he thought he had insulted him. *Journal of Philosophy* 72:5–15.

Pastin, M. 1974. About de re belief. *Philosophy and Phenomenological Research* 34:569–575.

Perry, J. 1977. Frege on demonstratives. *Philosophical Review* 86:474–497.

——. 1979. The problem of the essential indexical. *Nous* 13:3–21.

Plantinga, A. 1978. The Boethian compromise. *American Philosophical Quarterly* 15:129–138.

Pollock, J. 1980. Thinking about an object. In *Midwest Studies in Philosophy* 5, ed. P. A. French, T. E. Uehling, Jr., and H. K. Wettstein, pp. 487–499. Minneapolis: Univ. of Minnesota Press.

Putnam, H. 1975. The meaning of "meaning." In *Minnesota studies in the philosophy of science*. Vol. 7, *Language, mind and knowledge*, ed. K. Gunderson. Minneapolis: Univ. of Minnesota Press.

——. 1978. *Meaning and the moral sciences*. London: Routledge and Kegan Paul.

Pylyshyn, Z. 1980. Cognitive representation and the process-architecture distinction. *Behavioral and Brain Sciences* 3:154–169.

Quine, W. V. O. 1966. Quantifiers and propositional attitudes. In *The ways of paradox and other essays*, pp. 183–194. New York: Random House.

_____. 1979. Intensions revisited. In *Contemporary perspectives in the philosophy of language*, ed. P. A. French, T. E. Uehling, Jr., and H. K. Wettstein, pp. 268–274. Minneapolis: Univ. of Minnesota Press.

Schiffer, S. 1978. The basis of reference. *Erkenntnis* 13:171–206.

Searle, J. 1979. Referential and attributive. *Monist* 62:190–208.

_____. 1983. *Intentionality.* Cambridge: Cambridge Univ. Press.

Sellars, W. 1963. Some reflections of language games. In *Science, perception and reality,* 321–358. London: Routledge and Kegan Paul.

_____. 1967. *Science and metaphysics.* London: Routledge and Kegan Paul.

_____. 1973. Reply to Quine. *Synthese* 26:122–145.

Sober, E. 1984. *The nature of selection.* Cambridge: MIT Press, Bradford Books.

Sosa, E. 1970. Propositional attitudes *de dicto* and *de re. Journal of Philosophy* 67:883–896.

Sosa, E., and M. Pastin. 1981. A rejoinder on actions and de re belief. *Canadian Journal of Philosophy* 11:735–739.

Sterelny, K. 1983. The language of thought revisited. Unpublished.

Stich, S. 1983. *From folk psychology to cognitive science.* Cambridge: MIT Press, Bradford Books.

Wallace, J. 1975. Response to Arnaud. *Nous* 9:427–428.

Thought and Object:
De re Representations
and Relations

When we perceive something, we can think about it in a fundamentally different way than if we thought of it merely by description. To think of something by description is just to think of whatever happens to have the properties expressed by the description. But to perceive something is to be in a real relation to it, to be in a position to think of that object in particular, no matter what its properties. While attending to it, somehow (I hope to explain just how) we can think of it as "that," not merely as "the F." Our thoughts about it are not *descriptive*[1] but *de re*.

Thoughts about objects of perception make up the basic but not the only kind of *de re* thought.[2] We can have *de re* thoughts also about things we have perceived before and now remember and even about things others have perceived and have informed us of. Still, any object of *de re* thought must be or have been an object or perception, if not one's own thinking then someone else's. Of course this does not apply to *de re* thoughts about oneself or about abstract objects, but these will not be taken up here. My theory is intended to apply only to *de re* thoughts about concrete individuals other than oneself. I will first schematize the general form of *de re* thought and then characterize the *de re* representations and relations associated with each of the three kinds of *de re* thought: *perception based, memory based*, and *communication based*. I know all three have been recognized by others, but I believe that my view is different and not just in detail. In order to highlight its distinctive features, I will compare it briefly with various common conceptions and more fully with Gareth Evans' superficially similar approach. The difference stems from the distinction between identifying an object and merely thinking of one, and I will argue that the identity of the object of a *de re* thought does not depend on one's beliefs about its identity.

The Nature of *de re* Thought

If you could not have *de re* thoughts about things in the world, you could think of them only by description, each merely as something of a certain sort. If *all* your thoughts about things could only be descriptive, your total conception of the world would be merely qualitative. You would never be related in thought to anything in particular. Thinking of something would never be a case of having it "in mind," as we say colloquially, or as some philosophers have said, of being "*en rapport,*" in "cognitive contact," or "epistemically intimate" with it. Picturesque phrases aside, just what is this special relation? Whatever it is, it is different from that involved in thinking of something under a description. If we can even speak of a relation in the latter case, it is surely not a real (or natural) relation. Since the object of a descriptive thought is determined *satisfactionally*, the fact that the thought is of that object does not require any connection between thought and object. However, the object of a *de re* thought is determined *relationally*. For something to be the object of a *de re* thought, it must stand in a certain kind of relation to that very thought.

The relation that makes something the object of a *de re* thought is a causal relation, of a special kind to be explained in due course. We do not need to know its precise nature to appreciate the crucial fact that, being causal, it can connect objects with thought *tokens* only, not with thought *types*. Abstract entities simply cannot enter into causal relations. This fact has the important consequence that different tokens of the same type can have different objects, hence different truth-conditions. Of course this cannot be true if types of *de re* thoughts are individuated in part by their objects, but I will defend the view that they can (and should) be individuated narrowly, without mention of their objects.[3] The idea is that a type of *de re* thought consists in a way of thinking of an object, together with a way of thinking of a property.[4] What I am claiming, then, is that a way of thinking of an object does not determine the object of a thought token. In other words, if we call (following Frege) a way of thinking of something its *mode of presentation*, the object is not determined by its mode of presentation alone.

De re modes of presentation function as mental indexicals. They determine the contextual relation that something must bear to a thought to be the object of that very thought. And as Colin McGinn so aptly puts it, the object "is determined by the occurrence of a representation *in* a context, not by way of a representation *of* the context" (1982, p. 209). As we will see, the way in which the object is thus determined is remarkably similar to the way in which, according to proponents of the so-called causal theory of reference, the referents of proper names are determined.

Since *de re* modes of presentation function as indexicals, the thoughts in which they occur are not propositional. All I mean by this (I am making no assumptions about the ontological status of propositions) is that they do not have context-independent truth-conditions, as expressible by "eternal" sentences. As Tyler Burge (1977) first pointed out, they must be contextually related to an object for a truth condition to be determined. There is nothing in the content of a nondescriptive, *de re* thought that makes it about some object in particular. There is no kind of thought symbol, as Burge says, that must designate a certain object and no other. The same thought symbol can pick out different objects in different contexts.[5] Moreover, the object it picks out in a given context is a matter of which object stands in the relevant relation to the token of that symbol occurring in that context.

What *de re* Thought Is Not

Before spelling out my conception of *de re* thought, I will try to motivate it further by way of dispelling some common misconceptions. Since I have discussed them in some detail before (Bach 1982), here my description of them and their defects will be brief.

i. Intuitively, thinking of an object *de re* is having it "in mind," which if construed literally is a rather more intimate relation than the one I am suggesting. So construed it can only mean that the object itself is a constituent of the thought. This is reminiscent of Russell, who held that basic constituents of propositions must be objects of acquaintance, in his special sense. The trouble is, physical objects don't qualify, and the only particulars that can be constituents of one's thoughts are oneself (at least as Russell once held) and one's sense data.

ii. However, we don't have to take "having an object in mind" literally. It can be taken merely to suggest the familiar idea that the content of a *de re* thought is a singular proposition, as expressed by a sentence of the form "*a* is G." Here "*a*" is an individual constant of standard first-order logic, what Russell called a "logically proper name," whose sole semantic role is to introduce an object into a proposition. If it fails to denote, any sentence containing it fails to express a proposition.[6] The trouble with the view that the complete content of a *de re* thought is a singular proposition is that it violates what Stephen Schiffer calls Frege's Constraint (1978, p. 180).[7] It fails to account for the fact that one can think contradictory things of the same object without being guilty of logical inconsistency—one can think of the same object in different ways, under distinct modes of presentation. For example, you might think someone you see is clean and someone you smell is filthy without realizing that the one you are looking at is the one you are smelling. In general, without inconsistency you can think of *a* under m_1 and take it to be F while thinking of *a* under m_2 and taking it to be not-F, provided you are ignorant of the fact that $m_1 = m_2$. As Schiffer points out, since the singular proposition theory provides no place for modes of presentation, it can represent what you think only as the blatantly inconsistent "*a* is F" and "*a* is not F" and what you are ignorant of as "*a* = *a*." It neglects the fact that for an object to be thought of at all, it must be thought of in some way or another, and the fact that a physical object can be thought of in various ways.[8]

iii. Then there is the idea that *de re* thoughts, unlike descriptive ones, are essentially about their objects. Though true in one respect, this idea does not qualify as an adequate conception of *de re* thought, since, as is typical with essentialist claims, it is false in another respect. It is true of *de re* thought tokens since the object enters into the token's truth-condition. However, it is not true of *de re* thought types, since different tokens of the same type can have different objects. Insofar as *de re* thought tokens are type individuated by their (narrow) contents, as they should be for psychological purposes, they are not essentially of their objects. Their (narrow) contents do not fix their truth-conditions (wide contents). From a semantic standpoint, of course, they can be individuated by their truth-conditions, and in this respect they are essentially about their objects.[9] True though that is, it doesn't help us with the problem of characterizing their contents and of explaining how their objects are determined.

iv. Sometimes it is suggested that having a *de re* thought about an object is to be in some special cognitive relation to it. This is not as intimate a relation as acquaintance in Russell's sense, but it is cozy enough to have been called such things as "rapport" (Kaplan 1968), "direct cognitive contact" (Kim 1977), and "epistemic intimacy" (Chisholm 1980). Chisholm and Pollock (1980) have each offered what they take to be necessary and sufficient conditions for thinking of an object in what Pollock calls a "*de re* way." I can't go into the details of these epistemic approaches to *de re* thought, but a simple example will show why they are on the wrong track.

Suppose you see a tomato and take it to be red. Later you look back at the same spot, again see a tomato, and take it to be red. Unbeknownst to you, however, it is not the same one. Your two thoughts, being of the same psychological type, have the same (narrow) content but not the same objects (even if you believe that they do).[10] Still, they are paradigmatic cases of *de re* thoughts. Without spelling out the requirements imposed by the epistemic conception of *de re* thought, suffice it to say that the second *de re* thought in our example does not meet them. So that conception cannot be accepted.

v. Perhaps the most widespread misconception is that *de re* thoughts are what *de re* ascriptions ascribe, while *de dicto* (descriptive) thoughts are what *de dicto* ascriptions ascribe. This misconception comes in two forms, that "believes-that" locutions can be used literally only to ascribe *de dicto* beliefs, whereas "believes-of" (or "believes-to-be") locutions can be used literally only to ascribe *de re* beliefs, and that whether a singular term in the "that"-clause of an ascription occurs opaquely or transparently determines whether the belief being ascribed is *de dicto* or *de re*.

It is easy to show (Bach 1982, pp. 129–131) that these distinctions in belief-ascriptions do not reflect the *de re/de dicto* distinction in beliefs ascribed. An ascriber can use a singular term (in subject position of a "that"-clause) either to express an element in the content of the ascribed belief, i.e., how the believer is thinking of an object, *or* to express how he the ascriber is thinking of the object. And the belief can just as well be *de re* as *de dicto*. Similarly, using a singular term opaquely in a "believes-that" ascription does not imply that the belief being ascribed is *de dicto*. Its occurring opaquely means only that the ascriber is not using it to refer. Even then, he need not be using it to exhibit an element of the content of the thought being ascribed. He could be using it to express a concept (that he takes to be) coextensive with that element. And even if the singular term occurs transparently, the thought being ascribed could still be *de dicto*. The ascriber could be using the singular term to refer to the object of a *de dicto* thought, whose content he is not fully specifying.

In short, different forms of belief sentences do not mark differences in kind of belief. Neither the grammatical form of a belief sentence nor how a singular term occurs in it determines the kind of belief ascribed. So it is a mistake to suppose, as John Searle does, for example, that the distinction between *de re* and *de dicto* belief is an illusion arising "from a confusion between reports of beliefs and features of the beliefs being reported" (1983, p. 157). Rather, we must be careful to distinguish *de re*–belief ascriptions from *de re* belief-ascriptions and *de dicto*–belief ascriptions from *de dicto* belief-ascriptions.

The Form of *de re* Thought

Recognizing the indexical character of *de re* thoughts, Burge suggests we represent them with predicates or open sentences. "*De re* locutions are about predication broadly conceived. They describe a relation between open sentences (or what they express) and objects" (1977, p. 343). However, as Burge himself recognizes, there is more than one kind of *de re* relation, and a representation giving only the predicative content does not specify how that content is being applied to an object. If a *de re* locution is to give the complete content of a *de re* thought, it must specify the element of content that determines the relevant relation. Otherwise, there would be no difference in content between, for example, believing of a certain object you are looking at that it is G and believing of a certain object you are recalling, which happens to be the same object, that it is G. Accordingly, the complete content of a *de re* thought cannot be expressed simply by a predicate or an open sentence of the form "x is G." We must include an indexical element expressing the mode of presentation determining the relation which, in the context of thought, determines the object (if any) the thought is about. So, letting t be the time of the belief and R be the relation, as determined by m_R, that contextually fixes the object of the belief, the natural way to specify the belief is by "s believes (at t) under m_R that is x is G." For simplicity I am assuming a present-tensed belief content ("is G"), but allowances could easily be made here and in (DR) below for past-tensed ("was G"), future-tensed ("will be G"), and time-indexed ("is G at t_0") belief contents. The object of a *de re* belief need not still exist at the time of the belief, but of course such a belief cannot be of something that does not yet exist.

A *de re* belief is true iff there is (was) a unique object fixed by R and this object is (was/will be) G. Its truth-condition can be expressed in Russellian style by (DR).[11]

> (DR) At t, s's belief under m_R that x is G is true iff $(Ex)(Rx[m_Rs]$ & $(y)($if $Ry[m_Rs]$ then $y = x)$ & $Gx)$,

or, more perspicuously,

> (DR) At t, s's belief under m_R that x is G is true iff G(the x such that $Rx[m_Rs]$).

(DR) does *not* imply that in order for s to have this belief, the belief must have an object. Quite the contrary, it allows for the possibility that s could have had just that belief without thinking of any object. Equally, if the belief does have an object, (DR) allows for the possibility that it could have had a different object, had something else been the unique object bearing R to the belief token. (DR) specifies the object descriptively, but of course that is not how the object (if any) is represented by *s*. Something is the object of *s*'s belief not by being represented in *s*'s belief token by an individual concept but by actually bearing R to that very belief token.

In this way, then, (DR) captures the fact that *de re* thoughts are indexical. "*x* is G" is the open sentence that Burge took to express the full content of such a thought, while, "m_R" represents the mode of presentation that determines the relation in which the token of that mode of presentation must stand to an object for this object to be the object of *s*'s thought token.[12]

De re Representations and Relations

Now I will distinguish the various types of *de re* representations and the *de re* causal relations they determine. If we can have *de re* thoughts about (*i*) objects we are presently perceiving, (*ii*) objects we have perceived before, and (*iii*) objects we have been informed of,[13] there should be a specific *de re* relation for each case. For the purpose of formulating a specific version of (DR) for each, along with a recursive definition of the *of* relation, in this section I will merely sketch my accounts of each. I have stated my account of the first previously (Bach 1982), and so I will go into detail later only on the second and third cases.

Perception

Beliefs about objects being perceived are the paradigm case of *de re* belief and yet even they, like *de re* beliefs generally, can fail to have objects, as in realistic hallucinations. Accordingly, we should describe their contents so as to allow that a person could be in the same belief state whether or not he is actually perceiving a physical object.[14] Without committing ourselves to any particular philosophical theory of perception, we can do this by applying Chisholm's "adverbial" method (1957), whereby types of perceptual states are individuated by the way in which the perceiver is "appeared to."[15] Let us call these contents of perceptual states *percepts*, which for our purposes should be limited to ways in which individual physical objects can appear. With the schema "*s* is appeared$_k$ to *f*-ly" we can represent a person's being in a certain type of perceptual state, as determined by the kind *k* of percept (its sense modality) and the value of "*f*",[16] and abbreviate the whole schema by "$A_k fs$."

This schema applies equally to perceptions of physical objects and to realistic hallucinations. If the content of a perceptual state, the percept, is represented by "$A_k f s$," we can represent the state of affairs in which a physical object x actually appears$_k$ f to s as "$Cx(A_k f s)$," where "C" means, roughly, "causes in the way appropriate to perception." Explaining what *that* means would be tantamount to formulating a causal theory of perception that satisfactorily handles the notorious problem of deviant causal chains, but not having a solution I can only assume the causal theory to be correct in principle.[17] With that understood, for convenience I will paraphrase "C" simply as "causes." Then "$Cx(A_k f s)$" says "x causes s to be appeared$_k$ to f-ly," or, "x appears$_k$ (looks, feels, etc.) f to s." Along the lines of (DR) above, the truth-condition of s's belief of the object appearing$_k$ to him that it is G may be represented as (PB).

(PB) At t, s's belief under $A_k f$ that x is G is true iff G(the x such that $Cx[A_k f s]$).

(PB) makes clear that a perceptual or other perception-based belief[18] can be true or false of something only if s is perceiving it but that s can be in his belief state without even perceiving anything. That is, specifying the perceptual and conceptual contents of s's belief is enough to identify the type of belief state he is in. It is possible for there to be nothing that he is believing to be G, because the content of the belief is not a singular proposition. Indeed its content is not a proposition at all, since its perceptual component functions as a mental indexical.

To appreciate (PB) contrast it with its descriptive counterpart, formerly endorsed by Stephen Schiffer (1978), according to which the content of a perception-based belief is the same as its truth-condition, G(the x such that $Cx[A_k f s]$). The trouble with this view is that to believe something of an object one is perceiving does not require thinking of it under any description—the object is already singled out perceptually. By suggesting that there must be an individual concept, formed from the percept, that determines (satisfactionally) the object of belief, the descriptive view gets things backwards.[19] For by having the percept, the perceiver is already in a position (assuming the percept is appropriately caused by the object) to form beliefs about the object, which is determined relationally. Percepts function in belief as mental indexicals, and the object of a percept token is whatever bears C to it. To be the object of a perception-based belief, an object need not be represented as being in that relation; it need merely be in that relation.

How does (PB) deal with problem cases, such as believing contradictory things about the same object without being irrational? Suppose s is perceiving an object twice at the same time but does not realize this. He might be feeling it as well as seeing it; he might be seeing it straight on and in a mirror; he might be "seeing double." Suppose he is perceiving it in the same modality but that it appears in two distinct ways, f and f'. Then according to (PB), s believes of the x such that $Cx(A_k f s)$ that it is G and believes of the y such that $Cy(A_k f's)$ that it is not G. (PB) does not imply or even suggest that s believes that $x = y$. He might have no belief about the identity or even disbelieve it. In any case, so long as s is ignorant of the identity, it is not irrational of him to believe of what in fact is one and the same object that it is G and that it is not G.

Now recall the example in which you see a tomato and take it to be red, and later see a tomato in the same spot and take it to be red, but fail to realize that it is not the same one. Then s believes at t_1 of the x such that $Cx(A_k f s)$ and at t_2 of the y such that $Cy(A_k f s)$. The first belief is true iff at t_1 G(the x such that $Cx[A_k f s]$), and the second belief is true iff at t_2 H(the y such that $Cy[A_k f s]$). The contents of the two beliefs are the same, and the difference in their truth-conditions is due entirely to the different times of the beliefs. And because there is no implication as to the identity or distinctness of the objects being perceived, the first belief could be true of one object and the second false of another without s being any the wiser.

A perception-based belief is about an object without being about the identity of its object, but of course we have beliefs about the latter as well. Otherwise, since perception-based beliefs are as short-lived as the perceptual states they involve, their contents could not be integrated into our system of beliefs. That requires conceptualizing or otherwise transforming their perceptual contents so that the information they provide can be retained beyond the context of perception.[20] However, if we are to maintain over time a coherent model of things in the world, we must be able to form beliefs about objects we have previously encountered in perception. Although I have rejected the descriptive theory of perception-based belief, certainly descriptive beliefs, including those of the form of (PB), can play a role here, since they are beliefs about objects represented *as* objects of current perception. Moreover, such beliefs can be updated and thereby represent things as objects of past perceptions. However, we can also have *de re* beliefs about objects we have perceived before, insofar as we can *remember* them.

Memory

Without either endorsing or proposing a theory of what it is to remember an object, I will simply make three assumptions about this, I hope safely.[21] First, we can remember an object only if we have perceived it before. For example, I remember my father Karl Bach but not the composer Karl P. E. Bach. I remember *that* the composer was the second surviving son of J. S.

Bach, but I don't remember *him*. Next, to misremember something is still to remember *it*. What makes a memory a (mis-)representation of a certain object is that it is a *trace* of a perception of that object. Finally, remembering something often consists in but does not require having (or being able to have) an image of it. Instead, we can conceptualize how it appeared. Either way, however, the object remembered is the object whose perception led causally to the memory, not necessarily the one that best fits the memory. A memory-based[22] belief can derive either from a perception-based belief (though perhaps with not the same predicative content) or from a mere perception. After all, even if one formed no beliefs about the object when originally perceiving it, one could still form beliefs about it upon remembering it. And as we will see later, any beliefs you might form about the identity of the object of a memory-based belief have no bearing on which object that belief is about—but they readily lead to false inferences about that object.

What is the form of a memory-based *de re* belief? It parallels the schema (PB) for perception-based belief:

(MB) At t, s's belief under $W_k f$ that x is G is true iff G(the x such that $Mx[W_k fs]$).

"M" stands for the relation *causes in the way appropriate to memory*[23] (the converse of the relation *being a memory of*), and "$W_k f$" schematizes a way of having been appeared$_k$ to, i.e., a memory mode of presentation. Thus "$Mx[W_k fs]$" abbreviates "s remembers x having appeared$_k$ f."

I am supposing that *being a memory of* is a causal relation between memory tokens and objects of past perception. I may have suggested that this relation is the relative product of the relation *being a trace of*, which we took to be between memory tokens and prior percept tokens. and *being a percept of*, holding between percept tokens and objects of perception, but surely *being a trace of* can just as well hold between two memory tokens. In general, then, a memory token of an object is a trace of a memory token which . . . is a trace of a memory token which is a trace a percept token of the object. So letting "T" represent *being a trace of*, "P" *being a percept of*, "O" the *of* relation, and "m" and "m'" modes of presentation, we can recursively define the *of* relation for memories:

(R_M) (m)(if mPx, then mOx), and $(m')(m)$(if $m'Tm$ and mOx, then $m'Ox$).

This recursive definition will be generalized later to cover the case of communication.

Communication

We can have *de re* thoughts not only about things we perceive or remember but also about things of which we have been informed. If a speaker refers to something by name and expresses a *de re* thought about it, he thereby puts his audience, who may have never perceived it, in a position to form *de re* thoughts about it as well. If the hearer is in that position already, either because he has perceived and not forgotten it or because he knows it by some other name, at least the speaker is putting him in the position of thinking of it under a new *de re* mode of presentation. In any event, to understand the speaker fully the audience must think of the referent in the same way as the speaker.[24]

When the audience has no independent *de re* way to think of the referent (call this the "pure" case), the speaker must use a name[25] to succeed in expressing a *de re* attitude about it. The reason, as I will explain more fully later, is that names are the only kind of *de re* mode of presentation that a speaker can actually display to a hearer. You can *express* a percept or a memory but you can't *display* one—you can't produce a public token of a percept or a memory. In thinking of something by name, a speaker entertains a mental token of the name; in using it to refer, he produces a physical token of it; in hearing that token, the hearer forms a mental token of the same name. If instead of using a name the speaker used a definite description referentially, then even if the hearer took the speaker to be expressing a *de re* thought,[26] he could think of the referent only descriptively (at least in the pure case).

Again we can follow the pattern of (DR) to represent the form of communication-based *de re* thoughts. Letting "*n*" schematize a name (or any singular term used as a name) and "H" represent the relation *having* (for *s*), the converse of the *of* relation for names, we have:

(CB) At *t*, *s*'s belief under *n* that *x* is G is true iff G(the *x* such that H*x*[*ns*]).

I can make (CB) clearer by extending our recursive definition of the *of* relation. Let us distinguish two relations, the relation *being dubbed* (D) between the object and the initial token of the name,[27] and the relation *being linked to* (L) between a token of the name and its immediate predecessor in the causal process. Ordinarily, an individual is dubbed while being perceived, but not always. It can be dubbed by virtue of still being remembered, and even if no longer remembered it can be given one name by virtue of already being thought of by some other name. In any case, a name can function as a *de re* mode of presentation only of something that someone has perceived.[28] Tokens of a name can be linked inter- or intrapersonally: L can hold between a mental token and a heard (or read) physical token, or between an uttered (or written) physical token and a mental token, or between two mental tokens. Now we can extend our recursive definition of the *of* relation. Let us restrict the "*m*'s" to percepts and memories, and for clarity use "*n*" and "*n'*" for tokens (physical or mental) of the same name and subscripts to indicate different names. With (R_M) repeated as the first two lines, we have a branching recursive definition:

(OF) (m)(if mPx, then mOx),
         $(m')(m)$(if $m'Tm$ and mOx, then $m'Ox$),
         $(n)(m)$(if xDn by virtue of mOx, then nOx),
         $(n_1)(n_2)$(if xDn_2 by virtue of n_1Ox, then n_2Ox), and
         $(n')(n)$(if $n'Ln$ and nOx, then $n'Ox$).

I have not yet said what it is to think of something by name. In the section after next, we will investigate the psychological role of names and of expressions used as names, but first we should take a closer look at memory-based *de re* thoughts.

Memory-based *de re* Thoughts

I remember very little about a certain boyhood friend of mine. I think his name was "Dick Holloway," and I recall that he lived about three doors down the block, that he and I were in the same third- or fourth-grade class, and that he believed the largest number in the world to be infinity twelve (how could I forget *that*?). These beliefs are about him not because they contain an individual concept that applies to him alone, a concept expressed by a description like "my boyhood friend who thought the largest number to be infinity twelve." I *remember* Dick Holloway, and that is not a matter of thinking of him descriptively.

It might be suggested that if we construe individual concepts so broadly as to include images, then my beliefs about Dick Holloway *are* descriptive: I think of him as "the boy who looked thus-and-so," where "thus-and-so" expresses a certain way of looking.[29] My visual image of him may be dim and vague, but I'm pretty sure I could pick him out of our class picture. I think I'd recognize him if, somehow, I saw him unchanged from when I knew him, but I don't doubt that I could mistake many other boys for him. So his looking thus-and-so cannot be what makes the above beliefs about him. Even if my image matched him and him alone, only a causal connection would make it an image of him. Besides, he might not have looked the way I remember him as much as some other boy, but this would not make my beliefs about the other boy instead. So when I think of him under an image, his fitting that image (or a description verbalizing that image) is not what makes my beliefs about him. Rather, it is the fact that this memory image is causally connected in a certain way to how I perceived him. It is a *trace* of my percept of him.[30] Whatever the causal relation appropriate to memory is exactly, it explains the way in which an image can literally be a preservation in memory of a percept of a certain individual. Whatever the psychological story of how memories change over time, surely there must be some set of facts in virtue of which a certain one of my memory images, inaccurate though it may be, counts as the trace of my percept of Dick Holloway. Only thus can the image function in thought as a mode of presentation of him.

To be a memory of some individual in particular, a memory need not include anything about the identity of its object (nor must one be able to "place" that individual). Any beliefs I have about the identity of the object of the memory-based beliefs I take to be about a boy named "Dick Holloway" have no bearing on who those beliefs are about. So, for example, I believe that Dick Holloway was my only friend who said the largest number in the world is infinity twelve, but this is not what makes my memory-based beliefs about Dick Holloway. For among those memory-based beliefs is the belief of someone I am thinking of under a certain memory image that *he* was Dick Holloway and that *he* was my only friend who said the largest humber in the world is infinity twelve.

However, despite the fact that one can be ignorant or even mistaken about the identity of the object of a memory-based belief, identity beliefs are still important. For they enable these memory-based beliefs to be integrated inferentially. For example, I believe of Dick Holloway, whom I think of under an image, that he was Dick Holloway, that he was my boyhood chum who lived three doors down the block, that he was in my third- or fourth-grade class, and that he said the largest number is infinity twelve. I believe them all of the same individual, but without the appropriate identity beliefs I would fail to realize that. Now it might be objected, considering all the combinations of pairs of things I believe of Dick Holloway, that to ascribe the required number of identity beliefs is psychologically implausible. This would be so if they were all individually represented, but I don't mean to suggest that. Rather, these identity beliefs are jointly constituted by the fact that all the memory-based beliefs in question are stored in one *file*.[31] I will develop this intuitively attractive idea when we take up the subject of thinking of an individual by name.

A Case of Mistaken Identity

Suppose you once knew the tennis player Tim Gullickson. You didn't know then and still don't know that he has a twin brother Tom, also a tennis pro, who is not quite identical: Tom is left-handed, Tim right-handed. One afternoon you show up late for a tournament and see what you take to be the player you remember (Tim) in the midst of a tennis match. To your amazement he is playing left-handed and winning, the scoreboard showing Gullickson leading Glickstein, 6–3, 4–1. What do you believe about whom?

Because you are already acquainted with Tim and have *de re* beliefs about him, as you watch what you take to be Tim,[32] you form many new beliefs about him, including the belief that he has developed a remarkable left-handed tennis game. It just doesn't occur to you that he might have a left-handed twin. Now these new beliefs are about Tim under a memory image (how you visualize Tim), and each is the result of a perception-based belief about Tom and the identity belief that the player you are watching is the player you remember. That is, for each perception-based belief (about Tom) there is a memory-based belief (about Tim) with the same predicative content. I don't mean to suggest that there are two distinct sets of mental representations in your head, one functioning as the contents of your new beliefs about Tim and the other as the contents of your beliefs about Tom. Rather, your identity belief has led your perception-based beliefs about Tom to have become *merged* with your memory-based beliefs about Tim.[33] Notice that your having two sets of *de re* beliefs, memory based and perception based, does not depend on the fact that the player you remember is distinct from the one you are watching. Even if Tim had developed a left-handed game and it was he you were watching, you would still have distinct memory- and perception-based beliefs, even though their objects (as well as their predicative contents) would now be the same. Only this time both sets of beliefs would be about Tim, your identity belief would be true, and the merger resulting from it would not lead to confusion. As things are, however, your identity belief is false, as are your new memory-based beliefs about Tim (unless true fortuitously, e.g., that Tim is still playing tennis). So, for example, you believe falsely of Tim that he is beating Glickstein but truly of Tom that he is beating Glickstein (under different modes of presentation, of course, a memory and a percept).

Now suppose a friend comes by and says, "That's one of the Gullickson twins, whom I can tell apart only because Tom is left-handed." Your prior amazement over Tim's development of a left-handed tennis game quickly gives way to embarrassment over your ignorance. You abandon your identity belief and with it all the new memory-based beliefs you formed about

Tim. But you retain all the perception-based beliefs you have formed about Tom and add to them the belief that he is Tim's twin brother.

In one last variant, suppose you later think you recall (you haven't been told of Tom) that your old acquaintance Tim once beat Glickstein left-handed, but you no longer remember seeing the match. Who is this memory-based belief about: Tim, Tom, or both? Even though it resulted from watching Tom's match with Glickstein, I say it is about Tim—not because of your present identity belief that it was Tim you remember but because of whom your memory image is. To be sure, your original perception-based beliefs about Tom, though no longer retained, did play a role here, but the role they played, with the support of your *original* identity belief, was to lead to the memory-based belief (about Tim) that you have retained.

Communication-based *de re* Thoughts

Objects of perception-based thoughts are represented by percepts, and objects of memory-based thoughts by images or concepts are derived from percepts, but either way, the object is something encountered by the thinker himself. Can one also have *de re* thoughts about things one has not encountered but has merely been informed of? It might seem that you can think of such a thing only descriptively, even if you hear of it from someone who has encountered it; for if it is not there to point to, what more can the speaker enable you to do than think of it under a description? In referring to it, whether he provides you with a description under which to think of it or refers to it in some other way, surely he cannot put you into a position comparable to that of having encountered it yourself. *He* may be in a *de re* relation to it, but how can he put *you* in such a relation? You can think of the referent as the individual that he has encountered and is now telling you of, but that is to think of it under a description.

This objection to the very possibility of communication-based *de re* thought may seem plausible but it rests on a mistake. It implicitly assumes that reference to something not present and not familiar to the hearer must be *identifying* reference.[34] That is, to succeed in referring the speaker must enable the hearer to determine what he is talking about, and the objection is that under the circumstances, the hearer can do so only by description. The speaker is thinking of the referent in a certain *de re* way, but he cannot provide the hearer with that or any other *de re* way to think of it. He can express how he is thinking of it and the hearer can identify how, but that is to think of it only descriptively, as the object the speaker is thinking of in that way: the object of the hearer's thought is determined satisfactionally, not relationally.

What this objection overlooks is that a speaker cannot just express but actually *display* his *de re* way of thinking of the object and thereby enable the hearer to think of it in the same way. To do this the speaker must use either a proper name or some other singular term "as a name," as Russell (1919, p. 175) described using a term "merely to indicate what we are speaking about" (for convenience I will use the word "name" for any singular term so used). Now if the speaker is thinking of something by name, he is entertaining a mental token of the name; when he refers to it by name, he produces a physical token of that name; and the audience, upon hearing that token, forms a mental token of the same name, which can then be retained in memory. Since the hearer's mental token of the name "inherits" the same object as the speaker's, the object of the hearer's thought is determined relationally, not satisfactionally.

The reason the object is not determined satisfactionally is that the meaning of the name (even a description used as a name) does not enter into the content of the hearer's thought, hence not into the determination of the object being thought of by that name. A token of a name can function as a *de re* mode of presentation because its reference is determined not by its meaning but by its ancestry. It plays this role by being of a certain form (sound or shape), generally the same as the one to which it is linked.[35] When the meaning of the token does not matter, its referent cannot be determined satisfactionally. Indeed, that only its form matters is what constitutes its being used as a name. And that is what enables one to form *de re* thoughts about an unfamiliar object referred to by that name. Since the token of name represents in virtue of its form, not its meaning, its representational features can be perceived by the hearer, who can then and thereafter use mental tokens of the same name to think of the same object.

Singular terms of any kind can function as mental names and as means for enabling others to have *de re* thoughts about unfamiliar things. However, proper names are the only singular terms made to order for these roles. The reason is simple: individuals *have* names. Pronouns and descriptions can and often do play these roles within a given context of thought or utterance, but they are ill-suited to work as *de re* modes of presentation or identification of the same individual on diverse occasions. There is simply no way for a pronoun to inherit its reference from a use of the same pronoun on a previous occasion. And generally there are too many descriptions, often idiosyncratic, which people form of things they remember or have heard of, and too many things of which different people form the same description. However, descriptions can become proper names and thereby function as such. Good examples of descriptive names are "The Sultan of Swat," a name of Babe Ruth, and "The Chairman of the Boards," a name of Moses Malone. A descriptive name can work as a *de re* mode of identification (in reference) and as a *de re* mode of presentation (in thought) of the same object on various occasions. Also, a description can be conjoined to a proper name, especially a name belonging to more than one individual, to yield a hybrid singular term that functions as a name. There is "Aristotle the shipping magnate," for example, which distinguishes Onassis from Aristotle the philosopher.[36] Finally, it seems we each use descriptive and hybrid names privately, for people and things we can no longer visualize and whose proper names we do not know.

How can a name function as a *de re* mode of presentation of the same individual on various occasions? I suggest that names play this role by serving as labels, so to speak, on the mental files we have on individuals, including individuals we have never encountered or no longer remember.[37] To think of an individual by name just *is* to call up a file on that individual. We should not take the term "file" too literally, of course, but it suggests that information about an individual thought of by name is all stored together (I mean functionally, not necessarily spatially). If so, this would explain the apparent phenomenon (attested to from my experience) that you cannot think of a familiar individual by name without further thoughts about that individual occurring spontaneously. For example, when Fritz Kreisler's name occurs to me, I cannot help but think that he was a great violinist but a mediocre composer. The file model offers a much more natural explanation of the fact that many bits of information about an individual tend to get called up together than do sentential or so-called propositional models, on which each item of information is stored separately. What's more, in order to explain the fact that one takes them all to be about the same individual, the sentential model requires a combinatorily explosive hypothesis about the number of identity beliefs involved here, assuming they are individually represented.[38]

The role of names in language is quite different from their role in thought. The semantics of a linguistic name, considered independently of which mental name it is being used to express, consists in its contribution to the meanings of the sentences in which it occurs. I have defended the view, the "Nominal Description Theory" (NDT), that a name "N" makes the same contribution as the metalinguistic description "the bearer of 'N'" (Bach 1981a), and to suppose otherwise leads to the palpably absurd position that a name with many bearers (most do have many) is semantically ambiguous in as many ways as its number of bearers.[39] I argue that NDT does not have this consequence[40] and is immune to Kripke's (1980) various objections to description theories generally. NDT does not have the false implication that *linguistic* understanding of a sentence containing a name, e.g., "Veracruz Fettucini is bald," requires knowing whose name it is. Kripke's own theory does seem to imply that you don't understand the sentence unless you know who Veracruz Fettucini is, as if that is a piece of linguistic information. Further, his view suggests that if you asked "Who is Veracruz Fettucini?" you wouldn't understand your own question, and that the sentence would not even be meaningful if there were no such person (there is!).

Since NDT applies only to proper name types in language, it surely does not commit me to a description theory of mental tokens of names. The reference of a mental token of a name, and derivatively that of a physical token used to express it, is determined relationally, not satisfactionally, as the object of the percept token to which it is ultimately linked. Since the relation *being linked to* (as well as the relation *being a percept of*) is a causal relation, for mental names I am thereby endorsing a causal theory of reference, according to which they function as rigid designators. Because a name's reference, if any, is fixed by that of the original percept and not by its linguistic meaning, it refers to the same object in any possible world in which it refers at all. If the original percept to which the name is linked had no object (or if there were no original percept, as with fictional names), neither would the name itself.

Mental names can represent particular individuals, for their psychological role is quite unlike the semantic role of linguistic names. When a mental name "N" occurs to you, you don't start using the concept "the bearer of 'N'." Rather, its occurrence calls up the file it labels, thereby causing you to think of the subject of that file. This is why I suggest that thinking of an individual by a name just *is* to call up a mental file on that individual which is labeled with that name.[41] Mental names play this role in communication as well. When you hear a name that labels an existing file, that file immediately gets called up. But if there are several individuals with that name on whom you have files (distinctly labeled, e.g., "Aristotle the philosopher"), the sorts of things being said should, in the context, lead to just one file being called up. And if the speaker cannot plausibly be taken to be talking about the subject of any such file, a new file must be created. That also happens, of course, when you hear an unfamiliar name and do not take it to belong to anyone on whom you already have a file (of course with a different label). Either way, the speaker has put you in a position to use that name to have *de re* thoughts about the referent, not just in the context of utterance but thereafter, provided you retain the new file or the new label on the old file. New information can be added whenever the file is reopened, and that can happen either spontaneously or when you identify or others refer you to someone you take to be the same individual. And of course *you* can use the name to refer others to that individual, thereby causing either an existing file of theirs to be called up or a new one to be created.

So mental names are used to create new files on individuals and to call up old ones for additions, alterations, or just inspection. Files labeled with names (proper names or descriptions used as names) are relatively permanent ones, stored in long-term memory, but we have temporary files as well. Their natural labels are pronouns, which work on a short-term basis. Demonstratives and indexicals often serve to create temporary files, and personal and relative pronouns serve to keep them open—or to keep open recently reopened permanent files.

Nothing I have said should be taken to suggest that a file, temporary or permanent, must actually be on someone. You can have a file on a figment of your imagination or a fiction of someone else's. If you take one person for another (mistaken identity) or simply confuse two people (as with identical twins), you will have a file containing information derived from both and thus not determinately on either. For that matter, you can have two files on the same individual, e.g., your friendly neighbor and a notorious war criminal. Here, if you came to believe that they were one and the same, the two files would become merged.

Another Case of Mistaken Identity

A good illustration of mistaken identity (and of the role of identity beliefs in connection with communication-based *de re* beliefs) is Kripke's story of Godel the impostor. As Kripke tells it, Godel betrayed his friend Schmidt, the real discoverer of the incompleteness of arithmetic, by murdering him and taking credit for that discovery himself. Since our concern is not with the reference of the name "Godel," let's alter the story slightly and suppose that the discoverer of incompleteness was named "Godel" but that his murderer assumed the name (perhaps he was his brother and it really was his name). To avoid confusion I will use "Godel" to refer only to the discoverer of incompleteness. Suppose you were never acquainted with either man, but you do have a "Godel" file, a file containing beliefs that you express when using the name "Godel." You believe such things as that the subject of your "Godel" file discovered incompleteness, spent his later years at the Institute for Advanced Study, and died a few years ago. Now which man are your "Godel"-beliefs about? Are some about Godel and some about the imposter, or are they all about the same man—in which case, who? If their original sources are all people acquainted only with the impostor, it seems that they are all about the same man, the impostor, and Kripke would agree.[42]

Now suppose that your "Godel"-beliefs had several sources, one the author of a logic book written prior to the impostor's dastardly deeds, the other an acquaintance of the impostor on the IAS campus. Some of these beliefs came from one source and some from the other, with some coming from one having been "confirmed" by the other. They are all in the same file, but whom is each about? The source of the ones about the incompleteness proof, the device of Godel numbers, and so on is the author of the logic book, and the source of the ones about appearance, manner, and personality is the man from IAS. So it might seem that the first ones are about Godel and the second about the impostor. You may believe them all to be about the same man, but that doesn't mean they are, for at least some of your beliefs about the identity of the object of some of your "Godel"-beliefs are false. Yet if they are all stored in the same file, how could some be about Godel and some about the impostor?

It might be suggested that while your identity beliefs explain why your "Godel"-beliefs all go into one file, they also imply that you believe of both Godel *and* of the impostor (though under different modes of presentation, of course) that he was born in Vienna, discovered incompleteness, worked at the IAS, and had a quiet manner. It is not being suggested that each "Godel"-belief is unwittingly about both men—that would not make sense—but that each "Godel"-belief about one man has a counterpart about the other. If one is about Godel, its counterpart about the impostor results from an inference from it and the identity belief involving each man's respective mode of presentation. And, after all, this was the situation in the Gullickson case, which showed that there is nothing implausible about duplication of beliefs once we distinguish the modes of presentation operative in the two sets of beliefs.

The trouble with this suggestion is that here, as opposed to the Gullickson case, there aren't two modes of presentation to be distinquished, hence no counterpart of each *de re* belief about one man that is about the other. Your "Godel" file is simply labeled "Godel," and that name is the only *de re* mode of presentation available. Not being attached to two different files, it is not a mode of presentation of two different individuals. Since there is no reason to say that it is a mode of presentation of one man rather than the other, it cannot be a mode of presentation of either. So your "Godel"-beliefs are about neither.[43]

A variant of this last version of Kripke's story provides a final illustration of how identity beliefs can work. This time suppose that when you first heard of Godel, you were told about the murderous impostor. So you were careful about your sources of "Godel" information and kept two files, one on Godel and one on the impostor. However, the story was only a story. As a result, the beliefs in your "Godel's impostor" file are really about Godel. However, thanks to your belief that they are about someone else, they don't get put into your "Godel" file and you don't make the inferences that would be made by someone who took them to be about Godel.

Thinking of and Identifying:
A Comparison with Evans

Gareth Evans (1982) and I agree that thoughts about objects can be based on perception, memory, or communication. However, the requirement he imposes on what it is, in any of the three ways, to think of an object is far stronger than anything I have suggested. I can best explain this requirement and why I reject it by first making some elementary observations about reference, specifically to explain how referring to something is fundamentally different from, yet essentially connected to, thinking of something.

Strawson (1950) developed the thesis, which I have defended in Bach (1983), that reference is ultimately not a two-place relation between a word and an object but a four-place relation between a speaker, a word, an audience, and an object. That is, a speaker uses a word (or other expression) to refer an audience to an object. *Denotation* is a relation between a word and an object, but a speaker can use a word that denotes one thing to refer to something else or use a word that does not denote to refer to something anyway. So when we speak of an expression referring, we are speaking elliptically for its being used to refer someone to some object.

Understood as something speakers do, referring must be explained in terms of the notion of thinking of an object. For referring to an object just *is* the component of the communicative act of expressing an attitude about something one is thinking of. A speaker's intention in using a referring expression is fulfilled only if his audience forms an attitude about the same thing and takes it to be the same. This is not by magic: the utterance, perhaps accompanied by gestures or glances, must enable the audience to infer, in the context of utterance, what the speaker is talking about.

Since thinking of something is necessary for referring to that thing, we shouldn't expect to understand it on the model of referring. In order to think of something, as opposed to referring someone else to it, surely you don't have to refer yourself to it. Whereas there is something for an audience to aim at, to get right or get wrong (namely to think of what you are thinking of), there is nothing for you to aim at, to get right or wrong, when you are thinking of the object already. But you can do something else: wonder about its identity, about who or what it is. Thinking of it in one way, you can ask yourself whether it is the same individual as one you are thinking of in some other way. Is this my long lost cousin, is that my umbrella, is this politician the actor I saw on the Late Show the other night? But you don't have to know who they are to think of them in the first place.

Plain as it is, this point is not always appreciated. For example, Strawson's "descriptive metaphysics" (1959, chap. 1), which is meant to capture the essential features of how we conceptualize the basic features of the world and its occupants, is built around the notion of identifying reference, as if thinking of an object were a matter of being able to refer to it. At least he does not suggest this when he takes up reidentification, which he does not construe as an interpersonal phenomenon. Still, Strawson does not draw the distinction between thinking again of an object and the further achievement of thinking that the object is the same one. The ability to reidentify, together with possessing the underlying concept of reidentifiable, persisting objects, may be necessary for maintaining a coherent conception of the world over time, but it does not seem necessary merely for thinking of the objects.

These points all pertain to Evans. Developing an account of what he calls "information-based particular-thought" (IPT), he contends that thinking of an object requires identifying it or at least being able to identify it. He endorses what he calls "Russell's Principle," that "in order to have a thought about a particular object, you must *know which* object it is about which you are thinking" (1982, p. 74).[44] Although Evans and I agree that the thoughts in question can be based directly on perception or derivatively on memory or communication, where I speak of modes of presentation he speaks of *modes of identification*, or *Ideas*.

IPTs yield information about objects by way of causal links with their objects. Evans and I agree about the ways, but the difference between us is that for him IPTs are *Russellian*, in the sense that like sentences containing logically proper names, if they lack reference they lack content. But whereas Russell held that particular thoughts can only be about sense data,[45] as required by his restrictive doctrine of acquaintance, IPTs can be about external objects. However, the Ideas that enter into IPTs are not like Russellian proper names, in that the sense of an Idea is not exhausted by its object. For ideas are ways of identifying an object, and there can be various ways of identifying the same one: different Ideas of an object can enter into different IPTs that ascribe the same property to the same thing.

An Idea is of the object to which it is "informationally linked," but being "a discriminating conception" of an object, an Idea can be "adequate" only if it satisfies Russell's Principle. It must enable one "to distinguish the object of his judgment from all other things," so that one can "know which" object it is. Therefore, if a thought does not have the object one thinks it has, because it has some other object or even none at all, one can fail to have the thought one thinks one has. Indeed, Russell's principle not only implies that the identity of a thought depends on the identity of its object, but as understood by Evans it has the controversial consequence that the very *existence* of the thought depends on the existence of its object.

For Evans there are three kinds of IPTs. A perceptual demonstrative thought contains an Idea consisting in the ability to locate an object in "egocentric space" (i.e., objective space from an egocentric frame of reference) on the basis of current perception (pp. 143–151). Since this requires the maintenance of a *continuing* information link to the object (p. 146), such an Idea is adequate only so long as it enables one to maintain a conception of the object as the same one. Similarly, a demonstrative thought based on memory requires a "recognitional capacity" to identify the object (pp. 267–271). Here Evans makes allowances both for the possibility of duplicates—a capacity is relativized to contextually relevant objects (pp. 278–284)—and for the possibility of an object's changing beyond recognition—one need merely be able to think of it as the same object as what *was* recognizably such and such (pp. 272–273). Now an IPT based on communication contains a name of the object, and here (p. 373ff.) Evans appeals to the notion of a practice of using a name "N" to refer to an object x. Such a practice depends on there being (or having been) "producers" of the name who originally identified x demonstratively. Then a "consumer," having acquired the name from a producer, or a producer who is no longer identifying x demonstratively, can use "N" to think of and to refer to x and thereby have an adequate Idea of x.

Evans insists that thinking of an individual requires, in each case, knowing which individual it is. This may involve thinking of it in some other way as well, but as we will see, for Evans this is not necessary. For surely you can have an Idea "I_1" of something without also having another Idea "I_2" of it and believing that the object I_1 is of = the object I_2 is of. However, although Evans *says* that having a single Idea of something suffices for knowing which thing it is, it is quite unclear what he *means*. An Idea is a "discriminating capacity," but being able to discriminate something does not entail knowing which thing it is, at least not in any familiar sense of "knowing which." So what could Evans mean? One clue is that he often uses "discriminate" and "identify" interchangeably. He says, for example, that possessing an Idea of an object is to have a capacity for discriminating it and that using an Idea of an object is to identify it. He seems to equate identifying something with merely individuating it.

Let me explain this contention. "Identifying an object" here does not mean referring to it, i.e., identifying it for an audience so that they can think of it. Nor does it mean characterizing it in some interest-relative way (Boer and Lycan 1975), e.g., identifying your neighbor as a certain murder suspect. As I understand Evans, what it does mean, depending on the case, is either of two things: (*i*) reidentifying an object or (*ii*) thinking of an object so as to be able to reidentify it.

(*i*) Reidentification is taking an object you are presently thinking of under one mode of presentation to be a certain object about which you already have beliefs and which you think of under some other mode of presentation. The latter mode of presentation functions as a mode of identification in the the first way. For example, you might take the umbrella you are looking at as the one you remember losing (your percept matches your memory). Or you might take the man introduced to you as Richard Holloway as your boyhood chum Dick Holloway. Reidentifying an object (correctly) enables you to connect your new beliefs about it to the ones in your file on it. Being about the object under one mode of presentation "m_1," it cannot be inferentially integrated with your other beliefs about the same object but under another mode of presentation "m_2" unless accompanied by the identity belief that this is the same object, i.e., that the object presented by m_1 = the object presented by m_2. For the beliefs under "m_2" make up your existing file on the object, and unless a belief that the object presented by m_1 is F is accompanied by such an identity belief, the belief that the object presented by m_1 is F will not be added to that file. The belief that the object presented by m_1 is F may be retained but only in a new file labeled "m_1," since you have failed to identify the object presented by m_1 as the one presented by m_2.[46]

(*ii*) The second kind of identification is thinking of an object in such a way as to be *able* to reidentify it later. Say a cardsharp shows you three playing cards, an ace and two tens, and places them facedown. They look alike but you think of the ace as the one on the right. He then interchanges them, but so long as you keep your attention on the ace, you can continue to think of it under the same percept, which thereby functions as a mode of identification of the second kind. A memory can do likewise. If you notice that the ace has a bent corner, unlike either of the tens, you don't have to maintain your attention in order to identify it later as the one with the bent corner. Your memory of it enables you to recognize it (unless you are another loser in the con game of three-card monte) and thus serves (for better or worse) as a mode of identification.[47] Thus a mode of presentation of an object need not qualify as a mode of identification of that object. One can think of something without knowing which thing it is.

So the trouble with Evans' view is that what he regards as necessary conditions for using an Idea to think about an object are too strong and are, in fact, necessary conditions for something more. As many of our examples have suggested, one can think of an object without being able to identify it, that is, without knowing which object it is (in any useful sense of "knowing which"). You can think of a perceptual object merely by attending to it. If you look away and then turn back, you needn't be able perceptually to pick it out of a crowd, even if in the midst of look-alikes. Similarly, you can think of an object you have perceived before merely by remembering it. That you remember something, hence your ability to think of *it*, does not require that how you remember it distinguishes it from other things. All that matters is that it caused the percept that resulted in the memory. And if someone refers you to something by name, you can think of it simply by name. Of course if you know of several individuals with that name, you may not know which one he is talking about, if any, but this does not prevent you from thinking of it. Rather, this prevents you from knowing into which file, if any, to put the information he provides you about that individual.[48] In all three cases, then, you can think of an individual without knowing which one. Of course if its mode of presentation does not enable you to know which individual it is and you cannot identify it otherwise, your new beliefs about it cannot be integrated inferentially with any old ones you might have. But all this means is that its mode of presentation does not qualify as a mode of identification.

De re thoughts do not literally contain their objects, and their contents are not singular propositions in that or any other sense. Indeed, they are not propositional at all. For they include modes of presentation that function as mental indexicals, and different tokens of a mode of presentation of the same type can present different objects. The object of a *de re* thought is determined not satisfactionally but relationally, as the one standing in the appropriate causal relation to the very token of the mode of presentation contained in the thought. Which relation this is depends on the kind of mode of presentation, but whether it is a percept, a memory, or a name, one does not have to know what one is thinking of in order to be thinking of it. [49]

Notes

1. I prefer the term "descriptive" over the usual "*de dicto*," which misleadingly suggests that descriptive thoughts are about sentences (*dicta*).

2. I intend the phrase "*de re* thought" to apply not just to (occurrent) *de re* beliefs but to *de re* attitudes of any kind, though my examples will mainly be beliefs. Also, *de re* thoughts include occurrences too fleeting to qualify as attitudes at all.

3. For the distinction between narrow content and wide content and the corresponding ways of individuating types of thoughts, see Fodor (1980) or McGinn (1982).

4. That's for the monadic case, but obviously the same idea applies to individuating *de re* thoughts about *n* objects in an *n*-ary relation. For simplicity, in this paper

I will stick to the monadic case. Also, I will not take up the subject of predicative contents of thoughts, of what it is to think of a property (or a relation).

5. If I may wax metaphysical, there is no such thing as a representation (linguistic or mental) of an object's essence, particularity, or haecceity (to use some old terms enjoying undeserved revivals). Nothing in the content of a *de re* thought about an object makes the thought about *that* object. There is no way to capture in thought the "particularity" of an object, for as far as the content of the thought is concerned, the thought could just as well have been about a different object, had a different object been in its place.

6. As Russell showed, not all referring expressions have this feature. If we replace "*a*" with a definite description, the resulting sentence, of the form "The F is G," expresses a proposition even if nothing fits the description. Since "the F" introduces not an individual but an individual concept into the proposition, this is not a singular but a general proposition.

7. It is similar to what Evans calls the Intuitive Criterion of Difference (1982, p. 18ff.). I should note here that Evans' view of *de re* thought, though observant of Frege's constraint, does have the feature that the object enters into the type individuation of the thought. Whereas for me modes of presentation are individuated independently of the objects they present, Evans' "modes of identification" are not, as we will see when we take up his view later.

As for Schiffer, not only does he reject the singular proposition view of *de re* thought, he claims [at least in Schiffer (1978)—in this volume he takes it back] that the only way one can think of an object (other than oneself) is under a description, hence that one have "irreducibly" *de re* thoughts only about oneself (and the present moment).

8. This suggests a corollary to Russell's view, noted earlier, that physical objects do not qualify as objects of acquaintance. Since a physical object can be thought of in different ways, these ways of thinking of it cannot be expressed by logically proper names for it. For if one thing has two names, the same proposition is expressed no matter which name is used (1919, p. 175).

9. Distinguishing psychologically from semantically motivated ways of individuating types of beliefs provides a ready reply to Stich's (1978) and Perry's (1979) denial that belief is a properly psychological notion. They both rely on the arbitrary assumption that beliefs are or ought to be type individuated by truth-conditions only. However, like anything else beliefs can be type individuated in different ways for different purposes. Rather than conclude that for the purposes of explanation and prediction psychology does not need belief, Stich and Perry ought to have concluded that psychology should individuate types of beliefs in a way suitable to these purposes, namely by contents. People's behavior is intelligible only if we understand how they represent the world and particular things in it. How they do that consists in the contents of their beliefs and other attitudes, not in the objects of these attitudes.

10. Of course if you believe the tomato you are now looking at is the one you saw before, you may make false inferences, e.g., that it mysteriously changed shape.

11. For simplicity (but, as they say, without loss of generality) I am sticking to

one-place predicates and to *de re* beliefs about one object. (DR) could be suitably elaborated to cover *de re* thoughts about more than one object, as when you believe of two objects you are looking at that one is larger than the other.

12. Here I should mention a recent argument of Searle's (1983, pp. 213–214) against "irreducibly" *de re* beliefs, on the grounds that their

> contents are sufficient to determine the entire sets of conditions of satisfaction . . . not by setting purely general conditions, but rather by indicating relations in which the rest of the conditions of satisfaction must stand to the Intentional state or event itself.

Searle's view sounds so similar to mine that at first I thought we differed only in his unwillingness to call beliefs "*de re*" because they contain modes of presentation of their objects rather than the objects themselves. Obviously I agree that "a change in the world would [not] necessarily mean a change in the [content of a] belief," but I would qualify his claim that "all of our beliefs consist entirely in an Intentional content" (1983, p. 214). For as (DR) makes explicit, the content of a *de re* belief does not determine its truth-condition. Searle holds that it does, evidently because the content not only indicates the "relation in which the rest of the conditions of satisfaction must stand to the Intentional state or event itself" but is somehow "self-referential." I agree that the condition of satisfaction (truth-condition) refers to the state itself, but I deny that the content of the state refers to that very state. That is why I claim, contrary to Searle, that the object of such a belief is determined relationally, not satisfactionally. So far as I can tell, this is the main difference between my view and his. But it is a big one.

13. Burge (1977), Beebe (1979), and Evans (1982) accept all three, but as we will see below under Communication-Based *de re* Thoughts, case (*iii*) can seem dubious, even to those not generally skeptical of *de re* thought about external objects.

14. As Descartes let us never forget, you cannot tell merely from having a perceptual experience that you are not hallucinating: any perception of a physical object can be matched by a qualitatively indistinguishable hallucination. This may or may not lead to skepticism, but here we are concerned with the content of perception-based beliefs, not their justification.

15. The adverbial *method* does not commit us to Chisholm's adverbial *analysis*. It is compatible with such other ontological analyses of perception as sense-data theories, whether representative (causal) or phenomenalist, and direct realist theories, be they act-object or adverbial. The adverbial analysis may make the least ontological commitment, but that does not make it right (the claim that nothing exists is ontologically parsimonious).

16. We need not limit the range of "f" to purely sensible qualities, as the classical empiricists would have insisted, but can let it include properties like being waxen, rotten, or tomato-ish. There seems to be no definite psychological limit on the complexity of values of "f".

17. I can't take seriously the objection to my view based merely on the absence to date of an adequate formulation of the causal theory of perception, but I would

take seriously any plausible in-principle objection or alternative to the causal theory. In any case, I think something like Christopher Peacocke's (1979) notion of differential explanation could well lead to an adequate formulation.

18. It should be noted that what I am calling "perception-based" beliefs are not limited to perceptual beliefs proper, whose predicative contents, we might say, are formed solely as the result of how the object of perception appears. There is no limit to the predicative contents of perception-based beliefs.

19. For further discussion see Bach (1982, pp. 139–143) and Evans (1982, p. 173n.)

20. I believe that Schiffer's argument against irreducibly *de re* thought about objects of perception (1978, pp. 194–196) depends on a conflation of perceptual beliefs with their conceptualization. And even if he is right in maintaining that our *knowledge* of such objects can only be under (indexical) descriptions, like "the tomato I am now looking at," it does not follow that our *thoughts* of them can only be under such descriptions.

21. They recall Martin and Deutscher's (1966) well-known causal account.

22. Just as not all perception-based beliefs are perceptual beliefs, so not all memory-based beliefs are memories-that. But they all must contain memories-*of* (their objects).

23. Obviously I am assuming, as I did earlier in regard to the causal theory of perception, that the causal theory of memory is correct in principle, though it too awaits a formulation that solves the problem of deviant causal chains.

24. When indexicals, demonstratives, or descriptions containing them are used, full understanding requires thinking of the referent only in the same kind of way. For allowances must be made for person (e.g., "you" for "I"), perspective ("there" for "here"), etc.

25. Or use a singular term "as a name," in the sense of the section on Communication-Based *de re* Thoughts, below.

26. It is not necessary for a thought expressed when one uses a description referentially to be *de re* (Bach 1981b, pp. 221–222).

27. This label is convenient but strictly speaking it is a bit misleading, since it normally applies to a relation between an object and a name *type*.

28. A name can be given to something known only by description but then it does not qualify as a *de re* mode of presentation of that object.

29. Schiffer suggests a different description, "the person your image is a memory image of" (1978, p. 197), and proceeds to argue that your knowledge of the person must be under such a description rather than under the image itself (he seems to suppose that such a description is always available, even though it is clearly much too sophisticated for small children and for many larger people). Even if Schiffer is right to insist that having the description is necessary for knowledge of the person, nothing he says even suggests that you could not use the image itself merely to *think* of the person.

30. Strictly speaking I should say "percepts," since he did, after all, appear to me in many ways. But these ways of appearing were close enough (he didn't wear disguises, for example) that I could always recognize him. Thus it seems that my image of him was an abstraction from those percepts (yes, there is the still unsolved

problem of abstraction posed long ago by Berkeley), which though not identical were of a certain general type (I mean qualitative type, not the type *being of Dick Holloway*). So to be precise I should say that my image now is a trace of my image then, not of the various percepts, and that my image then was of him because it was an abstraction from percepts of him.

31. This is John Perry's (1980) term, which I prefer over Paul Grice's (1969) "dossier" and Michael Beebe's (1979) "cluster." One is too suggestive and the other not suggestive enough.

32. I will assume that you remember Tim Gullickson under an image, even if not by name, but for convenience, as I did with in Dick Holloway example, I will use the name in connection with how you think of him.

33. Daniel Dennett (1982, pp. 54–58) uses a case of mistaken identity ("The Ballad of Shakey's Pizza") to attack the whole idea of *de re* belief, on the grounds of implausible duplication of beliefs in such cases. However, he finds this implausible only because he overlooks the role of modes of presentation in *de re* beliefs, and thus he supposes that their contents could only be singular propositions. It is easy to object to that. Also, Dennett thinks that the very idea of such a duplication of beliefs presupposes a "theory that atomizes psychological processes into successive moments with certain characteristics" (1982, p. 58). However, our notion of merging files assumes nothing of the sort.

34. This is Strawson's phrase, and it was he who insisted that nondemonstrative reference can only be descriptive (1959, p. 7ff). Moreover, he maintained that the only not purely descriptive way to think of an object not in one's presence is to think of it in terms of a spatiotemporal relation to objects that are present. In effect, then, he denied the possibility of both memory- and communication-based *de re* thought.

35. The form is not the same when indexicals are involved and adjustments must be made for person or place, e.g., "your" for "my" and "there" for "here." Also, when a proper name is misremembered, the name confused with it can still function as a mental name of the same object.

36. Notice, however, that the hybrid "Aristotle the shipping magnate" is not itself a proper name, unlike "Jack the Ripper," which is.

37. The idea of names as labels on files on individuals goes beyond the Millian view of names as tags on the individuals themselves. Interestingly, modern proponents of the Millian view, such as Saul Kripke (1980) and Michael Devitt (1980), don't seem concerned about how information on an individual thought of by name gets stored. And their formulations of the causal theory of reference, which is commonly incorporated into the Millian view, emphasize interpersonal, communicative links in the chain of reference and neglect the intrapersonal role of memory.

38. Such considerations support the notion of *frames* and similiar notions in Artificial Intelligence, which I discuss in Bach (1984). One can think of files (on individuals) as a special case of frames.

39. No less absurd is Kripke's (1980, p. 8) and Evans's (1982, p. 384) suggestion of distinct but homonymous words (each with its own phantom subscript, no doubt).

40. If "N" has many bearers, then "the bearer of 'N'" is not a *complete* definite description, in the sense of applying to one thing uniquely. However, this presents no problem for NDT, just as incomplete descriptions in general do not present a problem for Russell's Theory of Descriptions (Bach 1983, pp. 198–199).

Also, as argued in Bach (1981a), unlike Kripke's view NDT is not troubled by the problems of existence, identity, and belief sentences or by the problem of vacuous names. Moreover, by assimilating standard uses of names to referential uses of definite descriptions, we can explain what I call the "illusion of rigidity." For the fact is that in referring to an object by name, generally a speaker thinks of it in some other, more informative way than simply as the bearer of that name.

41. Schiffer maintains that thinking of an individual by name, e.g., "Richard Feynman," requires using a metalinguistic description like "the person such that (a) that person is named 'Richard Feynman,' and that (b) my familiarity with the name of a physicist, derives from my having encountered references to that person by that name" (1978, p. 198). Schiffer has no doubt that he has knowledge of Feynman under that description, but most people who think of individuals by name are surely not as conceptually sophisticated as Schiffer. He astutely observes that when we know of someone by name only, we could not have thoughts expressed by sentences containing the name if we didn't have the name, and perhaps this *is* "nicely accounted for on the hypothesis that my only knowledge of Feynman is under a description which mentions his name" (1978, p. 199). However, Schiffer has not shown that *thinking* of Feynman by name involves the use of any description, much less such an elaborate one, and what I am suggesting seems much more realistic psychologically.

42. Even if it turned out that Kripke's story were really true and accepting the story you wondered whom your belief concerning the discoverer of incompleteness was about, you would have to say it was about the man known at the Institute as "Godel." You would realize that your identity belief that the man known at the Institute as "Godel" was the discoverer of incompleteness was false.

43. Strictly speaking, this point applies only to "Godel"-beliefs that have been filed. If one of your sources uses the name "Godel" in an utterance about the object of his "Godel"-beliefs (here I am assuming that the first source's beliefs are about Godel and the second source's about the impostor), whatever "Godel"-thought you entertain *then*, prior to filing (which is tantamount to taking the token of "Godel" you heard as of the same type as that which labels your "Godel" file), is about the same man. However, without being filed it cannot be integrated inferentially with your "Godel"-beliefs, but once it is filed and thus integrated, it no longer has a determinate object. When that happens, it can have only what Dennett calls a "notional object" (1982, p. 38).

44. Hereafter all references to Evans are to Evans (1982).

45. Originally Russell held that they can also be about oneself, but later he abandoned this view.

46. You could *later* identify an object as the object presented by m_1 (it could *then* function as a mode of identification), but at the same time the belief that m_1 is F is formed, you have not identified the object at all.

47. Of course, your ability to reidentify the ace (your recognitional capacity) is,

as Evans points out, relative to the context. If the three cards were returned to the deck containing other cards with bent corners and the deck were shuffled, you would no longer be able to reidentify that ace. On the other hand, if the ace were lying facedown by itself, you would not have to notice its bent corner or locate it in relation to other things in order to be able to reidentify it.

48. In your own thinking, having files on several individuals with the same name does not present a comparable problem. There is no problem for you which individual you are thinking of by that name. For as we saw earlier, each file must have a distinct label, e.g., "Aristotle the philosopher," and since each file's history determines whom it is on, once you have opened a file you are *ipso facto* thinking of its subject. You do not have to ask yourself of whom you are thinking, e.g., the philosopher or the shipping magnate.

49. This paper would not have been the same without the invaluable advice and encouragement of Mike Harnish, notwithstanding the outside chance that he might, just possibly, not agree with every single word.

Bibliography

Bach, K. 1981a. What's in a name. *Australasian Journal of Philosophy* 59:371–386.

_____. 1981b. Referential/attributive. *Synthese* 49:219–244.

_____. 1982. *De re* belief and methodological solipsism. In *Thought and Object*, ed. A. Woodfield. Oxford: Oxford Univ. Press.

_____. 1983. Russell was right (almost). *Synthese* 54:189–207.

_____. 1984. Default reasoning. *Pacific Philosophical Quarterly* 65:35–56.

Bach, K., and R. Harnish. 1979. *Linguistic communication and speech acts*. Cambridge: MIT Press.

Beebe, M. 1979. How beliefs find their objects. *Canadian Journal of Philosophy* 9:595–608.

Boer S., and W. Lycan 1975. Knowing who. *Philosophical Studies* 28:299–344.

Burge, T. 1977. Belief *de re*. *Journal of Philosophy* 74:338–362.

Chisholm, R. 1957. *Perceiving: A philosophical study*. Ithaca, N.Y.: Cornell Univ. Press.

_____. 1980. The logic of believing. *Pacific Philosophical Quarterly* 61:31–49.

Dennett, D. 1982. Beyond belief. In *Thought and Object*, ed. A. Woodfield. Oxford: Oxford Univ. Press.

Devitt, M. 1980. *Designation*. New York: Columbia Univ. Press.

Evans, G. 1982. *The varieties of reference*, ed. J. McDowell. Oxford: Oxford Univ. Press.

Fodor, J. 1980. Methodological solipsism considered as a research strategy in cognitive psychology. *The Behavioural and Brain Sciences* 3:63–73.

Grice, P. 1969. Vacuous names. In *Words and objections*, ed. D. Davidson and J. Hintikka. Dordrecht: Reidel.

Kaplan, D. 1968. Quantifying in. *Synthese* 19:178–214.

Kim, J. 1977. Perception and reference without causality. *Journal of Philosophy* 74:606–620.

Kripke, S. 1980. *Naming and necessity*. Cambridge: Harvard Univ. Press.

Martin, C., and M. Deutscher. 1966. Memory. *Philosophical Review* 75:161–196.

McGinn, C. 1982. The structure of content. In *Thought and Object*, ed. A. Woodfield. Oxford: Oxford Univ. Press.

Peacocke, C. 1979. *Holistic explanation*. Oxford: Clarendon Press.

Perry, J. 1979. The problem of the essential indexical. *Nous* 13:3–21.

———. 1980. A problem about continued belief. *Pacific Philosophical Quarterly* 6:317–332.

Pollock, J. 1980. Thinking about an object. *Midwest Studies in Philosophy* 5:487–499.

Russell, B. 1919. Descriptions. Chap. 16 of *Introduction to mathematical philosophy*. London: George Allen and Unwin.

Schiffer, S. 1978. The basis of reference. *Erkenntnis* 13:171–206.

Searle, J. 1983. *Intentionality*. Cambridge: Cambridge Univ. Press.

Stich, S. 1978. Autonomous psychology and the belief-desire thesis. *The Monist* 61:573–591.

Strawson, P. F. 1950. On referring. *Mind* 59:320–344.

———. 1959. *Individuals: An essay in descriptive metaphysics*. London: Methuen.

Woodfield, A., ed. 1982. *Thought and object*. Oxford: Oxford Univ. Press.

LYNN NADEL
JEFFREY WILLNER
ELIZABETH KURZ

The Neurobiology
of Mental Representation

Although few would dispute that our thoughts, feelings, and beliefs are realized in neural machinery, many nonetheless suppose that these mental states do not relate in any interesting way to their underlying biology. Historically acceptable assumptions about brain structure and dynamic organization encouraged this lack of concern with the neural bases of representation. When cognitive scientists attended to biology they typically "assumed that the hardware of the brain was general enough to support almost any proposal that we found useful to postulate" (Rumelhart and Norman 1981, p. 2). In this way, the contents of mental states have been sought not in the biological hardware, but rather in the symbolic software. Recent research leaves little doubt that many of the assumptions upon which this abiological view is based are wrong, but the implications of these new findings for the relation between mental and biological states remain unclear.

We review some of these findings here and attempt to relate them to issues of mental representation. We begin with a brief exposition of the traditional views which sanctioned a lack of concern with biology, and the ways in which these views have been proven inadequate. In the second section we analyze neural representations in sensory/perceptual systems, in particular those which show the striking feature of maintaining in an apparently isomorphic way some of the spatial or temporal aspects of experience. The possible functions of these internal "maps" are analyzed in some detail, especially as they shed light on the ways in which neural activity might "represent" knowledge. In the third section we discuss mental imagery and evaluate some of the implicit neurobiological claims made by the participants in the debate over the internal mechanisms responsible for the "analog" properties of imagery. We turn from there to a discussion of several contemporary approaches to representation—Connectionism and Computationalism—and how they square with contemporary neuroscience. Finally, we discuss briefly some of our own tentative answers to the mysteries of mental representation.

Background

Brain Theory Circa 1945

After the acceptance of the neuron doctrine at the end of the 19th century, a mechanistic associationism emerged. All psychological phenomena were viewed in terms of sensory inputs, motor outputs, and the neural associations needed to bring about a complex "mapping" of sense data onto actions (Køppe 1983; Greenblatt 1984). Acceptance of this view was hastened by its apparent success in accounting for certain language disorders (aphasias) being uncovered by Broca, Wernicke, and others at the turn of the century.

The neurology of associationism (cf. Buckingham 1984) went like this: the most prominent feature of the human brain was the cerebral cortex, and in particular the *neocortex*, which was assumed to have evolved most recently in vertebrate phylogeny; within neocortex there were areas "dedicated" to particular functions such as vision, audition, fine thumb movement, and the like, and "undedicated" areas reserved for the formation of associations. These associations were the hallmark of higher mental capacity, and the more undedicated cortex a species had, the more *intelligent* it was assumed to be. For the empiricist, undedicated association areas were the blank slates upon which experience wrote. Humans had the most of this kind of brain substrate, as befit our status in phylogeny.

Associations in the Brain and Mind

Classical neuroanatomy provided the foundation for these neurological speculations by viewing the functional organization of the brain in terms of several central postulates:

1. Sensory inputs are relayed over a few subcortical regions to a sole neocortical receiving area for each modality—*primary* sensory cortex.

2. Primary cortex directs its outputs to adjacent *secondary* or *psychic* cortex for further perceptual analyses.
3. Psychic cortex sends its outputs to multimodal *association* areas where integration across sensory modalities occurs.
4. These association areas are the highest level of analysis and abstraction. They are the source of outputs to the motor system controlling complex behaviors such as language or object manipulation.

Within this view, neocortex is divided into sensory, association, and motor areas. Association cortex was assumed to have expanded greatly in vertebrate and mammalian evolution, mirroring the ever-more-complex cognitive functions seen in these species. For example, the ability to integrate abstract information from two or more senses—what is known as cross-modal integration—was deemed essential to language by Geschwind (1965). He linked the absence of language in nonhuman primates to the supposed inability of these animals to integrate cross-modally; this inability itself reflecting the absence of appropriate association cortex.

The Contemporary Scene

Each of these tenets of classical theory has been called into question (Diamond 1980; Merzenich and Kaas 1980; Clemo and Stein 1982). Most areas of cortex previously called associative and assumed to be informationally undedicated have now been shown to receive inputs directly from parts of the thalamus (Diamond 1980) and to contain dedicated neural elements not unlike those seen in primary sensory cortex. It now seems clear that numerous parallel projection systems pervade the sensory systems (Lennie 1980), leaving almost no room for the undedicated associative regions—the blank slates—of classical theory. Merzenich and Kaas (1980) estimate that there are on the order of ten visual maps, seven somatosensory maps, and at least four auditory maps, and these estimates have already been revised upwards to account for new findings. Comparative neuroanatomical studies offer little support for the phylogenetic part of the argument; contrary to its claims, the relative proportions of allegedly "higher" and "lower" brain areas remain fairly constant across wide phylogenic gaps (Northcutt 1981). Comparative analyses of cross-modal integrative capacity also fail to support the traditional view. Animals other than humans have now been shown to integrate sense data from several modalities (cf. Davenport and Rogers 1970; Davenport, Rogers, and Russell 1973).

Associations among undedicated neural elements have figured in behavioral as well as neuropsychological thinking, as exemplified by traditional learning theory (cf. Hilgard and Bower 1975). The view that *any* stimuli, responses, and consequences could be interchangeably associated—a position thought to require undedicated elements—has been seriously undermined in recent years (e.g., Garcia and Koelling 1966; Shettleworth 1983; Domjan and Galef 1983). The search for universal laws of associative learning has given way to analyses of the properties of particular knowledge systems and their (possibly specific) modes of acquiring information (O'Keefe and Nadel 1978; Oakley and Plotkin 1982).

New Thoughts on the Neurology of Association

It is important to be clear about our use of the term association. There is a theory of how the brain works—let's call it *associationism*, or better yet, *connectionism*—which asserts that within the nervous system there are "elements" and "connections" between those elements. All mental phenomena are said to result from the interplay, or associating, of these elements and their connections. This is, simply, the *neuron doctrine*, and it is the generally accepted view.

There is, as well, a theory about *how* we acquire information—let us call it *Associationism*—which asserts that "associations" in the brain result from rather specific arrangements of external events, and only those arrangements. In particular, contiguity relations between events are stressed. An extensive reservoir of informationally undedicated neurons, whose content could somehow be imprinted upon them by experience, permit considerable flexibility with respect to the particular elements, connections, and circuits activated by any experience—for example, the neural activities initiated by the auditory and visual information involved in learning the referents of new words. This flexibility with respect to content made traditional association cortex the best measure of "general intelligence" but it required undedicated neurons. We have noted that "undedicated" cortex is in ever-shorter supply: the ability to conjoin internal representations of arbitrarily related events must be accounted for in some other way.

The outlines of an alternative have begun to emerge in recent syntheses of neuroscientific work on neocortex (see Oakley 1979; Whitfield 1979; Swanson 1983; Phillips, Zeki, and Barlow 1984). Associations are achieved through selective processes acting on what are essentially combinatorial networks of dedicated neurons. These dedicated cortical circuits are specialized for convergence–divergence relations by virtue of their extensive interconnectivity. At the outset integration occurs within modalities (unimodal association), then between modalities (polymodal association), and finally between polymodal inputs (supramodal association). The establishment of connections between neural activities representing arbitrarily related events—the formation of Associations—is said to reflect the *selective* strengthening of pre-existing, dedicated circuits rather that the *instructive* specification of previously undedicated circuits (Jerne 1967; Edelman 1981; Edelman and Finkel 1984; Nadel and Wexler 1984; Changeux 1985; but see Greenough 1984). The mental content of the associations selected in this way would appear to be a function, however complex or disjunctive, of the particular elements comprising them. Things are probably not that simple (see Fodor, this volume), yet the fact remains that neural circuits provide little basis for the general-purpose "blank slates" demanded by traditional theory.

In sum: the implicit brain theory of the 1940's and 1950's which legitimated the abiological stance of cognitive science appears to be wrong in all important respects. The brain is not wired up in a way which could support the general-purpose functions of classical Associationism. Rather, it is prewired in a highly precise way, utilizes content-addressable circuits, and accomplishes flexibility in learning and behavior through selective strengthening of appropriate sets of pre-existing circuits. What then of the relation between mental states and the biological hardware subserving them?

Mental States and the Brain

According to Marr, a representation is a "formal system for making explicit certain entities or types of information, together with a specification of how the system does this." The system itself is merely "a set of symbols with rules for putting them together" (Marr 1982, pp. 20–21). It has been apparent since the work of McCulloch and Pitts (1943) that the nervous system could support such formally defined representations. It was, and remains, unclear just how to talk about the relation between mental states—such things as beliefs, fears, hopes, and the like—and the biological substrates within which they are apparently symbolized.

The early Greeks (Epicuros, Empedocles, and Democritos) held that "objects give off faint images of themselves, simulacra or eidola, which, on being conducted to the mind, acquaint the mind with the nature of the objects which they simulate" (Boring 1950, p. 672). The temptation to look for facsimiles in the mind/brain in order to explain perception and thought is persistent, yet obviously flawed. The problem, as we see below, is not that such facsimiles do not exist, but that their mere existence explains nothing. Indeed, their existence itself becomes a fact in need of explanation.

If you close your eyes and gently press one eyelid, you experience visual sensations. Evidently, subjective experiences can be independent of the external physical events which triggered them. This simple observation led Johannes Muller and Charles Bell to propose, apparently independently, that the specific subjective quality attending any particular neural activity must owe to *where* the activated neurons terminate, rather than to the nature of the stimulus that caused them to be active. Thus, stimulation of retinal elements, by whatever means, gives rise to visual experience. Muller's Doctrine of Specific Nerve Energies rules out the eidola of the early Greeks, and rejects any form of simulative representation, going beyond the position adopted by Locke a century earlier. Locke argued that in the case of secondary qualities such as color, taste, or temperature, it would indeed be implausible to assume that representation is by simulation. But, in the case of the primary qualities—extent and location in space and time—representations could actually simulate what they were representing.

What makes the notion of representation by simulation seem so implausible is its apparent dependence upon an internal agent capable of "looking at" the neural representation and "seeing" what it looks like. From the point of view of neurons what one sees, or more properly feels, is simply a stream of inputs to various parts of one's surface, all of which have more or less the same sort of feel about them. Fodor (this volume) rightly points out that the labels we put on neurons to fix their information content are not visible to the neurons themselves. In the same way, neurons cannot *see* the global patterns of brain activity simulating spatial and/or temporal features of external stimuli. At best they can be taken to "see" that "this input is on, and that input is off, etc.," which is enough for the kind of symbolic representation envisaged by McCulloch and Pitts (see below).

All this having been said, how can we now explain the fact that there are regions in the brain within which spatial and temporal patterns of external stimulation are simulated? Scarcely a text on biological psychology, neurology, or neuroanatomy exists which fails to include pictures of the two best-studied regions: the sensory and motor strips located on either side of the central gyrus. In the nineteenth century Fritsch and Hitzig discovered that electrical stimulation in specific areas of what has come to be called the *motor strip* elicits movements in various parts of the body. An obvious structure to the distribution of these parts has been uncovered. The motor cortex can be portrayed in terms of the parts of the body affected by stimulation in specific regions. The resulting "body schema," though rather distorted, looks something like a body. Similarly, the sensory strip behind the central gyrus is also organized with reference to the body. Here, specific cortical regions are activated by stimulating particular parts of the body surface. As in the motor strip there is considerable distortion, with some parts of the body being heavily represented, while others are scarcely represented at all.

Though distorted, these neural "representations" seem to "look like" what they are representing. They preserve, by resembling, what most call the *topology* of the input.[1] Since this global resemblance can be of little interest to individual neurons themselves, it is reasonable to wonder why such topology-preserving representations exist at all. We take this issue up at some length for three reasons. First, it does present an intriguing puzzle. If you have ever wondered why we see the world rightside-up even though images on our retina are upside-down, you are amongst the puzzled. Second, this is where many of the neuroscientific data have been collected. A discussion of neural representations within these apparently simulative sensory systems broadens into an analysis of neural representation *per se*. And, third, by assessing the view that these "*homunculi*" play some functional role we are led to consider data from the study of mental imagery, on the basis of which claims about the functional efficacy of *isomorphic* internal representations have also been made (e.g., Shepard 1984).

Topological Representations

The essential feature of topological representations are their preservation of the relative spatial positions among inputs. They have been studied extensively in the visual system (the retinotopic projection) and the somatosensory system (the somatotopic projection). A similarly topological projection is seen in the auditory system, and indeed in many other brain systems, but with an important difference. Because of the spatial distribution of retinal and somatosensory receptors, they can convey certain spatial attributes of visual and tactile stimuli. The location of an object in the organism's (egocentric) spatial field, as well as information about the object's spatial extent and movement, can all be related in some lawful fashion to similarly spatial and temporal distributions of receptor activity. In the auditory system there is considerable organization within the receptor surface as well, but the cochlea is segmented in terms of the frequency of the sound stimulus to which its receptors are sensitive, rather than the spatial location of the sound source. Even though the projection from the cochlea into central brain regions concerned with audition is highly topological, there is no possiblility of the direct, simulative preservation of spatial information in this cochleotopic projection that exists in the retinotopic projection. Representation of the location of sounds in space does appear later in the auditory system, contributing to a multimodal spatial respresentation in the superior colliculus (Stein 1984), which we discuss below. This is an interesting observation in itself, for it demonstrates that spatial information could be internally computed in some way from the integration of nonspatial inputs. Why then are the visual and somatosensory systems organized in ways which preserve spatial information from the receptor stage inwards?

Why Topologies?

> If the problem is to connect a million sense cells to a million cells in the brain, one of the simplest solutions is of course to let a whole bundle of fibers find its way, instead of specifying the address for each individual fiber. The preserved order in the projection may just be due to the preserved neighborhood relations of the fibers in the bundle, and it would be idle then to speculate about the functional meaning of the resulting map. (Braitenberg 1984, p. 121)

The simplest account of the maintenance of topological relations in the visual and somatosensory projections holds that it is a by-product of developmental constraints, and plays no functional role in the workings of the system itself. There appear to be four other possibilities, each of which we will briefly discuss. These are (1) use of the resemblance information, (2) map comparison, (3) sensorimotor integration, and (4) local computations. We begin with the possibility that the apparent preservation of topological information is naught but a result of developmental economy—that is, it is simply easier to grow this way.

Developmental Economy—Doing What Comes Naturally

Interest in the functional significance of topological projections has been scant in comparison to that shown in the question of how these orderly patterns actually arise. Much of the early research focused on visual projection systems of fish and amphibia which show marked capacity for topological regeneration after experimental section (e.g., Sperry 1943, 1944, 1963); a wide range of explanations has been offered to account for the orderly patterns of new growth seen in these studies. Topological relations could be maintained by such things as: (1) time of outgrowth of the projection fibers, the *axons*; (2) pre-existing fiber order in the incoming nerve; (3) interaction between fibers in the target area; (4) functional tests of neighborhood relations; and (5) interaction between spatial "markers" carried by incoming fibers and spatial markers in the target area itself. Evidence has been provided for all these possible mechanisms, and it seems likely that several are involved.

Sperry's early results were generally interpreted in terms of the chemo-affinity hypothesis—the idea that there is a match between specific incoming fibers and their appropriate target cells [(5) above]. Most recently, the specific markers envisioned by this hypothesis have been replaced by concentration gradients (Bonhoeffer and Gierer 1984), for which there is both empirical support and greater plausibility. More attention, however, has been focused on the ordering of fibers that exists in the projection system even before it reaches its target, and on the role played in this ordering by various mechanical factors (Holt 1983; Martin and Perry 1983; Walsh and Guillery 1984). This work focuses on patterned projections forming during normal development and suggests that spatial patterning could derive from various mechanical and physical factors constraining the direction of fiber growth.

All this suggests that it is quite natural for topological projection patterns to emerge during development, obeying both mechanical constraints imposed by the medium and chemical constraints imposed by incoming fibers interacting with particular target areas in the brain. The naturalness of such pattern formation has been affirmed in more formal treatments: both mathematical models (Gierer 1981; Hausler and von der Malsburg 1983) and computer simulation (Kohonen 1982) indicate that topologically correct projection patterns can emerge in a self-organizing fashion from arrays of neural elements interacting only locally with one another. Note that these various factors contributing to the emergence of topological projections need have nothing to do with any spatial *content* of the information in the system itself. There is a match between the topological ordering of the fibers, and the spatial distribution of the external objects initiating activity on the visual and somatosensory receptor surface, but this is not a universal trait. Orderly projection patterns exist as well in neural systems uninvolved with spatial information. One might be tempted to wonder: are there systems which do not have this sort of precision? Briefly, the answer is yes—the olfactory system, at least, and probably several others (cf. Martin and Perry 1983; Lynch, in press).

This brief review of the development of projections preserving topological relations indicates that such patterns emerge easily and are the rule rather than the exception. The existence of such a pattern does not mean that the system is necessarily concerned with spatial information.

Resemblance

This oft-discredited but remarkably resilient idea suggests that topological projections pass to the higher brain (read mind) what can be called a replica of the sensed object, if only in terms of its extent and current location.

Thus, "the visual brain is able to recreate a map of its receptive sheet and *thereby perceive* the external world" (Kandel and Schwartz 1981, p. 237, our italics). As the weaknesses of this extreme reductionist position are clear, and have been clear for centuries (see Boring 1950), we discuss it no further.

Comparing Maps

Consider the problem of depth perception. As Marr (1982) pointed out, the 2-D world we receive on the retinal surface must somehow give rise to the 3-D world we subjectively inhabit. How might this be done? For animals with front-facing eyes (rats, cats, monkeys and humans, but not rabbits or fish) binocular disparity information appears to be a large part of the answer. Binocular disparity can be defined as the difference map of the views of a three-dimensional scene by the two eyes (Julesz 1971). Schwartz (1980) detailed a simple algorithm which could generate such "difference maps" by interlacing strips of the cortical maps from the two eyes. This proposal takes advantage of the topologically correct visual maps in both hemispheres and the well-known ocular dominance columns in the visual cortex (alternating columns of neurons preferentially activated from one or the other eye; see Hubel and Wiesel 1962, 1974).

Though the specific details of the processes generating and comparing "maps" may differ from case to case, the capacity to make such comparisons is a very powerful one, providing possibilities beyond mere difference extraction. Each sensory system is comprised of a cascade of "maps" which can be compared, contrasted, or concatenated. When the maps preserve relative spatial position, they permit the integration of activities from different modalities into multimodal representations of the external environment.

The auditory system offers an interesting example because the initial "mapping" at the sensory surface in this modality is not in terms of spatial locations, as we noted earlier. Instead, spatial gradients in the cochlea reflect differential sensitivity to specific frequencies of sound. This frequency-specific, or *tonotopic*, coding is maintained through many strata of the auditory system, comprising as many as six separate levels (Merzenich, Jenkins, and Middlebrooks 1984). Auditory representations sensitive to sound location must be constructed on the basis of minute differences in the intensity and time of arrival of a sound at the two ears. In the barn owl, for example, the initial stages of the auditory system are comprised of neural elements sensitive to specific frequencies, with little regard for the source of the sound. Further into the system a transitional stage appears, in which neurons remain narrowly "tuned" to certain sound frequencies but begin to demonstrate some spatial selectivity as well, responding best to sounds emanating from any of several sources. Finally, at the level of the inferior colliculus and optic tectum one discovers neurons lacking precise frequency specificity—hence "broadly tuned"—but which show considerable spatial specificity. This transition within the auditory system from coding specifically (and only) in terms of sound frequency to coding in terms of the external location of the sound source has two major advantages. First, a quite precise spatial map could result, enabling the organism to locate objects in space purely on the basis of the sounds they emit. This is exactly what one observes in the barn owl (Knudsen and Konishi 1978a, 1978b, 1978c; Knudsen and Knudsen 1983; Knudsen 1982, 1984). Second, once such a topologically correct map is constructed within the auditory system, it could be integrated with the already existing topology-preserving "maps" in the visual and somatosensory systems, yielding a multimodal representation. This too happens in the barn owl, and in many other species as well (Stein 1984; Merzenich, Jenkins, and Middlebrooks 1984).

The above indicates that the preservation of topological features within the nervous system is important. Whether or not this internal topology actually corresponds to an external spatial arrangement of stimuli is only part of the story. Even in systems, such as the auditory system, in which there is no particular relation between the internal spatial ordering of neurons and the external spatial ordering of stimuli activating these neurons, the preservation of internal order seems necessary. This, of course, is just what one would expect if one takes Muller's Doctrine of Specific Nerve Energies seriously—part of what any particular neural activity "means" owes to the location of the active neurons.

Sensorimotor Integration

Few behaviors are more ubiquitous, or more central to survival, than is the deceptively simple *orienting response*. When an animal sees/hears/touches something unexpected, a rapid sequence of behaviors ensues, incorporating both autonomic and somatomotor responses. The former prepare the animal in terms of energy use, while the latter improve the animal's information gathering capacity by appropriate adjustments of the sensory apparatus. The eyes are shifted to bring the new stimulus into the center of the visual field, where more detailed analysis of its features is possible. The ears are shifted to receive sounds more efficiently.

These adjustments, and other motor responses, are all generated from the same midbrain region known as the *optic tectum* in frogs and the *superior colliculus* in mammals. Most of the neurons in the deeper layers of this system are responsive to inputs from any of several modalities—a property seen in even quite primitive species. The critically important feature of these neurons is that they are activated by stimuli from different modalities but occurring in the same part of egocentric space. Intercalated with these neurons responding to inputs from particular spatial locations are others, sources of efferent fibers to as many as fifteen motor areas, in each case eliciting an orientation toward the part of egocentric space "mapped" by the neurons responding to afferent input (Gaithier and Stein 1979; Harris 1980; Harris, Blakemore, and Donaghy 1980; Newman and Hartline 1981; Meredith and Stein 1983; Stein 1984; Fries 1984; Huerta and Harting 1982; Stein, Spencer, and Edwards 1984).

The utility of these exquisitely constructed sensorimotor orienting systems needs little comment. Questions remain about the way in which different sensory inputs are integrated into a single spatial framework, given that the spaces they represent are quite different and that the representations are systematically distorted as well (see below). If we can take a clue from the pattern of development of this system in ontogeny, we might guess that the tectum/colliculus is a kind of "production system" which contains the rules governing a wide variety of orienting behaviors in local, egocentric space. Stein, Spencer, and Edwards (1984) have shown that the motor projections from the colliculus in the cat are in place within a few days of birth, while the sensory inputs grow into place later, modality by modality.

Are Topological Maps Representations?

Spatial maps appear widespread throughout the nervous system. Though developmental economy might be enough to account for some of these maps, it cannot be the only explanation, since the auditory system goes to the trouble to construct such a "map" in the absence of any developmental advantages. Some of these maps seem to resemble what they represent from the receptor surface inwards, others only acquire such a property after considerable integration, while still others seem to subserve spatially appropriate reflexive behaviors. Are any of these maps legitimately called representations? Many cognitive scientists might agree with Pylyshyn (1984, p. 48):

> Describing a certain neural pattern as representing the position of a limb is exactly the same as describing the pattern of gears in a clock as representing the position of the hands on the face of the clock or of the time of day; both are a derivative sense of representing which gains us no explanatory advantage over a neurophysiological or mechanical description.

Whether or not the topological maps we have been discussing are to be called representations, they are the bearers of considerable information for the organism and are the basis for much of its adaptive, even goal-seeking, behavior. Because topological maps can resemble what they "represent," there has been a tendency not to view them as real representations (e.g., Somjen 1972). The foregoing should have made it clear that the functions and characteristics of these maps do not depend upon the resemblance relation itself—we should not be misled by its presence into downgrading the functional importance of the preservation of topological relations. These relations are critical in providing a common framework within which inputs from diverse systems can be integrated in the service of adaptive behavior. And, as we see now, they permit interactions of computational importance between neighboring neural elements.

Local Computations

Neurons can interact with their neighbors in either of two ways: directly through specialized *synaptic* contacts which are usually, but not always, chemically mediated, or indirectly through the spread of current in the extracellular medium. Perhaps these forms of interaction permit the organism's nervous system to capitalize on the topological arrangement of neural elements to accomplish some computational goal.

It is clear that neurons often interact synaptically with their neighbors. Hartline (1938) demonstrated in the horseshoe crab that neurons inhibit their laterally placed neighbors and that this functions as a contrast-enhancing mechanism which "sharpens" the border between areas of differing excitation as a result of unequal inhibition generated on either side. Mechanisms which function in this way are seen throughout the nervous system. But, they have a unique impact within the topology-preserving sensory systems. Here, lateral inhibition networks make these systems particularly interested in *edges* in the environment—surfaces and lines of maximal contrast.

Demonstration of lateral inhibition required the development of new technology—in particular, the ability to record the electrical activity of individual nerve elements. Once this was accomplished (and it is now a relatively routine affair to record from single neurons of awake, behaving, largely unrestrained animals), it became possible to pose the following kind of question: what specific external "feature" elicits activity in the neurons of a given brain region? The simple intuition behind this research was that these neurons could be seen as *detectors* of the features in question, and that with enough of these detectors we could explain perception. It was hoped that the study of feature detectors would relate neural activity to mental representation in the broadest sense.

Hubel and Wiesel (1974) and many, many others have contributed to our knowledge of the features which best activate neurons in different parts of the brain [see Orban (1984), for an up-to-date review of this approach to visual system function]. There is evidence of highly complex "feature detectors" in the furthest reaches of the perceptual systems—e.g., the visually driven "monkey hand" and "face" detectors reported in the inferotemporal neocortex (Gross, Roche-Miranda, and Bender 1972; Gross, Bender, and Gerstein 1979; Perrett, Rolls, and Caan 1982), and the multimodal "place" detectors reported in the hippocampal formation (O'Keefe and Dostrovsky 1971; Ranck 1973; O'Keefe 1976, 1979).

Initial enthusiasms notwithstanding, it is now generally accepted that an understanding of perception will not result simply from analysis of ever more complex "feature detectors" in the brain. As Fodor and Pylyshyn (1981) argue, the mere presence of neurons which "detect" such things as lines, curves, faces, or grandmothers in the external world provides an explanation neither for perception nor for the bases of internal representation.

If objects and events are not "detected" and "encoded" by the activity of individual neurons, how then are they represented by the nervous system? One alternative suggestion focuses on so-called "spatial frequency" channels in the visual system (Campbell and Robson 1968). Any visual input can be decomposed into a set of pure spatial frequencies, cycles of brightness and darkness. Regions of the visual world with rapid transitions in brightness—e.g., edges and the like—are composed of high spatial frequencies. Regions with gradual transitions are composed of low spatial frequencies. Campbell and Robson claimed that these perceptual "channels" have a neural reality; brain circuits were said to be prewired to respond maximally to spatial frequencies of certain values. There is good evidence, in fact, that part of the vertebrate visual system—the *lateral geniculate nucleus* of the thalamus and its projections to the cortex—is segregated along such lines (cf. Sherman and Spear 1982). Visual perception might then be accomplished by decomposing the ambient optic array into its spatial frequency components and by using this componential information to interpret the world. That such decomposition is theoretically and mathematically plausible is clear, but there do not appear to be any neurobiological mechanisms which could globally integrate these local analyses (Uttal 1973; Schwartz 1980).

Feature detection and spatial frequency analysis will not, by themselves, explain perception. Many workers now hold, with Marr (1982), that adequate understanding of perceptual function—indeed cognitive function in general—will require description and explanation at several different levels: (1) that of a *computational theory* (the function or goal of some mental capacity—the *what* and *why* of it); (2) that of *representations* and *algorithms* (the "interpretation" of inputs and outputs, and the transformation of the former into the latter—the programmatic *how* of it; and (3) that of *implementation* (the hardware, the physical *how* of it). Computational problems, for example transforming the two-dimensional information received at the retina into three-dimensional perception of the visual world, are usually open to a variety of solutions. In this sense, computation can be independent of implementation. An actual implementation demands a specific means of representing information, and algorithms appropriate for transforming this type of representation in ways which will achieve the desired computational goal. As long as one assumed that the neural structure of representation made no contribution to its content—the assumption of undedicated neural elements—it made sense to emphasize the purely arbitrary relations holding between the computational and neurobiological levels. However, if the form in which information is represented neurobiologically has something to do with its content, this would limit the range of useful algorithms. Perhaps a particular form of representation *demands* a certain algorithm, and the two together are suited only for a specific computational goal. This version of the "modularity" thesis (see Marr 1976) implies that mental capacities could have characteristic neuroanatomical or neurophysiological signatures, notwithstanding the logical independence of these two levels. We will return to the issue of modularity later. Here, we present a few recent examples of what might be called *computational neuroanatomy*—the study of the relation between neurobiological structure and computational function. Though speculative, they indicate ways in which structure and function might ultimately be linked.

Schwartz (1977, 1980) has considered the details of the projection from the retina to the visual (striate) cortex in some depth. Though topological, it is grossly distorted, riven with anisotropies, and subject to a surprising amount of individual variation (Van Essen, Newsome, and Maunsell 1984). The significance of these distorted simulative "maps" lies not in what they look like, of course, but rather in the role they might play in perceptual analyses. Schwartz (1977) showed that the retinotopic projection can be described analytically as a complex logarithmic (conformal) mapping, which has the effect of converting angular strips into parallel ones. It can be approximated by a single mathematical equation, is fundamental to many biological, especially developmental, phenomena,[2] and apparently characterizes a number of other sensory (and motor!) regions. Its existence in the visual system was confirmed by Van Essen et al. in their study of anisotropies and individual variability. They reported only modest deviations from the conformal principle, and agreed that the visual projection "can to a first approximation be described by one rather simple equation" (p. 446).

Although the exact functional significance of this arrangement is unclear, Schwartz has pointed out that in this logarithmic domain size changes reduce to simple translations, while image size itself remains constant. Such a property could be useful in providing a basis for size invariance—the fact that we treat stimuli activating retinal areas of different size as the same object, depending on our knowledge of the distance of the stimulus at any given moment (but see Cavanagh 1982). Perhaps more important, the common logarithmic code seen in sensory and motor systems could provide the basis for appropriate intermodal mappings. Recall that even though topology is roughly preserved within the visual and somatosensory systems, the distortions are extensive and quite different for the two senses. How are these distorted representations to be integrated? The common property of conformal mapping could help solve this problem.

Another example of computational neuroanatomy concerns the local features of neuronal architecture in the cerebellum—a brain structure whose internal organization has attracted many attempts at correlating structure and function (e.g., Marr 1969; Pellionisz and Llinas 1979). One recent attempt focuses on the several somatotopically arranged "maps" interdigitated in the anterior lobe of the cat's cerebellum (Braitenberg 1983). One of these maps uses the entire lobe to represent the animal's length, another fits the cat into an area no bigger than 1 mm. Braitenberg has suggested that these particular body maps could be parts of a system computing some function in three orthogonal dimensions. He pointed out that every time an animal moves, making contact with other surfaces, passive shock waves propagate through its body. The animal's purposeful movements would be open to interference from these waves unless they were programmed with the resulting shock waves taken into account in advance. Hitting the ground running, a critical ability in many predator and prey species, depends upon the ability to circumvent such interference. Braitenberg suggests that the cerebellum accomplishes this by coupling the passive mechanical waves with sequences of motor commands. Within the topological maps in the cerebellum, appropriately organized arrays of neurons could act as "velocity gates," adjusting the characteristics of outputs so that they mesh with, rather than work against, the effects of the passive waves accompanying movements. A similar claim concerning the direct computation of velocity within the visual system has been made by Ganz (1984).

These examples indicate that the local organization among an array of neural elements can determine their involvement in things like edge detection, velocity of movement, and so on. Although there is no logical necessity for neural arrays to be organized topologically in order to accomplish these functions, such organization certainly simplifies the process. Since the "computation" of velocity, for example, depends upon the sequential activation of neighboring receptor elements, and the transmission of this spatiotemporal pattern of activation to the interior, considerable difficulties would arise if adjacent receptor elements projected to nonadjacent neurons.

More on Representations

Most of the functions we have been discussing—the computation of velocity, adjustment to passive shock waves, binocular disparity—are not the kinds of things populating other chapters in this volume. Interesting though these mechanisms might be, they shed little light on the internal representation of beliefs and the like. What is more, they fail to tell us very much about the basic "units of representation" in the nervous system. Neither individual "feature detectors" nor global spatial frequency analyses will account for both the facts of perception and the known features of the visual parts of the brain. There are benefits obtained by preserving topological relations within internal representations, but the role played by the *isomorphism* between what is being represented and what is doing the representing remains a matter for speculation.

Mental Images

The study of *mental imagery* provides another approach to the role of isomorphic representation, one which seems to make a rather different set of claims about the relation between mental and biological states. The mental rotation studies of Shepard and his colleagues (Shepard and Metzler 1971; Shepard 1975, 1984; Cooper and Shepard 1978), and the mental scanning studies of Kosslyn and his co-workers (Kosslyn 1978, 1980; Kosslyn, Ball, and Reiser 1978), have been interpreted to mean that mental "images" behave *as though* they were embedded in a medium with explicit spatial properties.

Many of the data suggesting this conclusion consist of a linear relation between the spatial extent of manipulations upon internal images and the time to perform such functions. Thus, rotating an internal model of an object, or determining the distance between points on an internal cognitive map, takes more time when greater rotations or distances are involved. Considerable confusion exists over exactly how this linear relation is to be explained. The most concrete interpretation suggests that isomorphic images are literally *rotated* or *moved* within a spatial medium and that the variations in latency simply reflect these physical processes. At the other extreme, latencies are held to reflect the computational complexity of internal manipulations upon representations which are propositional rather than imagistic in form. Increased distances or rotations lead to longer latencies because they require additional computation, not because the physical distances have increased. The long debate between these two positions (see Pylyshyn 1973, 1981; Kosslyn 1981) will not be exhumed here. Our interest lies in assessing the claim that the psychological characteristics of mental imagery somehow reflect the spatial properties of the underlying neural substrate within which images are realized. Most pertinent is the intuition that the smoothly increasing rotation and scanning latencies reported by Shepard, Kosslyn, and others reflect the action of analogue rather than digital processes.

Ever since McCulloch and Pitts (1943) it has been the accepted wisdom that neurons are essentially on–off devices communicating with each other through specific contact points (*synapses*). Acceptance of this idealization provides the basis for most current computational approaches. Assumptions about analogue properties fly in the face of this accepted wisdom.

Analogue Processes in the Brain

It has been known for some time that neurons interact with one another in ways other than through discrete synaptic contacts. Electrical interactions between neighboring neurons have been demonstrated in invertebrates (e.g., Korn and Faber 1979), and more recently in vertebrates[3] (Shepherd et al. 1985). In addition to such nonsynaptic couplings, the field effects generated by all-or-none (digital) *action potentials* could influence the excitability of other neural elements nearby. Such effects would depend upon the way in which collections of neurons are oriented—when all the cell bodies and neural processes are lined up the same way, interactions of this sort would be facilitated. It is worth noting that in most regions of the cortex the neurons *are* organized this way.

Electrical potentials generated by brain activity can be monitored on the surface of the skull: the functional significance of these global patterns of activity remains uncertain. Few accept the Gestaltist position that information is actually represented in these large-scale supraneuronal patterns—which is *not* to say that patterns of electrical activity (EEG) could not serve as perfect harbingers of underlying brain states that *do* have functional significance.

In sum, there is evidence for interactions between neural elements beyond the discrete coupling at synaptic junctions, but no reason to suppose that such interactions could permit large-scale analogue functions. If mental images are not literally being rotated within a spatially extended neural medium, how does one account for the results?

Representing and Resonating

Shepard (1984) has proposed that the brain networks responsible for sensing and responding appropriately to significant stimuli can be said to be *tuned* to *resonate* at specific *natural modes*. These natural modes can be said to "represent" those stimuli (or responses) with which they resonate best, and they behave the same whether one is perceiving or imagining, seeing or dreaming. However, Shepard dissociates himself from any version of resonance based purely on field effects exerted upon individual neurons. Resonance refers instead to "information," and the charactertistics of the natural modes of particular "resonating representations" are "determined by the connectivity and synaptic transmission coefficients of the neural circuit" (p. 437). In other words, Shepard is making no claims about analogue functions in the nervous system. Resonance occurs in terms of dynamic patterns of activity between neurons, interacting with one another in neurobiologically acceptable (e.g., synaptic) ways.

Kosslyn (1981) also refuses to tie the analogue properties of mental images directly to underlying neurophysiology. The "functional relations of loci . . . need not be determined by actual physical relations any more than the functional relations of cells in an array in a computer need to be determined by the physical relations among the parts of core memory" (p. 49). There is nothing, then, in current conceptions of mental imagery which requires a departure from contemporary neurobiology. Resonant modes—particular dynamic patterns of neural activity—can be realized within neural networks functioning in classical all-or-none fashion. Clark (1984) has argued that the opposition between analog and digital, or pictorial and propositional, sets up a false dichotomy. Demonstrations that imagery and perception share similar neural substrates (e.g., Farah 1985), are not pertinent to the underlying analog/digital nature of the representation (cf. Pylyshyn 1984, p. 241).

Representations as Patterns of Activity

Although the analogue vs. digital debate fueled by research on mental imagery settled very little, it did bring to light aspects of psychological function which were incompatible with the view of the brain as something like a digital computer working largely in (admittedly rapid) serial fashion.

And, the notion that information is represented in terms of *patterns* of neural connectivity and activity offers a third way to conceive of neural representation. This approach avoids the pitfalls of pure feature detection hierarchies on the one hand, and neurophysiologically implausible analogue mechanisms on the other.

> The "neuron doctrine" . . . is basic to the connectionist view. The dynamic pattern concept does not contradict this view and, in fact, is compatible if rates of change in neuronal activity are regarded as the "flows" dynamically maintaining a pattern. (Blumenthal 1974, p. 74)

Still More on Representations

It would be wise to regroup here. We have argued that contemporary neuroscience forces one to reconsider the relation between mental representations and their neurobiological substrate. The apparent absence of traditional "undedicated" association cortex, the parallel processing charactertistics of brain, and the iterative, convergent–divergent nature of cortical circuitry suggest that representations reside in patterns of connectivity and activity within extensively interconnected neural arrays. On this broad point there is general agreement.

Is Knowledge Localized or Distributed In the Brain?

However, there remains considerable disagreement about the extent to which knowledge is really distributed. Feature detector theory lies at the localization end of the continuum, asserting at its apogee that each thought had its own cell, each cell its own thought (e.g., Barlow 1972). Spatial frequency theory relies on global representations which are distributed in ways short on biological plausibility. Modern *Connectionist* theories, which we discuss below, encompass both localized and distributed notions of representation.

In the 19th century this issue was framed in terms of *phrenology*—the view that the brain was divided into faculties, each localized to a specific region. Marshall (1984) points out that Gall's faculties were primarily defined in terms of *content domain*. Many of his contemporaries divided the mind into faculties defined *not by their contents*, but rather by their *functions*. This, of course, makes all the difference, as the latter but not the former view biases one toward notions like "undedicated" neurons and leaves the issue of the localization of knowledge aside. As Marshall points out, the modern "modularity" thesis is a resurrection of sorts for Gall's position (see below).

Lashley (1929) posed the question directly: if information is localized in the brain, restricted brain lesions should have selective effects, different for lesions in different areas. If not, then the deleterious effects of brain damage might be expected to reflect the extent of the lesion rather than its location, and to be general rather than specific in nature. Lashley's results did little to settle the question, though he interpreted them as favoring the view that information was not highly localized within given brain regions. He later equivocated with regard to the localization of information in topologically organized systems (Lashley 1937), and his work on the effects of cortical damage was itself criticized for various methodological shortcomings.

Hebb's (1949) classic *Organization of Behavior* proposed a novel quasi-connectionist hypothesis which sought to account for the apparent absence of strict localization of function in the brain. Assemblages of neurons, called *cell assemblies* and *phase sequence*, were set into motion by particular experiences. Such assemblies were composed of neurons distributed widely through the brain which, once started, were capable of sustaining their own activity via reverberatory loops. With enough repetition these loops would become permanently "cohesive," allowing partial inputs to initiate activity in the entire loop. Thus, information was both localized in specific neurons *and* distributed throughout the brain. Hebb's model has a remarkably modern flavor to it [see Goddard (1980) for an updating of cell assembly theory in light of recent neuroscientific data], not least because the assumptions it made about neural plasticity continue to stimulate research (e.g., Marr 1969; Grossberg 1970, 1976; Kohonen 1982; Easton and Gordon 1984).

Cell assemblies have multiple points of entry and often several pathways through which activity could continue to circulate. In this way, the information represented by a particular assembly could survive the loss of some of the assembly's elements. This was Hebb's way of dealing with facts indicating that behavioral functions often survived brain damage. It was known that gaps in the visual representation, caused by migraine headaches or actual brain damage, had virtually no effect on perception (Lashley 1941). The gaps are simply filled in. Similarly, lesions in the frontal cortex could be without apparent effect (Hebb 1945).

The idea that the brain is organized so as to resist the impact of damage has had a surprisingly large impact—surprising because it is a highly ambiguous notion.[4] At one end of the scale are those, like Edelman and Finkel (1984), who are concerned with the fact that individual neurons are continually dying. There *must* be some redundancy built into any representation; otherwise ideas would disappear left and right. Edelman's solution to this problem is "group neuronal selection" theory, which accounts for the way in which groups of neurons are *selected* to represent some external stimulus as a joint function of initial hard-wiring and the organism's unique experiences. Within such groups there is enough redundancy so that the representation can survive local damage.[5]

Shepard (1984) wondered how, despite damage, "the brain can often re-establish more or less normal functioning," and presumed that the brain "has evolved to serve the organism under less favorable conditions. . .even, of structural damage to the brain itself" (p. 419). His answer is that information must be represented in "partially redundant resonant subsystems, loosely coupled to each other and capable of autonomous excitation" (p. 438). In this he makes common cause with *Connectionist* models (e.g., Anderson 1983; Wood 1978, 1983), to which we turn shortly.

Damage resistance of another sort influenced Simon (1962) and Marr (1976) in their analyses of the distribution of information in the nervous system, and they came to rather a different conclusion. Complex systems should be "implemented as a collection of small sub-parts that are as nearly independent of one another as the overall task allows" (Marr 1976, p. 485). By isolating subsystems from each other, the effects of damage can be limited to directly affected areas only.

These two kinds of theoretical responses to the challenge posed by the facts of damage resistance—distribution of knowledge across many elements (or connections) and isolation of functional subsystems—are characteristic of two apparently opposed views of mental representation which stress *connections* or *computations*.

Computations and Connections

To put it most bluntly: the contemporary scene reflects an emerging struggle between "Connectionist" and "Computational" approaches to mental representation. Both seek to incorporate what they consider to be the lessons of modern neurobiology; both fall somewhat short of this goal. We consider each briefly in turn.

The New Connectionism

Renewed interest surrounds the view that information is represented in the nervous system in terms of connectivity patterns among large numbers of neural elements (see, e.g., Feldman 1982; Hinton and Anderson 1981; McClelland and Rumelhart 1981). What differentiates this position from the generally accepted claim that the brain works with elements and their interconnections (the neuron doctrine itself) is the notion that information is internally represented in terms of sets of *connection weights* between elements, rather than in terms of the activity of elements themselves. This claim has a number of implications, not all of which are favorable (see Fodor, this volume).

Connectionists "assume that the computational power of the network arises directly from its connection structure and not through complex symbolic signals or a higher-level interpreter" (Feldman 1982, p. 27). The initial impetus to this approach was the realization that the brain must process information in a massively parallel fashion. Any complex function, therefore, would necessarily be distributed across many circuits. A major goal of Connectionist models, as clearly enunciated by Feldman above, is the rooting out of any hidden homunculi. Connectionism forges complex behavior, even consciousness, out of the combined efforts of a collection of quite "stupid" elements (cf. Dennett 1978; Rumelhart et al., in press). It is this very stupidity which is both the strength and the weakness of the connectionist approach.

The first models (Feldman 1981; Hinton 1981; Kohonen 1980, 1984; Feldman and Ballard 1982) were consistent with the emerging view that combinatorial networks of neurons are *hard-wired* to represent information in specific connections. However, this feature brings with it some serious problems. In particular, since "the knowledge which guides processing is hard-wired into the connections between the processing units" (McClelland 1985, p. 116), considerable duplication of information would be needed to enable parallel processing to occur. Another problem derives from the assumption that learning involves changes in connection weights in such networks. How could prior states of the network, including those necessary for storing the information guiding processing, ever be retrieved? McClelland's (1985) solution is to abandon, for some parts of the network, the view that connections are hard-wired, replacing it with a mechanism which "distributes connections" among an array of undedicated elements. This relapse into what appears to be a neurobiologically untenable position suggests that Connectionist theory has serious limitations.

Connectionist models are currently popular largely because they are very good at abstracting prototypes, reflecting their lineage in *Perceptron* theory (Rosenblatt 1961; Minsky and Papert 1969). This strength has been confirmed in a variety of treatments (e.g., Anderson and Mozer 1981; Reilly, Cooper, and Elbaum 1982; Nelson 1983; Anderson 1983). However, problems surface with any attempt to go beyond this impressive capacity to categorize and abstract prototypes—Connectionist models have difficulty with the representation of individual events. Since experience continually adjusts the connection weights between neurons, it seems impossible to retrieve specific prior states of the network.

In sum: modern Connectionist models originated in attempts to make theories of cognition biologically plausible. Parallel processing and hard-wired architecture were emphasized. The extent to which information is actually distributed remains a matter of debate. Some adopt a local-network view (e.g., Ballard, in press), while others opt for extensive distribution. However configured, these models have problems yet to be surmounted, only some of which are discussed by Fodor (this volume). Coping with change within a fully connected network remains problematic (Barnden 1984), in much the same way that Gestalt field theories could not cope with learning. Taken to its extreme, Connectionism threatens a return of the blank slate:

> The general recognition and association capabilities of the neural network function with a minimum of bias and are as content to make one association as any other. The biological machinery has evolved in such a way as, so to speak, to be ready for anything . . . A child seems willing to accept any connection, marvelous or trivial, if it is repeated and part of his world. (Cooper 1980, p. 15)

Computations

Computational theory could be said to have started with the idea of a blank slate. Turing (1950) certainly appears to have felt that way:

> Presumably the child brain is something like a notebook as one buys it from the stationers. Rather little mechanism, and lots of blank sheets. (p. 456)

Computational theory is *not* simply the assertion that the brain "computes," though of course it does just this. As expounded by Marr (1982) and others, computational theory refers to the view that understanding some cognitive function demands analysis at three separate levels, as we outlined earlier. These are the levels of *computational theory*, *representation and algorithm*, and *implementation*. A computational approach is compatible with many of the assumptions of connectionism. In fact, there are some who consider them interchangeable (Arbib and Caplan 1979), arguing that they are merely different ways of talking about the same thing. Others suggest, quite reasonably, that they are simply addressing different levels of the problem. Certainly computational theories permit at least some parallel mechanisms, though they continue to emphasize sequential processing.

Feldman's (1982) contention notwithstanding, computational theories do not suppose that little symbols move about the brain, using neurons and synapses like freeways and on-ramps. Neural activity itself is taken as *symbolizing* or *encoding* something. This is saying little more than Johannes Muller said nearly two centuries ago: the meaning of a given form of neural activity is to be found in which neurons are active.

Connections and Computations Compared

We have meandered through battlefields historical and rhetorical. The outlines of a convergence seem clear. Knowledge is represented within neural aggregates and is expressed through their action and interactions. These neural representations *necessarily* have the character of symbols—there is simply no other way to talk about them.

Connectionist models, interpreted in computational terms, provide a reasonable approximation to much of neocortical function, as currently viewed by neuroscientists. Long considered the crowning achievement of evolution, most of the neocortex is more properly seen as an analyzing device, capable of detecting and adjusting to a wide range of environmental invariances. These adjustments are what Shepard, and Gibson and Lashley before him, mean by the term "resonance." Connectionist networks *relax* into these resonant modes by moving towards stable (energy) states. One can safely predict that future years will see a great expansion of research on these networks.

Beyond these concept-forming, prototype-extracting systems there must lie combinatorial networks which provide in some way for the representation of nonprototypical things—the unique and singular which cannot be reduced to an exemplar of something else. There are many reasons to believe that there are separate knowledge systems organized with respect to categories on the one hand and unique occurrences on the other (cf. O'Keefe and Nadel 1978; Tulving 1983). The amnesic syndrome confirms this conjecture by devastating the patient's ability to learn that some particular event occurred while sparing pattern-analyzing abilities (e.g., Cohen and Squire 1980). We know about unique events, we remember them, and they intrude on our waking and sleeping moments. Such memories, and their specific contents, seem to stretch beyond the limits of Connectionist theory, demanding separate representation.

Beyond Connectionism—With a Capital C

Realizing the inherent limitations of fully connected networks is one thing—providing alternatives is another. Edelman and Reeke (1982) and McClelland (1985) have found it necessary to go beyond their Connected nets to incorporate some *outside signal* which acts upon the net, influencing its activity and, presumably, any changes which occur in its connection weights.

The introduction of a "teaching input" pays very big dividends. Formal mathematical models (Miyake and Fukushima 1984), computer simulations (Granger 1983), and neurally inspired hypotheses (Edelman and Reeke 1982) show the gain in discriminatory power offered by allowing each level in the sequence of combinatorial networks to "talk back" to areas providing its inputs. The "reentry of outputs from one set of networks to other preceding or parallel networks makes possible spatiotemporal correlations of features from representations of the same object in different networks" (Edelman and Reeke 1982, p. 2091). In this way, reciprocal interconnection allows for the registration of both invariant and unique aspects of experience.

What is perhaps most attractive about this sort of hypothesis is that it is neurobiologically plausible. Everything we have learned in recent years points in the same direction: information in much of the brain is processed within a series of densely interconnected (combinatorial) structures. The "syntax" of these mental representations is provided by a fixed neural architecture whose structure permits only certain combinations. Lynch (in press) has begun to spell out some of the neural mechanisms instantiating these combinatorial nets, but we are far from being able to specify the precise rules governing the actions of any particular network. One further problem remains:

> If the representational theory of the mind is true, then we know what propositional attitudes are. But the net total of philosophical problems is surely not decreased thereby. We must now face what has always been *the* problem for representational theories to solve: what relates internal representations to the world? What is it for a system of internal representations to be semantically interpreted? (Fodor 1981, p. 203)

If we view at least some of these combinatorial networks as the bearers of internal representations, and hence propositional attitudes, we may find a partial answer to this question by investigating what the prewired elements in these nets are "connected" to in the external world. Similar moves within philosophy (e.g., Dretske 1981, this volume; Fodor, forthcoming) encourage this approach. A full answer awaits analysis of the syntax of neural representation—the rules which determine how particular combinatorial systems can, and cannot, put things together.

A Tentative Neurobiological Hypothesis

Consider these ideas in the context of recent work on the neural representation of space. The *hippocampal formation* receives inputs from throughout the neocortex, thus serving as a supramodal convergence area. It can, on the basis of its pattern of inputs, be described as the most advanced cortex in the brain (cf. Swanson 1983), and thus the most "abstract" of the brain's combinatorial nets (cf. Lynch, in press). We have suggested that this brain system is central to the construction of *cognitive maps*—internal representations which capture the spatial layout of scenes and events (O'Keefe and Nadel 1978). This theory is based on the presence of neurons in the hippocampus which act as "place" detectors (cf. O'Keefe 1979 for a review) on the highly organized internal wiring of this structure (cf. Teyler and DiScenna 1984), and on the profound disruption in spatial behavior following damage to this brain region in a number of species, including humans (Sutherland and Dyck 1984; Morris et al. 1982; Squire and Zola-Morgan 1983; Smith and Milner 1981). Though the hippocampus is stocked with neurons which are activated by the animal's presence in a particular location, these are *not* spatially arranged within the hippocampus to resemble the shape or layout of the environment. Adjacent neurons can "detect" places nearby or far apart.

Damage to the hippocampal formation leads to the amnesic syndrome mentioned above: preservation of the ability to "learn how" with a concomitant loss of the ability to "learn that." We supposed that the hippocampal *cognitive map* was intimately involved in establishing new representations of momentary "states of affairs." These internal models would link together the neural representations of all those things coexisting at that moment, creating the unique record which survives to remind us of the event.

Here, then, is a neural system well suited to the task of representing propositions about the world—knowledge that "such-and-such" is the case. It is encouraging that in the absence of the hippocampal formation animals and humans can continue to learn discriminations, benefit from the use of category inclusion, and acquire complex motor, pattern-analyzing, and cognitive skills. The brain systems which remain, neocortex most prominently, apparently contain the "modules" required for these forms of learning. They do not contain modules capable of replacing the lost functions of the hippocampal system—such rehabilitation as amnesic patients are capable of reflects the very real limits of learning in these surviving networks (Schacter and Glisky, in press), when deprived of their interactions with the hippocampal system.

Put most succinctly, the idea is that a network of elements in the hippo-campal formation establishes a temporary "relation" with a network of elements in the neocortical projection areas. By so doing, it helps bind them together (literally and figuratively; cf. Squire, Cohen, and Nadel 1984; Nadel and Wexler 1984), and it imposes upon them an *interpreta-tion*. This interpretation, borne by the hard-wired internal workings of the hippocampus, enriches the cortical representation by enmeshing the things it represents in an objective spatial framework (cf. Nadel, Willner, and Kurz 1985). This nonegocentered map of the external world can be viewed as the last in a series of mental representations of the organism's spatial world. The earliest in the series are the topologically organized systems discussed at the outset—these represent space in purely egocen-tered ways. We should not be surprised that a neural system which creates a unified spatial representation of the world in which we move and act is also central to learning and remembering personal aspects of experience.

Some Final Thoughts

Though one could say that the brain is full of nothing but "representat-ions," this would strain the accepted use of the term. On the other hand, Connectionism and other approaches eschewing all talk of representations are incomplete. Contemporary analyses of representational function in the brain emphasize not only the richly interconnected neural networks de-manded by Connectionist theory but also the dynamic interplay of num-bers of these networks, linked together by precise patterns of reciprocal innervation. Further, neurobiological analyses serve to remind us that the brain is evolving piecemeal, each piece serving some need in the animal's natural world, but in ways compatible with already existing structures. Such a perspective helps one understand why there are so many neural systems representing spatial knowledge.

Fodor (this volume) notes that in Connectionist models "the labels are for us, not for the machine." To the neuroscientist, labels are the chemicals one uses to stain and thereby identify the precise neurons one has been studying. It remains easier to detect labeled neurons than it is to know what they "say." Though the hippocampus might be in a position to read the labels, we may have to be satisfied with an answer like this: what it means to think, feel, or actively believe X is for a specifiable set of some millions of neurons to fire ensemble. In some cases most of these neurons will be in more or less the same vicinity, taking advantage of the benefits of topological representation, and we will be able to see them in action with our instruments, for what it is worth. In most cases only some of these neurons will be in the same vicinity, and we will be reduced to talking about mental states. One cannot help being on the side of reduction in this instance.

Notes

We gratefully acknowledge the help of many colleagues in formulating the ideas expressed in this paper. Dale Sengelaub carefully read and improved an early version. Seminar discussions with Tom McKenna, Marcus Kessler, Steve Hampson, Howard Henry, and Steven Guich helped us understand some of the implications of recent neuroscientific research in this area. Don Hoffman shared his thoughts on computations and connections. Gary Lynch provided intellectual encouragement, and access to his recent thinking in this area. Our debts, of course, are far greater than these few credits suggest. We are grateful for grants from NINCDS (NS-17712) and the March of Dimes Birth Defects Foundation which supported our work during the writing of this chapter. L.N. thanks Maria Cadaxa for her unselfish contributions of time and energy, when both were in short supply. Without her support this paper could not have been written.

1. The terms *topology* and *topography* are often used interchangeably in the neuroscientific literature. This usage is unfortunate. Topography refers to the detailed features of a local region—topographic maps show these features, while topographic mappings preserve their integrity. By contrast, topology refers to the study of properties of (geometric) forms which remain invariant under transformations, such as bending, twisting, etc., thereby preserving neighborhood, but not necessarily metric, relations. This latter is the proper term to use for neural *projection* systems.

2. This equation describes structural patterns that emerge during morphogenesis, and accounts for the ubiquity of certain forms, e.g., spirals, in nature (Thompson 1961).

3. One does not want to rule out the possibility that local nonsynaptic interactions play a role in normal neural function. The important question is whether such interactions would measurably change the way a system works. Consider the situation where local interactions of the sort described by Shepherd et al. (1985) occur within a "sheet" of relatively similar neurons. These interactions might influence the output of the sheet, but the output of cells in the sheet would still take the form of all-or-none action potentials. Thus, we can imagine the following situation: at each level of a "hierarchy" of separate sheets of neurons the inputs will interact in a local, seemingly analog, fashion to influence the shape of the output.

That output, however, will still be digital. We end up with a completely mixed system—analog inputs, digital outputs.

As noted in the text, these local effects should be most pronounced in brain regions where the neurons are organized in a highly regular fashion. And, local nonsynaptic interactions should be prominent in the topological systems, but *not* in nontopological systems. In the latter, evidence suggests that local synaptic interactions serve largely to isolate and perhaps highlight the active neurons. Again, this is pretty much what one would expect when the activity of individual neurons is important. It is all the more likely to be important when the precise pattern of outputs is crucial. Goddard (personal communication) has uncovered evidence for inhibitory interactions within the hippocampus which could easily serve this purpose, as they seem to isolate active elements, maintaining the remainder in a relatively quiet state. O'Keefe (1985) has raised the intriguing possibility that the active elements in the hippocampal "cognitive map" could be picked out by the interaction of two "beams" of input activity. He notes that this system is close to optical holography, and provides some evidence that the internal physiology of the system works in the right way. The holographic idea has been suggested within purely cognitive, connectionist models, too (e.g., Eich 1982).

4. There is a widespread feeling that the brain is rather resistant to various kinds of malfunction, including actual damage or destruction to some of its elements. This "fact," which appeals to arguments based on adaptiveness, is taken as a given; it poses little trouble for traditional theory, since most circuits were supposed to be initially undedicated anyway.

Distributed processing models scatter information thoughout the brain, avoiding serious loss until serious damage is incurred. Modular models isolate systems from each other, so that local damage, even when severe, is restricted in its effects. Another possibility, of course, is that remaining circuits take on some of the functions of those that have been lost—that there is "takeover of function." Yet another is that the circuit regenerates—a common-enough event for some species, but still quite controversial for humans. Most likely of all, it appears, is a solution at the functional/behavioral level. Recovery often consists of *finding another way to do the job*. The neurobiological implications of these various models are quite different.

5. Edelman and Finkel (1984) make much of a set of data purporting to show the extensive redundancy, or "degeneracy," of neural networks. Peripheral nerve section or amputation of a finger cause considerable reorganization in the somatosensory cortex (Kaas, Merzenich, and Killackey 1983; Merzenich et al. 1983)—the topological maps in this region *move*. For Edelman and Finkel these data are proof of the degeneracy inherent in the somatosensory maps, and they provide clues to the neuronal selection rules assumed by these authors to control the "entry" of particular neurons into particular representations during normal development. While these speculations are interesting, they may be premature. At least some of the changes occurred so rapidly that they must have involved the "unmasking" of already-existing connections. Longer latency changes were also seen, and the careful study of these might shed light on the development of cortical representations.

Bibliography

Anderson, J.A. 1983. Cognitive and psychological computation with neural models. *IEEE Transactions on Systems, Man and Cybernetics* SMC-13:799–815.

Anderson, J.A. and M.C. Mozer. 1981. Categorization and selective neurons. In *Parallel models of associative memory*, ed. G.E. Hinton and J.A. Anderson. Hillsdale, N.J.: Erlbaum.

Arbib, M.A., and D. Caplan. 1979. Neurolinguistics must be computational. *The Behavioral and Brain Sciences* 2:449–483.

Ballard, D.H. In press. Cortical connections and parallel processing: Structure and function. *The Behavioral and Brain Sciences.*

Barlow, H.B. 1972. Single units and sensation: A neuron doctrine for perceptual psychology? *Perception* 1:371–394.

Barnden, J.A. 1984. On short-term information-processing in connectionist theories. *Cognition and Brain Theory* 7:25–59.

Blumenthal, R. 1974. Discontinuous systems. *Neurosciences Research Program Bulletin* 12:65–77.

Bonhoeffer, F., and A. Gierer. 1984. How do retinal axons find their targets on the tectum? *Trends in Neurosciences* 7:378–381.

Boring, E.G. 1950. *A history of experimental psychology*. 2d ed. Englewood Cliffs, N.J.: Prentice–Hall.

Braitenberg, V. 1983. The cerebellum revisited. *Journal of Theoretical Neurobiology* 2:237–241.

———. 1984. *Vehicles: Experiments in synthetic psychology*. Cambridge: MIT Press.

Buckingham, H.W. 1984. Early development of association theory in psychology as a forerunner to connection theory. *Brain and Cognition* 3:19–34.

Campbell, F.W., and J.G. Robson. 1968. Application of Fourier analysis to the visibility of gratings. *Journal of Physiology* 197:551–566.

Cavanagh, P. 1982. Functional size invariance is not provided by the cortical magnification factor. *Vision Research* 22:1409–1412.

Changeux, J.-P. 1985. *Neuronal man*. New York:Pantheon.

Clark, A. 1984. Seeing and summing: Implications of computational theories. *Cognition and Brain Theory* 7:1–23.

Clemo, H.R., and B.E. Stein. 1982. Somatosensory cortex: A "new" somatotopic representation. *Brain Research* 235:162–168.

Cohen, N.J. and L.R. Squire. 1980. Preserved learning and retention of pattern-analyzing skill in amnesia: Dissociation of knowing how and knowing that. *Science* 210:207–210.

Cooper, L.A. and R.N. Shepard. 1978. Transformation on representations of objects in space. In *Handbook of perception*. Vol. 8, *Perceptual coding*, ed. E.C. Carterette and M.P. Friedman. New York: Academic Press.

Cooper, L.N. 1980. Source and limits of human intellect. *Daedalus* 109:1–17.

Davenport, R.K., and C.M. Rogers. 1970. Intermodal equivalence of stimuli in apes. *Science* 168:279–280.

Davenport, R.K., C.M. Rogers, and I.S. Russell. 1973. Cross modal perception in apes. *Neuropsychologia* 11:21–28.

Dennett, D. 1978. Artificial intelligence as philosophy and as psychology. In *Philosophical perspectives on artificial intelligence*, ed. M. Ringle. New York: Humanities Press.

Diamond, I.T. 1980. The subdivisions of neocortex: A proposal to revise the traditional view of sensory, motor, and association areas. *Progress in Psychobiology and Physiological Psychology* 8:2–43.

Domjan, M., and B.S. Galef. 1983. Biological constraints on instrumental and classical conditioning: Retrospect and prospect. *Animal Learning and Behavior* 11:116–121.

Dretske, F.I. 1981. *Knowledge and the flow of information*. Cambridge: MIT Press, Bradford Books.

Easton, P., and P.E. Gordon. 1984. Stabilization of Hebbian neural nets by inhibitory learning. *Biological Cybernetics* 51:1–9.

Edelman, G.M. 1981. Group selection as the basis for higher brain function. In *Organization of the cerebral cortex*, ed. F.O. Schmitt, F.G. Worden, G.M. Edelman, and S.G. Dennis. Cambridge: MIT Press.

Edelman, G.M., and L.H. Finkel. 1984. Neuronal group selection in the cerebral cortex. In *Dynamic aspects of neocortical function*, ed. G.M. Edelman, W.E. Gall, and W.M. Cowan. New York: Wiley.

Edelman, G.M., and G.N. Reeke, Jr. 1982. Selective networks capable of representative transformations, limited generalizations, and associative memory. *Proceedings of the National Academy of Science* 79:2091–2095.

Eich, J.M. 1982. A composite holographic associative retrieval model. *Psychological Review* 89:627–661.

Farah, M.J. 1985. Psychophysical evidence for a shared representational medium for mental images and percepts. *Journal of Experimental Psychology: General* 114:91–103.

Feldman, J.A. 1981. A connectionist model of visual memory. In *Parallel models of associative memory*, ed. G.E. Hinton and J.A. Anderson. Hillsdale, N.J.: Erlbaum.

———. 1982. Dynamic connections in neural networks. *Biological Cybernetics* 46:27–39.

Feldman, J.A., and D.H. Ballard. 1982. Connectionist models and their properties. *Cognitive Science* 6:205–254.

Fodor, J.A. 1981. *Representations*. Cambridge: MIT Press, Bradford Books.

――――. Forthcoming. Psychosemantics: Or where do truth conditions come from? In *Essays for Donald Davidson*, ed. E. LePore.

Fodor, J.A., and Z.W. Pylyshyn. 1981. How direct is visual perception? Some reflections on Gibson's "Ecological Approach," *Cognition* 9:130–196.

Fries, W. 1984. Cortical projections to the superior colliculus in the macaque monkey:A retrograde study using horseradish peroxidase. *Journal of Comparative Neurology* 230:55–76.

Gaithier, N.S., and B.E. Stein. 1979. Reptiles and mammals use similar sensory organizations in the midbrain. *Science* 205:595–597.

Ganz, L. 1984. Visual cortical mechanisms responsible for direction selectivity. *Vision Research* 24:3–11.

Garcia, J., and R.A. Koelling. 1966. Relation of cue to consequence in avoidance learning. *Psychononic Science* 4:123–124.

Geschwind, N. 1965. Disconnexion syndromes in animal and man. *Brain* 88:237–294, 585–644.

Gierer, A. 1981. Development of projections between areas of the nervous system. *Biological Cybernetics* 42:69–78.

Goddard, G.V. 1980. Component properties of the memory machine: Hebb revisited. In *The nature of thought. Essays in honor of D.O. Hebb*, ed. P.W. Jusczyk and R.M. Klein. Hillsdale, N.J.: Erlbaum.

Granger, R.H. 1983. Identification of components of episodic learning: The CEL process model of early learning and memory. *Cognition and Brain Theory* 6:5–38.

Greenblatt, S.H. 1984. The multiple roles of Broca's discovery in the development of the modern neurosciences. *Brain and Cognition* 3:249–258.

Greenough, W.T. 1984. Possible structural substrates of plastic neural phenomena. In *Neurobiology of learning and memory*, ed. G. Lynch, J.L. McGaugh, and N.M. Weinberger. New York:Guilford Press.

Gross, C.G., D.B. Bender, and G.L. Gerstein. 1979. Activity of inferior temporal neurons in behaving monkeys. *Neuropsychologia* 17:215–230.

Gross, C.G., C.E. Roche-Miranda, and D.B. Bender. 1972. Visual properties of neurons in inferotemporal cortex of the macaque. *Journal of Neurophysiology* 35:96–111.

Grossberg, S. 1970. Pavlovian pattern learning by nonlinear neural networks. *Proceedings of the National Academy of Sciences* 68:828–831.

――――. 1976. On the development of feature detectors in the visual cortex with applications to learning and reaction-diffusion systems. *Biological Cybernetics* 21:145–159.

Harris, L.R. 1980. The superior colliculus and movements of the head and eyes in cats. *Journal of Physiology* 300:367–391.

Harris, L.R., C. Blakemore, and M. Donaghy. 1980. Integration of visual and auditory space in mammalian superior colliculus. *Nature* 288:56–59.

Hartline, H.K. 1938. The response of single optic nerve fibers of the vertebrate eye to illumination of the retina. *American Journal of Physiology* 121:400–415.

Hausler, A.F., and C. von der Malsburg. 1983. Development of retinotopic projections: An analytical treatment. *Journal of Theoretical Neurobiology* 2:47–73.

Hebb, D.O. 1945. Man's frontal lobes: A critical review. *Archives of Neurology and Psychiatry* 54:10–24.

———. 1949. *Organization of behavior*. New York: Wiley.

Hilgard, E.R., and G.H. Bower. 1975. *Theories of learning*. 4th ed. Englewood Cliffs, N.J.: Prentice-Hall.

Hinton, G.E. 1981. Implementing semantic networks in parallel hardware. In *Parallel models of associative memory*, ed. G.E. Hinton and J.A. Anderson. Hillsdale, N.J.: Erlbaum.

Hinton, G.E., and J.A. Anderson. 1981. *Parallel models of associative memory*. Hillsdale, N.J.: Erlbaum.

Holt, C.E. 1983. The topography of the initial retinotectal projection. *Progress in Brain Research* 58:339–345.

Hubel, D.H. and T.N. Wiesel. 1962. Receptive fields, binocular interaction, and functional architecture in the cat's visual cortex. *Journal of Physiology* 160:106–154.

———. 1974. Uniformity of monkey striate cortex: A parallel relationship between field size, scatter, and magnification factor. *Journal of Comparative Neurology* 158:295–306.

Huerta, M.F., and J.K. Harting. 1982. Tectal control of spinal cord activity: Neuroanatomical demonstration of pathways connecting the superior colliculus with the cervical spinal cord grey. *Progress in Brain Research* 57:293–328.

Jerne, N.K. 1967. Antibodies and learning: Selection versus instruction. In *The neurosciences: A study program*, ed. G.C. Quarton, T. Melnechuk, and F.O. Schmitt. New York: Rockefeller Univ. Press.

Julesz, B. 1971. *Foundations of Cyclopean perception*. Chicago: Univ. of Chicago Press.

Kaas, J.H., M.M. Merzenich, and H.P. Killackey. 1983. The reorganization of somatosensory cortex following peripheral nerve damage in adult and developing mammals. *Annual Review of Neuroscience* 6:325–356.

Kandel, E.R., and J.H. Schwartz. 1981. *Principles of neural science*. New York: Elsevier/North-Holland.

Knudsen, E.I. 1982. Auditory and visual maps of space in the optic tectum of the owl. *Journal of Neuroscience* 2:1177–1194.

———. 1984. Synthesis of a neural map of auditory space in the owl. In *Dynamic aspects of neocortical function*, ed. G.M. Edelman, W.E. Gall, and W.M. Cowan. New York: Wiley.

Knudsen, E.I., and P.F. Knudsen. 1983. Space-mapped auditory projections from the inferior colliculus to the optic tectum in the owl. *Journal of Comparative Neurology* 218:187–196.

Knudsen, E.I., and M. Konishi. 1978a. Space and frequency are represented separately in the auditory midbrain of the owl. *Journal of Neurophysiology* 41:870–884.

――――. 1978b. A neural map of auditory space in the owl. *Science* 200:795–797.

――――. 1978c. Center-surround organization of auditory receptive fields in the owl. *Science* 202:778–780.

Kohonen, T. 1980. *Content-addressable memories*. Berlin: Springer-Verlag.

――――. 1982. Self-organized formation of topologically correct feature maps. *Biological Cybernetics* 43:59–69.

――――. 1984. *Self-organization and associative memory*. Berlin:Springer-Verlag.

Køppe, S. 1983. The psychology of the neuron: Freud, Cajal, and Golgi. *Scandinavian Journal of Psychology* 24:1–12.

Korn, H., and D.S. Faber. 1979. Electrical interactions between vertebrate neurons: Field effects and electrotonic coupling. In *The neurosciences. 4th Study Program*, ed. F.O. Schmitt and F.G. Worden. Cambridge: MIT Press.

Kosslyn, S.M. 1978. Measuring the visual angle of the mind's eye. *Cognitive Psychology* 10:356–389.

――――. 1980. *Image and mind*. Cambridge: Harvard Univ. Press.

――――. 1981. The medium and the message in mental imagery: A Theory. *Psychological Review* 88:46–66.

Kosslyn, S.M., T.M. Ball, and B.J. Reiser. 1978. Visual images preserve metric spatial information: Evidence from studies of image scanning. *Journal of Experimental Psychology: Human Perception and Performance.* 4:47–60.

Lashley, K.S. 1929. *Brain mechanisms and intelligence: A quantitative study of injuries to the brain*. Chicago: Univ. of Chicago Press.

――――. 1937. Functional determinants of cerebral localization. *Archives of Neurology and Psychiatry* 38:371–387.

――――. 1941. Patterns of cerebral integration indicated by the scotomas of migraine. *Archives of Neurology and Psychiatry* 46:331–339.

Lennie, P. 1980. Parallel visual pathways: A review. *Vision Research* 20:561–594.

Lynch, G. In press. Synapses, circuits, and the beginnings of memory. Cambridge: MIT Press, Bradford Books.

Marr, D. 1969. A theory of cerebellar cortex. *Journal of Physiology* 202:437–470.

――――. 1976. Early processing of visual information. *Philosophical Transactions of the Royal Society of London B.* 205:307–322.

――――. 1982. *Vision*. San Francisco: Freeman.

Marshall, J.C. 1984. Multiple perspectives on modularity. *Cognition* 17:209–242.

Martin, K.A.C., and V.H. Perry. 1983. The role of fiber ordering and axon collateralization in the formation of topographical projections. *Progress in Brain Research* 58:321–337.

McClelland, J.L. 1985. Putting knowledge in its place: A scheme for programming parallel processing structures on the fly. *Cognitive Science* 9:113–146.

McClelland, J.L., and D.E. Rumelhart. 1981. An interactive activation model of the effect of context in perception. Part I. An account of basic findings. *Psychological Review* 88:375–407.

McCulloch, W.S., and W.H. Pitts. 1943. A logical calculus of the ideas immanent in nervous activity. *Bulletin of Mathematical Biophysics* 5:115–133.

Meredith, M.A., and B.E. Stein. 1983. Interactions among converging sensory inputs in the superior colliculus. *Science* 221:389–391.

Merzenich, M.M., W.M. Jenkins, and J.C. Middlebrooks. 1984. Observations and hypotheses on special organizational features of the central auditory nervous system. In *Dynamic aspects of neocortical function*, ed. G.M. Edelman, W.E. Gall, and W.M. Maxwell. New York: Wiley.

———, J.H. Kaas. 1980. Principles of organization of sensory-perceptual systems in mammals. *Progress in Psychobiology and Physiological Psychology* 9:1–42.

———, J.H. Kaas, J.T. Wall, R.J. Nelson, M. Sur, and D.J. Felleman. 1983. Topographic reorganization of somatosensory cortical areas 3b and 1 in adult monkeys following restricted deafferentation. *Neuroscience* 8:33–55.

Minsky, M., and S. Papert. 1969. *Perceptrons*. Cambridge: MIT Press.

Miyake, S., and K. Fukushima. 1984. A neural network model for the mechanism of feature-extraction. *Biological Cybernetics* 50:377–384.

Morris, R.G.M., P. Garrud, J.N.P. Rawlins, and J. O'Keefe. 1982. Place navigation impaired in rats with hippocampal lesions. *Nature* 297:681–683.

Nadel, L., and Wexler, K. 1984. Neurobiology, representations, and memory. In *Neurobiology of learning and memory*, ed. G. Lynch, J.L. McGaugh, and N.M. Weinberger. New York: Guilford Press.

Nadel, L., J. Willner, and E.M. Kurz. 1985. Cognitive maps and environmental context. In *Context and learning*, ed. P.D. Balsam and A. Tomie. Hillsdale, N.J.: Erlbaum.

Nelson, T.J. 1983. A neural network model for cognitive activity. *Biological Cybernetics* 49:79–88.

Newman, E.A., and P.H. Hartline. 1981. Integration of visual and infrared information in bimodal neurons of the rattlesnake optic tectum. *Science* 213:789–791.

Northcutt, R.G. 1981. Evolution of the telencephalon in nonmammals. *Annual Review of Neuroscience* 4:301–350.

Oakley, D.A. 1979. Cerebral cortex and adaptive behavior. In *Brain, behaviour, and evolution*, ed. D.A. Oakley and H.C. Plotkin. London: Methuen.

Oakley, D.A., and H.C. Plotkin. 1982. Learning in the context of a hierarchy of knowledge gaining processes. In *Learning, development, and culture*, ed. H.C. Plotkin. New York: Wiley.

O'Keefe, J. 1976. Place units in the hippocampus of the freely moving rat. *Experimental Neurology* 51:78–109.

———. 1979. A review of the hippocampal place cells. *Progress in Neurobiology* 13:419–439.

———. 1985. Is consciousness the gateway to the hippocampal cognitive map? *Brain and Mind*, ed. D. Oakley. London: Methuen.

O'Keefe, J., and J. Dostrovsky. 1971. The hippocampus as a spatial map. Preliminary evidence from unit activity in the freely moving rat. *Brain Research* 34:171–175.

O'Keefe, J., and L. Nadel. 1978. *The hippocampus as a cognitive map*. Oxford: Clarendon Press.

Orban, G.A. 1984. *Neuronal operations in the visual cortex*. Berlin: Springer-Verlag.

Pellionisz, A., and R. Llinas. 1979. Brain modeling by tensor network theory and computer simulation: Distributed processor for predictive coordination. *Neuroscience* 4:323–348.

Perrett, D.I., E.T. Rolls, and W. Caan. 1982. Visual neurones responsive to faces in monkey temporal cortex. *Experimental Brain Research* 47:329–342.

Phillips, C.G., S. Zeki, and H.B. Barlow. 1984. Localization of function in the cerebral cortex. *Brain* 107:327–361.

Pylyshyn, Z.W. 1973. What the mind's eye tells the mind's brain: A critique of mental imagery. *Psychological Bulletin* 80: 1–24.

———. 1981. The imagery debate: Analogue media versus tacit knowledge. *Psychological Review* 87:16–45.

———. 1984. *Computation and cognition. Toward a foundation for cognitive science*. Cambridge: MIT Press.

Ranck, J. B., Jr. 1973. Studies on single neurons in dorsal hippocampal formation and septum in unrestrained rats. *Experimental Neurology* 41:461–555.

Reilly, D.L., L.N. Cooper, and C. Elbaum. 1982. A neural model for category learning. *Biological Cybernetics* 45:35–41.

Rosenblatt, F. 1961. *Principles of neurodynamics: Perceptrons and the theory of brain mechanisms*. Washington, D.C.: Spartan.

Rumelhart, D.E., and D.A. Norman. 1981. Introduction. In *Parallel models of associative memory*, ed. G.E. Hinton and J.A. Anderson. Hillsdale, N.J.: Erlbaum.

Rumelhart, D.E., P. Smolensky, J.L. McClelland, and G.E. Hinton. In press. PDP models of schemata and sequential thought processes. In *Parallel distributed processing: Explorations in the microstructure of cognition*, ed. J.L. McClelland and D.E. Rumelhart. Cambridge: MIT Press, Bradford Books.

Schacter, D.L., and E.L. Glisky. In press. Memory remediation: Restoration, alleviation, and the acquisition of domain-specific knowledge. In *Clinical neuropsychology of intervention*, ed. B. Uzzell and Y. Gross. Boston: Martinus Nijhoff.

Schwartz, E.L. 1977. Spatial mapping in the primate sensory projection: Analytic structure and relevance to perception. *Biological Cybernetics* 25:181–194.

———. 1980. Computational anatomy and functional architecture of striate cortex: A spatial mapping approach to perceptual coding. *Vision Research* 20:645–669.

Shepard, R.N. 1975. Form, formation, and transformation of internal representations. In *Information processing and cognition. The Loyola Symposium*, ed. R.I. Solso. Hillsdale, N.J.: Erlbaum.

———. 1984. Ecological constraints on internal representation: Resonant kinematics of perceiving, imagining, thinking, and dreaming. *Psychological Review* 91:417–447.

Shepard, R.N., and J. Metzler. 1971. Mental rotation of three-dimensional objects. *Science* 171:701–703.

Shepheard, G.M., R.K. Brayton, J.P. Miller, I. Segev, J. Rinzel, and W. Rall. 1985. Signal enhancement in distal cortical dendrites by means of interactions between active dendritic spines. *Proceedings of the National Academy of Sciences* 82:2192–2195.

Sherman, S.M., and P.D. Spear. 1982. Organization of visual pathways in normal and visually deprived cats. *Psychological Reviews* 63:738–855.

Shettleworth, S. 1983. Function and mechanism in learning. In *Advances in analysis of behavior*. Vol. 3, *Biological factors in learning*, ed. M.D. Zeiler and P. Harzem. New York: Wiley.

Simon, H.A. 1962. The architecture of complexity. *Proceedings of the American Philosophical Society* 106:467–482.

Smith, M.L., and B. Milner. 1981. The role of the right hippocampus in the recall of spatial location. *Neuropsychologia* 19:781–793.

Somjen, G. 1972. *Sensory coding in the mammalian nervous system*. New York: Appleton–Century.

Sperry, R.W. 1943. Visuomotor coordination in the newt (*Triturus viridescens*) after regeneration of the optic nerve. *Journal of Comparative Neurology* 79:33–55.

———. 1944. Optic nerve regeneration with return of vision in anurans. *Journal of Neurophysiology* 7:57–69.

———. 1963. Chemoaffinity in the orderly growth of nerve fiber patterns and connections. *Proceedings of the National Academy of Sciences, U.S.A.* 50:703–710.

Squire, L.R., N.J. Cohen, and L. Nadel. 1984. The medial temporal region and memory consolidation: A new hypothesis. In *Memory consolidation*, ed. H. Weingartner and E.S. Parker. Hillsdale, N.J.: Erlbaum.

Squire, L.R., and S. Zola-Morgan. 1983. The neurology of memory: The case for correspondence between the findings for human and nonhuman primates. In *The physiological basis of memory*. 2d ed., ed. J.A. Deutsch. New York: Academic Press.

Stein, B.E. 1984. Development of the superior colliculus. *Annual Review of Neuroscience* 7:95–125.

Stein, B.E., R.F. Spencer, and S.B. Edwards. 1984. Efferent projections of the neonatal cat superior colliculus: Facial and cerebellum-related brainstem structures. *Journal of Comparative Neurology* 230:47–54.

Sutherland, R.J. and R.H. Dyck. 1984. Place navigation by rats in a swimming pool. *Canadian Journal of Psychology* 38:322–347.

Swanson, L.W. 1983. The hippocampus and the concept of the limbic system. In *Neurobiology of the hippocampus*, ed. W. Seifert. London: Academic Press.

Teyler, T.J., and P. DiScenna. 1984. The topological anatomy of the hippocampus: A clue to its function. *Brain Research Bulletin* 12:711–719.

Thompson, D'Arcy W. 1961. *On growth and form*. New York: Cambridge Univ. Press.

Tulving, E. 1983. *Elements of episodic memory*. London: Oxford Univ. Press.

Turing, A. 1950. Computing machinery and intelligence. *Mind* 59:433–460.

Uttal, W.R., 1973. *Psychobiology of sensory coding*. New York: Harper and Row.

Van Essen, D.C., W.T. Newsome, and J.H.R. Maunsell. 1984. The visual field representation in striate cortex of the macaque monkey: Asymmetries, anisotropies, and individual variability. *Vision Research* 24:429–448.

Walsh, C., and R.W. Guillery. 1984. Fibre order in the pathways from the eye to the brain. *Trends in Neuroscience* 7:208–211.

Whitfield, I.C. 1979. The object of the sensory cortex. *Brain Behavior and Evolution* 16:129–154.

Wood, C. 1978. Variations on a theme by Lashley: Lesion experiments on the neural models of Anderson, Silverstein, Ritz, and Jones. *Psychological Review* 85:582–591.

———. 1983. Implications of simulated lesion experiments for the interpretation of lesions in real nervous systems. In *Neural models of language processes*, ed. M.A. Arbib, D. Caplan, and J.C. Marshall. New York: Academic Press.

Mental Muddles

Lately, a number of investigators in cognitive psychology and artificial intelligence have proposed that some puzzling facts about thinking can be explained through what they call "mental models." People's ability to understand connected discourse, their knowledge of science, and their skill in reasoning are all topics that mental models are supposed to elucidate. Mental models are held to be responsible for both the successes people have and the errors they make when they are faced with logical, scientific, or probabilistic questions. To further whet our curiosity, some of the proposals advanced by the mental modelers are really quite startling. As an example, one claim is that when you reason about a problem, what you're doing is manipulating in your head working models of the domain in question. If you're reasoning about an electronic circuit, then you're performing quite literally a thought experiment with a mental circuit. Similarly, if you're trying to produce a conclusion for a classical syllogism—for example, the syllogism in (1)—then you're mentally shuffling tokens corresponding to artists, beekeepers, and clerks.

> (1) None of the artists are beekeepers.
>   All of the beekeepers are clerks.
>   ---
>   Therefore, ???

A second remarkable claim is that ordinary sentence understanding involves the same kind of internal models. So if I tell you that there's a cup on the table and you understand me, that's in part because you have constructed an internal scale model containing entities corresponding to the cup and the table, spatially arrayed.

A difficulty for those who want to understand or to appraise mental models is that their proponents seem to have somewhat different views. The term "model" has, of course, lots of current uses—compare "model" in "model theory," "mathematical model," "simulation model," or "scale model"—and the notions of mental model differ in a parallel way. Examples of these varied uses can be found in the contributions to Gentner and Stevens (1983), in Johnson-Laird (1983), and in Kahneman and Tversky (1982). To help get a grip on these differences, we can begin by making a coarse distinction among these theories according to whether or not mental models are supposed to be representations in formats distinct in kind (and perhaps with different representational powers) from more familiar formats (e.g., networks or propositions).[1]

For many mental modelers representational format is not an essential issue: These investigators have been struck by the role that world knowledge or domain-specific knowledge plays in cognitive activities like problem solving or comprehension, and they have offered some plausible hypotheses about the scope of this knowledge. For example, Hayes (1979) and many of the contributors to Gentner and Stevens (1983) are interested in explaining common-sense conceptions of physical phenomena in domains like electricity, heat, and motion. The emphasis is on the content of these beliefs, however they happen to be represented, and with the development of the beliefs with increasing expertise. However, other mental modelers take a much more literal approach, and it is really to this group that my comments apply about thought experiments and internal models. According to this group, mental models are quite unlike the usual propositions or networks and promote a kind of reasoning that is different from standard or probability systems.[2]

In what follows, I'll use "literal mental model" to refer to those conceptions in which the models are unique representations in the above sense and "figurative mental model" for those in which no representational uniqueness is implied. "Figurative" in the latter phrase does not mean that the phenomena studied by these investigators are illusory. On the contrary, these phenomena (some of which are discussed in the next section of this chapter) are of genuine psychological interest, and the case for domain-specific knowledge is persuasive. The question that I wish to raise is whether the evidence warrants more than this—whether the knowledge needs to be packaged in the special purpose representations that the literalists posit. To answer this question, I'd like to examine some arguments that have been advanced to support literal models: that these representations are needed in order to provide a psychological semantics for natural language (Johnson-Laird 1983) and to explain probabilistic (Kahneman and Tversky 1982) and deductive reasoning (Johnson-Laird 1983; Johnson-Laird and Bara 1984). These claims are discussed in turn in the third, fourth, and fifth sections below. The point that I hope will emerge is that the advantages of mental models can all be obtained without commitment to literal models-in-the-head, and that the figurative position is therefore the more reasonable one.

Why Mental Models?

Even when we restrict our attention to literal mental models, we still find some important differences among these theories. For Johnson-Laird (1983), mental models have affinities to methematical model theory, whereas the mental models of de Kleer and Brown (1981, 1983) and Kahneman and Tversky (1982) are more like computer simulation models. I'll return to these differences presently, but in the meantime it's worthwhile noticing a commonality that may help explain what motivates the literalists. This characteristic is that (literal) mental models are typically claimed to mirror quite directly the structure of the domain they represent. For example, a mental model of a circuit contains parts that correspond to those of the circuit: resistors where the circuit contains resistors, capacitors where the circuit contains capacitors, and so on. Because mental models are tailored in this way to the referent domain, they are consistent with evidence from a variety of subfields in cognitive psychology that domain content often plays a large role in comprehension and reasoning.[3]

It's unclear how much weight this notion of domain specificity will bear but it is easy to cite examples that accord with this intuition. In categorization research, for instance, investigators like Medin and Schaffer (1978) have proposed that mental representations of natural categories such as *apple* or *trout* might consist, not of abstract lexical entries, but of sets of remembered exemplars—memories of apples and trout actually encountered. A judgment about whether a new instance is a member of a category is then made by computing its similarity to these remembered instances. Similarly, a good deal of research on the comprehension of discourse suggests that one's memory of a passage includes facts that are not directly expressed by the sentences, but that are imported from one's prior knowledge of the passage's subject matter. A well-known example is that subjects presented with the sentence *Two robins crouched on their nest as the hawk flew above them* have great difficulty discriminating it from *Two robins crouched on their nest as the hawk flew above it* (Bransford, Barclay, and Franks 1972). Since there is much less confusion when "beside" is substituted for "on" in the above sentences, it seems reasonable to think that the difficulty is caused by subjects remembering descriptions of the spatial layout that the initial sentence implies, rather than by subjects remembering the sentence itself. Literalists tend to read these demonstrations as evidence that there is something wrong with propositional or network representations: Because these abstract formats don't by themselves predict memory confusions, they fail to capture some significant psychological generalizations.

Further support for domain specificity comes from studies of probabilistic and deductive reasoning. Thus, Kahneman and Tversky's (1972) research suggests that estimates of the frequency and probability of an event are ordinarily calculated on the basis of intrinsic characteristics of the event rather than on the basis of abstract properties like the base rate of its occurrence or the variance of the relevant distribution, properties that are required for normatively appropriate judgments. Research on deductive reasoning has also uncovered clues that the specific subject matter or content of a set of premises can influence judgments about the soundness of a conclusion drawn from them. Since the interpretation of these results will be important later in this chapter, we need to pause to consider these findings in more detail.

I can most easily illustrate these content effects through some data that Sandra Marcus and I collected as part of an investigation of reasoning with conditional sentences (Marcus and Rips 1979; see also Rips and Marcus 1977). The experiment itself was quite simple. We gave subjects a series of arguments, each consisting of two premises and a conclusion, as shown in the top half of Table 1. The first premise was always a simple conditional and the second premise was either the antecedent or the consequent of the conditional in negated or unnegated form. If the second premise was the antecedent, the conclusion was the consequent, which again could appear negated or unnegated. If the second premise was the consequent, the conclusion was the antecedent, negated or unnegated. Subjects' task was to read the arguments and to decide whether they were logically sound. For our purposes, the main manipulation in this experiment consisted in the way that the arguments were framed. In one of our conditions, subjects saw the arguments phrased in terms of the disposition of letters and numbers on a set of cards. For instance, a modus ponens argument (Argument 1 in Table 1) would appear as in (2). The subjects were told that the sentences referred to a pack of cards that could contain any of the letters A, B, or C on the left side and any of the numerals 1, 2, or 3 on the right. In a second condition, the same arguments were framed in terms of the actions of a pinball-type device that contained three channels along which a ball-bearing could run and a set of three differently colored lights. In this condition, the same modus ponens inference would have appeared as in (3).

(2) If there's a B on the left side of the card, then there's a 1 on the right side.
There's a B on the left side.

There's a 1 on the right side.

(3) If the ball rolls left, then the red light flashes.
The ball rolled left.

The red light flashed.

As a subject in this experiment, the responses that you give should, of course, depend on your interpretation of the conditional. For example, if you understand the first premise as a material conditional, then you should respond that the modus ponens and modus tollens arguments are sound and that the other arguments are not (i.e., you should accept Arguments 1 and 8 of Table 1 and reject the rest). Using this kind of correspondence, we were able to classify the subjects into those who responded as if they were taking the first premise to be a material conditional, those who understood it as if it were a material biconditional, and others. In the bottom panel of Table 1, you'll see the distribution of subjects in these categories for each of the two types of content. These distributions are based on 54 undergraduate subjects, none of whom had taken a course in formal logic. The obvious fact about these data is that the distributions are diffferent for the card and machine contexts. For the cards, Material Conditional responses outnumber Material Biconditionals by more than four to one. For the machine, on the other hand, the proportions are exactly the same.

The point of this illustration is that the subjects were responding, not just to the conditional form of the sentence, but also to the subject matter of the problem. One might be tempted to dismiss the results of one experiment; however, content effects like these are pervasive. Results like ours had previously been obtained by Staudenmayer (1975). Marcus and I also found content effects when subjects were asked to determine the truth of conditionals, given truth values for their antecedents and consequents, and similar results have been reported by Johnson-Laird and Tagart (1969) and by Legrenzi (1970). Other investigators have obtained content effects in Wason's well-known selection task (Wason and Johnson-Laird 1972, chap.

Table 1. **Argument forms (Panel A) and distribution of responses (Panel B) for the conditional reasoning task**
from Marcus and Rips (1979)

A. 1. If A, C.   5. If A, C.
       A.   C.
       ———   ———
       C.   A.
    2. If A, C.   6. If A, C.
       A.   C.
       ———   ———
       Not C.   Not A.
    3. If A, C.   7. If A, C.
       Not A.   Not C.
       ———   ———
       C.   A.
    4. If A, C.   8. If A, C.
       Not A.   Not C.
       ———   ———
       Not C.   Not A.

B.

Problem Content	Material Conditional	Material Biconditional	Other
Cards	.296	.074	.630
Machine	.278	.278	.444

14), as well as in experiments on classical syllogisms (e.g., Wilkins 1928). Whatever its cause, the effect is clearly robust.

Literalists see these content effects as further evidence that something is wrong with propositional or network representations. According to the literal approach, reasoning isn't a matter of proof based on abstract logical formulas but of the creation and manipulation of internal analogues. In terms of the experiment that I described, a subject forms a model of a pinball machine in one condition and a model of a card in another. The subject will then agree that the sample argument about the pinball machine is sound only if in every internal model (or simulation) in which the premises come out true, the conclusion is true as well. Since the pinball machine model will presumably produce different results from the card model, we should expect corresponding differences in subjects' performance. Thus, mental models handle content effects by building the content into the reasoning process itself. Content influences reasoning because reasoning is accomplished by transforming (domain-specific) content.

The foregoing discussion points to several aspects of literal mental models that contrast them with more familiar assumptions in cognitive science. In the rest of this chapter, I'd like to focus on three of these, all of which are quite controversial and which raise some thorny issues about cognitive representation in general. The first is that mental models provide a kind of classical, referential semantics for linguistic forms. Roughly, understanding a sentence is a process that includes two steps. First, input sentences of natural language are stored in memory in the form of propositions; then, optionally, these propositions are interpreted with respect to a mental model of the referents of these sentences. This is the model-theory-in-the-head idea that I spoke of earlier and that is championed by Johnson-Laird. The second issue has to do with models as simulations or thought experiments—a point of view that's common to psychologists like Kahneman and Tversky (1982) and to AI researchers like Forbus (1983) and de Kleer and Brown (1981, 1983). The emphasis here isn't on models as interpretive devices but on models as a way of reasoning or answering questions about complex systems. The third issue is closely tied to the problem of content effects that we have just looked at. The claim is that when people are faced with a deduction problem, they solve it by manipulating mental models. Thus, mental models allow us to eliminate the need to posit internal versions of rules like modus ponens or universal instantiation in favor of a procedure that consists in constructing and rearranging a model's components. What I propose to do is examine each of these issues in turn and then see what can be made of the literalists' case.

Before getting down to work, though, a preliminary comment is in order concerning the relationship between mental models and mental imagery. Like the mental modelers, advocates of imagery hold that networks and propositions do not exhaust the possible formats for cognitive representations. Moreover, both images and models are domain-specific, since the formal properties of these representations are supposed to mirror those of the objects and relations they stand for. Similarly, proponents believe that imagery is implicated in various problem-solving tasks, especially ones that have a spatial component. These points of resemblance may lead you to suppose that mental models are images and to take evidence for and against the imagery hypothesis as bearing on mental models. But although it may be possible to reconstruct models as images, there are some reasons to keep the current formulations of mental models distinct from imagery theories. For one thing, mental modelers themselves insist that models differ from *both* propositions and images (Johnson-Laird 1975, chap. 7). For another, images don't have the power that has been imputed to mental models. As an example, mental models (conceived as internal simulations) are supposed to be responsible for people's predictions about uncertain singular events, such as whether the marriage of a friend will end in divorce (Kahneman and Tversky 1982). It seems unlikely that conventional imagery could be behind such judgments; for although you may be able to image the end of a marriage as a kind of internal movie, the imagery in this situation doesn't seem instrumental in the prediction. The plausibility of the image is more likely to be a function of the prediction than the other way round. For reasons like these, I propose to take the arguments for mental models on their own merits rather than assimilate models to images. As for the imagery hypothesis itself, I would like to remain agnostic for purposes of this chapter. In particular, references to "perceptual representations" should be understood to mean representations *derived* from perception, not representations with an imaginal character.

Muddle I: Mental Models as Semantic Models

As I have already indicated, mental models are advertised as a "semantic" method that is inherently distinct from the "syntactic" method that is more usual in cognitive psychology. Whereas most cognitive psychologists believe that information is mentally represented in terms of networks or logical forms, which are syntactically described strings of internal symbols, mental modelers like Johnson-Laird (1983) claim that they're attempting to explicate notions like truth and reference and to incorporate these notions in a cognitive account of comprehension. The argument is that a psychological account can't do without these semantic properties, since there are purely psychological phenomena that depend on them.

At first glance, these claims of mental modelers may seem odd since they appear to violate a basic tenet of cognitive psychology: what Fodor (1980) calls the "formality constraint." This is the idea that the business of cognitive psychology is to describe computational processes that operate on mental representations and that the only computationally relevant properties of these representations are structural ones internal to the representations themselves. In particular, cognitive psychology must do without semantic notions like truth and reference that depend on the relationship between mental representations and the outside world. Most cognitive psychologists probably accept this formality constraint, though they might not put it in exactly this way. They believe, in other words, that what's cognitively relevant are representations (perceptual representations, for example, or representations derived from discourse), that people can compare these representations in various ways, but that they don't have cognitive access to the external relations these representations bear to the world. This makes it surprising that mental modelers—and especially the cognitive psychologists among them—would appeal to semantic properties.

To determine whether literalists are correct in their demand for referential semantics within cognitive psychology, we need to take a closer look at their proposals. The basic argument (due to Johnson-Laird 1983, chap. 10) is that the usual psychological accounts of how people grasp the meaning of sentences—accounts based on network structures, semantic features, or meaning postulates—leave out facts about the referents of phrases and sentences. But an explanation of reference is needed to explicate even such basic notions as ambiguity and deductive inference. Therefore, the usual psychological explanations are no good. And in particular, what they're missing is exactly what mental models can provide, since mental models supply referents for expressions of mentalese. This conclusion clearly depends on whether Johnson-Laird is correct in asserting that the explanation of comprehension and inference requires a theory of reference, and by way of evidence he offers a number of examples that he believes make the case for incorporating reference within psychology. To see if this is right, let us examine two of these examples, the ones that seem to provide the strongest support for his position. The first concerns how people understand sentences with pronouns, and the second concerns inference with relational predicates.

To begin, then, consider the sentence *They are handsome*. This sentence seems to be ambiguous because *handsome* itself has two meanings: When applied to acts of various kinds, *handsome* means something like generous (as in *Their contributions were handsome*); whereas when applied to people, *handsome* means attractive. So by knowing the referent of *they* in the original sentence, you can infer the correct meaning of the adjective and hence of the sentence as a whole. Conversely, if you happen to know which meaning of *handsome* is intended but aren't sure of the referent of *they*, then you can use that fact to narrow the possibilities. If it means *generous*, *they* will have to denote acts rather than people. Now, according to Johnson-Laird, this interplay between lexical meaning and referential context can't be handled by meaning rules expressed as features or meaning postulates, since these lexical meaning rules don't have access to facts about what the word *they* refers to. But mental models can again come to the rescue. If you happen to know the referent of *they* from nonlinguistic context, then you can put this information into your mental model and use it in the interpretation of the sentence.

Johnson-Laird is short on the details of how mental models are supposed to effect this marriage of reference and lexical analysis. You might also legitimately wonder whether this example shows a fundamental flaw with internal meaning rules. You might feel, for example, that there is a

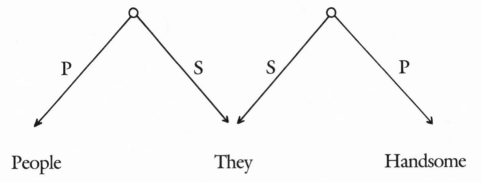

Fig. 1. An ACT-like representation of the sentences *They are handsome* (at right) and *They are people* (at left).

reasonable sense in which *They are handsome* really is ambiguous, no matter how much a speaker or listener knows about the surrounding referential context. However, the present point is that even if you believe there *is* a problem, there is nothing about mental models that make them especially well suited to solve it. The relevant contextual features of such an utterance could just as easily be spelled out mentally as a logical formula or as part of a network. For instance, if *They are handsome* can be represented in the network shown on the right of Figure 1 (based on Anderson 1976), then it seems that we should also be able to encode the relevant contextual information (that "they" are people, say) as in the left half of this structure. The network should then be sufficient to trigger whatever inference procedures are necessary to select the correct meaning of the sentence.

As we will see, similar conclusions apply to the second example, which centers on the relation *x is on y's right* (or *x is to the right of y*). Suppose Ann, Beth, and Cathy are sitting on a bench such that Ann is on the right of Beth and Beth is on the right of Cathy. Then surely Ann is on the right of Cathy. However, Johnson-Laird points out that this conclusion does not follow if some other seating arrangement is adopted. For example, if the three were evenly spaced around a circular table, then when Ann is on Beth's right and Beth is on Cathy's right, Ann is not on Cathy's right. Plainly, too, we could alter the size of the table and the number of people seated around it so that Ann is to the right of the first k individuals but not to the right of person $k + 1$. What Johnson-Laird (1983, p. 241) concludes from this is that "the extent of the transitivity of the relation varies as a function of the seating arrangements up to an arbitrary number of individuals, and would accordingly require an infinite number of different meanings in order to cope with each possible extent from zero upwards." Since an infinite number of meaning postulates for *to the right of* is out of the question, meaning postulates must go. What should replace them are mental models, which can incorporate contextual information about the exact nature of the seating arrangement.

Someone who believes in meaning postulates might respond to such an argument like this: "What Johnson-Laird's example proves is not that 'the extent of the transitivity of [*to the right of*] varies'—whatever that might mean—but simply that *to the right of* is intransitive. What he has done is provide a counterexample showing that for some *x*, *y*, and *z*, *Right-of (x,y)* and *Right-of (y,z)* but not *Right-of (x,z)*, and this exactly meets the definition of an intransitive relation. The fact that it is *sometimes* true that *Right-of (x,z)* couldn't be more irrelevant. This being so, meaning postulates can hardly be faulted for failing to state under what circumstances, when *Right-of (x,y)* and *Right-of (y,z)* are true, *Right-of (x,z)* is true as well. Indeed, the situation is exactly the same as with any more obviously intransitive predicate—say, *can win against* (e.g., in tennis). It's notorious that Ann can win against Beth and Beth against Cathy, but Ann can lose to Cathy. It would be absurd to require that a lexical semantic formalism predict who would win in this third match—that's the job for a theory of tennis skill, not for a theory of meaning."

This objection looks convincing, but a further point that needs to be emphasized is that, even if the objection were mistaken, nothing about Johnson-Laird's example requires literal mental models. For instance, we could specify by means of a network or by separate propositions the position of the individuals and the directions they face (e.g., as vector coordinates). Then questions about who is to the right of whom can be solved by computations on these values. Of course, there may be empirical problems with such a propositional representation—for example, it might mispredict reaction time data when subjects are asked to decide about *Right-of* relations—but the round table example in itself is no argument against it.

Exactly the same deficiency recurs for all of the other examples that Johnson-Laird mentions as reasons for abandoning a psychosemantics based on meaning rules; that is, none of them call for anything more than a mechanism that can compare representations derived from discourse to representations derived from perception. Disambiguation of *They are handsome* requires only that comprehenders (a) have some way of representing the perceptual context in which *they* is specified, and (b) have a way of relating it to the representation of the sentence. Believing that Ann is (or is not) on the right of Cathy demands only that a representation of the sentence match one derived from perception or earlier discourse. The need for such a comparison process is no news, and it has been the subject of a great deal of research in cognitive psychology (e.g., Clark, Carpenter, and Just 1973). The examples provide no grounds to suppose that either perceptual or discourse representations are other than propositions or networks, and thus they are no evidence for literal mental models.

A number of philosophers have argued that a semantics for natural language is incomplete without a theory of truth to show how expressions of the language are connected to the world (Davidson 1967; Lewis 1972). Johnson-Laird's plea for a semantics based on mental models often appears to echo these ideas. For example, Johnson-Laird (1983 p. 259) complains that networks, meaning postulates, and decompositional theories "purport to capture the semantic properties and relations of expressions, but they give no account of their truth conditions," whereas mental model theory can. But it is essential to notice that mental models—even literal ones—are just representations too. Although it might be possible to construct a theory of what it means for one mental representation (e.g., a mental proposition) to be true in relation to another (e.g., a mental model), this clearly wouldn't fulfill the goal of connecting mental representations to the external world. For precisely the same problem about truth would arise with respect to the mental models.[4] Thus, if meaning postulates and other schemes can be faulted for not dealing with referential semantics, mental models can be criticized on the same basis. To provide a referential semantics for mental representation, one must show how to get around a number of forceful objections that appear to doom any such project from the start (e.g., Putnam 1983; Quine 1969; Stich 1983). And to provide such a semantics within cognitive psychology, one must also get around additional obstacles concerning the limits of computational theories (Fodor 1978, 1980). As far as I can see, mental models are of no help in resolving any of these difficulties.

In short, anyone interested in selling mental models is probably well advised not to base his pitch on similarity to referential semantics. Fans of reference-and-truth are unlikely to find internal models to be fair substitutes. Furthermore, whatever mental models appear to be able to do in the line of explaining psychological semantics can already be done by the old notational systems. If mental models do have an advantage, it is more likely to be in explaining reasoning, so it's to this topic that we should turn.

Muddle II: Mental Models as Simulations

A better case for mental models can be built around the way we reason about certain sorts of physical systems. There is an intuition that in thinking about systems we know well, we are able to trace mentally the causal sequence of events that take place during the systems' operation. This kind of thinking can prove useful in correcting faults in a device or in anticipating how the device will perform in some new situation. I'm going to assume that this sort of reasoning is familiar—perhaps from program debugging or from other sorts of troubleshooting (e.g., figuring out why your doorbell isn't working). The important thing is that this sort of reasoning *doesn't* feel like carrying out a derivation in some sort of internal logic or probability calculus. In AI this kind of reasoning has been called "envisioning" or "running" a mental model, and it is the subject of current research by Forbus (1983) and by de Kleer and Brown (1981, 1983). For example, de Kleer and Brown have constructed programs that can answer questions about circuits by simulating their operation in a qualitative model. The question I want to raise concerns how easily this simulation idea can be extended as an account of actual human performance. How much of human reasoning can be reduced to performing a simulation in a mental model of the target domain? This question is highlighted by Kahneman and Tversky's (1982) claims that many tasks calling for prediction and evaluation rest on mental simulations. They mention in particular predicting how well two friends of yours who haven't yet met will get along when you introduce them, assessing the likelihood that the United States will invade Saudi Arabia in the next decade, and evaluating counterfactual statements such as "he could have coped with the job situation if his child hadn't become ill." All of these tasks are supposed to be solved by running a mental model of the situation and seeing how easily such outcomes can be produced.

The trouble is that the AI research on mental models itself casts doubt on the generality of mental simulation. In the complex social–political contexts that Kahneman and Tversky discuss, mental simulation may just be too hard. In order to make mental simulation even remotely plausible, both Forbus and de Kleer and Brown limit the envisioning process to qualitative facts about the device or system in question. For example, the circuit simulations don't have access to exact values for circuit parameters but only to information about whether these parameters are going up or down. This moves the envisioning process away from simulations of the sort that an expert might perform on a computer (simulations involving the solution of large systems of differential equations) and toward psychologically plausible simulations. But lack of precise parametric values means that the performance of simulation is underdetermined. Although you don't have to solve lengthy systems of equations in your head, qualitative simulation requires you to consider multiple possible realizations of the system. The difficulty of so doing is amply demonstrated by the same AI research.

As an example, consider Forbus's program FROB. This program is able to describe and answer questions about the behavior of balls (actually point masses) bouncing around in a two-dimensional plane bounded by arbitrary line segments. In the part of the program that is relevant to us, the plane is divided into nonoverlapping regions that Forbus calls "places." The trick is to predict the places a ball can reach, given a qualitative description of its motion: For example, can the ball reach Place Number 1 if it is currently at Place Number 3 headed northeast? The obvious difficulty is that this qualitative information doesn't constrain the ball's trajectory sufficiently to allow an unambiguous prediction of its motion. The program therefore has to keep track of all possible paths through the space, which is infeasible in any but a very limited terrain. Of course, you can reduce the number of paths by re-introducing quantitative information about energy or elasticity—FROB actually does this in its nonenvisioning mode—but the process then reverts from mental simulation to solving equations in textbook mechanics.

Forbus's conclusion from this is that "although envisioning is an important technique, . . . the burden of building a complete description of possible states is too onerous outside very small domains, and is too restrictive a style to capture all of the ways people use qualitative physical knowledge" (Forbus 1983, p. 70). Similarly, de Kleer and Brown mention that "although one would intuitively expect qualitative simulations to be simpler than quantitative simulations of a given device, they turn out to be equally complex, but in a different way" (de Kleer and Brown 1983, p. 155). The moral is that unless you know a great deal about a system, even qualitative simulations are off limits, given the normal memory and processing limits that humans have to contend with. For any system that is the least complex, we're thrown back on crude rules of thumb that are far from literal simulation. For example, I suspect that although most people know a little about what the parts in their car do, if anything goes wrong they have to rely on simple-minded heuristics such as "if nothing happens when I turn the key and if it's a cold day, then maybe it's the battery."

Some initial empirical evidence against mental simulation comes from an experiment conducted with Dedre Gentner. In this study, college-age subjects were told that the experiment concerned a closed room containing a pan of water and that they would be asked questions about the relation between physical variables that describe this room. These variables were temperature of the air, temperature of the water, air pressure, evaporation rate, and relative humidity. On each trial in the experiment, subjects were presented a pair of these variables and were asked to decide whether a change in the first variable would cause a change in the second. For example, if air pressure goes up, would that cause a change in the room's relative humidity? Since each subject answered a question for each pair, it's possible to examine a subject's entire set of answers for consistency. In particular, we can look for possible violations of transitivity of the causal relations in the subject's responses. Suppose, for example, that the subject stated that a change in variable x causes a change in variable y and that a change in variable y causes a change in variable z. The subject should then agree that a change in variable x will also cause a change in variable z, barring coincidences such as exact cancellation of effects from different causal pathways between x and z. If in these circumstances the subject says that a change in x causes no change in z, we count the triple $<x,y,z>$ as an intransitivity for that subject. It turns out that the maximum number of intransitivities of this sort is 18 for a five-variable set-up like the one we are using; the minimum number is of course 0 intransitivities, which is the score that subjects should receive if they were successfully simulating this system. Chance performance is 7.5 intransitivities; that is, subjects would have an average of 7.5 intransitivities if they answered the questions by flipping a coin.

Our 16 subjects were deliberately chosen to be intelligent nonexperts in this domain. The were all college students at the University of Chicago who had no college-level courses in physics or chemistry. However, most had had at least one high-school chemistry or physics course. Several of them knew enough to volunteer that temperature measures the mean kinetic energy of air or water molecules. For our purposes, the main facts about the experiment are these: None of the subjects in this experiment were perfectly transitive. In fact, no subject had fewer than 3 intransitivities, and the most intransitive subject had 12. The average number of intransitivities was 6.8, which is not significantly better than chance performance. As examples of what these intransitivities were like, in 34% of the response sets subjects affirmed that water temperature changed air temperature and that air temperature changed air pressure but denied that water temperature changed air pressure. Similarly, in 31% of the sets subjects affirmed that water temperature changed evaporation rate and that evaporation rate changed air pressure but denied that water temperature changed air pressure. There are several routes you could take in trying to explain this poor performance. This domain is somewhat technical and perhaps beyond what our naive subjects could envision. Or perhaps they did some mental simulation, but only in a piecemeal way. However, it is difficult to see how these intransitivities could come about if subjects were answering the questions by inspecting a coherent running model of the entire system. Global mental simulation could produce inaccurate responses, but if the simulation is runnable at all, the responses should at least be consistent. Given the obtained inconsistencies, the evidence is better explained on the view that subjects were relying on simple, error-prone rules of thumb that could easily by expressed propositionally.[5]

The thing to reflect on is that if mental simulation breaks down even in this austere system, it seems hopeless when applied to systems that are as complex as the social and political ones that Kahneman and Tversky discuss. The amount of knowledge required to make the models runnable is just too great, if the AI work that I've mentioned is any guide. Defenders of mental simulations are likely to object that in these social–political contexts, people revert to very simplified models of the domain and run their simulations on these stripped-down models. However, at some point it becomes difficult to tell whether processing of this kind is literal simulation or is more like the rule-of-thumb reasoning described above. For example, take Kahneman and Tversky's (1982, p. 203) own evidence on this issue. In one of their experiments, subjects were given the following problem:

> Mr. Crane and Mr. Tees were scheduled to leave the airport on different flights, at the same time. They traveled from town in the same limousine, were caught in a traffic jam, and arrived at the airport 30 minutes after the scheduled departure time of their flights.
> Mr. Crane is told his flight left on time.
> Mr. Tees is told that his flight was delayed, and just left 5 minutes ago.
> Who is the more upset?
> Mr. Crane   Mr. Tees

Not unexpectedly, 96% of the subjects stated that Mr. Tees was the more upset; and according to Kahneman and Tversky, this is because the subjects tried to imagine how close each traveler came to making his flight. But assuming this is true, are subjects literally simulating a further delay in the flight (e.g., a further problem with the aircraft) or an event that would permit the limousine to get to the airport sooner (e.g., a new route that the limousine could take)? Or rather are they reasoning with simpler plausible rules—for example, reasoning that any flight that is delayed by 25 minutes could easily be delayed by 30 or more, thus permitting Mr. Tees to get on board.

Mental modelers' loose talk about mental simulations or simulation heuristics is of little use unless it can be translated into a plausible psychological mechanism that is capable of doing the simulating, where by "plausible mechanism" I mean one that is framed in terms of the ordinary cognitive vocabulary of elementary information processes—for example, comparison and storage operations. But the best examples we have of how this translation would go—the AI research just described—puts these simulations out of the reach of all but experts in a given domain. Of course, people do make predictions about what will happen in complex physical and social interactions. They plan actions and evaluate the probable consequences. If you like, you can refer to these projections as "simulations based on mental models." But in doing so, you forfeit the claim that "simulation" should be taken literally as a distinct type of reasoning. You have become a figurative, rather than a literal, mental modeler.

Muddle III: Models vs. Inference Rules

I mentioned at the beginning that a main attraction of mental models for psychologists is that they seem to provide a way of dealing with the effects of content in deductive reasoning tasks. The hope is that this problem can be explained if we conceive of deduction as a matter of manipulating models, which wear their content on their sleeves. Furthermore, once we have switched to mental models as a deductive method, we can eliminate the need to posit mental inference rules that carry out mental derivations. In Chapter 2 of his book, Johnson-Laird explicitly contrasts the mental-models idea with what he calls "the doctrine of mental logic," the notion that people possess internal deduction schemata. These rules might be mental analogues of the ones you find in Gentzen- or Jaskowski-style natural deduction systems. They might include rules like modus ponens, conjunction introduction, universal instantiation, and so on, that are familiar from introductory texts in predicate logic. In order to decide if an argument is sound, you apply these rules to the premises in an attempt to find a mental derivation of the conclusion. Psychological theories of this type have been proposed by Braine (1978), Osherson (1974–1976), and me (Rips 1983), but also by Johnson-Laird himself in earlier work (Johnson-Laird 1975). What Johnson-Laird now believes is that mental logic was just a mistake—that, in short, deductive reasoning is not a matter of mental *proofs* but of mental *models*.

One way in which mental models could be responsible for subjects' performance in deduction tasks is if subjects treat the tasks as thought experiments about the domain in which the problem is framed—for example, packs of cards or pinball machines in Examples (2) and (3). But the difficulty with this line is the one that we've just encountered in discussing the AI results: Literal mental simulation is implausible for most domains. It's highly unlikely, for example, that naive subjects know enough about a pinball machine's innards to be able to construct a workable mental simulation. To make matters worse, the deduction-as-simulation idea makes it impossible to explain why certain inferences seem so easy, no matter what domain they're applied to. For example, subjects' recognition of the validity of an argument of the modus ponens form does not depend on the complexity of its content (Rips and Marcus 1977). But we ought to predict such dependence if this inference had to be checked by running a mental simulation. You might counter by saying that a statistically null effect is weak grounds for rejecting the mental-simulation idea. Perhaps the simulation need only be run once per domain and the results of the simulation stored for later use. But even this possibility is ruled out by the fact that such inferences are readily carried out even for domains for which you've had no previous exposure and have no model to employ (Evans 1977; Taplin and Staudenmayer 1973). Deduction-as-simulation explains content effects, but unfortunately it does so at the cost of being unable to explain the generality of inference.

It appears that the only way to achieve this generality is to drop mental simulation and adopt some more abstract procedure, and this is exactly what Johnson-Laird has done in the explanations he offers for deductive reasoning. His account relies, not on the notion of mental models as simulations, but on the idea of mental models as a kind of semantics, the same idea we looked at earlier. To see what mental models of this sort are supposed to look like and how they eliminate inference rules, let's consider a specific example. It's unfortunately true that psychologists have devoted a great deal of effort to studying classical syllogisms, even though syllogisms comprise only a tiny subset of deductive inferences. Johnson-Laird is no exception to this trend and in fact his theory of syllogisms is the central example of mental models in his book.[6]

Let us suppose that you are the subject in an experiment in which you are given on each trial a pair of syllogistic premises and are asked to produce a conclusion that follows from these premises. On one of the trials, you receive the pair in (4), the same problem we saw in Example (1):

(4) None of the artists are beekeepers.
    All of the beekeepers are clerks.

    Therefore, ???

According to the theory, the first thing to do in this situation is to interpret the individual premises, and you do this by configuring a set of mental exemplars that correspond to particular artists, beekeepers, and clerks. The theory stipulates that the model for the first premise is the one in (5), and the model of the second premise is that of (6).

(5) $artist_1$
    $artist_2$

$$\text{beekeeper}_1$$
$$\text{beekeeper}_2$$

$$(6) \quad \text{beekeeper}_1 = \text{clerk}_1$$
$$\text{beekeeper}_2 = \text{clerk}_2$$
$$0 \, \text{clerk}_3$$

In these diagrams, the exemplars are indicated by words, though the words themselves have no significance other than to differentiate exemplars of different types. To indicate identity among the exemplars, you place an equal sign between them; so the equal sign between beekeepers and clerks in (6) represents the fact that those beekeepers also happen to be clerks. The zero in front of clerk 3 indicates that this individual may or may not exist; that is, there may or may not be a clerk who is not a beekeeper. In (5) the line in the middle of the diagram indicates that these artists and beekeepers are distinct individuals. The models in (5) and (6) are those of Johnson-Laird and Bara (1984), who present a more detailed and somewhat revised version of the theory described by Johnson-Laird (1983) and Johnson-Laird and Steedman (1978).

After you've formed these representations of the premises, you have to combine them into a unified model of the problem as a whole. One way to do this is according to the diagram in (7), and it's easy to see that this is a perfectly good model in the sense that it makes both of the premises true.

$$(7) \quad \text{artist}_1$$
$$\text{artist}_2$$

$$\text{beekeeper}_1 = \text{clerk}_1$$
$$\text{beekeeper}_2 = \text{clerk}_2$$
$$0 \, \text{clerk}_3$$

In order to generate a conclusion to the syllogism—which is your task as a subject in this experiment—you try to read from this model the relationships that hold between the outer terms, *artists* and *clerks*. The conclusions that suggest themselves on the basis of this diagram are *None of the artists are clerks*, *None of the clerks are artists*, *Some of the artists are not clerks*, and *Some of the clerks are not artists*. However, in order to be sure that these candidate conclusions are valid, you need to check that there are no alternative models of the premises that make these conclusions false. You therefore need to look for new ways of combining the premises, and one such possibility is given in (8):

$$(8) \quad \text{artist}_1$$
$$\text{artist}_2 \qquad\qquad 0 \text{ clerk}_3$$
$$\overline{\qquad\qquad\qquad\qquad\qquad\qquad\qquad}$$
$$\text{beekeeper}_1 = \text{clerk}_1$$
$$\text{beekeeper}_2 = \text{clerk}_2$$

We've moved the position of the optional clerk_3, and the juxtaposition of clerk_3 and artist_2 is supposed to represent an "indeterminate" relation between them: Artist_2 may be the same person as clerk_3. According to this new model, it is no longer necessarily true that none of the artists are clerks nor that none of the clerks are artists. However, the conclusions *Some of the artists are not clerks* and *Some of the clerks are not artists* remain true in (8).

Finally, by adding a new optional clerk token to the first line of the diagram, we can create the model in (9), in which only the conclusion *Some of the clerks are not artists* holds.

$$(9) \quad \text{artist}_1 \qquad\qquad\qquad 0 \text{ clerk}_4$$
$$\text{artist}_2 \qquad\qquad\qquad 0 \text{ clerk}_3$$
$$\overline{\qquad\qquad\qquad\qquad\qquad\qquad\qquad}$$
$$\text{beekeeper}_1 = \text{clerk}_1$$
$$\text{beekeeper}_2 = \text{clerk}_2$$

Boolos (1984) has noted in a critique of Johnson-Laird and Bara (1984) that even this latter conclusion is invalid, since the premises of Syllogism (4) could be true and the conclusion false under circumstances where there are no beekeepers. However, Johnson-Laird and Bara assume that subjects treat all three classes (artists, beekeepers, and clerks) as nonempty, and under this assumption *Some of the clerks are not artists* is valid, since there are no further models of the premises that make this sentence false.

Johnson-Laird claims that the theory can successfully predict the difficulty people have in producing correct conclusions. The key notion is that the larger the number of models that you must consider, the greater the demand on memory, since memory is required to keep track of them. Because working memory is limited in capacity, the greater the number of models, the more likely you are to overlook one or more of them and produce an inappropriate conclusion. In the above example, you supposedly need to consider at least three models—the ones in (7)–(9). Other syllogisms require from one to three models and should vary accordingly in their solution difficulty. For reasons that I'll mention in a moment, my own view of the evidence is that Johnson-Laird simply hasn't given us enough information to be able to assess the prediction. However, we can grant that some proposal of this type is workable in principle and that it may be able to predict syllogism difficulty successfully.

The important question is whether mental models of this sort are more plausible components of a theory of deduction than mental inference rules such as modus ponens, and it seems to me that there are at least four reasons for being suspicious about this possibility. The first is that mental modelers get rid of traditional inference rules only at the expense of positing some rules of their own. Procedures are necessary to specify how the models should be used to represent the premises, how these premise models should be combined, how one combined model should be transformed into another, and how potential conclusions should be evaluated for consistency with a combined model.

To see that this isn't a trivial task, let's return to Syllogism (4). An important feature of Johnson-Laird's theory is that the probability of a correct response depends crucially on which model of the premises is considered first. For example, subjects who initially construct Model (7) should have a relatively difficult time with this syllogism; for as we've seen, there are four potential conclusions that hold in this model, only one of which is a valid conclusion to the argument. Two additional models [i.e., Models (8) and (9)] must be considered to eliminate the invalid conclusions and ensure a correct answer. On the other hand, subjects who start with Model (8) should be somewhat more successful. There are only two potential conclusions that are true of this model, and only a single additional model—Model (9)—is needed to determine the correct one. Thus, predictions about the difficulty of this syllogism depend on whether Model (7) or Model (8) is taken up first. In fact, Johnson-Laird and Bara (1984, p. 34) mention only one principle that is relevant to determining the order in which models are constructed: "in forming an initial model, reasoners are guided by the heuristic of trying to maximize the greatest number of roles on the fewest number of individuals." This means that, all things being equal, subjects should opt for models in which tokens are identified—for example, where a given artist also has the role of a beekeeper or a clerk (see also Johnson-Laird and Steedman 1978). However, it is not clear whether this principle can decide between Models (7) and (8) in our example. To the extent that it applies at all, it would seem to favor (8), since in this model clerk$_3$ might also be an artist. However, if this is the case, Johnson-Laird and Bara's own prediction about the difficulty of this syllogism comes out wrong: Instead of having Difficulty Level 3, it should have Difficulty Level 2. In other words, it's unclear what the basis is for ordering the search of possible models of premises, and this ambiguity about the procedures makes the empirical content of the theory uncertain.[7]

A second problem is that, although the elements in a model are supposed to be objects that provide the referents for the premises and conclusions, the rules that make use of them have to respect properties that seem much like those of standard logical syntax. The equal sign in the syllogism example has to be interpreted in a way that enforces the idea that the two tokens refer to the same individual, and the line between the artists and beekeepers must be interpreted to indicate that the separated tokens cannot refer to the same individual. Because of these features, manipulation of mental models isn't fundamentally different from manipulation of mental propositions. To the extent that the rules that operate on the models are sensitive to these logical constants, they just *are* inference rules. If I'm right about this, the contrast that Johnson-Laird sets up between mental logic and mental models collapses. Of course, the inference rules that mental models employ are nonstandard, and such rules may certainly be worth study. But there appears to be no principled difference between mental logic and mental models of the sort that distinguishes formal proof theory from formal model theory.

Third, although this sort of mental model is more general than the simulation approach, it sacrifices the ability to account naturally for content effects. That is, if the terms of a syllogism are interpreted simply as tokens, then it's no more obvious why content should influence reasoning with mental models than reasoning with standard inference rules. Representations like (7)–(9) are quite abstract and drift away from the idea of domain specificity that provides the underlying motivation for mental models. So, contrary to Johnson-Laird's claims, content effects can't be used as an argument for the superiority of (these sorts of) mental models over inference schemata.[8]

Fourth, what's so bad about inference rules, anyway? In point of empirical evidence, mental logic greatly outscores mental models. Although this isn't the place for a thorough review (see Rips 1984), theories of mental logic successfully predict the validity judgments that subjects give for a fairly wide range of propositional-logic-type arguments (Braine, Reiser, and Rumain 1984; Osherson 1974, 1975; Rips 1983); they account for reaction times (Braine, and Reiser, and Rumain 1984), as well as intersubject differences on problems of this type (Rips and Conrad 1983); and they help explicate what subjects say when they're made to think aloud while they're making validity decisions (Rips 1983). They even predict which lines subjects will recall when they have to remember a natural-language proof (Marcus 1982). Braine and Rumain (1983) propose a way in which mental logic could handle classical syllogisms, and Osherson (1976) has described a mental logic for monadic predicate calculus (which includes classical syllogisms as a special case), showing that it accounts for subjects' judgments of difficulty in evaluating a broad sample of arguments. By comparison, the only tasks for which we have anything approaching a fleshed out mental-model theory are classical syllogisms and transitive inferences.

Although it has been claimed that content effects pose a problem for mental logic, this approach has at least two options for dealing with content. One obvious way is to follow the lead of logicians and absorb content into the logic by adding operators that formalize important relations such as causality and temporal precedence. Both Osherson and I have proposed mental logics of this sort (Osherson 1976; Rips 1983). The other way of dealing with content effects is to regard them as a result of additional premises that subjects bring to the task. Although subjects are told in reasoning experiments to decide whether the conclusion follows on the basis of the premises alone, they may well find this instruction difficult to follow and treat the stimulus argument as an enthymeme. For example, subjects may implicitly use rules of thumb about the likely workings of the pinball machine to eliminate some of the contingencies in our earlier example.

A more serious objection is that the inference rules posited in a mental logic (and the control procedures that apply these rules) are ad hoc—arbitrarily selected to fit the data—and hence are uninformative about the actual procedures that subjects use in reasoning. This is true insofar as the initial selection of rules is based on their ability to account for some body of preliminary data or intuitions. But the selection is also constrained by the ability of these rules to fit together into a system that can account for the infinite number of arguments that people are capable of recognizing as sound. There has also been an attempt to constrain the systems even more tightly by enforcing symmetry relations between the introduction and elimination rules for each connective or quantifier (Osherson 1977). Furthermore, as in any other psychological theory, empirical constraints are added as the system is applied to a larger range of phenomena—in this case, a larger set of logic tasks—and as I have mentioned, mental logic has already been used to predict the outcomes for a fairly reasonable sample of problems. Mental logic hasn't evolved into a completed scientific theory; but neither is it any more ad hoc than its competitors. In brief, although mental models could conceivably be used to banish mental proofs, it's not clear why you would want to.

In the Mental Model Mood

Researchers who subscribe to mental models have offered a number of insights into human cognitive processes. One of their basic themes is that many psychological activities are less isolated than one may have guessed: Language understanding and reasoning (at least at higher levels) proceed against a background of common-sense knowledge. This knowledge is sometimes analogous to theories in substantive domains like mechanics or economics. The positive contributions of mental modelers lie in working out the details of these ideas, and there has been some progress along these lines, as several of the papers in Gentner and Stevens (1983) attest. This chapter is certainly not meant to belittle these achievements but to point out some problems that can arise from taking mental models too literally. Perhaps one could summarize these problems by saying that literal versions of the mental model approach promise much more than they can deliver. They promise to give psychology a referential semantics, explain probabilistic reasoning, and eliminate psychological rules for deductive and lexical analysis. A theory that could do all this would indeed be appealing, but in the case of mental models the promises are spurious. Looking closely, we find: (a) There is no account at all of reference or truth, if we take these notions to be relations between expressions and external objects. The semantic work that models *can* do can be accomplished through propositional or network mechanisms. (b) For most realistic situations, probabilistic reasoning is more plausibly explained through simple rule-of-thumb heuristics rather than through simulation in mental models. (c) Mental model approaches to deduction are restricted to a small subset of inferences, are not clearly formulated, and falter in accounting for the content effects that motivate them. Moreover, "mental model" is not a unitary concept but requires ad hoc assumptions for each domain to which it has been applied. Why would anyone suppose that a representation that seems so clearly limited could carry out such a grand design?

You can put yourself into a mental model mood by concentrating on the varied roles that perceptual representations play in cognition. It's surely possible to form perceptual representations from external information and compare these representations to others that we've constructed from discourse. Perceptual representations are helpful in other ways too. For instance, if Chase and Simon (1973) are right, master chess players can store thousands of representations of board positions to guide them to a winning strategy. In certain reasoning tasks, we might also make use of perceptual representations to ease computational difficulties—keeping track of or transforming the premises. Although you might dispute the role of perceptual representations in particular kinds of problems, you would probably admit that they're sometimes useful.

Clearly, perceptual representations are important aspects of cognition, both when we have to compare sentences with the products of visual input and when we reason. And by the way, since it's a bit frumpy to have to refer to them as "perceptual representations," let's call them "mental models" instead.

This seems to be the intuition behind what literalist mental modelers believe, and up to this point it's unobjectionable. The controversy starts when you begin to take mental models as representations that are distinct in kind—formally unlike other representations. If you then endow them with imperialist ambitions over all of reasoning and psychosemantics, you get the muddles we've discussed.

Notes

This paper benefited from discussions with cognitive psychologists and philosophers at the University of Chicago, Bolt Beranek and Newman, MIT, and the University of Arizona. I'm especially grateful to Norman Brown, Rob Chametzky, Fred Conrad, Dan Garber, Dedre Gentner, Janis Handte, Mike Harnish, Reid Hastie, Gary Kahn, Philip Johnson-Laird, Linda Levine, Ron McClamrock, Greg Murphy, and Ed Smith for comments about earlier versions of this manuscript. Part of the research reported here was supported by US Public Health Service Grant K02 MH00236 and National Science Foundation Grant BNS 80-14131.

1. I use "proposition" (as do most psychologists) to mean what philosophers prefer to call "an internal sentence token" or, perhaps more accurately, "an internal sentence token in logical form." Since it is annoying to spell this out each time, I'll stick to "proposition" throughout this chapter.

2. By "standard deduction systems" I mean the types of axiomatic or natural proof methods described in logic texts (e.g., Mendelson 1964). Of course, by calling them "standard" I don't mean to imply that they are the only correct ways to arrive at deductive conclusions.

3. I owe this point to Edward Smith. See his review (Smith 1985) for some further examples.

4. For the distinction between "true in a model" and "true," see Wallace (1974). The closest Johnson-Laird comes to confronting these problems is in Chapter 15 of his book, and it boils down to the following "truth definition": "If a discourse has complete truth conditions, it is true with respect to the world if and only if it has at least one mental model that can be mapped into the real world. If a discourse has only partial truth conditions . . . , it is false with respect to the world if it has no mental model that can be mapped into the real world . . . " (Johnson-Laird 1983, p. 442). Since there is no explicit account of what this "mapping" amounts to, this definition is not very helpful.

5. Although I'm supposing that these rules of thumb can be expressed in logical form (either as propositions or as production rules), I'm certainly not assuming that only deductive operations are involved in answering the test questions. Expressing information in logical form does not carry with it a commitment to purely deductive procedures (Israel 1984); and in the case of the questions about evaporation, it's natural to expect that inductive inference will come into play. Although I will later defend the plausibility of mental versions of deduction rules (e.g., modus ponens) as explanations of people's reasoning about deductive problems, I don't believe that the only inferences are deductive ones.

6. Johnson-Laird (1983, pp. 71–72) contends that syllogisms play a frequent part in everyday argumentation; yet it is significant that the examples he gives of everyday syllogisms are not of the categorical form that he proceeds to investigate. The real difficulty with the psychologists' emphasis on syllogisms, however, is not so much that they are "ecologically invalid," but that the conclusions reached in studying them do not generalize easily to other forms of deductive inference (Rips 1984). There are exactly 512 categorical syllogisms but an infinite number of deductive arguments.

7. It is also worth noticing that for the subjects to be confident that they have found the correct response to a give syllogism, they must either construct enough mental models to eliminate all possible conclusions (in which case a "no valid conclusion" response is warranted) or construct *all possible* models of the premises to ensure that a putative conclusion is true in all of them. However, there appear to be no theoretical limits to the number of mental models that can be constructed for a premise pair, since a new model can always be found by adding another optional token, as in the construction of Model (9). Only performance factors such as external deadlines or memory size can stop this search. This implies that subjects can never be certain of the validity of a conclusion, for some not-yet-constructed model might refute it. It also means that (contrary to Johnson-Laird 1983) mental model theory is not an effective procedure for syllogisms and is left open to some of the criticisms that he levels against earlier syllogism theories.

8. Of course, these objections are directed specifically at the mental models of Johnson-Laird, and it is always possible that another such formulation will succeed where this one fails. However, I know of no current theory that is both obviously nonpropositional and that accounts naturally for content effects. For example, Erickson's (1974) theory that syllogisms are solved by the mental manipulation of Euler circles has the same problem with content effects. All Euler circles are the same, whether they represent beekeepers or bedwarmers. (Erickson, incidently, doesn't claim to solve the content problem).

Bibliography

Anderson, J. R. 1976. *Language, memory, and thought*. Hillsdale, N.J.: Erlbaum.

Boolos, G. 1984. On "Syllogistic inference." *Cognition* 17:181–182.

Braine, M. D. S. 1978. On the relation between the natural logic of reasoning and standard logic. *Psychological Review* 85:1–21.

Braine, M. D. S., B. J. Reiser, and B. Rumain. 1984. Some empirical justification for a theory of natural propositional logic. In *The psychology of learning and motivation*. Vol. 18, ed. G. H. Bower. New York: Academic Press.

Braine, M. D. S., and B. Rumain. 1983. Logical reasoning. In *Handbook of child psychology*. Vol. 3, ed. J. H. Flavell and E. M. Markman, pp. 263–340. New York: Wiley.

Bransford, J. D., J. R. Barclay, and J. J. Franks. 1972. Sentence memory: A constructive versus interpretive approach. *Cognitive Psychology*, 3:193–209.

Chase, W. G., and H. A. Simon. 1973. The mind's eye in chess. In *Visual information processing*, ed. W. G. Chase, pp. 215–281. New York: Academic Press.

Clark, H. H., P. A. Carpenter, and M. A. Just. 1973. On the meeting of semantics and perception. In *Visual information processing*, ed. W. G. Chase, pp. 311–381. New York: Academic Press.

Davidson, D. 1967. Truth and meaning. *Synthese* 17:304–323.

de Kleer, J., and J. S. Brown. 1981. Mental models of physical mechanisms and their acquisition. In *Cognitive skills and their acquisition*, ed. J. R. Anderson, pp. 285–309. Hillsdale, N.J.: Erlbaum.

———. 1983. Assumptions and ambiguities in mechanistic mental models. In *Mental models*, ed. D. Gentner and A. L. Stevens, pp. 155–190. Hillsdale, N.J.: Erlbaum.

Erickson, J. R. 1974. A set analysis theory of behavior in formal syllogistic reasoning tasks. In *Theories in cognitive psychology*, ed. R. L. Solso, pp. 305–329. Potomac, Md.: Erlbaum.

Evans, J. St. B. T. 1977. Linguistic factors in reasoning. *Quarterly Journal of Experimental Psychology* 29:297–306.

Fodor, J. A. 1978. Tom Swift and his procedural grandmother. *Cognition* 6:229–247.

———. 1980. Methodological solipsism considered as a research strategy in cognitive psychology. *Behavioral and Brain Sciences* 3:63–73.

Forbus, K. D. 1983. Qualitative reasoning about space and motion. In *Mental models*, ed. D. Gentner and A. L. Stevens, pp. 53–74. Hillsdale, N.J.: Erlbaum.

Gentner, D., and A. L. Stevens. 1983. *Mental models*. Hillsdale, N.J.: Erlbaum.

Hayes, P. J. 1979. The naive physics manifesto. In *Expert systems in the micro-electronic age*, ed. D. Michie, pp. 242–270. Edinburgh: Edinburgh Univ. Press.

Israel, D. 1984. Some remarks on the place of logic in knowledge representation. Cambridge, Mass.: Bolt, Beranek and Newman.

Johnson-Laird, P. N. 1975. Models of deduction. In *Reasoning: Representation and process in children and adults*, ed. R. J. Falmagne, pp. 7–54. Hillsdale, N.J.: Erlbaum.

———. 1983. *Mental models*. Cambridge: Harvard Univ. Press.

Johnson-Laird, P. N., and B. G. Bara. 1984. Syllogistic inference. *Cognition* 16:1–61.

Johnson-Laird, P. N., and M. Steedman. 1978. The psychology of syllogisms. *Cognitive Psychology* 10:64–99.

Johnson-Laird, P. N., and J. Tagart. 1969. How implication is understood. *American Journal of Psychology* 82:367–373.

Kahneman, D., and A. Tversky. 1972. Subjective probability: A judgment of representativeness. *Cognitive Psychology* 3:430–454.

———. 1982. The simulation heuristic. In *Judgment under uncertainty: Heuristics and biases*, ed. D. Kahneman, P. Slovic, and A. Tversky. Cambridge: Cambridge Univ. Press.

Legrenzi, P. 1970. Relations between language and reasoning about deductive rules. In *Advances in psycholinguistics*, ed. G. B. Flores D'Arcais and J. M. Levelt, pp. 322–333. Amsterdam: North-Holland.

Lewis, D. 1972. General semantics. In *Semantics of natural language*, ed. D. Davidson and G. Harman, pp. 169–218. Dordrecht: Reidel.

Marcus, S. L. 1982. Recall of logical argument lines. *Journal of Verbal Learning and Verbal Behavior* 21:549–562.

Marcus, S. L., and L. J. Rips. 1979. Conditional reasoning. *Journal of Verbal Learning and Verbal Behavior* 18:199–223.

Medin, D. L., and M. M. Schaffer. 1978. A context theory of classification learning. *Psychological Review* 85:207–238.

Mendelson, E. 1964. *Introduction to mathematical logic*. New York: Van Nostrand–Reinhold.

Osherson, D. N. 1974–1976. *Logical abilities in children*. Vols. 2–4. Hilldsdale, N.J.: Erlbaum.

———. 1977. Natural connectives: A Chomskyan approach. *Journal of Mathematical Psychology* 16:1–29.

Putnam, H. 1983. Computational psychology and interpretation theory. In *Realism and reason*, ed. H. Putnam, pp. 139–154. Cambridge: Cambridge Univ. Press.

Quine, W. V. 1969. Ontological relativity. In *Ontological relativity and other essays*, ed. W. V. Quine, pp. 26–68. New York: Columbia Univ. Press.

Rips, L. J. 1983. Cognitive processes in propositional reasoning. *Psychological Review*, 90:38–71.

———. 1984. Reasoning as a central intellective ability. In *Advances in the study of human intelligence*. Vol. 2, ed. R. J. Sternberg, Hillsdale, N.J.: Erlbaum.

Rips, L. J., and F. G. Conrad. 1983. Individual differences in deduction. *Cognition and Brain Theory* 6:259–285.

Rips, L. J., and S. L. Marcus. 1977. Suppositions and the analysis of conditional sentences. In *Cognitive processes in comprehension*, ed. M. A. Just and P. A. Carpenter, pp. 185–220. Hillsdale, N.J.: Erlbaum.

Smith, E. E. 1985. Natural reason. *Contemporary psychology* 30:181–182.

Staudenmayer, H. 1975. Understanding conditional reasoning with meaningful propositions. In *Reasoning: Representation and process in children and adults*, ed. R. J. Falmagne, pp. 55–79. Hillsdale, N.J.: Erlbaum.

Stich, S. P. 1983. *From folk psychology to cognitive science: The case against belief*. Cambridge: MIT Press.

Taplin, J. E., and H. Staudenmayer. 1973. Interpretation of abstract conditional sentences in deductive reasoning. *Journal of Verbal Learning and Verbal Behavior* 12:530–542.

Wallace, J. 1974. Nonstandard theories of truth. In *The logic of grammar*, ed. D. Davidson and G. Harman, pp. 50–60. Belmont, Calif.: Dickenson.

Wason, P. C., and P. N. Johnson-Laird. 1972. *Psychology of reasoning*. Cambridge: Harvard Univ. Press.

Wilkins, M. C. 1928. The effect of changed material on the ability to do formal syllogistic reasoning. *Archives of Psychology* 16 (102).

ALVIN I. GOLDMAN

Constraints on Representation

Introduction

This paper has a somewhat different focus than most of the papers for this conference. It isn't concerned with mental representation *per se,* but with the relation between mental representation and epistemology. I take my topic to fall under the theme of the conference, since the conference theme is the representation of knowledge and belief and these are of central interest to epistemology. I am not concerned, however, with the standard epistemological task of giving an analysis of "*S* knows that *p*." Rather, the intent is to engage in epistemological reflection on selected aspects of mental representation. I shall begin by laying out some themes from the psychological literature on certain traits of human representation. Then I shall turn to some epistemological morals and implications of these themes.

To explain the rationale for this approach, a few comments are needed about my view of epistemology, which forms the backdrop of the discussion. (For further details, see Goldman 1986). First, I conceive of epistemology as an evaluative subject, not a purely descriptive one. Broadly speaking, it evaluates practices, processes, and methods in the conduct of intellectual affairs. Affairs of the intellect transpire in different "locations," especially the sphere of the mental and the sphere of public speech. The present discussion is restricted to the domain of the mental. One question epistemology asks in this domain is: How good are our cognitive processes—especially our native processes—at producing epistemically desirable outcomes? Which processes or proclivities promote epistemic ends more successfully, and which have qualified or even negative consequences?

A candidate epistemic end is the production of true *beliefs*. So epistemologists are often interested in methods or processes of belief formation. Now belief is usually construed as a relation between a cognizer and a proposition or between a cognizer and some other unit of representation (e.g., a sentence in the "language of thought"). But in order to *believe*, or accept, any unit of representation, one must first *form* that representation in the mind. So there's a sense in which the topic of representation formation is prior to that of belief formation. This prior topic—the formation of representations—is the locus of this paper.

Talk of "mental representation," and research into its nature, invite many philosophical and methodological questions. Is thought really representational? Does it have determinate semantical content? If we assume that it does, how does it get this content? These are obviously important questions but not the ones addressed here. They are questions for the philosophy of mind or the theory of interpretation, and these aren't areas I mean to explore. I am going to *assume* that cognition is representational and investigate specific styles of human representation formation. In identifying the styles in question, I shall draw on certain psychological research. Like any research, this material is open to methodological questions. But questions of this kind also fall outside my purview. I am simply going to assume that the studies cited here correctly identify some pervasive traits of human cognition. My purpose is to address epistemological questions that can be raised about these traits.

Epistemologists often discuss the topic of representation formation under slightly different headings than those used here, e.g. "concept formation" and "hypothesis formation." These phrases point to part of the territory I will be reconnoitering, but the phraseology is too restrictive. In particular, I mean to include the formation of mental representations in any kind of internal code, e.g., modality-linked codes such as visual or auditory codes. On some approaches, visual perception and visual imagery are contrasted with propositional forms of representation. My intention, though, is to include all such codes within the present topic. For this reason, I shall often use the phrase "cognitive units," which is meant to subsume whatever variety of modes of representation are in fact found in human cognition.

Hierarchies and Pattern Preferences

Virtually all theories of mental representation assume that the mind somehow decomposes experience into parts and that it somehow " analyzes" and "segments" the presented world. It is also assumed that the mind engages in "synthesizing" activities, constructing new units and structures out of antecedently formed units. In the history of philosophy, Kant laid great emphasis on the mind's synthesizing activity, specifically the mind's propensity to structure experience in terms of material "objects." The comprehension and production of speech is another salient area where segmentation and construction of formal units must play a critical role in the mind's activities. The mind's grasp of other temporal sequences—e.g., the sound patterns of music—is also readily treated in terms of various unitizing activities: breaking the experience into some set of elementary parts and interpreting larger arrays as structures formed from those parts. This kind of idea is very common in cognitive science. I shall select certain unitizing and constructional operations that cognitive psychologists have postulated and will explore their nature and breadth of application.

Specifically, I shall be concerned with three unit-forming and unit-exploiting traits that are widely postulated in the literature. First, human cognition involves preferences for *patterns* with certain properties, many of which were originally identified by Gestalt psychologists. Second, human cognition forms and groups representations into *hierarchical* structures. Third, human cognition makes heavy use of *analogies* in representation formation.

Let's start with hierarchical structuring. The literature is replete with instances of data structures, or cognitive units, which are organized hierarchically. In each case, some units are embedded in higher-level units, which may in turn be embedded in still higher-level units. Such embeddings can be postulated in the stages of (A) encoding, (B) storage, and (C) retrieval of information (or all three). Before proceeding to survey some of this literature, however, let me digress a moment on the metatheory of our topic.

In saying that certain cognitive units, or representations, are structured hierarchically, do we intend some "formal," or "syntactical," feature of these representations? Or does this characterization describe the representations in terms of their "content," their "semantical" dimensions? Although this is an overly neglected question, I think the latter is the proper understanding. In saying that an array of representations is structured "hierarchically," we give a characterization of the relationship between the meanings or referents of the representations, not their intrinsic, formal properties as data structures in a mental code.

Here now are some examples of representational contents which seem to be structured hierarchically: (1) The *phrase structure of sentences* (in natural languages) is hierarchical. A sentence is the highest-level unit, subordinating noun phrases and verb phrases, which in turn subordinate nouns, verbs, and other grammatical units. These units, of course, are categories of word sequences in natural language. But natural language is the product of the mind; so the presence of hierarchically related categories in the public code implicates a hierarchical organization of associated mental representations. (2) Another domain in which hierarchical structuring is widely postulated is semantic memory. The popular semantic memory "networks" (e.g., Collins and Quillian 1969; Collins and Loftus, 1975) include, in particular, the *class-inclusion* structure of common-sense concepts. Class-inclusion arrays such as "physical object," "living thing," "animal," "mammal," "dog," and "collie" are ubiquitous in natural languages. Aristotle was perhaps the first to stress concept hierarchies with his development of taxonomical systems. His emphasis, however, was ontological. Taxonomies are probably best seen as manifestations of deep-lying representational mechanisms of the human cognitive system. [For studies of the formal properties of natural language taxonomies, see Sommers (1959, 1963) and Keil (1979).]

Hierarchicalization is by no means confined, however, to representations associated with natural language. According to current theories, it's also found in the representation of all sorts of visual and temporal materials. (3) In the case of *visual* cognitive units, smaller visual parts are embedded in larger ones (Navon 1977; Bower and Glass 1976; Palmer 1977; Winston 1975; and others). (4) Similarly, the representation of *temporal* strings is organized hierarchically, with shorter units being subordinated to longer ones (Bjork 1968; Simon and Kotovsky 1963; Restle 1970; Greeno and Simon 1974; Deutsch and Feroe 1981). Detailed examples in these domains will be given shortly.

Many other domains of cognition are also the subjects of postulated hierarchicalization. (5) In the cognitive theory of *story understanding*, plots are said to be represented hierarchically, with smaller episodes embedded in larger ones (Kintsch and Van Dijk 1978). (6) The organization of behavior is achieved by hierarchical networks of *motives* and *submotives, plans* and *subplans* (Miller, Galanter and Pribram 1960; Goldman 1970). (7) Problem-solving tasks are structured by means of *problems* and *subproblems* (Ernst and Newell 1969; Newell and Simon 1972; Simon 1975).

Let me now flesh out some of these proposals, concentrating on (3) and (4). We begin with visual materials. The idea that visual representation—in both perception and imagery—involves multiple layers of embedding is very natural. Take the representation of a standing person. The whole is an elongated, ellipse-shaped object, oriented vertically. At a finer level of resolution, the parts of the body are delineated: a head, a torso, two arms, and two legs. Each of these parts has global properties. But each can also be considered a whole with further parts. The head, for example, has eyes, ears, a mouth, and a nose.

A tidbit of psychological lore testifies to the storage of imagistic information by hierarchically layered parts. When asked which is farther west, Reno or San Diego, the typical subject mistakenly chooses San Diego. The natural explanation is that San Diego and Reno are encoded as subunits of California and Nevada, respectively, and California is pictured as west of Nevada on one's mental map of the continent.

What is the experimental support for hierarchical organization in visual materials? The experimental studies I shall present are not only concerned with hierarchical organization. They also postulate preferences for the extraction and storage of patterns that accord with Gestalt principles. So before turning to these studies, let me mention and illustrate these well-known Gestalt principles, originally postulated for perception. Some of the principles are illustrated in Figure 1 (borrowed from Anderson 1980, p. 53.)

In part A, we perceive four pairs of lines rather than eight separate lines. This illustrates the principle of *proximity*: elements close together tend to organize into units. Part B illustrates the same principle. Five *columns* of dots are seen rather than five *rows*, because the dots in a column are closer together than the dots in a row. Part C illustrates the principle of *similarity*: objects that look alike tend to be grouped together. In C, we tend to see five rows of alternating Os and Xs, even though the rows are spaced similarly to those in B. Part D illustrates the principle of *good continuation*. We perceive part D as two lines, one from x to y and the other from w to z, although there is no reason why this could not represent another pair of lines, one from x to z and the other from y to w. But the line from x to y displays better continuation than the line from x to z, which has a sharp turn. Part E illustrates the principles of *closure* and *good form*. We see the drawing as one circle occluding another circle, although the occluded object could have many other possible shapes.

Let's now turn to the studies on hierarchical organization and segmenting of visual materials. Bower and Glass (1976) postulated hierarchical organization of visual units, in which larger patterns are mentally decomposed into subpatterns. In principle, larger patterns could be mentally dissected into all kinds of parts. But in fact, they proposed, only certain subpatterns are "naturally" represented as parts of the original pattern.

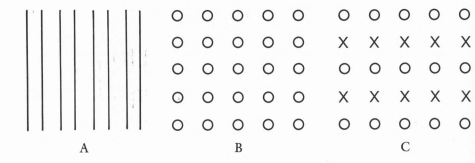

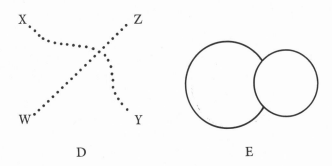

FIGURE 1

Their experiments had subjects study nonsense line drawings. Bower and Glass predicted that a "*natural*" part should serve as a strong retrieval cue for the whole pattern, whereas an *unnatural* fragment—even one of equal size—should lead to poorer recall of the original whole. After studying the nonsense line drawings, Bower and Glass's subjects were tested for recall on fragments which the experimenters had categorized as "good," "mediocre," or "bad" (misleading). The experimental results were that "good" cues had about five times more redintegrative, or retrieval, power than bad cues.

How did Bower and Glass choose the "good," "bad," and "mediocre" fragments? By application of Gestalt rules of common direction and minimal angle. As we saw earlier, the rule of common direction, or good continuation, states that line segments continuous in the same direction are combined and encoded as a single structural unit. The rule of minimal angle says that when three or more segments intersect at a point, the two with the minimal angle between them are combined to form a single structural unit. If part-segmentation accords with these rules, the figure in A would be parsed into the parts shown in B, and the figure in C would be parsed into the parts shown in D. Using this theme, Bower and Glass constructed picture fragments of C such as E, F, and G (cf. Fig. 1). E should be a good cue, F a mediocre cue, and G a bad cue. Experimental results confirmed this prediction.

A very similar set of results were reported by Stephen Palmer (1977). Palmer also was interested in different levels of mental representation of visual materials, corresponding to different subparts of a given figure. Like Bower and Glass, he suggested that only certain subparts are "natural," or

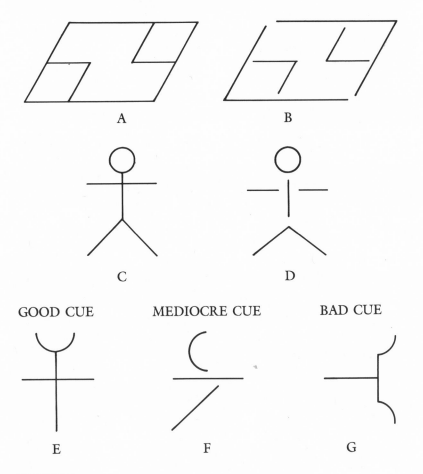

A   B

C   D

GOOD CUE   MEDIOCRE CUE   BAD CUE

E   F   G

FIGURE 2

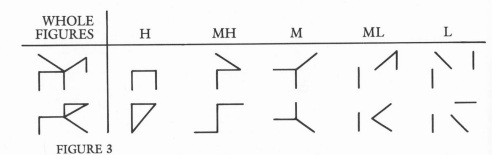

FIGURE 3

"good," decompositions of a larger figure. Palmer devised a measure of "goodness" based on Gestalt principles of grouping: proximity, closedness, connectedness, continuity, and so forth. Figure 3 displays some of the whole figures and respective parts which Palmer used, where the parts are rated for degrees of "goodness": high (=H), medium high (=MH), medium (=M), medium low (=ML), and low (=L).

Palmer then conducted a series of experiments to see whether observed results conformed with the part-ratings his scheme predicts. One experiment asked subjects to divide figures into their "natural" parts. A second task was to rate goodness of identified parts within figures. A third experiment was a reaction-time experiment. A fourth experiment involved a "mental synthesis" task, in which subjects were instructed to construct a figure mentally from parts. Palmer found substantial evidence for the kinds of selective organization in perception and imagery which he had postulated.

Another recent researcher who posits representational "preferences," though not hierarchical organization, is Shimon Ullman (1979). Ullman deals with the principles that underlie the visual system's interpretation of a sequence of two-dimensional stimuli, e.g., a collection of dots of light on a movie screen. How does a subject "see" such a succession of stimuli? One question is how the subject "matches" the parts of one frame in a motion picture with parts of a succeeding frame. Which parts of the subsequent frame are viewed as identical to parts of a preceding frame? Second, does the subject interpret these event sequences as representing a single three-dimensional object in motion or in change? If so, what governs the choice of a 3-D interpretation?

Ullman claims that the visual system displays at least three wired-in preferences: (1) In interpreting which dot-elements match which in successive arrays, there is a preference for seeing motion to nearest neighbors. (2) In deciding what matching to impute, motion along straight lines is preferred. (Notice that these first two principles echo Gestalt principles of proximity in space and common direction.) (3) Any set of elements undergoing two-dimensional transformation which has a unique interpretation as a rigid body moving in space should be so interpreted (i.e., "seen" as such).

This third principle is a version of the preference for seeing visual arrays as solid "bodies," a theme that many philosophers have stressed. I cited Kant for this earlier and might further mention more recent philosophers like Strawson (1959) and Quine (1973).

Let me turn next to temporal strings of events. Working on the hypothesis of hierarchical representation of serial patterns, Restle (1970) devised a formalism congenial to such representation. Let $E = [1\ 2\ 3\ 4\ 5\ 6]$ be a set of elementary events. "1", "2", etc, comprise the alphabet for representing these elementary events. Let X be a sequence of events from this set; for example $X = <1\ 2>$. A set of operations on this set is then introduced: *repeat* (R) of X, *mirror image* (M) of X, and *transposition +1* (T) of X. Each operation generates a new sequence from a given sequence and then concatenates the old and the new. For example, $R<1,\ 2> = <1\ 2\ 1\ 2>$; relative to the above-specified alphabet, $M<2\ 3\ 4> = <2\ 3\ 4\ 5\ 4\ 3>$; and $T<2\ 3> = <2\ 3\ 3\ 4>$. In this fashion, a lengthy and complex series can be represented economically by multiple embedding. For example, $T<1> = <1\ 2>$; $R<T<1>> = <1\ 2\ 1\ 2>$; $T<R<T<1>>> = <1\ 2\ 1\ 2\ 2\ 3\ 2\ 3>$; and $M<T<R<T<1>>>> = <1\ 2\ 1\ 2\ 2\ 3\ 2\ 3\ 6\ 5\ 6\ 5\ 5\ 4\ 5\ 4>$. Using sequences constructed in this way, Restle and Brown (1970) found evidence that subjects mentally encode temporal patterns in accord with a hierarchical structure indicated by the recursive format.

A number of recent writers have proposed that musical cognition reveals hierarchically organized representations. For example, Lerdahl and Jackendoff (1983) hold that there at least four components of the experienced listener's musical intuitions that are hierarchical in nature. "Grouping structure" expresses a hierarchical segmentation of a piece into motives, phrases, and sections. "Metrical structure" expresses the intuition

FIGURE 4

that the events of the piece are related to a regular alternation of strong
and weak beats at a number of hierarchical levels. And so on.

The bulk of my discussion will focus on the work of Deutsch and Feroe
(1981). Deutsch and Feroe suggest that people represent pitch sequences
in tonal music in abstract form. To illustrate, consider the pitch sequence
shown in Figure 4.

A musically sophisticated performer (or listener) would represent this
sequence at two or more levels of description. At the lowest level there is a
representation of the entire presented sequence. At the next higher level,
the representation would feature an arpeggio which ascends through the C
major triad (C–E–G–C). This more abstract representation registers the
fact that the entire sequence can be viewed as the four notes of this triad
each preceded by a neighbor embellishment. At the higher level of representation, the embellishments are deleted. The resulting hierarchical structure may be presented in tree form as in Figure 5.

Drawing on ideas of earlier authors, Deutsch and Feroe propose that
tonal music is represented with the help of several different (mental) "alphabets": e.g., major scale alphabets, minor scale alphabets, the chromatic
alphabet, and the triad alphabets. Different alphabets can be used at different levels of representation of the very same passage. Whereas the first-
level representation in the foregoing example occurs in the chromatic alphabet, the second-level representation could use the major triad alphabet.
In the major triad alphabet, C–E–G–C is a sequence of *successive* elements.
Employment of multiple alphabets facilitates conformity with laws of fig-
ural goodness. (Like other authors I have cited, Deutsch and Feroe postulate Gestalt-like laws of goodness.) For example, pitch sequences are more
efficiently perceived when their components combine to produce *unidirec-
tional* pitch changes and changes *proximal* in pitch. By treating the sample
passage in the major triad alphabet, it can be represented as a sequence of
successive—i.e., proximal—notes.

A major hypothesis of Deutsch and Feroe is that music sequences are
stored hierarchically and that a performer generates a learned composition

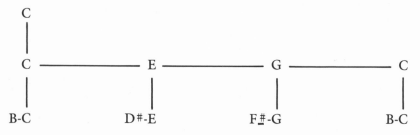

FIGURE 5

by accessing it in a top-down fashion. There are close analogies here, which Deutsch and Feroe note, with Chomsky's system of grammar. Similar ideas in music were anticipated by Heinrich Schenker (1935), who in turn credits C.P.E. Bach's Essay on the True Art of Playing Keyboard Instruments.

In addition to these studies of hierarchicalization in specific domains, John Anderson (1983) postulates hierarchical organization as a pervasive cognitive phenomenon. Anderson points out that even more complex structures can result when a single element occurs in several different hierarchical structures, thereby joining them to produce a "tangled hierarchy." Hierarchies can also contain units of multiple representational types: imaginal, temporal, and propositional. Finally, he postulates that people can retrieve elements from a hierarchical structure either through a top-down process (starting with the top structure and unpacking successively lower layers of elements)—or in a bottom-up manner (starting with a bottom node and retrieving higher-level units).

Operations and Analogies

Our discussion has been focusing on the mind's representational preferences. These might be stated as follows: the mind prefers patterns with certain properties, and the mind prefers groups of representations that can be ordered hierarchically. What really interests me now is a further speculation, which is implicit in some of the foregoing material: these preferences reflect certain *operations,* or *transformations,* that govern the formation of internal representations.

On this hypothesis, the preference for patterns conforming to the rule of *proximity* reflects an operation that searches for, or tends to generate, elements that are *"next"* to other elements within some relevant array. Another preference cited by the Gestalt psychologists but not previously mentioned here is the preference for *symmetry.* This preference might reflect an operation that looks for, or tends to generate, *inversions,* or *mirror images.* Such an operation was prominently featured in the material on serial patterns, especially musical patterns. But it also seems to have wide application in other areas of cognition. Our aesthetic response to symmetry in ornamental creations, and even in intellectual creations, may be symptomatic of some such deep-lying cognitive operation. Again, the preference for hierarchical orderings may reflect some such operations as *"abstraction"* and *"globalization,"* or their inverses, *"specification"* and *"localization."* All of these operations may function in one or more of the following contexts: (A) perception, (B) storage and retrieval from memory, and

(C) imaginative construction of new representational units out of pre-existing units.

It should be emphasized again that these "operations" are described here *semantically*, rather than *formally* or *computationally*. In describing an operation as "globalization," for example, I describe it in terms of semantic relations betwen input and output representations.There is no intended implication about the operation's intrinsic nature.

For present purposes, it is not crucial to fix the representation-forming operations precisely. What interests me here is the hypothesis that there is a determinate and fairly *narrow* set of such operations, *roughly* of the kind which I have been culling from the surveyed literature. Indeed, it is equally worth assessing the implications of a weaker hypothesis, viz., that there is a fairly wide set of available operations, or transformations, but with a *preference ordering* among them. On this latter hypothesis, the system's control processes effect a priority ordering among the transformations, so that higher ranked ones get applied earlier and therefore have a greater frequency of application.

Intimations of a narrow set of operations, at least for certain domains, were contained in the research we have presented. Deutsch and Feroe suggest that a great deal of observed pitch sequences in traditional music can be reconstructed in terms of elementary operations such as sameness in pitch, next in pitch (within a specified scale, or alphabet), predecessor in pitch, transposition of a phrase, inversion (mirroring) of a phrase, and so on. Similarly, Noam Chomsky and other grammarians postulate a fairly narrow set of operations to account for grammatical structures. Chomsky also suggests that analogous representational "constraints" may underlie art-forms (1980, p. 252):

> Certain conditions on the choice and arrangement of linguistic ex-pressions characterize literary genres intelligible to humans, with aes-thetic value for humans; others do not . . . . In these and many other domains, a certain range of possibilities has been explored to create structures of marvelous intricacy, while others are never considered, or if explored, lead to the production of work that does not conform to normal human capacities.

Citing Marshall Edelson (1972), Chomsky notes that Freud made simi-lar proposals in his work on dreams. In Edelson's interpretation, Freud's psychoanalysis was a sort of science of semiology, a dream being created by principles he calls "the dreamwork," which produce the manifest content of dreams from latent dream-thoughts. Finally, Chomsky proposes a "universal grammar" of scientific theorizing, by which he apparently means a set of hypothesis-constructing operations that I too mean to subsume under our discussion. Although the literature I have adduced focuses mainly on operations concerning visual or auditory patterns, the class of representation-forming operations I mean to address includes operations that take concepts or hypotheses as inputs and generate new hypotheses as outputs.

Notice that our conjecture is independent of the issue of modularity of mind. If the mind is modular, it would be natural to expect that distinct modules have distinct sets of operational, or transformational, repertoires. But a nonmodular theory is also compatible with a highly constrained set of operations. Nothing said here is intended to take sides on the modularity issue.

Distinct repertoires of operations might be associated with distinct representational *codes*, as opposed to distict *modules*. John Anderson, who opposes mental modularity, endorses a multiplicity of codes and takes these codes to have different sets of operations (Anderson 1983). Specifically, he postulates three types of representation: temporal strings, spatial images, and abstract propositions. For temporal strings, he suggests three probable operations: combination of objects into linear strings, insertion, and deletion. For imagery, he mentions synthesis of existing images, and rotation. For abstract propositions, he lists insertion of objects into relational slots and filling in of missing slots. He clearly thinks that the representational types, or codes, differ in their transformational repertoire.

The next theme I wish to discuss is analogy. This is a large topic, which has burgeoned in recent years. No attempt at comprehensive coverage of the literature is therefore contemplated. Furthermore, I will lump together the notions of analogy, similarity, and metaphor, though these can doubtless be distinguished.

The ubiquity of the similarity construct in psychology has been remarked upon by Amos Tversky (1977): "the concept of similarity is ubiquitous in psychological theory. It underlies the accounts of stimulus and response generalization in learning, it is employed to explain errors in memory and pattern recognition, and it is central to the analysis of connotative meanings." Other cognitive scientists have emphasized the centrality of analogy (A) in the phraseology of everyday language, and (B) in strategies of problem solving.

A recent book by Lakoff and Johnson (1980) traces the pervasiveness of analogy—or metaphor—in ordinary language and thought. A sample metaphorical pattern involves *orientational* metaphors: expressions rooted in spatial orientations such as up-down, in-out, front-back, on-off, deep-shallow, and central-peripheral. Innumerable expressions for nonspatial properties and events are built upon these orientational notions. For example, happy is up, sad is down ("I'm feeling up," "That boosted my spirits," "My spirits rose," "You're in high spirits," "I'm feeling down," "He's really low these days," "My spirits sank"); health and life are up, sickness and death are down. ("He's at the peak of health," "He's in top shape," "He's sinking fast," "His health is declining"); having control or force is up, being subject to control or force is down ("I have control over her," "I am on top of the situation," "He's at the height of his power," "He is under my control," "He fell from power," "He is low man on the totem pole"); good is up, bad is down ("Things are looking up," "We hit a peak last year, but it's been downhill ever since," "Things are at an all-time low," "He does high-quality work"). According to Lakoff and Johnson, a vast expanse of our conceptual territory is rooted in analogical extensions of more primitive conceptual contents. The linguistic patterns, then, may be taken as evidence for the pervasive employment of some sort of analogy-constructing operation in the cognitive system.

The use of analogy in problem solving is also widely remarked upon. Polya (1957) recommends searching for analogies as a strategy for solving mathematical problems. Analogical test items of the form A:B::C:D are widely used in intelligence testing, since a grasp of these sorts of relationships seems to develop quite early.

Experimental studies of problem solving also reveals a strong influence of similarity judgments in problem-solving strategies. In many problems, a person's task is to find a way of getting from one state in a "problem space" to the goal state. Typically, a long series of states must be traversed. How does the human problem solver choose, in any given state, what state to move to next? Apparently, people are strongly governed by similarity. They choose to move into new states that are more *similar* to the goal state than the present state, and more similar to the goal state than other possible candidates.

Here's an illustration from Atwood and Polson (1976). Subjects were given the following water-jug problem.

> You have three jugs which we will call A, B, and C. Jug A can hold exactly 8 cups of water, B can hold exactly 5 cups, and C can hold exactly 3 cups. A is filled to capacity with 8 cups of water. B and C are empty. We want you to find a way of dividing the contents of A equally between A and B so that both have 4 cups. You are allowed to pour water from jug to jug.

Atwood and Polson asked which move the subjects would prefer, starting from the initial state. Would they prefer to pour from A into C, thereby yielding state 2 (below); or would they prefer to pour from A into B, thereby yielding state 3?

State 2: A(5) B(0) C(3)
State 3: A(3) B(5) C(0)

Twice as many subjects preferred the move to state 3 as preferred the move to state 2. Notice that state 3 is quite similar to the goal, since the goal is to have 4 cups in both A and B, and state 3 has 3 cups in A and 5 cups in B. By contrast, state 2 has no cups of water in B. This illustrates a tendency to move to states that are as similar as possible to the goal state.

Recent work on scientific theory construction, both by cognitive scientists and by historians of science, also explores the importance of analogy, or similarity. For example, several authors trace the development of Darwin's theory to his finding an analogy betwen Malthus' theory of human population growth and the growth of species. [For other attempts to study the role of analogy in theory construction, see Gentner (1980) and Darden (1983).]

Analogy is often treated as a separate representation-forming device, and we could certainly place it alongside the other operations tentatively listed earlier. In other words, where it's assumed that one representation (be it a concept, a theory, an idea for a problem solution, or what have you) is obtained from another by some sort of operation, one candidate operation might be that of analogy. This might be regarded as a primitive, irreducible operation. But I want to advance another proposal: that the analogy operation is analyzable in terms of other operations.

One way of trying to flesh out this proposal would be to treat analogical representation formation as a *substitution* operation. Take Bohr's model of the atom, for example. This representation might be derived "by analogy" from a representation of the solar system. Wherein does the "analogical" construction consist? The suggestion would be that it consists in *substituting* a nucleus for the sun, electrons for the plants, and nuclear forces for the gravitational force.

But is this approach really plausible? A criterion of adequacy for any such theory would seem to be this: if representation R* is obtained from R "by analogy," then R* (or, rather, its putative referent) should be judged (quite) *similar* or *analogous,* to R, at least by the cognizer in question. But not every mental substitution yields a representation of a subjectively "similar" object. If R is a representation of a swan, and R* is obtained by first deleting everything in R except the eyes and then substituting a (representation of a) tiger, the new representation, R*, is hardly very similar to, or analogous to, the original.

What further constraints can be placed, then, on such substitutions, to yield a match with intuitive judgments of resemblance or similarity? One possibility would employ the notion of "natural parts." The greater the naturalness of the parts preserved under replacement, the greater the subjective similarity of the resulting representation.

I doubt, however, that judged analogies or similarities can be adequately recovered by the substitution operation, even conjoined with these additional devices. Other high-ranking or "preferred" operations, in addition to substitution, might have to be invoked. For example, assume that reversal, or inversion, relative to some natural axis or alphabet is a high-ranking transformation. Then an object obtained from another object by such a reversal should be judged very similar to it. With this in mind, we might try to generalize the approach along the following lines:

> The contents of representations R and R* are similar, i.e., receive a high similarity rating, if and only if the content of one is obtainable from the content of the other by application of a *high-ranking* cognitive transformation (or combination of transformations).

Notice the analogy between this idea and the one employed by topologists. In topology, two figures are said to be topologically equivalent (homeomorphic) just in case one can be obtained from the other by some sort of topological operation.

If this line of analysis proved promising, it might be exploited by turning it on its head. (I owe this suggestion, and the example that follows, to Charles Chastain.) Instead of studying similarity in terms of transformations, one could study transformations in terms of judged similarities. For example, given perceived similarities among faces, one might try to identify high-ranking transformations by seeing which would give rise to these similarity judgments.

These are some tentative thoughts about analogy. Their relevance stems from our interest in representation-forming operations. If analogy is related to such operations in the manner proposed, we gain new avenues for getting at the repertoire of operations. Furthermore, given the apparent ubiquity of similarity, or analogy, in cognitive phenomena, identification of this repertoire—and the most preferred members of it—would be quite important for cognitive science.

Epistemic Assets and Liabilities

It is time to turn to epistemological issues, which will occupy the last three sections. Recall that on my view epistemology is an evaluative subject. But there isn't just a single dimension, or standard, of epistemic evaluation. On the contrary, a number of standards can be used for evaluating cognitive processes, and it is doubtful whether these can be amalgamated into a unique index, or criterion, of epistemic worth. (For further details on this topic, see Goldman 1986.) At least three sorts of properties of a cognitive process seem epistemically significant. First, how does the process contribute to the *reliability* of the cognitive system, i.e., to the *truth-ratio* of the beliefs that it forms? Second, how does the process contribute to the *problem-solving*, or *question-answering, power* of the cognitive system? That is, how adept is the system at answering (correctly) the questions, or problems, to which it seeks an answer? Third, how does it contribute to the *speed* with which the system can get correct answers, and to the *timeliness* of its acquisition and deployment of these answers? Can it get answers to questions when it needs to have them?

This brief list may seem to omit the most central notions of epistemic appraisal, e.g., justification. But I believe that that notion can be explicated in terms of the standard of reliability. I will say a bit more about this under "Justification," below; a more complete treatment can be found in Goldman (1986).

Some of these standards—especially the reliability standard—are most naturally applied to *belief*-forming cognitive processes; yet this paper addresses *representation*-forming processes. Precisely this distinction is what motivates the formulation of our questions in terms of a process's "*contribution*" to the system's reliability, power, and speed. Representation-forming processes can make (positive or negative) *contributions* toward such properties of a cognitive system, even if they do not have such properties in and of themselves.

Our epistemological reflections will be directed at the sorts of representation-forming operations for which evidence has been adduced in the preceding sections. More specifically, I will be asking about the epistemic implications of a narrow, or highly constrained, set of representation-forming operations. In the present section, I will talk about an *assortment* of assets and liabilities that might be associated with such a set. In the next section, I will talk about the probable role of such operations in the evaluative dimension of "*originality*" (which I regard as a partly epistemic notion of appraisal). And in the last section, I will talk about the relevance of such operations to epistemic *justification*.

To begin our discussion, let's note a distinction between two types of belief, two "forms" or "locations" in which information can be retained by the cognitive system. On the one hand, the system can hold information in LTM (long term memory), an inactive form of storage. On the other hand, it can hold information in an activated form, in "short term," or "working," memory. The crucial point here is that (according to most theories) information is *usable* only if it is in working memory. Contents that are merely stored in LTM lie dormant and have no impact on new reasoning, new problem solving, or the choice of current behavior. Contents in working memory, by contrast, are able to interact and influence ongoing cognitive activities. However, working memory has a sharply limited capacity. Whereas LTM is practically unlimited in space, only a relatively small number of items can be retained in working memory at any one time. From the standpoint of *timeliness*, then, the cognitive system needs to have mechanisms by which it puts just the items it needs into working memory. If there is an overload, inaccuracies and confusions will probably result.

An example of this need occurs in the guidance of long and complex courses of behavior. To execute a complex course of action, one needs to be guided by a representation appropriate to the action. To be effective, we have said, the representation must be in working memory. On the other hand, a representation for the whole course of action might be too complex to be kept—in all its details—in working memory. How can this dilemma be resolved?

Hierarchical organization of representations is an excellent resolution of this dilemma. The musical performer, for example, can "chunk" her representation of the piece being performed into all sorts of units, moving from macro- to microunits as needed. The piece is represented in LTM at all sorts of levels, many encompassing different sized segments of the work. To guide performance of each local passage, a representation is brought into working memory that is specific to that passage: a representation detailed enough for performance guidance yet small enough for accurate retention in working memory. This point is highlighted by Deutsch and Feroe:

> Several investigators have shown that for serial recall of a string of items, performance levels are optimal when such a string is grouped by the observer into chunks of three or four items each (Estes 1972; Wickelgren 1967). Thus on the present system if a string of operators together with an alphabet were grouped together in chunks of three or four, superior recall would be expected . . . . When segments of tonal music are notated on the present (hierarchical) system, there emerges a very high proportion of chunks of three or four items each . . . . As pitch sequences become more elaborated, they are represented as on a larger number of hierarchical levels, but the basic chunk size does not appear to vary with changes in sequence complexity. This chunking feature therefore serves to reduce memory load.

Are there any other advantages of multiple layers of analysis? Many intellectual tasks can benefit from flexibility on the dimension of "resolution," or "grain," of analysis. Which details need to be attended to and which may be ignored varies from task to task. If I want to use a computer for a paper-weight, I can restrict my interest to its global size and weight. But if I want to run a program on it, I need to be concerned with its microcharacteristics. Hierarchicalization facilitates flexible movement from level to level, and the creation of superordinate and subordinate groupings ad libitum. There are many different types of questions for which answers can be represented.

But doesn't the preference for certain ways of decomposing wholes into parts reduce flexibility? Isn't constrained flexibility an implication of the system's instantiation of Gestalt-like principles of pattern preference? This constraint might be discussed in terms of Jerry Fodor's (1983) notion of *"epistemic boundedness"*: the inability of a cognitive system even to represent—and *a fortiori* its inability to believe—certain truths. If a cognitive system has a fixed set of representation-forming operations, there must be representations it is incapable of generating. This appears to imply a limitation on power.

But actually this isn't so, at least on my definition of power. On my definition, a system is completely powerful if it can answer (correctly) *every question it can ask*. This doesn't imply that it can answer *every* question. In other words, complete power doesn't entail unboundedness. Therefore, boundedness doesn't entail the absence of complete power.

Setting this point aside, how serious a defect is the absence of *"total"* power? Not much. When we're talking about finite minds, it isn't an alarming defect that omniscience is beyond reach. That's just the nature of the beast. The more important question is: Is it capable of getting true answers to the questions it wants to answer, to the problems it wants to solve? On this point, there is no glaring deficiency in the representational operations under discussion.

Hierarchical organization per se is neutral as to the substantive principles for forming subordinate or superordinate units. And even the Gestalt principles might be best interpreted as *preferred* operations, or default procedures, rather than mandatory operations. Take the wholes and parts that Palmer used in some of his experiments. (Cf. Fig. 3.) The parts are rated for goodness as either high (H), medium high (MH), medium (M), medium low (ML), or low (L). Subjects gave such ratings to the parts, which accorded with Palmer's Gestalt-inspired metrics. But subjects clearly can "see" *each* of these parts as a part of the whole, even the ones with the lowest ranking. So people aren't incapable of parsing the whole into the inferior segments; those parsings are just less "natural," or obvious.

Still, isn't it a vice of the system that it has "preferences" for certain parsings? Doesn't it inevitably betoken a *distortion* in the system's noetic relation with the world? Doesn't it mean that the mind can't "mirror" the world, and doesn't this necessarily breed error, not merely ignorance?

No. Representational preferences do preclude "mirroring," but mirroring isn't required for truth. You don't have to get *every* truth to get *some* truths. Parsing and synthesizing preferences may indeed imply that some "correct" parts and wholes don't get constructed. But the preferred parsings and syntheses may be perfectly accurate as far as they go.

Sometimes, however, preferences do seem to produce error, not just partial ignorance. Gestalt preferences apparently induce the visual system to "supplement," or "fill in," the stimuli it encounters to achieve "good continuation" or "completeness," even when the real figure has discontinuities or gaps. This is indeed distortion. Interpretation of two-dimensional arrays as three-dimensional solid objects can also lead to error— when the real stimuli are only dots of light.

But how serious are these error possibilities? As long as the organism's ecology is full of solid objects, which generally *do* instantiate "good continuation," these error-prospects won't be systematic. In terms of the *actual ecology* of human beings the preferences in question may be highly reliable. Furthermore, the tendency to "go beyond the information given" (in Bruner's phrase) helps on the timeliness dimension. Looking or waiting for further information can often waste valuable time and keep the system from proceeding to other, equally important questions. An occasional error is a worthwhile tradeoff for systematic and large-scale time-saving.

Is there anything useful about the *specific* pattern preferences human beings manifest? I have no inkling of the benefits or costs for the organism taken singly, but a definite plus can be assigned to the species *sharing* a narrow set of pattern preferences, no matter what they are. The plus is associated with *social coordination*. Shared pattern preferences promote successful communication; and successful communication provides enormous epistemic advantages.

The sort of point I have in mind is made, in essentials, by Chomsky and by Quine. Chomsky argues that human beings share a narrow set of grammatical universals. This facilitates language learning and thereby facilitates communication. Similarly, Quine (1969; 1973, p. 23) stresses the uniformity of people's innate quality spacings, or (we might say) pattern preferences. If the young child had a very different set of innate quality spacings from its elders, it might associate different units with its elder's words than the latter do. This would make it hard to achieve mutuality in sense or reference. Where the parent individuates in terms of rabbits, the child might individuate by rabbit-stages. Or the discrepancy might be much greater. (I here assume, unlike Quine, that it's determinate which style of mental individuation in fact characterizes a person.) But where innate pattern preferences are shared and are relatively small in number, the prospects for successful communication are greatly enhanced. Such communication has great epistemic benefits: so many truths can be acquired from other people via language. A noncommunicating creature would be at a severe epistemic disadvantage.

Originality

Although it's barely touched by philosophical epistemology, the category of originality is obviously a widespread term of evaluation in intellectual affairs. It is a dimension commonly invoked in the evaluation of both intellectual *products*—books, articles, ideas, and hypotheses—and intellectual *producers*. Since the progress of knowledge depends on the production of *new* knowledge, and since this often depends on original ideas (not merely new evidence for old ideas), originality is a proper subject of epistemological study. Of course, originality is also present in the sphere of the arts, which may not fall under the rubric "intellectual" and may therefore fall outside epistemology. But that needn't perturb us.

What do we mean when we call an idea "original" (whether it's a scientific idea, an artistic idea, or what have you)? One *minimal* meaning is that it's an idea nobody else has had before—at any rate, an idea which the thinker didn't *get* from anyone else. But there is another, stronger sense of the term "original." Within the class of ideas that aren't *directly* borrowed from others and that aren't mere duplicates, some strike us as more inventive, clever, surprising, imaginative, or creative than others. These we deem "original." Other ideas, which are equally nonduplicates, seem pedestrian, obvious, and trite. The term "original" is withheld from these. But how do we distinguish the inventive ideas from the pedestrian, the imaginative from the hackneyed?

Apparently we have some tacit *metric* by which we measure originality. Some ideas seem more "distant" from socially available ideas, harder to think up on one's own. Other ideas, even if they are original in the minimal sense, seem easy to think up; they seem "closer" to what has already been formulated. But what underlies this metric? What makes some ideas seem close to their predecessors and easier to think up, and others more distant and difficult? The answer is related to human representation-forming operations.

Suppose, as the preceding sections of the paper suggest, that human beings have a fairly delimited set of representation-forming operations, and there is a (substantially) fixed ranking of these operations. Finally, make the added assumption that in any scientific or cultural milieu, the stock of ideas antecedently available to cognizers is essentially the same. Then all new ideas must result from transformations of the same initial stock of ideas. If this is (largely) correct, one will expect certain new ideas to occur independently to many people in a given field. They all have roughly the same stock of initial information and previously tried ideas, and they have a largely shared set of problems they wish to solve. If so, when the highest-ranking—or most "natural"—operations are applied to people's initial stock of ideas, many will come up with the same (or very similar) new thoughts. But these will be the most *obvious* thoughts, the most straightforward extensions of pre-existing ideas.

The sociologist of science, Robert Merton, has remarked on the prevalence of multiple discoveries in science: the same discovery being made at roughly the same time by several independent researchers (see Merton 1973). In fact, historically significant multiples probably underestimate the prevalence of the phenomenon. Scientists and scholars are constantly coming up with very similar ideas; but many of these don't get published at all, or do not get published by everyone who thinks of them. People's minds run in very much the same channels.

How, then, are truly original ideas created? And why do certain individuals seem particularly adept at such inventiveness (a fact that ostensibly eliminates an explanation in terms of sheer *chance*)? Four possibilities come to mind. (1) Perhaps the ranking of operations isn't completely fixed, or isn't universal. Perhaps certain operations, which are unusual or low-ranking for most people, are higher in rank for others. The latter individuals apply these "unusual" operations more readily, and hence come up with ideas that others find surprising and inventive. (2) While there is no interpersonal difference in the ranking of operations, perhaps some individuals just try a larger number of operations, turning eventually to unusual operations that most people don't try at all. This could result in ideas that strike others as departures from the commonplace. (3) Perhaps the important difference lies in the *combinations*, or *permutations,* of operations that certain people employ. The generation of new representations, it may be suggested, are often the result of a series of transformations, not a single transformation. What may distinguish the creative thinker from the humdrum thinker is the transformational combinations, or permutations, he or she utilizes. All three of these possibilities are ways in which the *control* mechanisms differ interpersonally. A fourth possibility is that one of our prior assumptions is inaccurate, viz., that people have the same stock of initial ideas on which to operate. While there is doubtless much overlap in such antecedent resources, there are also normally some differences. Perhaps the distinguishing character of creative people is that they apply the same operations to unusual sets of initial ideas, thereby producing unusual outputs.

Whether this is an exhaustive list of possibilities doesn't much matter. It's clearly important to the understanding of creativity to determine which of these possibilities—or other such possibilities—is primarily responsible for differences in creativity. This is a future task for cognitive science but one which is continuous with work already undertaken on basic representation-forming operations.

How is this relevant to epistemology? I believe that an important part of epistemology should be the assessment of problem-solving procedures (cf. Goldman 1983). Problem-solving procedures include the formation of representations that are candidate solutions to problems. When problems are difficult and previously unsolved by others, this may mean that unusual solutions need to be constructed. So cognitive procedures requisite to such construction fall under the scope of epistemology.

Justification

Originality and creativity are nonstandard topics for traditional epistemology. Are there other, more traditional, dimensions of appraisal to which the study of representation-forming operations is also germane? As indicated earlier, yes. The highly traditional topic of justification can be illuminated by the psychology of representation formation.

One reason why people often believe a proposition is that the proposition, if true, would explain observed phenomena. But a person isn't *justified*, or *warranted*, in believing such a proposition P if there is a good *alternative* explanation in which P isn't true. So, at least, it is commonly said. But this principle isn't quite right. Even if there *is* an alternative explanation in which P isn't true, we wouldn't deny that a person's belief in P is justified unless we would *expect* him to *think up* the alternative explanation. A person is justified in placing credence in the only plausible explanatory hypothesis that occurs to him, as long as any alternative explanation is extremely difficult to construct (from his prior belief corpus).

Suppose a child (a 10-year old, say) has never paid close attention to objects partly immersed in water. Suppose also that he's never heard of laws of optical refraction or other such physical laws. Suppose he now sees an oar half-immersed in water and notices that it looks bent. He concludes that it *is* bent. It never occurs to him that there might be a law of physics which implies that a straight object partly immersed in different media, e.g., water and air, should look bent. He doesn't form a representation of any such alternative explanation of the oar's apparent bentness. Is his belief in the oar's being bent justified or unjustified? I think it *is* justified. Given his background information, it would be very difficult to think up any alternative hypothesis (other than bentness) to explain the oar's apparent bentness.

Suppose you too see the apparently bent oar, but you are familiar with laws of optical refraction; yet you too conclude that the oar is bent. Then we could say that your belief is unwarranted. You ought to be able to construct the alternative explanation, which should inhibit your belief.

Consider another example. Was Othello justified in believing that Desdemona was unfaithful? Apparently, Othello didn't construct any (plausible) alternative explanation of Iago's insinuations, of Desdemona's loss of her handkerchief, etc. It didn't occur to Othello, for example, that Iago might be a villainous fellow, that his being passed over for promotion might make him vindictive and lead him to deceive Othello about Desdemona. Most of Shakespeare's viewers doubtless find a singular paucity in Othello's imagination. It seems trivial to construct alternative hypotheses to the unfaithfulness hypothesis, but Othello fails to do so. Hence, his belief is unwarranted.

The point I wish to stress in all such cases is that judgments of justifiedness or unjustifiedness depend on the *ease* or *difficulty* of thinking up rival hypotheses. When a scientist's belief in a certain theory is subsequently shown to be wrong by the invention of a new and vastly more powerful theory, this needn't undermine the justifiedness of the earlier belief (i.e., the justifiedness of the first theory being believed *at* the earlier time). It depends on how hard it would have been for him to create the new theory.

Now the ease or difficulty of constructing alternative hypotheses is a function of (A) one's antecedent conceptual and doxastic corpus, and (B) the "naturalness," or probability, of applying a suitable combination of representation-forming operations to obtain these alternative hypotheses. Our intuitive judgments of justifiedness and unjustifiedness, I believe, rest partly on a tacit grasp of the ease or difficulty of constructing relevant rival hypotheses from the cognizer's (presumed) conceptual and doxastic corpus. However, if we want to spell out the basis for these intuitive judgments, we need to identify the repertoire of operations and their standard preference ordering. That would give us a systematic ground for the indicated judgments. But this job is a job for cognitive psychology. In this fashion, cognitive psychology is needed for two tasks: (1) to explain the basis for, and (2) to systematize, certain criteria of epistemic evaluation.

One final comment. Earlier I indicated that, on my view, justifiedness is linked to the *reliability* of the cognitive processes used. (This is the philosophers' sense of "reliability," which corresponds to what behavioral scientists call "validity.") How do the foregoing comments on justifiedness relate to reliability?

The idea is this. A belief-forming process that includes consideration of competing explanatory hypotheses is a more reliable process, in general, than similar belief-forming processes which ignore competing hypotheses. So we may expect only the former, but not the latter, to be licensed by suitable rules of justifiedness. However, it's not clear that such rules would require a cognizer to construct *all possible* competing hypotheses. For one thing, this might take too much time and would ultimately reduce the power and speed of the system. But secondly, at least on one conception of justifiedness, a person's belief is justified in case it's produced by a process that is reasonably reliable *relative to the resources of the human cognitive system*. That is, justifiedness is judged by the use of processes that are as reliable as can be expected, given the native endowments of human cognizers. Now, among the relevant resources are resources for hypothesis construction. Relative to these resources (and some initial corpus of concepts and beliefs), some hypotheses are easy and others are difficult to construct. The conception of justifiedness indicated above is sensitive to this relative ease or difficulty. A detailed identification of the dimensions of ease and difficulty, however, rests with psychology, for only psychology can illuminate the representation-forming repertoire that must be deployed for these tasks. In this way, psychology can contribute to epistemology.

Bibliography

Anderson, J. R. 1980. *Cognitive psychology and its implications.* San Francisco: Freeman.

_____. 1983. *The architecture of cognition.* Cambridge: Harvard Univ. Press.

Atwood, M. E., and P. G. Polson. 1976. A process model for water jug problems. *Cognitive Psychology,* 8:191–216.

Bjork, R. A. 1968. All-or-none subprocesses in the learning of complex sequences. *Journal of Mathematical Psychology* 5:182–195.

Bower, G. H., and A. L. Glass. 1976. Structural units and the Redintegrative power of picture fragments. *Journal of Experimental Psychology: Human Learning and Memory* 2:456–466.

Chomsky, N. 1980. *Rules and representations.* New York: Columbia Univ. Press.

Collins, A. M., and E. F. Loftus. 1975. A spreading activation theory of semantic processing. *Psychological Review* 82:407–428.

Collins, A. M., and M. R. Quillan. 1969. Retrieval time from semantic memory. *Journal of Verbal Learning and Verbal Behavior.* 8:24–247.

Darden, L. 1983. Artificial intelligence and philosophy of science: Reasoning by analogy in theory construction. In *PSA 1982,* ed. P. Asquih and T. Nickles. East Lansing, Mich.: Philosophy of Science Assoc.

Deutsch, D., and J. Feroe. 1981. The internal representation of pitch sequences in tonal music. *Psychological Review* 6:503–522.

Edelson, M. 1972. Language and dreams: The interpretation of dreams revisited. *Psychoanalytic Study of the Child* 27:249.

Ernst, G. W., and A. Newell. 1969. *GPS: A case study in generality and problem solving.* New York: Academic Press.

Estes, W. K. 1972. An associative basis for coding and organization in memory. In *Coding processes in human memory,* ed. A. W. Melton and E. Martin. Washington, D.C.: Winston.

Fodor, J. A. 1983. *The modularity of mind.* Cambridge: MIT Press.

Gentner, D. 1980. The structure of analogical models in science. Rep. 4451. Cambridge, Mass.: Bolt, Beranek and Newman.

Goldman, A. I. 1970. *A theory of human action.* Englewood Cliffs, N.J.: Prentice-Hall.

––––––. 1983. Epistemology and the theory of problem solving. *Synthese* 55:1, 21–48.

––––––. 1986. *Epistemology and cognition.* Cambridge: Harvard Univ. Press.

Greeno, J. G., and H. A. Simon. 1974. Processes for sequence production. *Psychological Review* 81:187–196.

Keil, F. C. 1979. *Semantic and conceptual development.* Cambridge: Harvard Univ. Press.

Kintsch, W., and T. A. Van Dijk. 1978. Toward a model of text comprehension and production. *Psychological Review* 85:363–394.

Lakoff, G., and M. Johnson. 1980. *Metaphors we live by.* Chicago: Univ. of Chicago Press.

Lerdahl, F., and R. Jackendoff. 1983. *A generative theory of music.* Cambridge: MIT Press.

Merton, R. K. 1973. Singletons and multiples in science. In *The sociology of science.* Chicago: Univ. of Chicago Press.

Miller, G. A., E. H. Galanter, and K. H. Pribram. 1960. *Plans and the structure of behavior.* New York: Holt, Rinehart and Winston.

Navon, D. 1977. Forest before trees: The precedence of global features in visual perception. *Cognitive Psychology* 9:353–383.

Newell, A., and H. A. Simon. 1972. *Human problem solving.* Englewood Cliffs, N.J.: Prentice-Hall.

Palmer, S. E. 1977. Hierarchical structure in perceptual representation. *Cognitive Psychology* 9:441–474.

Polya, G. 1957. *How to solve it*. Princeton, N.J.: Princeton Univ. Press.

Quine, W. V. 1969. Natural kinds. In *Ontological relativity and other essays*. New York: Columbia Univ. Press.

––––––. 1973. *The roots of reference*. LaSalle, Ill.: Open Court.

Restle, F. 1970. Theory of serial pattern learning: Structural trees. *Psychological Review* 77:481–495.

Restle, F., and E. Brown. 1970. Organization of serial pattern learning. In *The psychology of learning and motivation: Advances in research and theory*, ed. G. Bower, vol. 4. New York: Academic Press.

Schenker, H. 1935. *Der Freie Satz*. Vienna: Universal Edition. Trans. E. Oster. 1979. New York: Longman.

Simon, H. A. 1975. Complexity and the representation of patterned sequences of symbols. *Psychological Review* 79:369–382.

Simon, H. A., and K. Kotovsky. 1963. Human acquisition of concepts for sequential patterns. *Psychological Review* 70:534–546.

Sommers, F. 1959. The ordinary language tree. *Mind* 68:160–185.

––––––. 1963. Types and ontology. *Philosophical Review* 72:327–363.

Strawson, P. F. 1959. *Individuals*. London:Methuen.

Tversky, A. 1977. Features of similarity. *Psychological Review* 84:327–352.

Ullman, S. 1979. *The interpretation of visual motion*. Cambridge: MIT Press.

Wickelgren, W. A. 1967. Rehearsal grouping and the hierarchical organization of serial position cues in short-term memory. *Quarterly Journal of Experimental Psychology* 19:97–102.

Winston, P. H. 1975. Learning structural descriptions from examples. In *The psychology of computer visions*, ed. P. H. Winston. New York: McGraw-Hill.

The Aesthetic Basis
for Cognitive Structures

*A man does not show his greatness by being at one extremity, but
rather by touching both at once.*
PASCAL

Introduction and Summary

This paper concerns the cognitive, neurological, and formal bases for indigenous skills such as human language. In particular, which linguistic
universals are unique to language, and which are attributable to general
properties of human mind? Students of natural language with a wide variety of theoretical assumptions agree that grammars have several interesting
properties that must be explained.

(1) There are distinct systems of linguistic knowledge, e.g., phone-
    tics, phonology, morphology, syntax, semantics.
(2) No system can be induced from the others.

Grammars specify the relations between sounds and meanings. Each of
the systems of knowledge in (1) represents a logical stage in the
sound/meaning pairs: the existence of such systems has a clear functional
basis, allowing for representation of intermediate regularities. It is less
clear why the relevant regularities in one system cannot be defined as a
direct function of regularities in another system. For example, syntactic
categories cannot be defined in terms of semantic categories—syntactic
gender of nouns almost never completely reflects semantic gender, syntactic transitivity of verbs rarely follows from semantic transitivity.

The inability to induce one system from another is puzzling. If one could be derived from another, the expressive power of languages would remain unchanged, whereas the grammatical description would be simplified. A grammar in which semantic gender predicts syntactic gender and in which semantic transitivity predicts syntactic transitivity would be much simpler and presumably easier to learn. Yet, grammars never have such simplifying properties—why? In this paper, I suggest that the functional role of the existence of noninducible systems of representation is developmental: they facilitate the experience of language acquisition as an aesthetic and problem-solving activity. Such activities are intrinsically enjoyable in humans. That is, it is the very fact that systems of linguistic representation cannot be mutually defined that creates an intrinsic motivation for the acquisition of a multisystemed grammar.

The most natural way to investigate the uniqueness of linguistic structure is to compare it with structures found in other cognitive behaviors. However, there is a great difficulty that infuses the study of indigenous mental skills—each exists with a palpable function. For example, it is always a vexed question whether the regularity of language behavior is due to its structure or to the communicative and representational function it is serving. Similar problems arise in understanding the nature of object recognition, the use of the number concept, reasoning, and so on. In each case, the naturally occurring behavior is highly functional and may therefore have many properties that are uniquely shaped by its particular function, not by basic cognitive structures.

There are two standard methods to minimize the ways in which a skill's function obscures our insight into its mental nature. One is to examine the behavior of infants, before they have started functionally to apply a skill; much of the current attention to infant capacities exemplifies this approach (cf. Mehler 1984). The other technique is to construct arbitrary situations for adults to solve, which tap the structural properties of the skill without having any real function: linguists do this when they ask informants to render abstract grammaticality judgments; experimental psychologists do it when they require subjects to perform on otherwise meaningless laboratory tasks.

There is a third approach, which goes back to the initial stages of Fechnerian psychophysics—namely, the study of aesthetic judgments, a behavior with no apparent direct function. Aesthetic behavior reveals to us what the mind does when it has only its own purposes to serve and may thereby clearly reveal its real processes. Of course, nothing is *totally* pure in the life of the mind—even aesthetic activity can be viewed as serving the functions of conceptual hedonism. But, at least it must reveal to us what the waking mind likes to do when nothing external matters.

The structure of this discussion is the following. First, I briefly review the limitations of the current optimal-arousal-level model of aesthetically satisfying experiences. I then discuss simple demonstrations of two basic mental processes in perception—perceptual schemata automatically form representations and more conceptual levels of analysis integrate conflicts in those representations. Resolving a representational conflict by accessing a new overarching representation itself releases a momentary surge of enjoyable emotional energy, traditionally known as the "aha" or insight reaction when it occurs in explicit problem solving.

A definition developed with several colleagues (Lasher, Carroll, and Bever 1983; Bever, Lasher, and Carroll, in press) relates the two kinds of processes that occur during perception and problem solving to the processes involved in an "aesthetically satisfying experience." On this definition, such an experience stimulates a conflict in perceptual representations, which is resolved by accessing another representation that allows the two conflicting ones to coexist. As in explicit problem solving, it is accessing the conflict-resolving representation that releases the surge of enjoyable energy characteristic of a satisfying aesthetic experience. I will show that this definition allows for the explanation of the preference for certain traditionally preferred folk objects: the golden mean rectangle, the rhythm "shave and a haircut, two bits," the song "Happy Birthday," and the child's tale "Goldilocks."

The principles of aesthetic activity provide a cognitively intrinsic motive for the child to learn a form of language that has independent systems of representation: multisystemed language is learned because it is aesthetically—and therefore emotionally—satisfying to do so. In this way, the aesthetic principles constrain the form of learnable languages to have independently defined systems of representation.

Such a view has broader implications for the learning of abstract structures of many kinds—in general the successful application of a representation that integrates other representations releases an intrinsically reinforcing experience. Accordingly, we can view the child's acquisition of abstract representational structures as endogenously motivated by his* aesthetic impulses toward an integrated system of mental representations. This means that there is a strong constraint on the kinds of mental structures that children can learn to integrate—the structures must potentiate experiences that meet the aesthetic principles.

---

*A note on pronouns and their syntactic gender: The historic generic personal pronoun in English is syntactically masculine. This is a typical example of the mismatch between syntactic and semantic categories mentioned in this essay. I use the syntactically masculine pronoun to refer to all humans, while recognizing the linguistic arbitrariness of this choice.

The Current Theory of Aesthetic Satisfaction

A current psychological theory of the basis for aesthetic judgments is that we prefer an optimal arousal level (Berlyne 1971, 1974). This theory goes back to Wundt's notion that as stimulus intensity increases, it excites first a positive and then a negative affect. In the modern reformulation (Fig. 1), the optimal level is the result of summing a positive and negative function related to the intensity of an experience—preferred stimuli are those that involve an intermediate range of intensity. This is the "goldilocks" theory of aesthetic experience—what humans like must not be too intense, not too weak, but *juuuuuust* right. Such a theory is acceptable insofar as it is

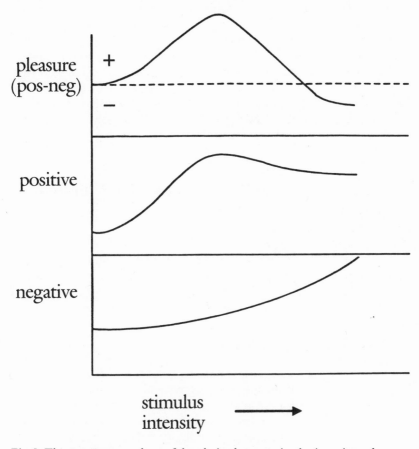

Fig. 1. The two-component theory of the relation between stimulus intensity and pleasure (Berlyne 1971, 1974).

nearly tautological, but difficulties arise as soon as one attempts to apply it to real art forms. Music is one of the flagship cases of this approach: an ideal melody is one of "optimal complexity." Optimal complexity is in turn defined as an "optimal level of predictability" of a note sequence—that is, we expect to hear a particular sequence but are most satisfied with a sequence that slightly departs from our expectation.

It is clear that this is wrong, even on trivial formal grounds. Often the musical form itself dictates what must occur, as may the listener: anybody who has endured the indeterminate end of a Bruckner symphony knows that expecting the final chord is best satisfied by in fact hearing it. The definition of ideal "melodic complexity" must lie in the interaction of perceptual and representational mechanisms with melodic form, not post hoc predictability. Even worse, the central assumption of the arousal theory of aesthetics cannot explain how one could possibly enjoy a melody the second time, never mind the thousandth time, since the expected tone sequence is the actual tone sequence once the melody has been memorized. It is striking how theorists in the optimal-arousal school deal with this simple fact—generally they argue that our memory is mercifully short, so we keep forgetting what we have heard and are able to be *re*-surprised by it afresh to *juuuuust* the right degree (Meyer 1967).

The Study of Mental Representations in Children and Adults

The optimal arousal theory flows from a general principle of behavior regulation enunciated by Wundt. Let us see if we can do better by considering more recent theories of mind. Existing research and theories exemplify two processes relevant for this discussion—representation formation, and conflict integration among representations.

Representation Formation

If current psychology accepts anything at all, like Helmholtz (1895, 1903) it accepts the view that the mind is a representation-bound organ. I wish to avoid entanglement in the many idiosyncratic and technical differences between competing psychological theories of perception—the formation of representations. Most theories generally agree that the mind forms partial representations of reality by transducing neurologically coded information in terms of internal schemata. Many arguments revolve around the question of whether such schemata have their effect before final recognition of an object (Helmholtz 1895) or after, if at all (Gibson 1962), but the theories agree that such schemata exist.

The most obvious of such schemata are gathered under the rubric of gestalt principles of basic form. An important gestalt principle for this discussion is the unifying force of unit repetition. For example, a series of repeating dark dots form a line, a series of repeating motives form a shape (repeating rectangles), a series of repeating pairs of weak–strong beats elicit perception of an underlying rhythm (Fig. 2). In each case, the repeating units are integrated into a larger whole: a line, an evenly divided figure, a rhythmic pattern beat that conveys a particular meter.

When a unit is repeated, but backward, it defines a "symmetry"—and symmetries are also powerful organizing principles for percepts. For example, a line that goes up and down can be perceived as unified, opposite motives are perceptually unified, a symmetrical pattern of beats is unified (' ''' ') (Fig. 3).

Gestalt schemata are characteristic of the output of systems that form representations—that is, gestalt properties are of theoretical interest because they attest to the existence of automatic representation-forming mechanisms, which impose immediate representational organizations on sensory information. The nature of these representation-forming mechanisms has also been the subject of recent discussion. In their purest form, they are described metaphorically as the output of opaque "modules," mechanisms that automatically transduce information of one kind into another (Posner 1980; Fodor 1983); alternatively, they can be viewed as

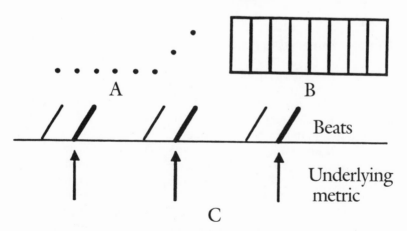

Fig. 2. Examples of the perceptually unifying role of the repetition of individual units; (a) repeating data form a line, (b) repeating rectangles form a larger rectangle, (c) repeating pairs of beats form an underlying metric.

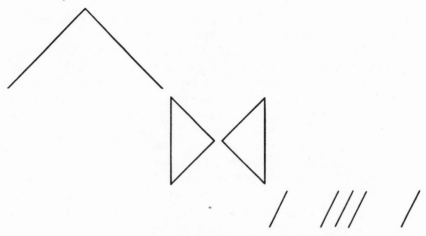

Fig. 3. Examples of the perceptually unifying role of symmetrical units.

"automatized" skills, cognitive mechanisms that have become so habitual that they operate autonomously, without conscious control (Neisser 1963; Posner and Snyder 1975; Shiffrin and Schneider 1977). This controversy revolves around the modularist's claim that the mechanisms are innate, involve unique processes, and are uninfluenced by current knowledge. In the present discussion, we can avoid this controversy: the crucial property of the perceptual systems is that once acquired, they characteristically operate *automatically* and autonomously. They provide an immediate cascade of partially independent representations coordinated with every input.

Conflict Integration (Conceptualization)

If the mind automatically forms representations, by way of distinct automatic mechanisms, the initial analysis of a single object will yield representations that conflict. Representations "conflict" when they present analyses that are incompatible along some dimension. For example, if I blink my eyes while a hummingbird moves from one flower to another, I am presented with two successive views of "hummingbird" in different locations and with differing silhouettes—the needs of worldly comprehension require that I make an intuitive decision about how many hummingbirds there are. In fact, hummingbirds move so fast that I might not even have to blink my eyes for this representational problem to arise. Accordingly, the mind must have a way of reconciling representational conflicts. The corresponding mental principle is that conflicts between representations can be resolved by accessing a separate conceptual representation that integrates the conflicting ones—for example, I might intuitively develop a representation of a single hummingbird in rapid motion between two locations. The conflicting representations are allowed to coexist within the overarching framework of a single-bird-in-motion.

Helmholtz (1903) assumed that such resolving entities are basically direct associations, underlying "unconscious inferences." It is interesting that whereas such inferences may affect our representation of the world through unconscious mechanisms, they have a direct impact on our conscious perception of reality. Indeed, we might suggest that the conscious organization of what is perceived as reality is often a representation that exactly reconciles apparent conflicts in other representations. This interpretation of consciousness reappears at the end of the paper.

Representational Integration in Adults

In everyday perceptual life, the autonomic and conflict-resolving processes occur so fast that they are difficult to observe and study. There are, however, simple laboratory demonstrations of their existence. Consider first an example of the extraction of "prototypes" from varying presentations of an object. If subjects successively view dot patterns in which the dot placements vary randomly from a single underlying pattern, the subjects eventually come to believe that they saw an exemplar of that underlying pattern, even when they never did (Fig. 4) (Posner and Keele 1968). This is a simple but precisely controlled demonstration of the extraction of prototypical representations from varying presentations of an oject. On the conflict-resolution analysis, the viewer abducts the underlying concept of the shape as an integrated representation of the conflicting images seen

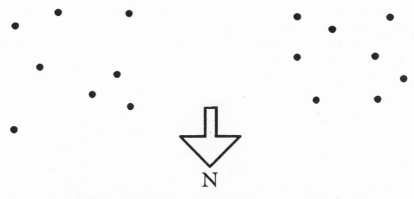

Fig. 4. Sequential perceptions of distinct data arrays are eventually organized in terms of the underlying figure from which each array randomly deviates (Posner 1969).

over time. I say "abducts" because no *exact* ideal instance of the underlying pattern could ever be presented.

In this case, the integrating representation is the presumption of a single static object pattern. There are other well-studied instances of representational conflict resolution that involve the abduction both of a presumed object and a directed dynamic relation between its different perceptual representations. A classic example is the "phi-phenomenon," the perception of an image of motion when an object is briefly presented first in one place and then in another. An everyday example of this is the perception of a yellow traffic light; if it blinks back and forth from one lamp to another we perceive back-and-forth motion, even though we know that the light does not move. Our analysis of this phenomenon is straightforward—one is presented with superficially distinct stimuli, a light on the left and then a similar light on the right. The initial perceptual mechanisms assign the two lights largely identical structure, leading to a representational conflict over where they are. The integration of this conflict is simply the perceptual assumption that the light moved from the first position to the second. The viewer automatically contributes the percept of motion that subsumes the otherwise conflicting percepts [see Rock (1983) for a wide-ranging discussion of perception viewed as problem solving].

Such an example of inferred motion might seem to be the quintessence of a laboratory curiosity, but, after all, it is the most typical of experiences. For example, if I pass one hand behind the other, you see the sequence as continuous, inferring the motion during the period that you cannot see the moving hand. Since much of our visual world is made up of partially obscured objects, it is clear how common the abduction of motion really is. It is no surprise that this phenomenon has become a major area of investigation of modern psychology.

One can use apparent motion between more complex figures to explore what kinds of motions the mind easily imposes (Shepard and Cooper 1982; Shepard 1984; Shepard and Metzler 1971). In a typical study, arbitrary block-figures like those in Figure 5 are presented to a subject. The task is to decide if the pair of figures indicates the same object in a different orientation. A striking result is that viewers assume that the object itself does not change, when a possible physical motion can be invoked to explain the shift from one presentation to another. This explains the demonstration that the amount of time it takes to decide that the second of two such figures is the same object as the first is the same relative time as it would take a constant-speed device physically to carry out the actual rotation. This reflects the intuition that when making such a same vs. different judgment, we imagine the motion of one configuration of the figure rotat-

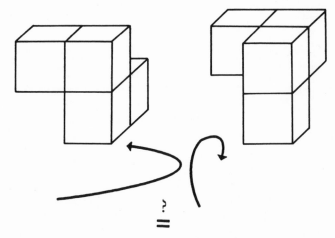

Fig. 5. Evidence for the image of motion: the time to judge if the figures are spatial rotations corresponds to the relative time to carry out the actual rotation (Shepard and Cooper 1982; Shepard and Metzler 1971; the actual studies characteristically use more complex figures).

ing towards the other. This time-taking abstract image of motion demonstrates the "psychological reality" of intermediating representational processes—in this case, an abstraction of the complex movement of a meaningless figure from one orientation to another.

Representational Conflicts in Infants

It takes a special situation like matching meaningless figures to bring out effects that one can study experimentally with normal subjects. Adults have organized the separate processes of representation formation and integration to a degree which ordinarily obscures their separate operation. Infants, on the other hand, can display behaviors that reflect the functions separately, drawn out in time.

Consider a standard example of an infant's behavior—the game of peek-a-boo. There are several things to explain about this game, how it works, and why the infant likes it so much. (This analysis comes more or less straight from Piaget, without any intention to endorse the Piagetian explanations of development, only their description.) On this view, the child playing peek-a-boo is playing with the problem of "mommy-permanence" (Piaget 1950, 1954). The presumption is that the child can develop a representation of what is in front of him, although there are not yet any visually accessible permanent concepts.

In the game, mommy appears as a visual image, then disappears, then

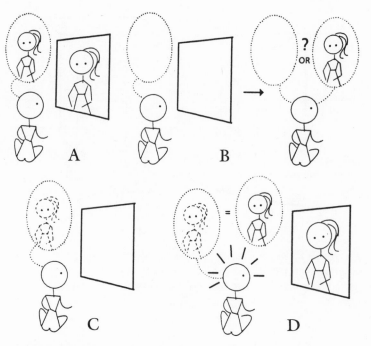

Fig. 6. Stages in the game of peek-a-boo. (a) The child represents the present mother; (b) the child contrasts the recent image of the mother with her absence; (c) the child formulates the concept of a permanent mother; (d) the child confirms the concept with the reappearance of the mother.

reappears, then disappears, etc. (Fig. 6). The child is left with a bewildering phenomenon—first mommy is there, then she isn't. This conflict raises the representational question, IS THERE A MOMMY OR ISN'T THERE? The resolution of the mommy-just-present and mommy-now-absent representations is an inner representation of a permanent mommy, resolving the appearance/disappearance representational conflict. A similar analysis explains the slightly older infant's frequently exasperating preoccupation with looking at a rattle in its hand, looking away, dropping the rattle, listening to the noise, and finally looking down to check where it went. The infant is experimenting with the integration of different kinds of sensory inputs from a single object. The perceptual concept of object permanence integrates the conflict between his visual, motor, and auditory representations. This kind of conflict-integration model is characteristic of Piagetian views of knowledge that emerge later, covering more abstract kinds of knowledge such as number and logic. In each case, a more conceptual mode of representation is accessed as the basis for resolving a representational conflict (Bever 1983). Of great importance for this discussion is the fact that the conflicting representations can remain in the child's mental repertoire, even while the more conceptual representational mode sets them in an orderly relation to each other.

Of course, playing peek-a-boo is manifestly a social activity, and here again we face the problem of a competing functional explanation of why the child likes the game. Clearly, the child is motivated to play the game at least in part because it is communicative. On my interpretation, a separate motive is that it allows the child to solve and re-solve the problem of person-permanence. Each time his expectation of mommy is fulfilled, the appearance/disappearance conflict is resolved again. And, as you can see, I assume it to be obvious that human beings get a charge out of solving problems—peek-a-boo is simply an early problem-solving game.

The Emotional Impact of Solving a Problem

It is useful at this point to review the structural and emotional phenomena that occur when an adult solves a problem. The original observations by Dunker reveal an initial formation of representational conflicts, discovery of a resolving representation, and an attendant "aha" reaction (Duncker 1945). For example, in trying to solve the problem of how to get X-rays to destroy an embedded tumor, subjects chracteristically waver back and forth between suggesting a hypothetical X-ray gun that would shoot the X-rays at the tumor, destroying both it and the intervening tissue, and a hypothetical gun that would send the X-ray only the right distance, so that it would not destroy the intervening tissue. The ultimate solution, of a focusing lens, resolves the two ways of thinking about the gun: the gun sends the rays at the tumor but does so in a diffuse way until the lens focuses them at the right spot. Finding the integrating solution to the problem also releases a surge of emotion, "aha," that accompanies problem solving. Characteristically, recognizing the solution occurs in two phases: first the subject has the intuition that he "sees" the solution, then he checks it out. It is the first, intuitive phase that is associted with the "aha" reaction.

The emotional force of problem solving is interesting in its own right. This discussion so far has presupposed that it is a basic property of human cognition to get a thrill from solving a problem. In the appendix to this paper, I speculate on why the problem-solving thrill exists. For the moment, I am using the formal similarity between early cognitive growth and natural problem solving to define a set of processes that may occur in aesthetic experiences. From that standpoint, what is important is that the first intuition that a problem is solved evokes a burst of pleasurable energy. Whatever its source, we know this to be true.

To summarize so far: there are two fundamental processes that occur when we perceive and represent the world. We automatically form representations of what we perceive. We integrate conflicts in those representations by accessing perceptual and conceptual knowledge of a variety of kinds. The integration of such representational conflicts is itself accompanied by a release of emotional energy. These processes are functional in everyday perception, conceptual development, and problem solving.

The formal similarity of the processes underlying these three kinds of everyday activities does not mean that they are theoretically identical. One difference between perception, cognitive development, and problem solving lies in the degree of automaticity with which the conflict-resolving representation is formed. In perception, forming a constant object, or one in movement, clearly draws on integrating mechanisms that are nearly as automatic as those which form the conflicting representations in the first place. Problem solving is at the other extreme; in that activity even some of the initial representation-forming mechanisms may be elaborate and conscious. The automaticity of the conflict-resolving mechanisms in cognitive development lies between these extremes: the child is solving intuitive problems and thereby is elaborating a growing permanent set of mediating and integrating systems of representation.

Aesthetic Judgments

The overall goal of this paper is to explore the possibility that basic mental operations can explain the existence of some specific properties of language. The preceding review summarizes the importance and pervasiveness of forming conflicting representations and integrating them. Yet, each of the examples I discussed has a clear functional role; without a theory of functions and their relation to behaviors, we cannot be sure that the representational processes are not adaptations to the functions they serve. I introduced this essay with the point that aesthetic activity may directly reveal the operation of the mind, free of worldly functions. Whatever the mind chooses to do during aesthetic activity might display its inner workings, unstressed and undistorted by the need to solve real problems. Accordingly, I now turn to examples of aesthetic activity. Drawing on the generally accepted processes just discussed, I am going to test, on everyday experiences, the principle of "The Aesthetically Interesting Experience" that my colleagues and I have been developing for the past few years (Lasher, Carroll, and Bever 1983; Bever, Lasher, and Carroll, in press).

On this theory, an experience is aesthetically interesting if it involves conflicting representations that are integrated within the organizing framework of a distinct representation. That is, it has exactly the same formal properties as perception, cognitive growth, and problem solving. It is important to note that we focus on the formal properties involved in the simultaneous presence of the distinct representations, rather than the exact temporal processes involved in forming their mental correlates. We are attempting to construct a "generative theory of aesthetics," with the virtues, as well as the limitations, of formal models of other kinds of mental activities. At the end of the discussion, I will point out some of the general features of aesthetic experiences that differentiate them from perception, cognitive growth, and problem solving.

My presentation focuses on examples of folk aesthetics rather than the fine arts because of my concern with objects of psychologically natural preference. Professional art reflects functional and historical influences of its own. Indeed, there is no reason to believe that professional art always follows any aesthetic principle whatsoever. But a simple object which is culturally and historically preferred over others is more likely to display the inner human aesthetic than is an arbitrarily motivated art object. Five folk objects display the operation of the aesthetic principles: the "shave and a haircut, two bits" rhythm, the golden rectangle, the song "Happy Birthday," the children's story "Goldilocks," and successful puns. In each case, the object stimulates a clear representational conflict and affords a resolution that integrates the initially conflicting representations. Furthermore, the integrating representation in each case is interpretably related to the social function that the object appears to serve.

Shave and a Haircut vs. Shave and a Massage

Consider the "shave and a haircut, two bits" rhythm. It has a definite social meaning: an attention-getting noise, "knock" or "honk." This is a widely known rhythmic tatoo: for example, in Latin American countries, motorists honk this at others whom they believe to have just behaved in a vehicularily miscreant manner (there is a ritual string of obscenities that go with it). What we must account for then is twofold. First, why is this rhythm so stable, even cross-culturally, and second, why does it have the functional meaning of a single attention-getting noise?

Consider a visual configuration of the rhythm and recall my discussion of rhythmic gestalt units (Fig. 7). The fifth beat divides the sequence into two parts of equal duration. But the first part is filled with two beats, whereas the corresponding portion of the second part is empty. This typical device opposes in time the two subsequences, identical except that the second has a gap where the first is filled. This, in part, explains the finality of the last two beats, since they occur just after an expectancy for beats has been failed.

Such a traditional analysis in terms of syncopation is consistent with the general representational view, but is not fully explanatory—it explains part

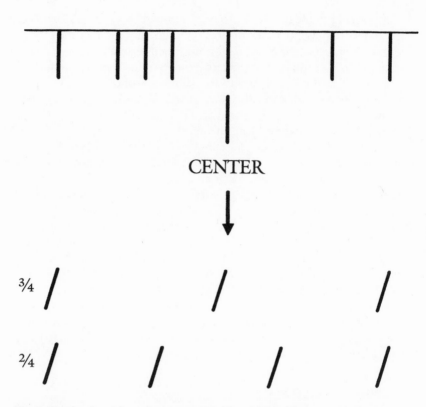

Fig. 7. Two metric analyses of a common attention-getting rhythm. The ²/₄ metric places strong beats as in "shave and a haircut (pause) two bits"; the ³/₄ metric places strong beats as in "shave and a massage (pause) two bits."

of the satisfaction of the last two beats but not in a way that accounts for the special status of the whole tatoo. To explain this, we must listen further. There is a temporal symmetry defined by the last four beats; this symmetry requires the fourth beat to be stressed, not the fifth (since the fourth beat corresponds to the final beat in this symmetric subpattern.) This interpretation imposes a ²/₄ rhythm on the sequence as shown in Figure 7. This stress pattern is conveyed by "sháve and a háircut (pause) two bits." There is a distinct symmetrical pattern, in fact the first five beats comprise the symmetric rhythm mentioned above. We can also see how the underlying rhythmic pulse coordinates with this, using the principle that stressed beats are interpreted as down-beats that begin each metric unit. On this interpretation, the whole sequence has a ³/₄ metric with the strong beats indicated as on the first, fifth, and seventh beats. This stress pattern goes with the phrase, "sháve and a masságe (pause) two bíts."

Hence, the organization in terms of symmetries imposes conflicting analyses of the underlying repeating metric. This conflict is itself resolved by the last beat, which is the first beat at which the two rhythmic representations both require a strong beat. Accordingly, the last beat is a satisfying resting moment: a brief representational conflict in the underlying rhythm is resolved at that point. This analysis of the last beat as a single conflict-resolving pulse also explains the general social meaning of the tatoo, namely as a single attention-getting noise.

The Golden Mean Rectangle

Consider a simple rectangle (Fig. 8). Why is it that certain ratios of sides seem to be more satisfying than others? Rectangles of approximately ratio 1.6:1 seem to be preferred over other ratios (Fechner 1897; Woodworth 1938). An ancient explanation is that the ratio of 1.6+:1 has an appealing pure property: this ratio guarantees that if a square of the short side is subtracted from the rectangle, it leaves behind another rectangle of exactly the same ratio (Fig. 9). This subtraction can be applied recursively: like turtles, it is rectangles all the way down.

In his investigation that confirmed the preference for the golden mean rectangle, Fechner argues similarly that 1.6:1 is the ratio which presents the greatest "purity" of rectangularity. Yet, this explanation does little to explain the preference for this particular purity—other ratios exhibit similarly pure mathematical properties of other kinds. The formal elegance of

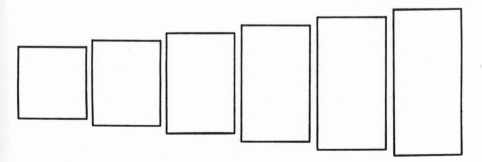

Fig. 8. Rectangles ranging in side ratios of 1:1 to 2:1.

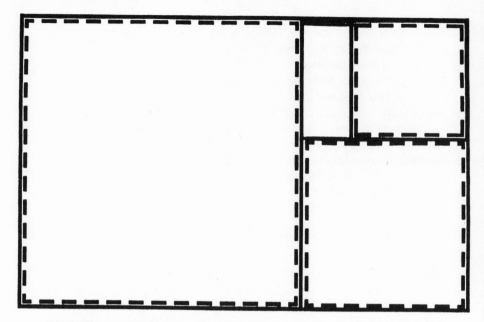

Fig. 9. *Three stages of the recursive reduction of the golden mean rectangle: subtracting the square (dotted line) formed on the short side of each rectangle leaves a smaller rectangle with the same side ratios as the original.*

such formulae does not reflect what the funtion of a rectangle might be, nor why the ideal ratio for that function is 1.6:1.

What, in fact, is the meaning of an ideal rectangle? That is, what does it convey? An intuitive description is that it is more than one square but less than two; somehow a rectangle signifies "two-ness" without actually dis-. playing it literally. This explains at the outset why rectangles that are slightly larger than a square or slightly smaller than two squares are not preferred examples—they are too close to the conventional extremes to be ideal. The quintessential rectangle lies between the extremes. Woodworth put it this way: "The golden section rectangle appears typical for a rectangle, slim enough to be a successful rectangle, without being extreme."

Clearly, the ideal rectangle must lie on an ideal ratio between 1.8:1 and 1.4:1 to avoid blending with one extreme or the other. What does our aesthetic principle have to say about why the ideal ratio is approximately 1.6:1, when other natural candidates might be 1.5:1 or 1.67.1? First, the representation-formation process will impose squares on the rectangle as an immediate simple gestalt form of representation [see the articles in Pinker (1984b) for general discussions of theories of visual perception, especially by Hoffman and Richards, and Ullman on the initial stages of perceiving simple figures. This initial analysis in terms of component squares is like the traditional analysis of the golden rectangle in terms of component squares. But what the traditional analysis missed is that there are *two* equally valid squares, one defined on the right side, the other on the left side.

This presents competing analyses, one in which the square is on the left and one in which the square is on the right. This does not set up a true representational competition for all rectangular ratios, however, because in some cases the overlapping squares themselves define a rectangle that can repeat to describe the whole rectangle in two dimensions. Rather than providing competing analyses, the overlapping squares yield a kind of representation that is identical to that of repeating rectangles. Thus, the simple gestalt law of repetition of elementary forms would provide a complete representation of such figures in two dimensions, with no need to access a different representational level to integrate initially conflicting representations.

Consider how this works for a rectangle with a ratio of 1.5:1. Overlapping squares imposed on this rectangle define three identical rectangles that exhaustively describe the figure (Fig. 10). Similarly, the ratio of $^5/_3$:1 defines a central rectangle of width $^1/_3$ and two bounding rectangles of

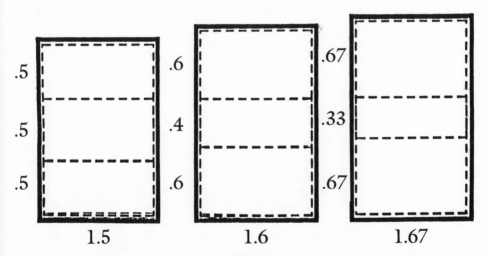

Fig. 10. Internal rectangles formed by overlapping two squares formed on the short sides of a large rectangle: in the 1.5:1 and 1.67:1 ratios the internal rectangle can repeat exhaustively and describe the entire large rectangle; in the 1.6:1 ratio (the golden mean ratio) the internal rectangle cannot describe the large rectangle.

width $2/3$ into which it can repeat and completely describe the figure. Here, too, the full rectangle is exhaustively described by repeating the small rectangle defined by the overlap of the squares. In each of these cases, the two-dimensional analysis in terms of overlapping squares is consistent with a simultaneous two-dimensional analysis in terms of repeating rectangles: hence, the squares do not yield a representational conflict that requires accessing another representational form.

Now consider a rectangle with a ratio of 1.6:1, roughly midway between the other two ratios. In this case, the overlapping squares yield a rectangle with length 0.4, that cannot describe the whole figure repetition in two dimensions—one would have to divide it in half and then repeat the result eight times to exhaustively describe the large rectangle in two dimensions. Accordingly, the initial two-dimensional analysis of the golden rectangle into two overlapping squares does not afford a simply derived complete description of it. Hence, the 1.6:1 rectangle presents conflicting representations in two dimensions—either it is the left-hand square plus a leftover, or it is the right-hand square plus a leftover. An obvious resolving integration is to analyze the figure as *having a third dimension*: this allows an analysis of the figure as having *two* overlapping squares, with one in front of the other. In this way, recourse to a conceptual third dimension affords a resolution of the representational conflicts yielded by the immediate two-dimensional analyses. This explains why the preferred ratio is 1.6:1 according to the aesthetic principle, which requires that conflicting perpetual representations be integrated by accessing a separate level of representation. It also explains the functional analysis of the rectangle as indicating "two-ness"—it evokes two simultaneous squares. (Note that it also predicts that the golden rectangle should excite more sensations of depth, a testable prediction.)

Happy Birthday!

Folk music is often composed but is usually culturally winnowed, so it can reflect the long-term effects of aesthetic principles. Consider as an example the song "Happy Birthday," which was originally composed but which seems to have taken on an aesthetically satisfying life of its own. That is, regardless of its origin, it has stood the test of aesthetically selective time. It has also acquired certain ritual functions that are explained by its particular aesthetic structure. Before reviewing the representational languages of music, notice what the social role of "Happy Birthday" actually is.

The most obvious fact about "Happy Birthday" is that it is a celebratory hymn, sung as a solemn recognition of somebody else's special day: the song puts the cap on the celebration. A birthday celebration is considered incomplete until "Happy Birthday" is sung—virtually every other convivial aspect can be dispensed with. Furthermore, the song is characteristically sung near the end of the festivity. To put it operationally, you can leave the party any time after the song is sung but not before: the song says "amen" to the happy occasion.

There is also a special kind of mystery-and-discovery ritual that goes with the singing of the song. Recall your youth of paper hats, rented magicians, rapidly melting ice cream, and mushy cake on floppy paper plates. The lights dim, a rustle approaches from the kitchen, an adult with a basso profundo starts intoning as a dirge, "happy birthday to you . . . ." You mouth along with the words until you get to the point where the person is named—at that point, everybody lets go with the worst string of obscenities that a five-year-old can muster ("happy BIRTHday dear Stinky-pants-in-his-underwear . . . "). That is, the song is really a mystery and a solution, revolving around whose birthday it is or what you are going to call the victim when you get there. The song really should be sung with the words, "Happy birthday to who? Happy birthday to who? Happy BIRTHday dear XXXXX, happy birthday to YOU." Even adults feel the naming tension: for example, when the song is sung at the next table in a restaurant, it is hard not to wait and see "who" the birthday celebrant is.

Now consider a little simplified music theory. [There are numerous ways to present the elements of music theory—in this case, I follow the style of Zuckerkandl (1959), which is appropriate for my purposes. I also use a pure graph notation to aid the nonmusical reader.] Melodies are composed out of scales defined along two dimensions, relative tone height and relative tone stability. Consider first tone height. Each melody is defined in part by a range of notes that it covers—a well-formed melody characteristically fills in all the notes in its range by the time it is over. That is, one of the representational schemata that listeners anticipate is a range of notes with the intermediate ones filled in. Consider "Twinkle Twinkle Little Star" (Fig. 11). The first phrase starts with an upward leap, and then the second descends and fills in all the intermediate steps.

This melody also illustrates that classical melodies are in a tonic key. A key is defined by a scale with seven notes dividing each octave. Characteristically, the tonic key is the first and last note of the melody, and often defines at least one end of the tone-height range. This is what occurs in the first phrase of "Twinkle Twinkle".

The analysis of a melody into a key gives a dimension to the notes in addition to their relative pitch: stability in the key. A functional way of thinking about the key stability of a note is in terms of the likelihood that a melody could stop at it. The most stable note is the tonic itself, the next most stable notes are the 3rd and 5th of the scale. The next most stable are the 2d, 4th, 6th, and 7th, and the least stable notes are those not assigned to the scale at all.

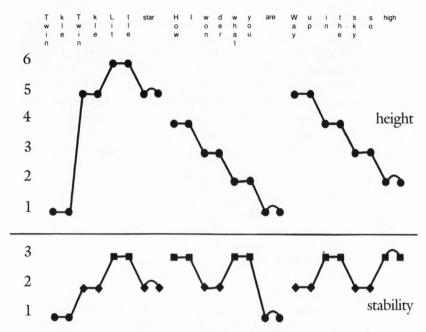

Fig. 11. Graphic representation of "Twinkle, Twinkle, Little Star," in which the notes of each melodic phrase are connected. The height dimension portrays the relative pitch of the notes. The stability dimension portrays the relative harmonic stability of the notes in the base key. (Note that the horizontal dimension portrays temporal order, but not exact rhythm.)

This notion of stability, sometimes referred to as "harmonic role" or "chroma," provides a representation of a melody independent of relative tone height, as shown in the chart for "Twinkle Twinkle." The most salient aspect is that the final settling phrase is one that starts harmonically stable, becomes instable, and returns to stability. The intermediate refrain ("way up in the sky so high . . . ") introduces a continuing harmonic instability on this dimension, which is then resolved by returning to the basic phrase at the ending on the harmonically stable tonic note.

This example illustrates that there are two kinds of information that contribute to perceptually determining the key of a simple melody: tone range is usually defined at one extreme by the tonic note of the key; harmonically, phrases tend to end on notes that are stable in the particular key.

Now again consider "Happy Birthday" (Fig. 12). First, in terms of tone range, it seems for the most part to be in the key of C. It starts on C, the first three repeating phrases all start on C, and the full range of seven steps between the two octaves of C are filled in by the end of the melody: all of these features of tone range suggest C. However, the analysis in terms of pitch stability suggests by the end of the second measure that the melody *might* be in the key of F. The third measure is most confusing: on the one hand it starts again on C, to which the previous two measures have also returned, and jumps an octave to another C. But then on its way down ("happy *BIRTHday dear* XXXXX") it defines an F major chord. Finally in the last measure, the first note, a B-flat, clinches the decision: the melody must now be in F, since the key of C does not have B-flat in it at all—C would require a B-natural. In fact the underlying chords (usually a B-flat triad) further determine that it is F, just at the point when the person is named. The conclusion is that the song ends in the key of F. In brief, the song presents an ongoing perceptual conflict in whether it is in C or F; the initial tone-height information suggests C, the stability information increasingly suggests F. That is, the song might be given the words, "Now this song is in C, now this song is in F, is it C or F major . . . ? This note says now it's F."

Heard prospectively, the song has perceptual cues suggesting it is in C; heard retrospectively it has cues suggesting F. What is the resolving integration of these conflicting representations? The resolution is the interpretation that the song presents a *harmonic progression* from the key of +F to +C. This progression itself is an example of the classical harmonic

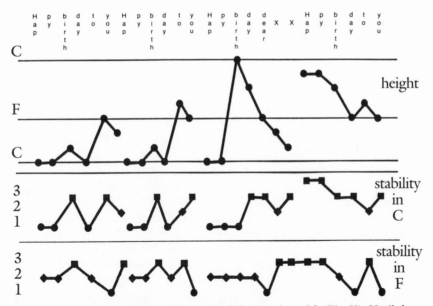

Fig. 12. Graphic representation of "Happy Birthday" (see legend for Fig. 11). Until the last phrase, the height dimension repeatedly suggests that the underlying key is C; the stability dimension increasingly requires it to be in F.

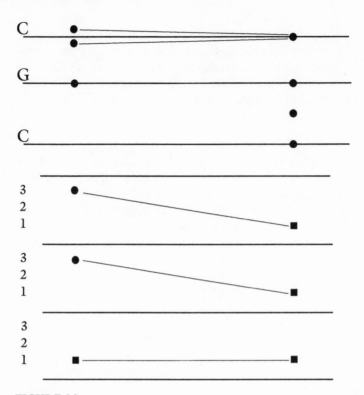

FIGURE 13

movement from a chord built on the 5th note to the tonic chord, a movement that underlies final progressions in virtually all of western folk and art
music. One reason for this can be seen in Figure 13—the fifth degree chord
presents a stable root (the 5th) with two maximally unstable notes of the
scale above it, each of which is one step up or down from the tonic (the 7th
and 2d). So, the fifth chord is stably rooted, yet its unstable upper notes
lead melodically to the tonic. One of the most typical occurrences of the
5th-to-tonic progression is the full-cadence "amen," which can end hymns
and other celebratory songs. Thus, in "Happy Birthday," the apparent
movement from the key of F to the key of C presents a melodically drawn-
out "aaaaamennnnnn" in celebration of a person's birthday. And that is
exactly the overall social function that "Happy Birthday" has.

We can see how this simple song satisfies the aesthetic principle. The
two tonal representations together subserve the harmonic salutation. The
analysis also explains why the song has the particular social ritual that it
does: the immediate perceptual representations of the song make it a tonal
mystery about the key it is in, and this mystery is resolved at the end of the

third phrase, just when the mystery celebrant is named. Thus, the ongoing perceptual analysis of the melodic structure of the song relates in a natural way to the mystery-name ritual that the song has acquired. Finally, the overall resolution of the tonal mystery in terms of a melodic movement from the 5th to the 1st notes reflects the celebratory conclusiveness of the song.

GOLDILOCKS—Why She Became a Little Girl and the Three Male Bears Became a Family

Cultural artifacts are modified to accommodate aesthetic needs. Children's stories are indicative examples of this kind of process. A fairy tale is successively passed on from generation to generation, much in the same way as language itself—successive pairings of parents and children reshape a story to fill the intuitive and aesthetic needs of both.

As in the previous examples, we must distinguish between the direct communicative appeal of a children's story and its representational structure. A recent version of the story of Goldilocks serves as a good example of such structures (Cauley 1981). It has several subevents.

> The three bears (father, mother, child) cooked some porridge. It was too hot, so they went out for a walk in the forest to let the porridge cool.
>
> Goldilocks was sent by her mother to go out and pick some flowers and keep out of mischief. She came across the bears' house, peeked inside, and went in.
>
> She tried the porridge in the three bowls:
> —the big one was too hot
> —the medium one was too cold
> —the small one was just right, so she kept tasting it until it was all gone.
>
> Then she tried to sit in the chairs:
> —the big one was too hard
> —the medium one was too soft
> —the little one was just right, so she sat in it but broke it by mistake.
>
> Then she tried out the beds:
> —the big one was too hard/rejecting
> —the medium one was too soft/enfolding
> —the little one was just right, so when she tried it she automatically went to sleep.
>
> The bears came home.
>
> First they noticed the disturbance of the porridge, in the order, father, mother, baby. ("Somebody's been eating my porridge and ate it all up!")

Then they noticed the chairs, in the same order. ("Somebody's been sitting in my chair and broke it!!")
Finally, they noticed the beds in the same order. ("Somebody's been sleeping in my bed, and there she is!!!")

Goldilocks jumped out of the window and ran back home. Her mother scolded her (but hugged her too).

Consider first what the real function of this story is—that is, why do children and adults like to share it? It seems intuitively clear that it is about "fitting in," a theme of the story which has been given a rich psycholoanalytic interpretation (Betelheim 1976; Betelheim argues that "Goldilocks" is actually an unsatisfactory fairy tale because it does not provide a complete dramatic solution—on his view, it has survived only because of its rich and analytically compelling imagery). Finding the right food, chair, and bed in the bears' family is an allegory about the child's place in the family. The story symbolizes that, in a family, relationships are three-way, not just a sequence of isolated two-way relations. The child's role is to be between that of the parents on each of several dimensions ("*juuuuust* right"). It is important that Goldilocks then systematically, though unintentionally, destroys the objects that instantiate her own position in the bear family (eating the porridge, breaking the chair, mussing the bed). This emphasizes the transitory nature of those objects and reinforces the fact that it is not the *bears'* family that she belongs in but her own, where she will be appropriately scolded for what she did but hugged at the same time.

To understand why a story survives, we must not only understand the deep symbolic themes it evokes, we must also understand how these themes are supported by its aesthetic properties. When we hear a story, we chunk it up into parts, that is, we apply an overall "story grammar" to it (Kintsch, Mandel, & Kozminsky 1977). Story grammars provide a basic organization of a narrative, and, complex as they are, they guide our initial perceptual organization of the story as we hear it. For example, Goldilocks in naturally chunked into segments that correspond to the separate items in the above summary. This represents the fact that the central theme of the story involves two orderly explorations of three triplets—first, Goldilocks explores three aspects of the bears' world, then the bears retrace her steps.

The three bears themselves specify an ordering that is obvious to a child, from father to mother to baby, big to medium to small. This order is explicit in the second triplet—the bears express their dismay in that order, and with an increasingly high-pitched voice. Goldilocks, however, originally chose the baby bear's possession as the final choice in a different ordering. The baby's object is actually between the other two in the order father–baby–mother: the ideal porridge is intermediately hot, the ideal chair is intermediately soft, and the ideal bed is intermediately resistant.

In this way, the most salient sections of the story have two conflicting representations of how the triplets of objects are ordered.This representational conflict meets one requirement of an aesthetic experience, but there must also be an integrating conflict-resolving representation. In this case, it is the number three itself, which subsumes both kinds of orderings. The number three is what the structure of the story presents and re-presents—not only are there three bears, there are three sets of objects, underlying two sets of three triplets. The result is that the representational structure of the story, brought out by the application of a story grammar, makes available a resolution of the primary semantic conflict within the story. We noted above that the number three is what the story is actually about—the notion that the child's relational world is a family, not a separable father, mother, child, nor a set of dyads.

"Goldilocks" has changed considerably since it was first widely published in 1843 (Southey 1836). Some of the changes may reflect general shifts. For example, the original protagonist was a little old lady, who was a very bad character—the content of the original story seems literally to be about the perils of bad deportment—and thus the reader's sympathy is entirely with the bears. Perhaps the little old lady was a child-surrogate in an age of nannies: this could explain the subsequent transformation of Goldilocks to a child with whom modern children can identify. Other changes in the story seem to be motivated by the aesthetic requirement, once one decides to make it about a child. For example, it is now important that the destructive things she does are "by accident." The original story had no clear beginning and ending; the protagonist wanders into the bears' house out of nowhere and disappears back to nowhere. Having the child partially "running away" from home, and returning with relief, gives an enveloping context that fits with the family-oriented main theme. Most interesting is the fact that the original version had three male bears, differing only in size, not in age or sex. The change to a family unit facilitates the allegorical theme that the story now has, which is supported by its aesthetic structure.

Puns and Jokes

My colleagues and I have argued that the essential elements of an aesthetic experience are rooted in representation-forming and integrating behavior that is typical of perception, cognitive development, and problem solving. It might seem that every time we change our minds about anything, it must be an aesthetic experience, since it involves a change in mental representations. It is important to consider some examples of why mere changes in representations do not lead to aesthetic experiences. Consider puns—for example, in the scene below:

> Q. Aren't all the mafiosi behind bars these days?
> A. Yes, serving drinks.
> Q. (Groan!)

Why is this sequence not aesthetic? It would seem that it involves two conflicting representations of a phonetic sequence ("bars"), with the phonetic sequence itself as the "resolution." This does not conform to the aesthetic principle for several reasons: first, the resolving structure is not itself a level of representation different from the one that presents the conflict; second, and most important, the two interpretations of a pun never coexist within the framework of a single representation—the listener first perceives one and then the other interpretation. It is a central feature of all the examples in this paper that the "resolving" representation creates a superstructure within which the conflicting representations can simultaneously coexist. It is for this reason that most merely ambiguous stimuli are not aesthetic. Similarly, perceptual and conceptual acts that involve merely replacing one representation with another do not conform to the aesthetic principle.

This predicts a situation in which the above sequence could be aesthetic and acceptable as a discourse of wit (in fact, the discourse below recently occurred).

> Q. Why does this restaurant have such a lousy wine list?
> A. I guess they haven't paid off the mob for a license.
> Q. Aren't all the mafiosi behind bars these days?
> A. Yes, serving drinks.
> Q. (Chuckle!)

Why is this pun more acceptable as a witticism than the above version with exactly the same phonetic basis? There might be many reasons, but the important one for our consideration is that it allows the change in representation of the crucial phonetic sequence ("bar") to fit with *either* interpretation in a way that makes sense in the overall context. (That is, if the mafiosi control liquor licenses and are behind bars as criminals, then it makes a punnish kind of sense that they serve drinks while in jail.) Such minor jokes are surely not the height of wit, but the example does clarify that a pun causes a groan if its alternate meanings do not have an overall sense that embraces them, whereas a pun is acceptably witty when the alternate meanings fit into a larger schema of the kind described by the aesthetic principle. This view also explains why the creator of bad puns always finds them funny—he perceives some connection in his mind between the two interpretations, even if the listeners do not.

This example clarifies why the experience of mere ambiguity is not necessarily aesthetic: there must be an overarching context which includes both interpretations. A Necker cube does not afford an aesthetic experience, because we perceive it as either having one orientation *or* the other. Yet, the same kind of three-dimensional ambiguity may allow an aesthetic experience, as in many paintings by Escher: Escher takes great care to provide local contextual support for the simultaneous acceptance of both three-dimensional orientations in different parts of the same pictures.

I have reviewed examples from five folk genres to illustrate a common set of principles underlying aesthetic experience. In each case, automatic representation-forming mechanisms provide conflicting perceptual analyses of an object, a separate level provides a representational framework within which the conflicting representations can coexist, and aspects of the integrating representation often have feautures that explain the function of the object.

The Roles of Art

The conflict-integration theory of aesthetic experience has several advantages over the optimal arousal model. First, the theory can explain the primary facts that are usually marshalled in favor of the more traditional arousal model—in particular, the role of optimal discrepancy between an expected and obtained stimulus. On our interpretation, the relation between an expected representation and an experienced one is simply a special case of integrating conflicting representations. If the representations are very close, little mental activity is involved in their integration and, hence, very little enjoyment will ensue; if the representations are too discrepant, no resolution at all can be found. The representational theory can also explain other facts; for example, simple preferences of a variety of kinds. We can also explain why art works can be re-experienced, without making the counterintuitive claim that audiences have forgotten a work each time they re-experience it. There are general reasons to believe that the historical resolution of a representational conflict can be re-enjoyed, even when it is well known—why else is history itself enjoyable, a mystery re-readable? Such examples demonstrate that we enoy re-solving *old* problems, just as we enjoy climbing the same mountain or re-experiencing the thrill of diving into the same pool from time to time. Similarly, we can re-enjoy a well-known art work simply by virtue of the fact that the representational conflicts it elicits are the result of highly automatized schemata which operate autonomously, even when we can anticipate the result of their operation.

Furthermore, a successful work of art is generally one that offers a variety of structural interpretations—that is, reappreciating an art work may sometimes rest on temporarily assigning it conflicting representations of new kinds. Even if the overarching resolution is the same, the pathway there is different. Of course, in the performing arts, this is just why performance matters—it guides the audience in forming intermediate and final representations of the work.

This theory explains the relationship between normal mechanisms of conceptual growth and aesthetic activity, in a way which may explain the cultural ubiquity of artistic enterprises. I have reviewed some basic processes which are allegedly typical of the mental growth of children as well as adult mental activities. Characteristically, the child resolves representational conflicts by abducing new conceptual representations that integrate the conflicts. The child's emerging conceptual mastery of the world results from a successive construction and abduction of conceptual levels that lead to effective resolutions. On this view, much of what we learn is self-willed, that is, we learn it to serve our own needs for mental consistency and not for any specific identifiable functional reason. I have tried to demonstrate that the same processes define the intuitive aesthetic activities of adults.

This leads to the conclusion that aesthetic experience continues in adulthood the recognition and solution of the kind of mental problems that are functional for us to solve during our childhood. That is, one role of art is to make us feel young. Of course, it may be that both young and old simply like to solve problems: we run out of real problems by the time we are thirteen years old, so we invent ones to solve via art.

The second interpretation of the role of art is that in stimulating the abduction of higher-order representations, art increases the scope of conscious experience. I have not said much about consciousness in this paper because it is even harder to deal with than aesthetic judgment. Nevertheless, on the conflict-resolution model of perception, the conscious inference of reality often reconciles conflicting sources of perceptual information. On that view, art stimulates an internal overarching structure in much the same way as ordinary conscious experience, but with the possibility of stretching the representation beyond the sensational present. To put it another way, by accessing a higher-order representation, an aesthetic experience allows one to transcend more momentary information [see Bever (1983) for a discussion of consciousness and relational processing].

Finally, one can argue that since many integrating concepts are themselves idealizations, art brings the mind into contact with uncaused Platonic universals—that is, it is one way we drag ourselves out of the shadows of Plato's cave.

Implications for Cognitive Theories, Language Acquisition, and Linguistic Structure

Few of these conclusions are novel, nor is the general theory of aesthetic experience that we are proposing without many precedents [see especially Croce (1922) and Langer (1967)]. What my colleagues and I are trying to do is show how the natural functions of mental life explain the structural and meaningful properties of aesthetic judgment. This has brought me far from my original reason for examining aesthetic activity. I started out using the structure of aesthetic judgment as a way of revealing function-free cognitive processes. I have ended up with a theory of aesthetic judgment that has some general implications for language acquisition, cognition, and learning in general.

It is a puzzling question why a child bothers to learn the abstract structures of his language, when he is quite successful at communicating with a rudimentary form of it. Two distinct answers to this problem have emerged in the last decade. On one view, the child learns the language as a function of "social interaction," sparked by his desire to communicate fully with the adult world (Bruner 1974–75; Bates 1976); on the other view, the manifest language capacity emerges as a reflection of the maturation of an innate linguist "organ" (McNeill 1970; Chomsky 1981; Pinker 1984a). It is beyond the scope of this paper to examine fully the limitations of each of these positions. We can briefly note that the social interactionist offers no explanation of the form of language that is arrived at except by granting the nativist's view of the ultimate structural goal of the child. The organicist offers no explanation of the dynamic role of the child and the specifics of his language, outside of the language organ—that is, it might explain why universal linguistic structures are the way they are, but not why language-specific patterns are acquired, nor *why the child likes to learn them*.

It is obvious what I am about to suggest: an important emotional source of language-learning zeal in the young child is the fact that it gives many rich opportunities to experience the conflict-integrating role of abstract levels of representation—that is, it offers many opportunities to enjoy aesthetically interesting experiences.

The formal description of how such experience might occur during language learning is a simple one. Consider, for example, a basic feature of language acquisiton, the learning of words during the first decade of life. Children easily learn three to five words a day, much more during certain periods. Such learning must be intrinsically motivating since it often occurs without an external motive. A few simple observations about what words are demonstrates how to relate their acquisiton to the aesthetic principles. Words characteristically specify the relations between semantic analyses and stereotypic concepts they convey. For example, "dog" has a technical definition ("domestic, canine," etc.) that covers a wide range of specific instance; our representation of the word also includes a standard stereotypic instantiation (e.g., "four-legged German Shepherd"). These obvious—largely theory-free—observations about the psychology of word meaning show that word learning involves the formation of categories out of conflicting instances ("cocker spaniel vs. dalmation"). On this view, the word, its technical definition, and its stereotypic application serve together as symbolic representations that unify the distince instances of its application. Accordingly, learning a word involves the kind of experiences characteristic of aesthetic enjoyment. The word binds conflicting representations as a symbolic fiat.

This exemplifies how the aesthetic principle can apply to acquisition phenomena: the levels of representation themselves are presupposed, as well as the conflicting representations at one of those levels—the critical learning process is the attachment of connections *between* the representational levels that integrates the conflicting representations. It is the formation of these connections that comprise specific learning; forming the specific connections releases the aesthetic thrill, providing intrinsic motivation to learn arbitrary lexical facts.

Consider now the child's discovery of phrase structure, the systematic hierarchical grouping and labeling of word sequences. Suppose, along with virtually all students of language acquisition, we postulate that the child has available an early "agent-action" schema that can be applied to the linguistic world. One of the most salient features of simple sentences is that the preverbal subject can very in length and complexity. Over a short period of time, the child can use the verb location to segment preverbal agents of varying lenth and complexity. This leads to a set of representations of the different kinds of word strings that can serve as agents—setting up a set of conflicting representations of what can be an agent, in the sense I have been discussing. The abstract phrase structure node, "NP," provides a structural resolution, embracing numerous lower level variants.

It should be clear that such a description is merely an account of the structural state of affairs that the child experiences. Arguments in language acquisition tend to center around the question of what *causes* linguistic structure; I have not made an argument here that the aesthetic principles cause phrase structure to have the properties that it does—I have only argued that phrase structure and the way that the child could discover its role in his particular language conform to the aesthetic principles.

A similar argument can be made about the integration of more abstract levels of representation. A transparent example would be the interrelation of varying syntactic forms with underlying semantic structures. For example, the variants of indirect object constructions ("John gave the book to Harry" vs. "John gave Harry the book") are resolved via the rule system that relates them systematically to the same propositional representation.

It seems possible that the formation of the psychological instantiation of an entire grammar is itself the result of successive conflict-resolving abductions that operate on separately developing kinds of language behaviors. The most obvious separate capacities that develop early are speech production and speech comprehension—clearly there are periods during childhood when these separate capacities compute different sets of sound/meaning pairs. There are sentence types which a child cannot say but understands, and conversely there are sentences which a child says that he does not understand. We know that the gradual resolution of representational conflicts can ultimately lead to the formation of complex and stable mental structures of representation—as in the emergence of naive number theory, naive physics, or naive logic. Continual application of the aesthetic processes would result in the abduction of an entire grammar, itself a gradual resolution of a series of such representational conflicts during childhood (Bever 1975).

Such formulations make predictions about the developmental course of language learning, in particular that new levels of representation are activated as representational conflicts clarify at other levels of representation. It is not obvious how the aesthetic principles could directly *explain* the structure of the abstract structural universals of language. However, it is clear that the language-learning child continually reshapes those structures to conform to the ways in which he learns it (see Halle 1962; Bever 1970). I have suggested that the aesthetic principles describe aspects of acquiring indigenous skills, such as naive mathematics and logic: insofar as discovering the structure of these skills affords aesthetically satisfying experiences, the child will learn the structure without extrinsic motivation. The principles may also determine some aspects of the structure of the skill as it is acquired. Accordingly, stages in the acquisition of language must provide the possibility of representational conflicts and their integration. This can lead to a number of predictions and experimental investigations, so my proposal is empirically demonstrable, at least in principle.

The conflict-integration model of acquisition leaves most nativist claims unscathed. I have argued that complex representational structures must have certain properties that intrinsically motivate children to learn how to interrelate them. This constraint on the structures does not explain them away as a mere by-product of individual acquisition: such a proposal *might* be true. A plausible alternative is that the constraint has operated over time, as one of the extrinsic requirements on the evolution of such innately prefigured skills as language. In this sense, the aesthetic constraint on language is like other usability constraints on the form of existing languages, notably learnability, comprehensibility, and producibility. Each system sets limits on what a human language can be, but none explains what it is.

The aesthetic constraint requires that language must conform to regularities that allow it to be described in terms of *levels of representation* which are independently defined and interrelated according to cognitively available principles. In the context of current generative theories of language, it may seem trivially true that grammars involve multiple levels of representation, but it is instructive to recall that many other kinds of grammatical descriptions have been proposed that do not have such properties (e.g., taxonomic phrase structure, string analysis, stratificational grammar, signals grammar). Many such nonrepresentational grammars have the everyday expressive power of a multileveled grammar, so there is no obvious evolutionary or ontogenetic explanation as to why they are not what children learn. On the view in this essay, the explanation lies in the aesthetic constraint.

This constraint may explain another prima facie odd property of grammars that I reviewed in the introduction—languages have multiple overlapping systems that partially describe the same facts (Sapir 1921–49; Sadock 1974). For example, syntactic gender almost never has complete overlap with semantic gender. Yet, the expressive power of a language with complete overlap of the two definitions of gender would not be impaired. It is hard to see how such a fact could be true if children constrained a language to be maximally straightforward. Indeed, it is a frequent goal of theories of language acquisition to show how syntactic knowledge emerges out of semantic knowledge—a goal that is never reached. According to the aesthetic constraint, the apparent complexity of multiple levels of representation is necessary because it makes language fun to learn.

Is the Aesthetic Principle General or Specific?

Many issues in cognition have recently focused on the question raised at the beginning of this paper—whether or not there are general mechanisms of representation and mental computation. On the "organ model," capacities such as language reflect the operation of unique and isolated computational systems that share no (interesting) properties with the systems that underly other capacities: on this view, there are no general cognitive mechanisms. The organ model addresses the genetic basis for special skills. The implications of the model for adult organization of behavior is expressed in theories of the "modularity" of mental organization—each behavioral capacity, like speech comprehension, operates separately from others, with rapid and efficient heuristics (Fodor 1983; Pylyshyn 1984). It is important to note that the aesthetic principle *presupposes* the availability of multiple representations of an object that cluster in natural forms; e.g., static vs. moving ones, two vs. three dimensions, momentary vs. durative, literal vs. metaphorical. The conflicting representations are derived independently of each other and *independently of familiarity with the art object*. That is, each of the representation-forming processes operate independently of the person's other knowledge—and that is a criterial definition for some versions of modularity.

The aesthetic principles, however, do not have the other important property of modularity—unique forms in each module. I have adduced examples of aesthetic processes that seem to operate in the *same* formal way in normal perception, cognitive development, and problem solving. One might be tempted to conclude that the representational conflict-resolving process *is* a general cognitive process that transcends any individual module, but I am not prepared to make that conclusion quite yet. In particular, aesthetic judgment may itself turn out to be a true general property of mental systems—a capacity that is not bound to specific modalities. Rather, it may operate on the output of modular processing systems, isolating *n*-tuples consisting of conflicting representations and their resolving integration.

This interprets the processes of aesthetic judgment to have a scope similar to psychophysical judgments, such as magnitude estimation, which appear to transcend single modalities: it is no accident that Fechner, who was concerned to create a science of aesthetics, devoted so much time to the science of judging intensity.

General Problem Solvers and Nativism

The predilection to search for general learning mechanisms corresponds to recidivist interest in showing that particular complex representational systems like language are acquired via "general" problem-solving systems (Anderson 1983). I have suggested that contingently specific representational systems are indeed acquired via normal problem-solving processes. It turns out, however, that the mechanisms for "general" problem solving themselves are not simple. The most natural form of general problem solving in humans itself follows the aesthetic constraint: it evokes abstract structures and integrating levels on problems as they are solved. Problem solving presupposes independent levels of representations and a set of available interrelations between the levels.

The Reintegration of Motivation and Learning

Behaviorism has died hard. The doctrine had two compelling attractions: it explained the structure of *what* is learned on the basis of *how* it is learned, and it explained *how* learning occurs as a function of *why* it occurs. Thus, behaviorism offered a continuous line of reasoning from functional motivation back to learned structure. Many investigations of behavioral structures have demonstrated the empirical inadequacy of what could be learned according to behaviorist principles; such demonstrations motivate the hypothesis that abstract representational systems must be innate rather than learned. But no proposals have been offered in the new cognitive vein to account for the relation between motivation and how learning occurs. I have argued that humans learn the interrelations between levels of representation because doing so releases an emotional surge. The present proposal provides a way of interrelating individual motivation with the view that the levels of representation are themselves both abstract and innate.

The construction of this essay has lead me a roundabout pathway that unexpectedly reunites the motive for learning a skill with the multileveled structure of what is learned. The concept of abstract levels of representation that map the relations between other levels of representation is common in current cognitive theories of mental life. The emotional excitement of representational integration can explain why humans learn such structures at all—it is not that we cannot help it, nor that it is recognizably functional; rather, abstract representational learning is essentially *thrilling*.

Acknowledgments

This essay was written while I was a sabbatical Fellow at the Center for Advanced Study in the Behavioral Sciences, jointly supported by the Center and the Trustees of Columbia University. It started as a lecture at the Arizona conference presented in this book and was refined in an informal talk to the 1984–1985 Center Fellows, to whom I am indebted for various comments. I am particularly grateful to Margaret Omara of the Center, who turned me into a "Happy Birthday" and "Goldilocks" pseudo-scholar. I also benefited from crucial conversations on specific topics with Janet Fodor, Randy Gallistel, LouAnn Gerken, Elizabeth Kaestner, Robert Krauss, Harry Reis, and Michael Tanenhaus. This essay owes most to my colleagues, Margot Lasher and Jack Carroll, with whom the basic aesthetic theory was originally worked out and applied to the fine arts. Finally, my original debt is to David Premack, who in a casual conversation about aesthetic capacity in nonhumans, made me realize that aesthetics in humans can be approached as a scientific topic.

Appendix: The Mechanisms of Arousal in Problem Solving and Aesthetic Experience

Throughout this paper, I have been assuming that it is thrilling to solve a problem, be it an implicit one of childhood, an explicit one of adulthood, or an artistic one in aesthetic experience. My claim for the structural link between problem solving, aesthetic experience, and structural acquisition only requires that all these behaviors elicit something like an "aha" thrill. I could stop my argument there, as the text does, simply postulating that the "aha" insight experience is enjoyable and explains the consequent urge to solve problems. However, it turns out that the formal relation between the various behaviors and the abduction of motion may provide an explanation for the "aha" thrill itself. I now turn to an explanation of what causes the thrill, based on the formal analysis of the processes involved in interrelating mental representations. (I include this discussion as an appendix because it is even more speculative than the nature of the aesthetic principles in their role in learning, which I outlined in the text.)

AHA! Emotion Out of Abstract Motion and Loss of Control

Emotional theories fall into two classes—causal and interpretive. Causal theories seek to explain different emotions as a function of biological factors: on this view, particular emotions are the mental expression of particular physiological states. Interpretive theories emphasize the importance of belief systems in designating emotions. Such a view usually differentiates two processes—mechanisms of arousal and mechanisms of interpretation (Mandler 1975). It capitalizes on the independent fact that general arousal mechanisms exist and that their behavioral indices are associated with strong emotions.

Most complete theories of emotion include elements of both causal and interpretive mechanisms. The modern tradition goes back to the James-Lange view that an emotion is the interpretation that we place on instinctual mechanisms: I impute fear to myself if I notice that I am withdrawing from some danger. On this view, the basic generator of the particular behavior is instinctive: the emotional interpretation merely symbolizes the behavior for the individual. A modern classic demonstration gives greater emphasis to the interpretive than the instinctive system: if a person is aroused (for example, by a chemical stimulant), he will both report and show signs of an emotion. Which emotion he feels is influenced strongly by his immediate context; if people around him are acting happy, so will he (Schacter and Singer 1962).

Emotions occur in broadly labeled categories, like "fear" and "happiness." What is at issue for this discussion is the arousal mechanism underlying momentary thrills that occur when we solve a problem. We can gain some insight into this by again considering the infant. Its first forms of interaction with the world are overwhelmingly physical: the infant is carried about, rocked to sleep, and so on. In all these cases, the world is interacting with the child by some manner of moving it: motion is a primary vehicle of social interaction. In fact, one of the earliest social achievements of the child is to get adults to pick it up.

Bodily motion controlled by others can be highly arousing—this may be directly caused, as by activity of the vestibular organs. It may also be independently magnified due to fear over temporary loss of control. We can see the importance of these concepts in one of the earliest occasions for smiling and laughing induced through social interaction. A fussing infant is picked up but continues to fuss. The adult jumps up and down slightly jiggling the child in a rapid motion, perhaps chanting some rhyme; the child quiets, looks at the adult, and smiles. Even more striking is the impact of picking up an infant rapidly and throwing it slightly in the air and catching it. The importance of brief loss of control is clearly strong in this case: only if the infant knows the adult, and is clearly aware of the game, does it enjoy the experience. Under those circumstances, the infant enjoys the game inordinately, as the adult increases the height of each toss.

It is tempting to wax poetic when discussing this kind of social and physical interaction. But, we can also subject it to an elementary formal analysis: on each cycle of the tossing game, the infant is in the adult's arms, then briefly flying, falling, then in the arms again. With repeated cycles, the exhilaration reaches a peak each time, just as the infant starts to fall. This experience seems paradigmatic of all thrills: they involve a brief moment of loss of control, bounded by safe havens. The safe surround creates a bridge of situational control across the moment of apparent danger, while basic somatic mechanisms are releasing strong emergency signals.

The conclusion is that the joy results from the release of instinctive emergency signals in a safe context. Why should the infant enjoy the discharge of emergency mechanisms, even it it is under controlled circumstances? The answer to this lies in a theory of emotions that is independent of the causal and interpretive theories (and therefore a theory that may be independently correct), the "opponent process" theory (Solomon 1980). On this view, brief experiences of intense negative arousal due to extreme loss of control are followed by a long "recovery" period of mild positive affect. A paradigm case is the emotions of amateur parachute jumpers. Although they are terrified during their early jumps, they eventually accommodate to the terror and enjoy a prolonged recovery period after each jump in which they experience confidence and joy.

We can combine our analyses of problem solving and perception with the thrill of losing control to explain how the problem-solving thrill is engendered. Consider again the phenomenon of motion perception, which has received so much recent attention—the resolution of two static images presented in time is that of an object that moves from one to the other. This is described by practitioners of the associated experimental art as "the image of a motion"; such a designation is distinguished from "the motion of an image" in order to avoid the homuncularily reductive requirement of having an internal observer who watches the image in motion (Shepard 1984; Kubovy 1983; Podgorny and Shepard 1975). The implications of this simple reformulation are tremendous—it postulates that an elementary object of perception is an abstract mental "resonance" of a physically possible movement. The perception of pure motion emerges out of an abstract movement from one stable image to the next.

The research on mental imagery and movement is based on the study of physical objects that could move in real space. Yet, the imagined movement that is evoked is in fact between two *abstract mental representations* of those objects. This demonstrates that the mental system has the capacity to form an *image of motion* between pure mental representations. I have noted that problem solving involves the formation of distinct representations and then an integrative resolution among the representations—a "leap of imagination" that allows abstract movement from one representation to the other representation. This is one source of excitement when we experience the solution of a problem—we briefly move from one representation of it to the other, via the just-intuited integrating representation. Leaps are associated with momentary loss of control and an associated excitement. When we take a dive, shutting our eyes tight, we briefly give ourselves over to unmonitored forces; like the tossed infant, between the point of loss of control and regaining it, we experience a brief thrill.

As in the infant, there is a separate, perhaps more physiological source of excitement that follows from the same basic principles. Consider, for a moment, the effect of perceived motion without the usual physically associated signals to our sense organs. It is just this that, in its extreme form, causes dizziness. The perception of motion induced by solving a problem, without proprioceptive or other cues, may elicit the same sort of disorientation, though to a much lesser degree.

This offers an explanation of why humans like to solve problems, even useless ones: we get a little thrill each time because the mechanisms of problem formation and resolution induce an inner percept of motion from one representation to another, with a momentary sensation of loss of control. It is a satisfying result of this proposal that the "aha" reaction to solving a problem occurs primarily just at the moment of initial intuition that one understands the solution. By hypothesis, it is at this point that one has arrived at an overarching representation that bridges the conflicting one. The image of motion from one representation to the other is emotionally effective until the structure of the integrating bridge becomes explicit—as one checks out the solution to the problem intuited in the resolving representation, the image of uncontrolled motion fades as the conflicting representations are explicitly integrated.

Coda—The Specific Emotions in Different Aesthetic Experiences

High art often elicits emotions of characteristic kinds. I suggested that problem solving is intrinsically thrilling because it evokes a feeling of inner motion on a freshly evoked dimension and a momentary loss of control. On this analysis, aesthetic experiences evoke the same mental mechanisms as problem solving and therefore the same emotional arousal. What remains is to explain the particular emotion that is felt—in problem solving, it is clear enough that we ultimately feel a mixture of pride and relief at having solved the problem. But what is the nature of the emotion evoked by aesthetic experiences, in which the "problem" exists only as a stimulus for the problem-solving activities themselves? That is, why do aesthetic experiences elicit emotions of particular kinds?

On the general theory of emotion, interpretive systems play a role in determining the emotion assigned to an aroused state. The everyday aesthetic objects shape the emotion as a function of their explicit or social content. Upon hearing the "shave and a haircut" tatoo, we experience a recognition that somebody wants our attention; the golden rectangle elicits a concept of "two-ness" and depth in a third dimension; "Happy Birthday" is a vehicle for saluting somebody else; "Goldilocks" tells an explicit story with the child's place in a family as the clear moral. Many high art works have even more explicit content: representational painting, litera-ture, and theater use the interplay between structure and content to guide the audience's particular feelings.

Some kinds of art lack such content, yet evoke strong emotional re-sponses. We can obtain the clearest picture of how the formal structure of aesthetic experience elicits and allows for the control of emotions by exam-ining such cases. Art-music is a striking example, since it has almost no semantic structure and yet can release turbulent feelings. There are several other notable facts: the same piece of music evokes different emotions in different people, and it evokes different emotions in the same person at different times.

There are several sources of the emotional arousal in response to music. First, music can directly excite the somatic and autonomic nervous systems via orienting and startle responses; Haydn exposes this in the "surprise" symphony, with loud chords at (expected) unexpected points. A gong in the middle of a quiet passage has the same effect: the blood races, the mind blanks out while the "fight or flight" system reaccommodates. Second, there is a rhythmic alternation of outer attention and inner mental process-ing paced by the perceptual analysis of each musical "phrase" (see Tan, Aiello, and Bever 1981; Bever, Lasher, and Carroll, in press). Finally, an effective musical work is one that elicits representational forms that fulfill the aesthetic principles, thereby stimulating the abstract image of motion, as discussed above.

Music has these three powerful mechanisms that can increase arousal and mental movement. But we must also account for the fact that not just general excitement but particular emotions are often felt, emotions such as elation and deep sorrow. First, there are a few conventions that depend on cultural motives—a march with a snare drum indicates a military image, whereas parallel fifths continually convey an oriental aura. Some of the motivic conventions are understandably related to basic physiological mechanisms, for example, different tempos: the perceived tempo of a piece can itself directly recruit rhythmic activities in a listener, as reflected in a tapping foot or nodding head. Once the rhythm is induced, it can resonate with different classes of emotions; for example, a quick tempo is unlikely to be perceived as lethargic and sad, whereas a harmonically slow-moving piece is unlikely to be perceived as energetic and happy. In addition, minor changes in the rhythm of the variation in processing load and attention may mimic some formal properties of emotional states.

Beyond conventional and physiological determinants of the emotion, a listener has his own prior emotional states as well: a person who is already depressed may take almost any piece of music as an occasion for sorrow. The very fact that music only vaguely guides the emotional content may account for its releasing power—the individual listener is free to attach his antecedently available emotions to the experience, thereby making it far more personally powerful than the usual response to an art work with explicit content.

This brief consideration of the sources of emotion in music outlines the kinds of factors which may play a role in other art forms, both high and low. Most important, it also highlights some emotional forces that can play a role outside of aesthetic experiences—most notably in problem solving and cognitive growth.

Bibliography

Anderson, J. 1983. *The architecture of cognition*. Cambridge: Harvard Univ. Press.

Bates, E. 1976. *Language and context: The acquisition of pragmatics*. New York: Academic Press.

Berlyne, D. 1971. *Aesthetics and psychobiology*. New York: Appleton–Century–Crofts.

———. 1974. *Studies in the new experimental aesthetics*. Washington, D.C.: Hemisphere Pub.

Betelheim, B. 1976. *The uses of enchantment*. New York: Knopf.

Bever, T. 1970. The cognitive basis for linguistic structures. In *Cognition and language development*, ed. R. Hayes, pp. 277–360. New York: Wiley.

———. 1975. Psychologically real grammar emerges because of its role in language acquisition. In *Developmental psycholinguistics. Georgetown University Round Table on Languages and Linguistics*, ed. D. Dato, pp. 63–75. Washington, D.C.: Georgetown Univ. Press.

———. 1983. Cerebral asymmetries, cognitive science and human consciousness. *Biology and language*, ed. J. Brown and E. Perecman, pp. 19–39. Cambridge: MIT Press.

Bever, T., M. Lasher, and J. Carroll. In press. A psychological theory of aesthetics. *Leonardo* 16:533–539.

Bruner, J. 1974–75. From communication to language: A psychological perspective. *Cognition* 3:255–280.

Cauley, L. 1981. *Goldilocks and the three bears*. New York: Putnam.

Chomsky, N. 1981. *Rules and representations*. New York: Columbia Univ. Press.

Croche, B. 1922. *Aesthetic as science of expression and general linguistic*. Trans. D. Ainslie. London: Macmillan.

Duncker, K. 1945. On problem solving. *Psychological Monographs* 58:(5).

Fechner, G. 1897. *Voschule der Aesthetik*. Leipzig: Breitkopf und Haertel.

Fodor, J. A. 1983. *The modularity of mind*. Boston: MIT Press.

Gibson, J. 1962. The problem of temporal order in stimulation and perception. *Journal of Psychology* 62:141–149.

Halle, M. 1962. Phonology in generative grammar. *Word* 18:3–16.

Helmholtz, H. 1895. Ueber den Ursprung der Richtigen Deutung unserer Sinneseindrucke. *Wissenschaftliche Abhandlungen*, vol. 3. Leipzig.

———. 1903. Ueber das Sehen des Menschen. *Vorträge und Reden*, vol. 1, 5th ed. Braunschweig.

Kintsch, W., T. Mandel, and E. Kozminsky. 1977. Summarizing scrambled stories. *Memory and Cognition* 5:547–552.

Kubovy, M. 1983. Mental imagery majestically transforming cognitive psychology. *Contemporary Psychology* 28:661–663.

Langer, S. K. 1967. *Mind: An essay on human feeling*. Baltimore: Johns Hopkins Press.

———. 1986. *The cognitive basis for aesthetic experience*. San Francisco: Freeman.

Mandler, G. 1975. *Mind and emotion*. New York: Wiley.

McNeill, D. 1970. *The acquisition of language*. New York, Evanston, and London: Harper and Row.

Mehler, J. 1984. *Human infancy*. Hillsdale, N.J.: Erlbaum.

Meyer, L. 1967. *Music, the arts and ideas*. Chicago: Univ. of Chicago Press.

Neisser, U. 1963. Decision time without reaction time: Experiments in visual scanning. *Journal of Experimental Psychology* 106:376–385.

Piaget, J. 1950. *The psychology of intelligence*. London: Routledge.

———. 1954. *The construction of reality in the child*. New York: Basic Books.

Pinker, S. 1984a. *Language learnability and language development*. Cambridge, Mass.: Harvard Univ. Press.

———, ed. 1984b. Visual cognition. *Cognition* 18.

Podgorny, P., and R. Shepard. 1975. Functional representations common to visual perception and imagination. *Journal of Experimental Psychology. Human Perception and Performance* 1:374–382.

Posner, M. 1969. Abstraction and the process of recognition. In *The psychology of learning and motivation*, ed. G. Bower and J. Spence, vol. 3, pp. 44–96. New York: Academic Press.

———. 1980. *Chronometric explorations of mind*. Hillsdale, N.J.: Erlbaum.

Posner, M., and S. Keele. 1968. On the genesis of abstract ideas. *Journal of Experimental Psychology* 77:353–363.

Posner, W. I., and C.R. Snyder. 1975. Attention and cognitive control. In *Information processing and cognition*, ed. R. Solso. Hillsdale, N.J.: Erlbaum.

Pylyshyn, Z. 1984. *Computation and cognition*. Boston: MIT Press.

Rock, I. 1983. *The logic of perception.* Boston: MIT Press.

Sadock, J. 1974. *Toward a linguistic theory of speech arts.* New York: Academic Press.

Sapir, E. 1921–49. *Language.* New York: Harcourt, Brace and World.

Schacter, S., and J. Singer. 1962. Cognitive, social and physiological determinants of emotional state. *Psychological Review* 69:379–399.

Shepard, R. 1981. Psychophysical complementarity. In *Perceptual organisation,* ed. M. Kubovy and J. Pomerantz. Hillsdale, N.J.: Erlbaum.

———. 1984. Ecological constraints on internal representation. *Psychological Review* 91:417–477.

Shepard, R., and L. Cooper. 1982. *Mental images and their transformation.* Boston: MIT Press.

Shepard, R., and J. Metzler, 1971. Mental rotation of three-dimensional objects. *Science* 171: 701–703.

Shiffrin, R., and W. Schneider. 1977. Controlled and automatic human information processing. *Psychological Review* 84:1–66, 127–190.

Solomon, R. 1980. The opponent-process theory of acquired motivation. *American Psychologist* 35(8):691–712.

Southey. 1836. *The doctor.* New York: Harper.

Tan, N., R. Aiello, and T. G. Bever. 1981. Harmonic structure as a determinant of melodic organization. *Memory and Cognition* 9(5):533–539.

Woodworth, R. 1938. *Experimental psychology.* New York: Holt.

Zuckerkandl, V. 1959. *The sense of music.* Princeton, N.J.:Princeton Univ. Press.

Subject Index

Name Index